S0-AXO-182

PROPHETIC WITNESS

The Boston College Church in the 21st Century Series

Patricia De Leeuw and James F. Keenan, S.J.,
General Editors

Titles in this series include:

Handing On the Faith:
The Church's Mission and Challenge
Edited by Robert P. Imbelli

Sexuality and the U.S. Catholic Church:
Crisis and Renewal
Edited by Lisa Sowle Cahill,
John Garvey, and T. Frank Kennedy, S.J.

Priests for the 21st Century
Edited by Donald J. Dietrich

Inculturation and the Church in North America
Edited by T. Frank Kennedy, S.J.

Take Heart:
Catholic Writers on Hope in Our Time
Edited by Ben Birnbaum

Voices of the Faithful:
Loyal Catholics Striving for Change
By William D'Antonio and Anthony Pogorelc

Two Centuries of Faith:
The Influence of Catholicism on Boston 1808–2008
Edited by Thomas H. O'Connor

The Church in the 21st Century Center at Boston College seeks to be a catalyst and resource for the renewal of the Catholic Church in the United States by engaging critical issues facing the Catholic community. Drawing from both the Boston College community and others, its activities currently are focused on four challenges: handing on and sharing the Catholic faith, especially with younger Catholics; fostering relationships built on mutual trust and support among lay men and women, vowed religious, deacons, priests, and bishops; developing an approach to sexuality mindful of human experience and reflective of Catholic tradition; and advancing contemporary reflection on the Catholic intellectual tradition.

PROPHETIC WITNESS

Catholic Women's Strategies for Reform

COLLEEN M. GRIFFITH, EDITOR

A Herder & Herder Book
The Crossroad Publishing Company
New York

The Crossroad Publishing Company
www.cpcbooks.com
www.crossroadpublishing.com

© 2009 by The Trustees of Boston College

All rights reserved. No part of this book may be reproduced, stored in a retrieval system, or transmitted, in any form or by any means, electronic, mechanical, photocopying, recording, or otherwise, without the written permission of The Crossroad Publishing Company.

In continuation of our 200-year tradition of independent publishing, The Crossroad Publishing Company proudly offers a variety of books with strong, original voices and diverse perspectives. The viewpoints expressed in our books are not necessarily those of The Crossroad Publishing Company, any of its imprints or of its employees. No claims are made or responsibility assumed for any health or other benefit.

Printed in the United States of America.

The text of this book is set in 9.75/12 Sabon.

Library of Congress Cataloging-in-Publication Data

Prophetic witness : Catholic women's strategies for reform / Colleen M. Griffith, editor.
    p. cm.
    "A Herder and Herder book".
    Includes bibliographical references and index.
    ISBN-13: 978-0-8245-2526-2 (alk. paper)
    ISBN-10: 0-8245-2526-4 (alk. paper)
    1. Women in the Catholic Church. 2. Women – Religious aspects – Catholic Church. 3. Feminism – Religious aspects – Catholic Church. I. Griffith, Colleen M. II. Title.
BX1397.P76 2009
282.082 – dc22
                                           2009000646

Contents

Part Three
INSISTENCE ON DIALOGUE

Part Four
POLITICS OF THE HEARTH

Part Five
FEMINIST ASCETICAL PRACTICES

Preface

Speaking as Women

Colleen M. Griffith

T HIS BOOK EXISTS in response to the hopes of hundreds of Catholic women
who over the past several years have participated in Boston College's programs aimed at addressing the concerns of Catholic women in the church. In
particular, this collection is the outgrowth of two conferences held at Boston
College. The first, "Envisioning the Church Women Want," took place in the
spring of 2004. It was sponsored by the Church in the 21st Century initiative
and led by Boston College's "Tuesday Morning Women," a university-wide
group of interested faculty, administrators, and students who come together
weekly for coffee, community, and conversation around women's issues. The
follow-up and second conference event, "Creating the Church Women Want,"
was held in the summer of 2006. Sponsored by Boston College's Institute of Religious Education and Pastoral Ministry (IREPM), in celebration of its thirty-fifth
anniversary, it was preceded by a week-long evening course titled "Prophetic
Witness: Catholic Women's Strategies for Ecclesial Reform." These gatherings met with overwhelming success and appreciation, generating renewed
commitment, dialogue, and goodwill.

Following the first conference, women participants noted that posing a more
inclusive and just vision of the church for the twenty-first century was a fine first
step, but that it would not be enough to bolster the necessary journey of reform
and renewal. They sought practical strategies that held the possibility of inspiring the ecclesial lives of Catholic women now. They expressed a strong desire
for imaginative proposals that could stimulate creative fidelity in challenging
ecclesial times.

This book is offered in response to their request. It brings together the voices
of leading Catholic women theologians from across the United States presenting
their particular strategies for reform and renewal of the church. The result is
an anthology that is strikingly different, direct, and practical. The contributing
authors hope that readers will find here significant resources that stimulate
more expansive ways of thinking and effective forms of praxis.

For his vision in launching the Church in the 21st Century initiative of which
this book is a part, I wish to thank William P. Leahy, S.J., president of Boston
College. I also express my gratitude to Patricia De Leeuw and James F. Keenan,
S.J., general editors of the C21 book series, for their outstanding leadership and
their commitment to Catholic women's concerns. For the exceptional support
shown for this book project and the attention to all logistics pertaining to the

conferences that served to launch it, I express my gratitude to my IREPM colleagues and to the Boston College "Tuesday Morning Women." I thank all of the outstanding women theologians who have contributed essays to this volume. I am especially grateful to my graduate assistant Glynn Forkey, whose organizational and technological assistance has been exceptional, and to Daniella Zsupan, who contributed much in the final stages of preparing the manuscript. Finally, I express my gratitude to my husband and life-partner, Thomas H. Groome, for his unwavering support and tireless spirit for a just and inclusive church.

Contributors

Susan Abraham, Assistant Professor of Ministry Studies, Harvard Divinity School

Karen A. Barta, Professor of Christian Scripture, Seattle University

Rosemary P. Carbine, Visiting Professor of Religious Studies, Whittier College

Francine Cardman, Associate Professor of Historical Theology and Church History, Weston Jesuit Department, Boston College School of Theology and Ministry

M. Shawn Copeland, Associate Professor of Theology, Boston College

Gemma T. Cruz, Assistant Professor of Systematic Theology, Saint Ambrose University

Colleen M. Griffith, Faculty Director of Spirituality Studies, IREPM Department, Boston College School of Theology and Ministry

Diana Hayes, Professor of Systematic Theology, Georgetown University

Mary Catherine Hilkert, Professor of Systematic Theology, University of Notre Dame

Jeannine Hill Fletcher, Associate Professor of Theology, Fordham University

Teresia Mbari Hinga, Associate Professor of Religious Studies, Santa Clara University

Lynn Jarrell, Associate Director for Canon Law, Legal Resource Center for Religious

Elizabeth A. Johnson, Distinguished Professor of Systematic Theology, Fordham University

Patricia Beattie Jung, Professor of Theology, Loyola University Chicago

Mary Jo Leddy, Director, Romero House Community for Refugees and Lecturer in Religion and Society, Regis College at the University of Toronto

Margaret R. Pfeil, Assistant Professor of Moral Theology, University of Notre Dame

Nancy Pineda-Madrid, Assistant Professor of Theology and Latino/a Ministry, IREPM Department, Boston College School of Theology and Ministry

Jane E. Regan, Associate Professor of Theology and Religious Education, IREPM Department, Boston College School of Theology and Ministry

Mary Margaret Doyle Roche, Assistant Professor of Religious Studies, College of the Holy Cross

Susan A. Ross, Professor of Theology and Director of the Gannon Center, Loyola University Chicago

Rosemary Radford Ruether, Carpenter Emerita Professor of Theology, Pacific School of Religion and Graduate Theological Union

Michele Saracino, Associate Professor of Religious Studies, Manhattan College

Angela Senander, Assistant Professor of Systematics and Moral Theology, Washington Theological Union

Cristina L. H. Traina, Associate Professor of Religion and Director of Graduate Studies, Northwestern University

Introduction

Creative Fidelity in Challenging Times

Colleen M. Griffith

THERE IS MUCH THAT twenty-first-century women who are Catholic and love their faith tradition find disheartening about the current institutional church. It is disappointing, for example, that the thousands of women who make up a majority of the workforce of the church have little or no voice at ecclesial polity tables. Canon law calls for consultation and cooperation of the Christian faithful in the exercise of governance, but these roles have opened to women only in a perfunctory way.[1] It is also unfortunate that despite widespread recognition of the formative power, and constructive nature of language across many disciplines of knowledge, church leadership has not chosen to adopt more expansive references for God and inclusive language for humankind in communal liturgy. Discussion of women's ordination remains a closed matter too, though the theological ground upon which this decision rests has been called into question by faithful and renowned Catholic theologians. In general, it is discouraging that the scholarship of today's most outstanding theologians is exerting little impact on the mind of the current magisterium.

Fortunately, these dispiriting dimensions of Catholic church life in the twenty-first century do not represent the full story. There are numerous signs of promise apparent as well. Small Christian faith communities, for example, are burgeoning; these serve as egalitarian examples of Christian community and are becoming significant ways for people to supplement parish life. Lay ministry is ever on the rise, and the numbers of women in ministerial positions continue to expand rapidly. There is increased interest in adult faith education, particularly among women, reflective of the desire to assume lives of mature Catholic Christian faith. Persons are taking more responsibility for their spiritual formation as well, through gatherings for Scripture sharing and prayer, retreat experiences, and spiritual direction.

A most notable sign of hope in our present ecclesial situation, something to which this book attests, is the presence of committed Catholic women doing theology. Without question, some of the most exciting and creative theological work being done on the world stage today is by Catholic women. One hundred years ago, women were not welcome in the theological community of discourse. Fifty years ago it was still most unusual for a woman to choose theology as a career. But today, in graduate programs throughout the United States, the number of women doing advanced theological degrees frequently surpasses that of men. In historically unparalleled ways, women theologians today, solidly trained and choosing theology as their vocation, invite us to stand up anew and reclaim the riches of the Catholic tradition in more emancipatory and expansive fashion. This volume gathers many of their voices.

On Women's Experience

Current interest in theologies written by women stems from a growing awareness that women's experience has not been represented adequately enough in theology heretofore. "Women's experience," of course, cannot be viewed as a universal category. It isn't the possession of any single group of women, nor is it the possession of men.

The contributing authors in this volume are committed to doing theology in a way that addresses and speaks from women's experience, construed in other than singular terms. Women's lives, as Emilie Townes notes, "are not a tapestried monolith."[2] Woman's spirit is manifest in plural form, and it gets spoken in multiple tongues. Diversity among women ensures a thick rendering of "women's experience." Being specific about one's location and contextual standpoint, therefore, becomes an important starting point for women theologians. Historical relevance and practical intent emerge as further hallmarks of the theologies of women, which seek to engage persons deeply at the level of agency.

In ancient Greek philosophy, *phronesis* was a term for the wisdom that emerged from the uniting of theory and practice. Aristotle described *phronesis* as "a truth-attaining rational quality concerned with action in relation to things that are good and bad for human beings."[3] When theology is done with this kind of practical wisdom, it engages persons in the realm of actual living. The authors assembled here aim for precisely this kind of engagement. They focus their conversation on strategies for ecclesial reform and renewal, and they do so with sensitivity and astuteness, intuition and practical imagination. They offer concrete proposals rather than abstract propositions. Thinking concretely in terms of strategies is, as the reader will readily note, no less rigorous than thinking in more general and abstract terms, and it holds the possibility of far greater relevance.

The strategies of hope proposed in this volume are represented under six headings:

1. Renewing the Vision

"Without a vision, the people perish" reads Proverbs 29:18. Amid challenging ecclesial times, having a vision becomes more necessary than ever. The authors assembled in Part One of the book offer orienting visions that serve to enlarge our range of vision. Their insights are communally wrought and not simply for women alone. At the same time, the vision articulated by these authors in relation to the creed, a culturally diverse church, and Catholic communities of the future is born of womanly sensitivities.

2. Knowledge as Power

Knowledge that carries practical intent is inherently powerful; it is also demanding. Knowledge of this sort refuses to be just informative. It seeks to influence people's heads and hearts and to invite personal and communal transformation. Women authors in Part Two recognize the practical intent and transformative possibilities in Scripture.

3. Insistence on Dialogue

There is no substitute for honest dialogue in community, and there are far too few opportunities for it in present Catholic ecclesial life. The *sensus fidelium* has long been prized as a central value and source of wisdom in Catholic ecclesiology. Yet dialogical vehicles for accessing the *sensus fidelium* remain scarce to nonexistent. Dialogue, as the women in Part Three of this book underscore, is a rich pearl of great price *and* a most effective strategy for change in the church. One can never fully predict the outcome of dialogue in terms of the collective intelligence to which it will give rise. One can expect it to be a source of empowerment, however, a shared exploration of previously held thoughts and feelings that helps to transcend limiting perspectives and assumptions.

4. Politics of the Hearth

Many concerns about the church raised by women impinge upon home life, family, and the raising of children. The public positions of Catholic communities carry significant implications in private life, something infrequently acknowledged. Underscoring the symbiosis between the public and the private, authors in Part Four note how Catholic ethical claims, and presumptions regarding handing on the faith, affect family politics.

5. Feminist and Womanist Ascetical Practices

Early Christians used the term "asceticism" to refer to intentional practices by which they conditioned themselves for living the Reign of God. Sadly, over time, asceticism came to be understood as a referent for penitential practices, and frequently body-disparaging ones.[4] Authors in Part Five seek to reclaim the original Christian understanding of asceticism, reformulating it in strongly positive terms as spiritual practice that is intentional, regular, and embarked upon in order to cultivate greater authenticity and integration.

6. Attending to Emerging Discourses

Coming into more inclusive ways of thinking, loving, and being community demands keeping an ear close to the ground. The potential for greater expansiveness of thought and action depends largely on careful discernment of and response to the movement of the Spirit of God in the specific historical cultural milieu in which we find ourselves. There are questions with which our communities of faith need to grapple, *as* they are being formulated and discussed in contemporary theological discourses. Authors in Part Six provide a sampling of some emerging discourses, inviting us to participate carefully in these conversations as a consciously chosen strategy for change.

The six strategic areas outlined above beckon the reader toward fresh places of exploration and appropriation. Each bears witness to the possibility of genuine and creative fidelity in challenging ecclesial times. Consideration of the various strategies found here fosters a listening to our own listening as women and opens up potential opportunities for ecclesial renewal and reform.

Flowering in the Burren

There is a well-known and beautiful spot in County Clare, Ireland, known as the Burren. Occupying an area of some 135 square miles, it is a bleak and stony place. The exposed limestone of the Burren stretches for miles with no visible topsoil, presenting a flat but jagged surface. In the Burren, rainwater penetrates lines of weakness in the limestone, and gradually vertical cracks, known as grikes, form in the rocks. Ironically these cracks in the rocks give rise to some rare and amazing wildflowers. A variety of unusual alpine and Mediterranean plants are apparent, growing from the spaces between the rocks.

The Burren in County Clare proved to be a big surprise to archeologists, botanists, and ecologists. I suspect that our present ecclesial time will prove a surprise as well. There is, after all, much that is flourishing in our "grikes," the cracks in the rocks of a bleak-looking ecclesial landscape. One unmistakable sign of rich flowering remains the prophetic witness of Catholic women, who in their prayer, praxis, and theological work remain committed to the vision of a Catholic Church at its best. The results of this commitment may seem incremental, but the prophetic power of such a stance cannot be missed.

The decision made by women in this collection to believe in and act out of hope for a future church now is a decision made not for themselves alone. It is a stance taken for the sake of thousands of other women and men, one that serves as an inspiration in the present and becomes an important lead for those yet to come. It is time to recognize the richness of our own Burren landscape, to find hope and enjoyment in the flowers growing in our grikes.

Part One

RENEWING THE VISION

Chapter 1

Articulating the Vision Anew

The Banquet of the Creed

Elizabeth A. Johnson

IN A SERMON delivered in the fifth century, Augustine reflected that early Christians in the land of Israel had no idea that one day there would be a church in North Africa, a community of believers praising God in a different language and culture. The church that he and his listeners now formed was to those ancestors in the faith still a "church of the future." Then he reached the heart of the matter, saying, "They weren't yet able to see it, and they were already constructing it out of themselves."[1] That, it seems to me, is a superb description of the responsibility we are here to consider.

The faith of the church is a two-thousand-year-old phenomenon, handed down from generation to generation. It has been carried through history in a living community of disciples who have expressed it in vastly different cultures and climates. In eras such as medieval Europe, when Christianity was culturally dominant, faith was passed on without much difficulty, the spark of belief catching hold through the practices of the whole society. In other times such as our own in the twenty-first-century United States, the ease is gone. But the church of the future still needs constructing, and the material is our own lives.

What are some of the obstacles to passing on the faith in our day? Among the more potent are these. Even everyday thought has to grapple with the historic challenge of Enlightenment atheism coming from the masters of suspicion: Feuerbach, Nietzsche, Marx, and Freud, along with their postmodern heirs. Culturally the air is colored by extremes: rigorous Christian fundamentalisms on the one hand, and on the other a certain agnosticism or comfortable indifference to religion conditioned by secular and consumerist values. Assumptions about how the world works, drawn from the practices of science and technology, rightfully place natural rather than supernatural powers at the center of attention. Religious pluralism adds a relativizing factor as we encounter the wealth of other world religions in our colleagues, neighbors, friends, and lovers. The institutional church itself often appears as an obstacle to faith, being mediocre in preaching and irresponsible, even sinful, in actions taken and scandalously not taken. We are in a new epoch that presents a challenge without precedent.

In this context, Karl Rahner's insight offers a modicum of wisdom: "The devout Christian of the future will either be a 'mystic,' one who has 'experienced' something, or he [she] will cease to be anything at all."[2] The Christian will be one who has *experienced* God. It is crucial to note, therefore, that the faith we are considering is not, first of all, assent to propositions, be they doctrinal or moral. Neo-scholastic theology defined faith this way, making it an intellectual act of the mind. Contemporary theology holds a more biblical view, seeing faith as assent with one's whole person to the mystery of the ineffable God who is unspeakably close in Jesus Christ and the Spirit. Faith is committing ourselves to this Mystery, risking a relationship that has the power to transform our lives. At the heart of it all, what does Christianity proclaim? It proclaims the reality of God as the self-giving nearness of forgiving Love in the midst of our darkness, injustice, sin, and death. All the doctrines and rituals aim to unpack this basic wonder. Faith means leaning our hearts on this Rock and responding with our life's prayer and praxis as part of the community called church.

Handing on the faith entails bringing the streaming new potential of the next generations into vibrant contact with the good news in such a way that they can experience how encounter with ineffable Love makes life meaningful, replete with care, and hopeful in the midst of struggle. For this to happen, we adults first have to know the experience of encounter with ineffable Love; the lamp of the word of God burns primarily with the oil of our own lives. Conscious of the challenges of our day, we then articulate a message of faith so that it can be heard. As in every era, a practice of discernment helps us to figure out which elements of faith need particular emphasis. Adults in the church who treasure their faith must make deliberate decisions not only about strategies but also about the very heart of what must be passed on in order to intrigue new generations into a life of relationship with the living God.

Toward that end, I propose to dwell on the Nicene Creed. One of the oldest professions of faith (fourth century) and widely used across the divided Christian churches, it provides one handy verbal nutshell of the faith to be passed on. Its three sections, corresponding to the three persons of the Trinity, offer a cornucopia of beliefs. There is much general understanding in the church regarding what these beliefs mean. But in my view the experience of God in our day raises new questions and brings forth fresh insights that give specific shape to what the creed confesses. Knowing full well that no one interpretation of the faith is adequate for all times and peoples, and that no one person can ever do justice to the full faith of the church, I will highlight two themes under each section that need to be woven into our inherited understanding in order to pass on the faith in a vibrant way.

First Affirmation

"We believe in one God...." The creed goes on to identify this one God as the Maker of everything, of all that exists in heaven and on earth, whether visible or invisible. It is a constant struggle in theology, preaching, and popular practice to understand this aright. God is not a being among other beings, even the first, highest, or greatest! God does not belong in the scheme of things at all!

Rather, God is incomprehensible mystery, the wellspring of being who creates, sustains, and is the goal of the world. Infinitely transcendent yet nearer to us than we are to ourselves, the living God is literally unimaginable, yet can be expressed in many images: mother, father, midwife, shepherd, lover, liberator, friend; blowing wind, blazing fire, flowing water; the One in whom we live and move and have our being. Besides getting right what we mean and do *not* mean when we say "God," there are two aspects we would be wise to weave into this first article of the creed as we hand on the faith: faith that loves the earth, and faith that stands open to the future.

Loving the Earth

Contemporary science is giving us a beautiful and dynamic picture of how our universe came to be. From the initial flaring forth of the Big Bang 13.7 billion years ago, to the formation of galaxies with their billions of stars, to the shaping of our sun and its planet 5 billion years ago, to the slow evolution of life over deep eons of time, the cosmic adventure has unfolded to display a dazzling array of plants and animals on earth, including the emergence of us humans a mere speck of time ago. Because we are the species now conscious of all this, Rabbi Abraham Heschel calls human beings "the cantors of the universe,"[3] that part of nature who can understand there is a Creator and give praise in the name of all the rest.

Telling the story of the universe in this evolutionary way makes us realize that the earth is not just a backdrop for the human drama of sin and redemption. Rather, earth has its own intrinsic value, loved by God for its own sake. Theology has been traditionally very anthropocentric, but a perhaps silly question puts this into proper perspective: what was God doing for billions of years before we humans came along? Not just "waiting" for the drama to begin. Sacramental theology has always taught that simple earthy things — bread, wine, water, oil, the embodied, sexual relationship of marriage — can be bearers of divine grace. We now realize that this is so, because the natural world itself is a primordial sacrament, a primary vehicle of God's blessed presence. Indeed this world "is charged with the grandeur of God,"[4] as Gerard Manley Hopkins poetically wrote.

In a terrible way, our human practices are wreaking unbearable damage on the life-systems of air, water, and soil, and on the other species that share one community of life with us on this planet. Why have we Christians who confess that God is Maker of this world not risen up *en masse* in its defense? One reason is that through theology's engagement with Greek philosophy, we have inherited a powerful dualism that devalues matter and the body and prizes the spirit as closer to God. The task now is to develop a life-affirming theology of the earth/matter/bodies, one that will do better justice to this world that God makes and so loves. We need to realize that a moral universe limited to the human community no longer serves the future of life. Countering the sins of ecocide, biocide, geocide, we must act on behalf of the natural world with care, protection, restoration, and healing, even if this action runs contrary to powerful economic and political interests, as it does.

In 1990 Pope John Paul II offered a radical principle: "respect for life and for the dignity of the human person extends also to the rest of creation."[5] We owe love and justice not only to humankind but to "otherkind." In such ethical reflection, the great commandment to love one's neighbor as oneself is extended to include all members of the life community. "Who is my neighbor?" asks Brian Patrick. "The Samaritan? The outcast? The enemy? Yes, yes, of course. But it is also the whale, the dolphin, and the rain forest. Our neighbor is the entire community of life, the entire universe. We must love it all as our very self."[6] The vision we much cherish is that of flourishing humanity on a thriving earth in an evolving universe, all together filled with the glory of God: such is the task faith calls us to in this critical age of earth's distress. If we truly believe in "one God, Maker of heaven and earth," then we will hand on a faith that loves the earth.

Standing Open to the Future

The stunning world opened up by Big Bang cosmology and evolutionary biology points to the Creator present and active not just in the beginning and not only in the present moment, but also in the future as our individual lives and the whole universe continue to take shape. This puts theology of the natural world, pregnant with surprise as its evolution has been, in tune with biblical history, where the one God is always on the move, out ahead, calling us forth. To illustrate this, let us recall two famous ancient stories about the meaning of life, one Greek and one Hebrew.

The Greek story opens at the end of the Trojan War when one of the fighters, Odysseus, sets out for home.[7] He spends many years and endures numerous hardships in his struggle to return to the island of Ithaca. There he hopes to rejoin his faithful wife, Penelope, his devoted son, and his irreplaceable dog. Along the way, he sees sights and finds himself in situations that are exciting. His journey is a grand adventure. However, in the end, his aim is to return to what he knows, to the joy and comfort of the past that he remembers.

The Hebrew story starts with an old husband and wife already settled in their home. Then God addresses Abraham, and by implication Sarah, with an invitation, "Leave, go forth" (Gen. 12:1). This invitation is accompanied by a concrete promise: descendants as numerous as the stars in the sky. It carries, too, an even deeper pledge that God will be with them. Centuries later, reflecting on this moment, the New Testament notes with amazement about Abraham: "and he went forth, not knowing where he was going" (Heb. 11:8). Overall, his journey is not as exciting as that of Odysseus. Yet called by God he dares to risk everything in trust, even when things got so bad that, as Scripture says, he had to "hope against hope" (Rom. 4:18). The steady drumbeat of his adventure, and that of Sarah, was faith in the ever-coming God who kept on meeting them in surprising ways.

Obviously, it is Abraham and Sarah, and not Odysseus, who exemplify the Christian understanding of what it means to be human in time. We humans have a passion to be — and to become — ourselves. This cannot happen if we try to simply return to the past or stay wedded only to the present moment. In the Bible, the present moment is a growing edge, opening us ever further to

God's dream for our becoming. "Leave, go forth," God addresses each of us. Come ahead to the place, the vocation, the relationships, the work, I will show you. Daring to respond, we find ourselves in situations we would never have imagined. When passing on the faith, our "We believe in one God" should be a call to adventure, a belief that not only remembers the great things God has done but also turns us to the future, where God still comes to meet us.

Second Affirmation

"We believe in one Lord Jesus Christ...." The creed goes on to affirm Jesus Christ's unity with God in the great, once-disputed term "one in being," and then recounts his life in history: born of Mary, suffered under Pilate, crucified and risen from the dead. For Christian faith, this historical story receives its power from the belief that here the transcendent God draws radically near by incarnation into human flesh. The historical story, then, matters greatly, for "Jesus [is] God's mercy in person."[8] Details from the historical story alert me to two accents that I hope we weave into this second article of the creed as we hand on the faith, namely, faith that does justice, and faith that loves life.

Doing Justice

Jesus' story starts out distressed. He was born into a poor family, laid in a manger, and soon became a refugee fleeing a ruler's murderous violence. In Gustavo Gutiérrez's memorable words, the advent of God in Christ is "an irruption that smells of the stable."[9] Years later Jesus set the theme of his own ministry with liberating words from the scroll of Isaiah: "The Spirit of the Lord is upon me, because he has anointed me to bring good news to the poor. He has sent me to proclaim release to the captives and recovery of sight to the blind, to let the oppressed go free, to proclaim a year of favor for the Lord" (Luke 4:18–19). What follows is indeed good news as suffering, evil, and despair in the concrete are met and transformed. The Messiah heals the sick, exorcizes those with demons, forgives sinners, cares for those whose lives are a heavy burden, and practices a table companionship so inclusive that it gives scandal. Illuminated by his thought-provoking parables centered in the coming kingdom of God, these merciful actions destabilize the prevailing norms of who is first and who is last. They establish beyond doubt divine solidarity with those who lack basic necessities: "I was hungry and you gave me to eat; I was hungry and you gave me no food" (Matt. 25:35, 42). Neglect of "the least of these" means turning your back on God.

In historical perspective, Jesus' death on the cross is the price he paid for his prophetic ministry. And again here, precisely where one would not expect to find divinity — amid torture and unjust execution by the state — the Gospel locates the presence of God. *Ecce homo:* behold the suffering face of Jesus, and the face of Christ desecrated in the emaciated, tear-stained, terrified faces of the world's poor, the crucified peoples. The resurrection irrevocably pledges that there will be a blessed future for all the violated and the dead, cast off as if their lives had no meaning.

This story of Jesus raises up a terrific countercultural challenge, one that raises significant questions with which communities of faith must grapple. How can we economically well-off Christians in the wealthiest nation in the world continue patterns of consumption that contribute to the destitution of millions of exploited poor people struggling for life both at home and abroad? A renewed emphasis on Jesus' prophetic preferential option for the poor in the name of God ought to summon our conscience to actions on behalf of justice that will transform oppressive economic structures on a global scale.

How can we white Christians in this country continue to support attitudes, actions, and inactions that diminish the well-being of African Americans struggling to live with full human dignity? During the time of slavery, the faith of black people understood the liberating message of Jesus better than their white masters did; an enslaved people intuited his cross in their suffering. Following Jesus entails solidarity in the struggle for human dignity for all God's people, whatever the color of their skin, country of origin, or legal status.

How can we in this hierarchical church continue to relegate women to second-class status governed by structures, laws, and rituals that privilege men (not meant in the generic sense)? Jesus called women disciples who were generous followers in his ministry, faithful witnesses of his death and burial, and commissioned witnesses of his risen life. Even apart from myriad Gospel examples of Jesus' beneficent relationship with women, his rejection of any relationship patterned on domination challenges the church to transformation. Doing justice entails making the community safe for women's psychological and spiritual well-being and empowering women's full participation in the ministries and offices of the church.

Divine predilection for history's lowest and least does not mean that God opts only for the marginalized in terms of sex, race, and class. God's love is universal, not exclusive. But it does mean that God has a particular care for those who are hurting. Listen to Mary's song of justice, the Magnificat, where she sings that God her Savior has brought down the mighty from their thrones and lifted up the lowly, filled the hungry with good things but sent the rich away empty, all in fulfillment of the ancient promise of mercy. Handing on a faith that does justice ensures that future generations will find a true path of discipleship in our day.

Healing Life

The most recognizable Christian symbol is an instrument of torture and death, turned into the flowering tree of life, the cross. I think one of the worst ideas we have passed on is that God needed and wanted the sacrifice of this bloody death in order to forgive sin. In the eleventh century Anselm took the idea of satisfaction as it was practiced under feudalism and crafted it into a powerful argument for the necessity of the cross. He meant this as a reflection on God's mercy, but in the hands of lesser preachers, this soon became a toxic idea, namely, our sins have so offended God that he demands death as recompense. Aquinas, Scotus, and others criticized this theory and the necessity that is so woven into it, but it won the day for the next thousand years.

Today, criticisms of this satisfaction theology of the cross are many. It makes it seem that the main purpose of Jesus' coming on earth was to die, thus diminishing the importance of his ministry. It glorifies suffering more than joy as a path to God and leads to masochistic piety. Liberation theology criticizes how satisfaction theology inculcates passivity in the face of unjust suffering rather than the will to resist. Feminist theology criticizes its portrait of a father handing over his son to death, seeing this in tandem with domestic violence and child abuse. Perhaps worst of all is the bloodthirsty picture of God that results, one who needs to be placated by suffering. Compare this to the idea of God present in the major parables of Jesus. It would be as if in the parable of the prodigal son, the father says to the returning runaway: No, you may not come in until you have repaid what you wasted; the older brother offers to help; he then works himself to the bone in the fields, finally dying of exhaustion; at which point the father says, all right, you can come in now. How contradictory this is to the God Jesus knew and taught!

One way forward is to return to the multitude of post-Easter metaphors that the New Testament uses to interpret the cross. Early Christians did indeed use the cultic metaphor of sacrifice drawn from the ritual slaughter of animals in the Jerusalem Temple and later pressed into service by Anselm. But they also used business metaphors such as buying back and redeeming; legal metaphors such as justification; military metaphors such as liberation and victory over the enemy; political metaphors such as mediation, peacemaking, and reconciliation; medical metaphors such as healing and making whole; family metaphors such as adoption; and even maternal metaphors such as giving birth (Jesus died so we could be born of God: the most frequently used interpretation in John's letters). As these metaphors work, we are subtly led away from a notion of the cross as a death required by God in repayment for sin and toward appreciation of the cross as an event of divine compassion in solidarity with our darkness, sin, and pain.

What does this mean? Jesus came not to die but to live and help others live in the joy of the reign of God. To put it baldly, God is not a sadistic Father, and Jesus was not a passive victim of divine decree. Rather, his suffering, freely borne in love, in fidelity to his ministry and his God, is precisely the way our gracious God has chosen to enter into solidarity with all those who suffer and are lost in this violent world, thereby opening up the promise of new life out of the very center of death. It is in this vein that we need to hand on the cross and resurrection, so that faith is lived in the joy of life and compassionate action with those who are suffering, rather than prizing pain in the name of God for its own sake.

Third Affirmation

"*We believe in the Holy Spirit. . . .* " The creed goes on to describe what the Spirit does: gives life, inspires prophets, upholds the church, renews life in baptism and the forgiveness of sins, and ensures the life of the world to come. Traditionally theology has linked this article of the creed with the church, seeing the church as a Spirit-filled community. Augustine used a particularly striking image to bring this point home. The Spirit is already at work among you, he preached to his congregation, cultivating you like an orchard, producing buds, strengthening your branches, clothing you with leaves, loading you with fragrant flowers and bringing forth fruit. Central to this flourishing is the Eucharist. We are invited to come and receive the consecrated bread and wine: "If you have received worthily, you are [yourselves] what you receive."[10] We are the Body of Christ, shaped by the Spirit. In our day Edward Schillebeeckx has also written movingly of the church: "By following Jesus, taking our bearings from him and allowing ourselves to be inspired by him, by sharing in his *Abba* experience and his selfless support for 'the least of my brethren (Matt. 25:40),' and thus entrusting our own destiny to God, we allow the history of Jesus, the living one, to continue in history as a piece of living christology, the work of the Spirit among us."[11]

In the context of this ecclesiology, two dimensions of faith in the Spirit that I see we need to hand on are faith that reverences the presence of God in the world's religion, and faith that dares to hope against hope for the resurrection of the dead.

Reverencing the World's Religions

In light of the universal presence of God in the world through Word and Spirit, theology today is increasingly realizing that the one salvific design of God for the world is not monolithic but multifaceted. This saving plan reaches its highest historical density in Jesus Christ with significance for all. We Christians are the bearers of this treasure; we witness and proclaim it. Yet the Word of God is not constrained by this particular history, nor is the Spirit of God limited by the church. Due to God's gracious initiative, different paths are laid down in different societies inviting people to share divine life. Thus the religions with their saving figures and sacred texts, their creeds, codes, and rituals, can be considered channels of grace set up by God's providence, intended to be ways people in different cultures encounter and respond to the Holy One. Put plainly, the religions are nothing less than expressions of God's presence in the world through Word and Spirit. Such diversity in the religious sphere gives dazzling expression to God's depth and mystery. It witnesses to the superabundant generosity of God who manifests divine purpose to the human race in such manifold ways.

It is odd, when you think about it, that for centuries the Christ event was used to obscure the work of God in other religions rather than to expand appreciation of it. Our presumption was that since the Word is present here, personally incarnate in Jesus Christ, and the Spirit is present here, poured out on the church, then God is not present elsewhere, or at least not so truly and lovingly present. We saw this as an either-or proposition. But the trinitarian God being infinite, this makes no sense. And the revelation in Christ of God's will to save all people actually postulates sweeping divine activity in the world, most notably in the other religions that lay down explicit paths of holiness. Not to recognize this is tantamount to being ignorant of the greatness of God.

Rabbi Jonathan Sacks proposes some arresting analogies.[12] What would faith be like if we acknowledged the presence of God in other faiths, whose truth is not our truth? It would be like feeling secure in one's own home, yet moved by the beauty of foreign places when we travel, knowing they are someone else's home, not mine, but still part of the glory of the world that is ours. It would be like realizing that our life is a sentence written in the story of our own faith, yet pleased to know that there are other stories of faith written in other lives, all part of the great narrative of God's call and humanity's response. Those who are confident in their faith are not threatened but enlarged by the different faith of others. As we discover ever more truth about God in each other, the dignity of difference can be a rich source of blessing. And we can work together in solidarity for the good of this broken world.

Hoping for the Resurrection of the Dead

There is a powerful logic that connects the opening of the creed, God creating heaven and earth, with the closing of the creed, the Creator Spirit bringing about the resurrection of the dead. In both cases we begin with virtually nothing: no universe, no future for the dead. In the first case the vivifying breath of the Spirit moves to create the world "in the beginning." In this end case, the Spirit moves again and, in a new act of creation, keeping faith with the beloved creature, carries a person through perishing into new life. The Nicene Creed traces this logic, from original creation through the story of Jesus Christ to the promise of the future. Hope in eternal life for oneself, others, and the whole cosmos, in other words, is not some curiosity tacked on as an appendage to faith but is faith in the living God brought to its radical conclusion. It is faith in the Creator Spirit that does not stop halfway but follows the road consistently to the end, trusting that the God of the beginning is also the God of the end, who utters the same word in each case: Let there be life. All the biblical images of the end-time — light, banquet, harvest, wedding feast, rest, singing, homecoming, reunion, tears wiped away, seeing face to face, and knowing as we are known — point to a living communion in God's own life. We die not into nothingness but into the embrace of God. There is reason to hope for more, then, even with tears of grief streaming down our cheeks. The conviction that the Spirit of God's purpose in creating the world is not annihilation but transformation into new creation sustains every moment of our vulnerable life.

Conclusion

Each age passes on the faith according to its own lights. In sharing these reflections about what is needed in our own day, I am awed by what a rich treasure we have in the Christian heritage. Extrapolating from the life and ministry of Jesus, Scripture dares to present the living God as fundamentally and essentially Love (1 John 4:8). Present as Spirit in the world, God is the lover of this world, including us human beings, and graciously desires the well-being of all. Faith then becomes the radical experience that at the heart of the world this kind of

Love exists as a reality greater than any other, and ceaselessly acts with compassion to heal, redeem, and liberate. This conviction is expressed in prayer — by turns silent, wildly lamenting, repenting, joyfully thanking and praising — in integrity of life, and in praxis that corresponds to God's own heart. In the biblical book of Wisdom, Holy Sophia goes to great pains to prepare a feast, setting the table, dressing meats, fermenting wine, and sending out her maids as messengers to gather all who will listen. Cognizant that the word of God lives from the energies of our own lives, we adults in the church join with each other in the Spirit of Sophia to set out a banquet of faith's good things and call to future generations to come and be nourished with wisdom for their life's journey.

Chapter 2

Knit Together by the Spirit as Church

M. Shawn Copeland

WHEN THE GIFT OF THE SPIRIT prompts men and women to confess Jesus as Lord, the community we call church comes into being. This confession lays the ground for a new common world of experience, understanding, judgment, decision, commitment, and love. In other words, the church is that community of human persons who hear Christ's message, respond to it under the power of the Spirit, and enter into a "new" and distinctive world of common meaning, commitment, love, and action. Theologians name this invitation the "inner gift of God's love";[1] believers experience that gift as being-in-love with God, which may be understood as Mystery, thematized as the work of grace, and realized in authentic living. The gift of God's loving Spirit creates a new basis for community. Women and men experience themselves as transformed persons who are called to live out this gift of love concretely through transformed human relations and who are knit together and empowered by that same Spirit to witness to a new reality.

The confession of Jesus as Lord, as Christ, does not deconstruct cultural or racial or gender or economic or political difference, but rather reorients such differences in light of a profound, transformative unity in Christ through the Spirit (Rom. 12:2; Gal. 3:28). The possibilities for such unity can be found in the earliest records of those who followed "the way" Jesus taught:

> Now there were devout Jews from every nation under heaven living in Jerusalem. And at this sound the crowd gathered and was bewildered, because each one heard them speaking in the native language of each. Amazed and astonished, they asked, "Are not all these who are speaking Galileans? And how is it that we hear, each of us, in our own native language? Parthians, Medes, Elamites, and residents of Mesopotamia, Judea and Cappadocia, Pontus and Asia, Phrygia and Pamphylia, Egypt and the parts of Libya belonging to Cyrene, and visitors from Rome, both Jews and proselytes, Cretans and Arabs — in our own languages we hear them speaking about God's deeds of power." All were amazed and perplexed, saying to one another, "What does this mean?" (Acts 2:5–12)

The followers of "the way" invited people of every tongue and custom, blood and land to the "good news" of salvation. None were to be excluded from God's compassionate embrace. The narrators of the Gospels identified the preaching of the apostles with the instructions of Jesus: "Go therefore and make disciples of all nations, baptizing them in the name of the Father and of the Son and of the holy Spirit, teaching them to observe all that I have commanded you" (Matt. 28:19–20a). "When the Advocate comes, whom I will send to you from the Father, the Spirit of truth who comes from the Father, he will testify on my behalf. You also are to testify because you have been with me from the beginning" (John 15:26–27). "Jesus said to [the disciples], 'Peace be with you. As the Father has sent me, so I send you.' When he had said this, he breathed on them and said to them, 'Receive the Holy Spirit' " (John 20:21–23).

The *ekklesia,* the church that emerged in the first century, was polyglot, culturally diverse, multiracial, flexible, economically and socially complex, experimental in its service and liturgy, daring in love of neighbor, and unafraid of the martyr's crown. This community lived out the compelling and dangerous memory of the crucified Jesus of Nazareth, whom they confessed as Lord and God. Yet we know how unwise it is to romanticize primitive Christianity and its growth and development. Human cooperation with divine grace, despite its abiding presence, is often slow, even difficult to discern, and, perhaps, even more difficult to realize. We have come to grasp, at least to some degree, the impact of the militancy of Constantine and Theodosius, of centuries of bitter doctrinal controversy, of persistent anti-Semitism, of crusades against the followers of Islam, of the torture of dissidents and women (and men) perceived as possessing strange powers upon "the spirit of the Church."[2]

Various and diverse peoples in antiquity practiced exclusion, but did not do so exhaustively, necessarily, or exclusively on the basis of race. Certainly, these same peoples expressed aesthetic preferences for the physiognomy of their own group. Yet scholarly opinions diverge on the meaning of race in antiquity. In a review of early Greco-Roman and early Christian literatures, theologian Robert Hood uncovered pejorative use of the term "black."[3] On the other hand, historian David Goldenberg concludes that in ancient Hebrew biblical literature as well as in Jewish-Hellenistic and rabbinic/targumic literature, race, in the modern sense, was of little importance.[4] But New Testament scholar Gay Byron argues that "assumptions about ethnic groups, geographical locations, and color differences" were appropriated and used rhetorically by early Christians to instruct and admonish followers as well as to signal and name threats and dangers to theological, spiritual, and devotional practices in their communities.[5]

Racism, as we know it, is a modern phenomenon that evolved from the sixteenth to the eighteenth century and is linked to European exploration. Kim Hall has shown how the colors white and black became the conduit through which the English began to formulate the notions of "self" and "other."[6] Soon "self" and "other" along with skin color became fixed denotative signifiers of racial and moral superiority, blurring into ontological notions about human being. Christian teaching joined merely conventional aesthetic taste to religious metaphor (i.e., white = pure = good; black = impure = bad) in order to justify biased ideas of Africa, its peoples and cultures, and, hence, the necessity of enslaving Africans. The religious and social blight spawned by this legacy extends even into our own day. Yet as church, we are called to witness to the message and mission of Jesus in the here-and-now, in the midst of cultural pluralism and diversity.

This essay is a modest effort in the service of a complex historical, theological, and sociological problematic — the challenge *to be church* in our time and place.

To that end, it explores meanings of culture, cultural diversity, and racist culture in order to offer some suggestions about how we as church, with the aid of the Holy Spirit, might be open to conversion for the transformation of ourselves and our situation. The first section briefly sketches some meanings of culture and distinguishes the authentic cultural diversity from a false multiculturalism. In order to open up our thinking about the way in which ideology penetrates our most basic assumptions, feelings, and behaviors, the second section probes the meaning of racist culture or a culture of racism. The third section assumes an integral role for the Spirit in knitting us together not so much across, but rather in and through our very cultural diversity of the church as we respond to the possibilities of new life in Christ.

Culture and Cultural Diversity

To speak about cultural diversity assumes some grasp of culture. Defining culture as a set of meanings and values that inform a way of life emphasizes it as a dynamic activity of critical imagination, understanding, judgment, and mediation. These meanings and values instruct and admonish, develop and sustain, form and transform, create and communicate. These meanings and values may be expressed in various ways — in art, language, symbols, ideas, attitudes, and, in the deeds and lives of women and men. At the same time, these meanings and values are conserved in the institutions, roles, tasks, operations, and cooperations of any group or society.

Culture-making is an essential aspect of our humanity. Theologian Orlando Espín makes this point when he states: "What is human in human life is that which is cultural."[7] Only through and within culture do we express common and complementary understandings of our collective experience, create true and beautiful expressions of that understanding, examine and change ourselves in light of that truth and beauty, and communicate that truth and beauty to others.

Certainly, "the cultural diversity of humankind is [self-evident]. . . . We have groups of people who are human, hence cultural in a wide variety of ways."[8] Each group's understanding of and formation in meaning and value differ and are distinct. Thus, through cultural meanings and values, one group of persons may be distinguished from another. Cultural diversity, then, implies a diversity or variety of cultures — a variety or diversity of meanings and values that are expressed by human beings through and within their lived experiences.

Human beings, even groups of human beings, can and often do function in more than one cultural setting, but this capacity ought not to be confused with multiculturality. For multiculturality, Espín states, is but a "theoretical image," an instance of wishing for what does not and cannot exist. Quite rightly, he questions the use of the term: "Who would benefit the most from the supposed implementation of multiculturality? In fact, who is in charge of defining multiculturality and judging when it has been sufficiently achieved?" Even if the term multiculturality implies "the quest for equality and inclusiveness, [it] assumes that there is an already established reality to which others are now welcome."

Thus, the rhetoric or language and action of multiculturality undermine cultural diversity on behalf of the dominant group and their preservation of the status quo. Multiculturality disguises the "fear of an inability to deal with cultural diversity.... [It] is a mechanism to co-opt the dominated into accepting as most real the social constructs and meaning[s] of the dominant."[9]

The United States like so many other nations is rich in culturally diverse human capital. This cultural diversity also characterizes the global Christian church *we are*. Yet we Americans seem to have great difficulty grappling with this diversity and difference. Women and people of color frequently bring a particular sensitivity to the matter of diversity and difference because they have had the experience of being "other" often. But generally speaking, we far too often focus on difference only to condemn or to ostracize; far too conveniently, we ignore or refuse to acknowledge that we diverse peoples and cultures may learn from one another. Political scientist Iris Marion Young perceptively observes that in our modern liberal consciousness, "the ideal of liberation [is equated with] elimination of group difference."[10] Subtly and blatantly we reward uniformity, endorse surrender to market values, and repress the creativity and possibility of diversity and difference.

Societal fear both of difference and of cultural diversity undermines any assertion that Christian living is inconsistent with powerlessness, dehumanization, and deprivation. Theologically, our fear of the "other" uncovers a form of despair at the power and grace of the Holy Spirit to change our hearts and lives — to transform us and our cultures from the inside out. As individuals and as community, we are set against ourselves, against one another, against unity in Christ: "so we, though many, are one body in Christ, and individually members of one another" (Rom. 12:5).

Racist Culture

What does it mean to speak about racist culture or culture as racist? How are we to account for the emergence, entrenchment, denotation of culture as racist? And how are we to bring about a change or transformation of racist culture? As bias, that is, a more or less conscious choice of an iniquitous way of living, racism in a given culture or society manifests itself through the "ideas, attitudes, dispositions, norms and rules, linguistic, literary, and artistic expressions, architectural forms and media representations, practices and institutions."[11] These manifestations or expressions convey meanings and values that affirm, promote, and reward an ideology of supremacy and dominance.

To qualify a culture as racist may well shock. But for a human being to live within and be formed by meanings and values inimical to one's very being does shock. When any one group of people coerces another people to live in and live out of meanings and values, which do not emerge from common and complementary fields of experience, of understanding, of judging, of deciding, then that group, which has assumed cultural and racial superiority, does grave damage. For the meanings and values that constitute a culture are not "mere accretions to [some] essential and indivisible humanity," writes Rabbi Jonathan Sacks, but rather "the very substance of how most people learn what it is to be human."[12] Emanuele Crialese's realistic and hauntingly magical film *Golden Door* depicts not only the fearful and fascinated yearning of a young widower, Salvatore Mancuso, and his sons for opportunities in the "new world," but also the condescending cultural and racist suspicions of the officials of Ellis Island. Confronted with tests of her "fitness" to enter America, the golden door, Donna Fortunata Mancuso, Salvatore's mother, with great dignity refuses to comply with what she recognizes as an assault against her person, against her culture. The meanings and values of white, Anglo-Saxon Protestant America set the measure of correct behavior, adequate responses, and appropriate reactions. Who and what diverged from this measure diverged from the measure of humanity.

On the whole, southern Europeans fared better than African Americans in the United States, perhaps because of their ability to establish enclaves of cultural distinctiveness and resistance, to maintain vivid personal memories and communal history, and to sustain emotional and physical connectedness to familial and affective relationships in the "old world." Unlike African Americans, who underwent severe, although never totalizing, cultural injury, southern Europeans were grounded securely in the meanings and values through which they expressed their humanity. And, unlike African Americans, southern Europeans, over time, both changed and were changed into racially acceptable members of American society.

Racist culture challenges the religious imagination. We must see, Rabbi Sacks writes, "God's image in one who is not in our image."[13] We are called to repudiate both a nationalism that oppresses and dominates the other, the stranger, and a putative universalism that eradicates difference and replicates the other, the stranger, in our image. The first exemplifies prejudice that when joined to power yields racist supremacy; the second defines intolerance. The parable of the good Samaritan checks the Christian failure to take difference seriously, to see God's image in the one who is not in our image. To quote Rabbi Sacks again: "Nothing has proved harder in the history of civilization than to see God, or good, or human dignity in those whose language is not mine, whose skin is a different colour, whose faith is not my faith and whose truth is not my truth."[14] This notion is reiterated in *Brothers and Sisters to Us,* the pastoral letter of the Catholic bishops of the United States condemning racism. The bishops state quite unequivocally: "racism is a sin: a sin that divides the human family, blots out the image of God among specific members of that family, violates the fundamental dignity of those called to be children of the same Father."[15]

This essay began with a notion of church as grounded by the work of the Holy Spirit in communal confession of Jesus as Lord. Then it sketched a definition of culture and cultural diversity, indicated the hazards of the notion of multiculturalism, and uncovered aspects of racist culture. Although this reflection assumes a role for the Holy Spirit in knitting diverse peoples together as church, just what that role may be has not been discussed. To this task I now turn.

Diversity as a Work and Gift of the Spirit

The Holy Spirit is the source and principle of the life of the church. The sign that the Holy Spirit is that source and that principle is manifest in transformed ethical and moral behavior. Cultural imperialism and racism constitute sins against the life of the community of Christ, the Resurrected Lord. As such, cultural imperialism and racism may be categorized as social sins. Moreover, these sins constitute sins against the Holy Spirit as they seek to thwart the power of the Spirit, deaden the minds, hearts, and actions of believers:

> And do not grieve the Holy Spirit of God, with which you were marked with a seal for the day of redemption. Put away from you all bitterness and wrath and anger and wrangling and slander, together with all malice, and be kind to one another, tenderhearted, forgiving one another, as God in Christ has forgiven you. (Eph. 4:30–33)

The social sins of cultural imperialism and racism disrupt our relationship with God and make it difficult, if not impossible, for us to open ourselves to God's reconciling love.[16]

As the source and principle of the life of the church, "the Spirit dwells [among us and] is at work in the most decisive acts of [our] life [as church]."[17] The energy or power of the Spirit "arouses [in us] not only a desire for the age to come, but, by that very fact, animates, purifies, and strengthens those noble longings ... by which the human family strives to make it is life more human and to render the whole earth [docile] to this goal."[18] Through the work of the Spirit, peoples of diverse races, ethnicities, and cultures hear and respond to Christ's message and experience this gift as being-in-love with God. The power of the Holy Spirit knits together people of diverse races, ethnicities, and cultures, dissolving every barrier, while regarding difference with dignity. The work of the Holy Spirit brings about unity in diversity and sustains diversity in unity.[19] "For in the one Spirit we were all baptized into one body — Jews or Greeks, slaves or free — and we were all made to drink of one Spirit" (1 Cor. 1:13).

The Gifts of the Spirit

The gifts of the Holy Spirit — wisdom, understanding, counsel, fortitude, knowledge, piety, and fear of or reverential awe before God — are given to individual women and men for the good of the community. These gifts promote and nurture the community's growth in the life of Christ. As gifts of the intellect, wisdom, understanding, counsel, and knowledge help us to discern and assent to the will of God, orient us toward moral living, nourish right conscience and prudence, and prepare us to do what is true. These gifts are mediated to us in African American Catholic communities through elders, women and men, who not only teach young people the demands of Christian living, but also embody those demands. These gifts are mediated through friends or spiritual directors or teachers, who help us to assess and understand our religious experiences and prod us toward continued growth in holiness and in truth. These gifts liberate us from ideology so that we might hear and respond to that Voice which runs counter to all the ideologies of this world.[20] They encourage our questions in pursuit of justice and the common good.

The gifts of fortitude, piety, and fear or reverential awe before God direct the will. Piety is the gift of the Spirit that moves us to love and worship God, who is the Father of Jesus Christ. Fortitude strengthens our resolve to do what is right and good, especially when what is right and good may be difficult to carry out. It supports critical discernment with regard to the historical situation in which we live and empowers us to join with others in creating and healing in history and society. The gift of reverential awe or wonder steadies us in seeking and doing what is right and good for love of God and in anticipation of the coming of God's reign. In relation to cultural diversity, the presence of these gifts manifest themselves in welcoming cultural and racial difference of the other; in generous concern concretely extended to the stranger; in joy in the gifts and growth of others; in humility about one's own cultural attainments. "For all who are led by the Spirit of God are the sons and daughters of God" (Rom. 8:14).

The Spirit of Our Resistance and Creativity

The Spirit calls us to openness to the other, to conversion of heart and mind — to transformation and change. The Spirit leads us *as church* to embrace the responsibility of resistance and creativity in order to honor the human other, to respect and enjoy cultural diversity. To resist cultural imperialism and racism, *as church* we must repudiate all exclusionary symbols, values, criteria, and practices. At the same time, we must support creative initiatives in the development of new symbols and practices, in the articulation of new values and criteria for a life of human flourishing. In this regard, let me offer three suggestions.

First, *as church,* in order to resist the powerful cultural imperialism and racism that have shaped our society, we must open ourselves to the Holy Spirit. We acknowledge the Holy Spirit as the God of life and in our quest for that which gives us life, we hunger and thirst for the Holy Spirit. Thus, in the struggle against cultural imperialism and racism, the Holy Spirit nurtures and sustains our desire for life — for freedom, for communion, for participation, for equality. The Spirit's work in us enables us to resist the reduction of human persons to statistics or social problems, to metaphors or attributes, to stereotypes or categories. The Spirit's work in us enables us to grasp women and men as instances of the intelligible, as intelligent in the world, instances of incarnate moral and ethical choice in a world under the influence of sin, yet standing in relation to a field of supernatural grace.[21] Such behavior emphasizes and engages humanity's essential humanness. Our resistance to racism as church must be rooted in a notion of person that acknowledges, confesses, testifies, and witnesses that all human beings are made in the image and likeness of God. This understanding of person acknowledges, confesses, testifies, and witnesses that our unity is incomplete unless we honor the riches of our differences, which are also gifts of the Spirit.

Second, as church, we must take the issues of cultural imperialism and racism seriously if we are to resist their corrosive influence on our daily living. *Golden Door,* the film mentioned earlier, accurately depicts a slice of immigration to the United States in the early twentieth century. The film's portrayal of the humiliation of the "other" evokes the current debate about immigration, undocumented workers, border crossing, and the building of barriers along the U.S.–Mexican border.

Taking cultural imperialism and racism seriously as church entails that we reject neutrality, that we take sides. Such an option calls for solidarity in act, which is practically intelligent and intelligently practical. To make such an option as church involves critical examination of conscience and of historical consciousness; to make such an option requires careful study and thoughtful grappling with the relevant issues in the context of a faith, which makes the stranger welcome and which understands that we are all strangers and sojourners for our true home lies in another realm. Moreover, as church such an option demands that we attend to the Spirit's energy and power, relinquish solutions produced by egoism, and commit ourselves to prayer as a condition for the possibility of bringing about the common good.

Third, in city after city in the United States, youth succumb to the lure of violence, and Latino, black, and poor white youth are especially vulnerable. As church, we must speak and act; already our silence and avoidance have sown a bitter crop. We need to seek the guidance of the Holy Spirit in order to learn how to be attentive to our youth. We not only must counsel young people but also live rightly in the midst of the vapid market values that swamp ordinary daily choices. We not only must advocate appreciation of the cultures, histories, and experiences of other and diverse peoples but also model hospitality, which encounters and dialogues with those whose national origin or culture or language or race or economic status differs from our own. We not only must denounce violence and brutality but also develop strategies that expose the corrosive impact of the gestures, dress, and rhetoric of gang life, which surrounds our youth. We must live a peace that does not merely suppress aggression but also creatively and actively befriends others and ourselves. With the help of the Spirit, we live the peace of Christ.

Conclusion

This brief essay on cultural diversity began by pointing to the action and power of the Spirit to bring about the *ekklesia* — the assembly of believers — as a community gathered around and grounded in the radical meaning of the "good news" of salvation in Jesus Christ. The transcultural, transhistorical intention of that message manifests itself in the Spirit's work of knitting us together *as church*. Next, the essay sketched out some definitions of culture and cultural diversity, probed the notion of racist culture or a culture of racism, and finally suggested some ways that an *inSpirited church* might respond to social predicaments of cultural imperialism and racism.

Like the church of the first century, the church of the twenty-first century is multilingual, culturally diverse, multiracial, flexible, economically and socially complex, experimental in preaching, service, and liturgy. But we are too rarely daring in our love of neighbor. We too often ignore the parable of the great banquet, reserving places for those who would advance our economic and social standing. We have grown cautious before the dangerous memory of the crucified Jesus. We confess Jesus of Nazareth as Lord and God, but do so in such a way that we have rendered being church as membership in just another volunteer organization claiming only some of our time.

We are church of the twenty-first century: only through our openness to and acceptance of the power of the Spirit shall we incarnate what it means "to be church," realizing through embodied concrete witness, worship, and work the meaning of the Gospel in our time and place. Only through the power of the Spirit shall we grow as origins of value in true love, to create spaces of freedom open to all — without regard to race or gender or culture or ethnicity or language — where the liberating work of Jesus may be lived, served, and communicated. Only through such living shall the gift of the Holy Spirit set free in us the reign of God.

Chapter 3

The Possibilities of Creating Church

A Personal Reflection

ROSEMARY RADFORD RUETHER

I AM HAPPY TO HAVE the opportunity to reflect on women and the church at this crucial time in the history of Roman Catholicism.[1] Let me begin by saying something of my context and intellectual history in relation to the Catholic Church. I come from an ecumenical family: a Catholic mother, an Anglican father, a Jewish uncle, a Russian Orthodox great-aunt, and Quaker relatives. There was never any doubt about what religious identity was strongest in this mix, namely, that of my mother's Catholicism, which was at the same time strongly committed and yet intellectually sophisticated. But it was also clear that the other family religious traditions were to be respected. This combination of being both Catholic and ecumenical is one that I have expanded, rather than rejected.

There was only one serious moment when I considered leaving the Catholic Church. This was about forty years ago when I realized that I did not believe in the doctrine of papal infallibility. It was not simply that I doubted this idea, but rather that it became clear to me that this was a serious ecclesiological error, theologically. I explored joining my father's Anglican Church, with which I was familiar having occasionally accompanied him to church as a child. In this process I became clear that I was simply uninterested in becoming an Anglican, much as I appreciated many aspects of this church. The only church that interested me, that held and still holds my loyalty, was and is Roman Catholicism.

My recommitment to Roman Catholicism was and is not based on the idea that it is the only true church or even the best church, but simply that it is a very important expression of historical Christianity in the West and that its reform and renewal are vital to Christian and human betterment. It is not that I expect that it is totally reformable according to my own vision of what the church should be, but rather that the reform vision of Catholicism that has been birthed in the last forty years needs to be defended as a vital option within world Catholicism. I am committed to keeping this reform option alive and to supporting that wing of Catholicism which expresses this vision, even while recognizing that there are those who seek to contest and even drive out this option. Today I would locate myself as an ecumenical Catholic Christian, who acknowledges the truth of other world religions, while at the same time being committed to this particular church as my immediate church context.

I prepare this article painfully aware that in the last twenty-five years in the pontificate of the previous pope (John Paul II) and his present successor, it seems unlikely that institutional Catholicism can move in any direction except backward, not back to the Gospels, but back to Vatican I, back to the defensive posture of an infallibilist papal monarchy seeking to impose its will upon the world church and even upon the world outside the Catholic Church. Opus Dei members have been placed by the Vatican in episcopal positions in country after country and also in delegations to the United Nations and the European Union in a bid to control world affairs in a reactionary way. This has meant not only an effort to place reactionary Catholic leaders in places of influence around the world, but also to dismantle those institutions and programs that have been developed to promote a Christian liberative vision of justice.

Many former Catholics that I know see any effort to stay committed to the reform of such a church as increasingly futile, perhaps even masochistic, and certainly a waste of energy best spent doing other more productive things. I think we need to look full in the face the negative character of this reactionary drive of the hierarchical church government without minimalizing its seriousness, but also without confusing it with the ultimate ground of our faith, hope, and love in and for the church. It is a firm rooting of ourselves in this ultimate ground that we most need if we are to be able to stay the course as prophetic reformers in the Catholic Church at this time.

My vision of the future church is shaped by the effort to respond to the *Kairos* of this period in human history, a time when the hopes released by the end of the Cold War have been betrayed by a new American imperialist militarism, a time when we must stand in horror at the increasing gaps between wealth and poverty in the world as a whole and at the increasing devastation of the earth caused by profligate and unjust materialism, as well as our sense of both urgency and helplessness before these challenges. It is also shaped by what I believe to be the perennial meaning of the Gospel, rooted in the person and ministry of Jesus Christ, ever new and yet ever one in a wisdom beyond passing historical changes in society and thought.

To me that transcendent wisdom — and I do consciously use the word "transcendent" here in what I regard as its authentic sense — is summed up by the word "grace." Grace is the authentic being of God made present to us in Christ's death and resurrection, which both liberates us from all the deformations of our power and security grabbing and returns us to our deeper and authentic self and calling as God's good creation. To me, being the church, the body of Christ, is basically about being the community who lives in and through that life of grace.

In discussing some of the characteristics of such a church, the church we need now, the church we have always needed, the church we were called to be from the beginning and are called to be today, both as local churches and as world church, I would like to explore briefly six elements.

The Church We Need Now

A Multicultural Church

We are called today to be authentically Catholic, not hegemonic white male Euro-Americans who confuse white male Western European culture with normative human and Christian culture to be imposed on Indigenous peoples, on Africans, Asians, Arabs, Polynesians, and women of all groups. This means really exploring, claiming, and celebrating the actual cultural diversity of our Catholic people in the world. This also means paying particular attention to the peoples who are the descendants from brutal colonization and enslavements imposed by European conquests over the centuries: the Indigenous peoples of the Americas, the Pacific, and elsewhere, and the African peoples brought in chains to the Americas and the Caribbean.

Globally Catholics are a people increasingly Hispanic, African, and Asian, even as the old heartland of European Catholicism in Italy, France, and Spain grows apathetic and their offspring in North America are following suit. Yet we are a people still wedded to cultural patterns shaped in the European Middle Ages, and ours is a church polity shaped by fourth-century Roman imperialism and eighteenth-century absolute monarchy seeking to live on as ecclesiastical fossils after the political substance has died. We need to acknowledge the relativity and even demonic character of these hegemonic cultural and political forms of the past and, at the same time, embrace a rich dialogue between the many cultures that make up the Catholic people, for the transformation and mutual enrichment of our whole cultural and social life.

A Church Committed to the Poor and the Oppressed

Since the birth of liberation theologies in Latin America, Africa, and Asia, brothers and sisters from these regions have been calling the church to renew itself in the preferential option for the poor. The Christian church is authentically the body of Christ by living in solidarity with those of our community who are treated most unjustly, who are most marginalized, despised, and destitute in the existing system of power and wealth. The foundational call of Christ to repentance, ministry, and service was and remains "good news to the poor, the liberation of the captive, the setting at liberty of those who are oppressed." Only by living that good news do we live the Gospel.

Yet to live that good news after twenty centuries of Catholic Christianity is also to live by repentance, to live in deep mourning and contrite struggle to change what has overwhelmingly been and still is a primarily contrary reality: the institutionalization of ecclesiastical power and privilege rooted in a preferential option for the rich and powerful. Since at least the Constantinian establishment of the early fourth century, if not before, Catholic Christianity has grown in wealth and power by blessing the power of aristocracies, of emperors and kings, of merchants and capitalist corporations, and their economic, political, and military might. It has mostly advised the poor and the oppressed to win favor with God by obeying their masters. If Christ calls us to be faithful by solidarity with the poor, then Christ calls us to be a repentant countersign to most of what we have been in history.

A Church Liberated from Sexism

To contemplate a future church liberated from sexism, a church that truly lives as a community of equality and mutuality of women and men, that is liberated from sexual pathology for the sake of healthy, loving sexuality, that is liberated from homophobia to acknowledge diversity of sexual orientations, this indeed is to be deeply repentant and transformed from much of what we have been through our history.

Ours is a time when sexism and sexual pathology seem more rampant than ever in church leaders. It is a time when the past and present popes cling to a misguided concept of unchanging truth by insisting on a male celibate priesthood against any possibility of married priests or women priests or acknowledging the existence of gay priests, while actual male celibate priests are increasingly discredited by charges of sexual abuse of youth, male and female. These same popes regard rejection of contraception and the ordination of women as if these were the first articles of faith. This era in the life of the church does not seem to be one in which there is much hope for repentance of the church's historical sins of sexism.

Yet it is precisely at such a time when we need to deepen our new recognition that Christian community means a community of equals, a community in which the distinctions of male and female, slave and free have been indeed overcome in the new Humanity, where we can celebrate that women as much as men are images of God and representatives of Christ. We need to affirm women as preachers, as sacramental ministers, and as theologians, bringing women's gifts of ministry fully into the church for the first time. We also need to affirm that being in Christ restores us to, and does not alienate us from the fullness of our embodied selves and the ability of our whole body to give love and pleasure to one another, without fear, and also without irresponsibility or exploitation.

A Democratic Church

Here too we seem to be on the horns of a contradiction, seeking a participatory and egalitarian church polity that has been the opposite of the historic church polity that patterned itself after patriarchy, aristocracy, and monarchy from the late first century to its incorporation into the system of the Roman Empire in the late fourth century and on through the medieval and early modern periods. When bishops thunder that "the church is not a democracy," they do not intend merely to speak about historical and social facts, but about divine intentions. In their mind, Christ founded the church to be a centralized feudal monarchy, of pope over bishops, bishops over priests, priests over laity, men over women and children. They believe that this is what Christ intended.

It is unthinkable to such bishops that this whole pattern of hierarchy might have been historically accidental, modeled on existing political systems, and, even worse, a betrayal of a deeper vision of the church as a community of equals better expressed in patterns of life where all members have a voice and a share in ministry. But it is precisely this unthinkableness of the historically accidental and non-normative nature of such a monarchical hierarchical structure that not only must be thought today, but is in a real sense obvious once one has a minimal acquaintance with the New Testament and church history.

A Church That Acknowledges Its Fallibility

A church that believes itself infallible in the pronouncements of its monarchical ruler is a church that has encapsulated itself in its own apostasy and made that apostasy irredeemable. In my view every other sin is forgivable except the sin of infallibility, for this is the sin against the Holy Spirit. This does not mean that we cannot repent of the mistaken claim of papal infallibility, imposed at a particularly bad moment in late nineteenth-century Italian Catholic history. Rather it means that we cannot repent of this or any other mistake that we have ever made, or are making, unless we acknowledge that we indeed can err, not simply as individuals, but as an institution acting in its formal and public institutional capacity. We need to clearly analyze and critique in detail these many mistakes, for examples in teachings about birth control, about the nonordainability of women, about the spiritual superiority of celibacy, about the divinity of patriarchal hierarchy, and finally the doctrine of infallibility itself, specifically, and not just in vague and abstract terms that leave in doubt what is being said.

To repent of the error of infallibility that fixates all other errors is also to liberate ourselves to be human, knowing ourselves to be finite, fallible, seeing in part and not totally, absolutely, or with final certainty. It is also to liberate ourselves to be Christian, to live by faith, repentance, and the grace of transformation without which we cannot be in authentic continuity with the new life in Christ. For new life in Christ can only be born and continually reborn through death to our idolatries and resurrection of a life that we hold only by not holding it, by being upheld by the One in whom alone we have ultimate trust. This ultimate trust excludes not only formulaic certainties of doctrines and teaching authorities, whether of pope or Bible, but also liberates us from infantile needs for such certainties. It liberates us to search intelligently for the perspectival truths that we can construct, without needing to cling to them absolutely and literally as the basis of our life.

A Church That Lives by Grace

All this is to say once again that the church we seek, in which alone we can have life, is the church that lives by grace, not in the sense of a grace that excludes knowledge, experience, historical change, but a grace that upholds us and supports us in and through both our searches for meaning and justice and our freedom to repent, liberating ourselves from misplaced ideas and systems and renewed in the miracle of life that wells up anew every day.

How Do We Get There from Here?

Once we have sketched something of a vision of authentic Christian community, the key question is how do we get there from here? What are the ways of moving toward that vision, given a present church polity and ideology that mostly institutionalizes and sanctifies the opposite? I would like to suggest four ways that we can begin to change ourselves and then some ways of building organizational bases to support such alternatives.

First, we need to *grow up*. I say this with no intention of demeaning middle-aged adults, including myself, who regard ourselves as already pretty grown up. Rather I am pointing out the great difficulty we have really liberating ourselves from the residue of a spirituality of infantilism that was deeply bred into our psyches in our traditional Catholic socialization.

Catholicism, like all patriarchal hierarchical institutions, re-creates relationships of domination and submission, modeled on a fusion of male over female with parent over child relations. We learn to dominate those below us and submit to those above us, but not how to be equals in mutually affirming relationships. We are not encouraged to become genuinely autonomous adults, but rather to remain always the dependent child under some kind of higher authority. These patterns of relationship are central to clerical culture.

This socialization into paternalistic dependency fixates us between rebellion and submission, ever reverting back to forms of submission as a way of assuaging feelings of guilt for rebellion, but not really being freed to be a responsible adult. By "responsible adult" I mean someone who has a confidence in one's own autonomous mind and agency, without either self-inflation or self-negation, and who is able to take responsibility for helping to develop the future of a community, without needing either to assuage guilt or assert power relations through such service. This is the kind of maturity required for real ministry, but it is difficult to develop in a paternalistic system.

Second, we need to be people of *prayer*. This requires that we overcome the kind of split between social action and spirituality that has been endemic in our culture. Real ability to stay the course of reform and service for the long haul is possible only if we have a deep grounding in the disciplines of daily prayer, meditation, and cultivation of the presence of God in our lives. This means resisting the demands for workaholism and endless achievement to find time for this kind of quiet meditation on a regular basis, and from these disciplines, beginning then to cultivate a sense of this presence of God even in the midst of activity.

These kinds of discipline were part of our traditional spirituality, but they were practiced often under compulsion and with an alienating spirituality. As we cast off these alienating power relations and ideas, we tended to let the patterns of prayer fall away, instead of finding out how to reclaim them through our own agency and with modes of prayer that would be nurturing.

Third, we need to have *critical knowledge* about church history and theology to be able to sort out adequately what Christian themes are really meaningful and what truth claims need to be questioned as assertions of power that are not conducive to spiritual health. As theologically trained people who have been in ministry, it may seem beside the point to say that we need to be better educated in theology and church history. But one of the things I learned from a dialogue that the Women's Ordination Conference conducted with the Catholic bishops of the bishops' committee on women some thirty years ago was that their seminary education was woefully inadequate.

The bishops did not have a critical education in Scripture or church history that would have enabled them to sort out the questions being put by feminist theology vis-à-vis assertions of the papacy that topics like women's ordination were against church tradition and so could not be discussed. In fact the general tendency was simply to say this could not be discussed because church authority had said so, without even being able to conceive of independent investigation of this claim from the standpoints of Scripture and church history.

Fourth, we as a people need to be *socially committed.* Like taking time for prayer, this calls for some rearrangement of our lives, and sometimes the way that we make a living, to find ways to connect at least part of our wealth and energy to solidarity with those less fortunate and to live more sustainably with the earth. Preferential option for the poor and an ecological lifestyle cannot be just rhetorical slogans. They have to relate to the way we live our lives. We need organized efforts to create an alternative society that stands up against the present global (dis)order being imposed by the World Bank and the powerful nations. We need a global uprising against the triumphalism of the rich and powerful who wish to make it appear as if there is no alternative possible to the neo-liberalism that is impoverishing the earth and the majority of people of the earth.

We need to take ecological impoverishment as seriously as the poverty of humans. These are not separate topics, but part of one and the same picture. We have to bring the ecological question home to our daily lives; this means examining how the way we live every day is part of the problem of global impoverishment of the earth and all its inhabitants.

Obviously ecological sustainability cannot be accomplished solely by changes in private lifestyle. Ours is a macrosystem of production, consumption, and waste. We need to cultivate a certain awareness of how we participate in this system, examining and making adjustments in how we transport ourselves, consume food and goods, use energy, discard wastes. We can and must find ways to build some of these shifts into our households, schools, offices, and local institutions over which we may have some influence. From this base in consciousness and our concrete struggles for ecological sustainability, we may be able to build larger networks to change patterns of earth-destruction that are diminishing the life of regions and the globe on a macro-level.

Living as Church

These four projects of maturity, prayer, knowledge, and social and ecological commitment need to be fleshed out in our social relations and, most particularly, in how we live as church. It seems to me there are two levels of living as church in a way that cultivates mature and liberating spirituality and social commitment to which we have access and power, regardless of what the official church institution is allowing or not allowing. These are base communities and parallel organizations.

Base Communities

Whether or not we have reasonable parish communities where we feel nourished in weekly worship, it seems to me that base communities in which small groups of ten to fifteen people covenant together for regular prayer, study, worship, discussion, and mutual support are an important foundation for Christian life. Such base communities were an integral part of the vision of the church created by liberation theology in the last two decades. But in my experience many of these base communities remained too clerical, too dependent on bishops, failing to address many sufficiently real issues of daily life, particularly concerns of women and of sexual and domestic abuse. We need to recommit ourselves to developing these communities in a way that will be deeper and more long lasting.

Parallel Organizations

In addition to the small covenant group, parallel organizations are important for projects of both church reform and social action. North American Roman Catholicism, with its tradition of volunteerism, is particularly rich in parallel organizations, which work to extend the boundaries of Roman Catholic activity in a way that is not dependent on hierarchical approval. Call to Action, peace and justice centers such as the Quixote Center in Washington, D.C., the Association for the Rights of Catholics in the Church, the Women-Church network, CORPUS, and Pax Christi are parallel organizations that are increasingly bonding together in national and international networks.

Parallel organizations are also developing all over the world among Catholics: the Catholic Women's Network in Britain, the Eighth of May movement in Holland, feminist theology networks in India and other Asian countries, *Católicas por el Derecho a Decidir* in Latin America, among others. Such parallel organizations might be seen as the Catholic expression of the creation of civil society. Such parallel organizations of Catholics operate within the Catholic community, but not under the juridical power of the hierarchy. They are vital expressions of democratization in the church.

Why Call Such Groups Catholic?

Basically such groups view themselves as Catholic because the membership comprises people of Catholic roots who are addressing reform issues in the Catholic Church, and because they are doing the direct work of ministry that is understood as inspired by Catholic Christian faith and life. Such groups see themselves as being church. Their Catholic Christian identity is self-chosen out of a sense of responsibility for both being church and calling the church as an institution to open itself to very real concerns. The groups are, at the same time, free of the sort of institutional control that could close them down or dismiss their leaders.

Ultimately we are engaged in a process the future of which cannot be predicted. It may be that Catholics concerned with such reforms will grow tired of institutional intransigence and go elsewhere, or it may be that at least parts of the official institution will open itself to more acceptance of such movements. We hope that we are engaged in a process that will lead to the kind of eventual transformation of the official institution that will allow a sufficient range of thought and life. But meanwhile we can and must carry on living ways of being Christian community that satisfy our vision of what is authentic and truthful; in short we need to insist on being the church today and not be just waiting to be allowed to do so tomorrow.

Part Two

KNOWLEDGE AS POWER

Chapter 4

Biblical Interpretation and Women's Experience

KAREN A. BARTA

"Let all who thirst come" (Rev. 21:17)

W HOSE EXPERIENCE COUNTS? Theologian Monika Hellwig asked this question a quarter of a century ago in her address as the first woman invited to give the Père Marquette lecture.[1] Hellwig questioned the adequacy of a theology that for centuries was "written, taught, studied and applied in preaching by men," and within Roman Catholicism, written mostly by a celibate clergy.[2] She raised concerns about those whose experiences remained invisible in this theological reflection: women, racial minorities, colonized peoples, and the poor.[3] Hellwig claimed that the marginalized would be the ones most capable of hearing the liberation message of the Bible. From the standpoint of their respective contexts, oppressed people would grasp fully the Bible's demand for justice. This call, asserted Hellwig, would be something they could "recognize without effort."[4]

Has Hellwig's prediction held true for women? Indeed, women have found hope in the biblical demand for justice and solace in the liberation strands of the Gospels. At the same time, women have struggled mightily with oppressive material in the Bible itself. The result, as Sharon Ringe notes, is that "many conclude that merely pointing to the portions of Scripture whose content supports justice and liberation is not adequate."[5] Beyond initial recognition of the promise apparent in core biblical texts, women still must reckon with much that is disturbing about the Bible.

I begin this essay with an acknowledgment of real challenges that women face both in reading the Bible and realizing how it has been appropriated. Biblical texts have been used frequently to support women's subordination to men. Selective renderings of the biblical material at the disposal of commentators and translators have served to oppress women. It becomes imperative, therefore, as Elisabeth Schüssler Fiorenza highlights, "to see the Bible as a perspectival rhetorical discourse that constructs theological worlds and symbolic universes, in particular historical and political situations."[6] One goal, when engaging biblical texts as women, is to note patterns of ancient patriarchal custom and sexist oriented rendering of texts and to identify the possibilities that biblical texts provide for changing these patterns and renderings.[7]

Taken as a whole, the Bible can be used as a significant corrective to sexist presentations of texts, allowing women again to catch sight of its more dominant liberating message. Only by growing in a deeper understanding of biblical texts and having knowledge of biblical interpretation will women be able to find fresh meaning in old texts. When the Bible has been freed from its oppressive uses, women will no longer feel they are "standing by a river, dying of thirst."[8]

Reading the Bible as Women

A majority of women worldwide have experienced some form of discrimination, be that societal, cultural, ecclesial, political, or a combination of these. As a result, reading the Bible as a woman becomes a very different experience from reading it as a man. One is more likely to pick up on what serves to negate the experiences of women.

When engaging Scripture, one cannot help but notice that God is referred to pronouncedly as "he" and not as "she." Yet the assumption that God is a male is neither doctrinally sound nor biblically arguable. The Bible, in fact, often presents God as Spirit, a word that in its original biblical language is feminine, despite the overwhelming translation of it in the form of the masculine. The church has never taught that God is male, even though male language for God remains dominant in the church's liturgy. There is an operative assumption at a popular level that God is male.[9]

As women pick up the Scriptures, they notice that Jesus is male[10] and they wonder why he chose men to be his twelve apostles, all duly named, with no women among them. They observe that men dominate in nearly every biblical narrative — with some wonderful exceptions, like Huldah and Esther in the Hebrew Bible and Mary Magdalene and the Samaritan woman in the Gospels. Still, Abraham is far more important than Sarah, the mother of his promised progeny, Isaac. Moses is the heroic figure of the Exodus story, and few remember much about his sister other than that she helped save *his* life as an infant. All book prophets are men — Isaiah, Jeremiah, Ezekiel, etc. The Gospels too all bear male names — Matthew, Mark, Luke, and John — followed by letters of Paul to Philemon, Timothy, and Titus, and letters ascribed to James, Peter, John, and Jude. While there are strong messages of inclusion and liberation from injustice to be found in the Bible, making one's way to these becomes challenging. Reading the Bible as a woman requires a clearing of some high hurdles; the experience of worship in a church that espouses only male sacerdotal leaders further raises the bar.

The Bible as Problem

The church's presentation of the Bible as "a pure and everlasting source of spiritual life" is a concern for women.[11] How do women draw from it without experiencing a degree of self-denigration in terms of their womanhood? It is unfortunate that women's voice is largely absent in the Bible and that the women that get mentioned are presented from a male point of view. Biblical women appear most frequently in relation to the men who have power over them.

There are few in-depth presentations of women's standpoints. Can a woman drink from the fount of biblical wisdom without swallowing too much? How can the Bible serve as a source of empowerment for women?

In the nineteenth century, during the first wave of the women's movement in the United States, it became commonplace to quote Scripture as a means of keeping women in their "proper place." Elizabeth Cady Stanton, champion of women's rights and daughter of the Enlightenment, responded with the publication of *The Woman's Bible* in 1895.[12] A great majority of women in Stanton's time were reluctant to join her effort. As a result, the Bible continued to be used to support women's subordination to male authority in many areas of everyday life. It took another twenty-five years for women to win even the right to vote. While women find themselves in a much different place in the twenty-first century, there are persons today still willing to quote problematic texts of the Bible in support of what they believe to be women's "proper place." This leads some women to conclude that the Bible is irretrievable. Is this so?

Three Necessary Claims

In order to move to a place where the Bible's revelatory power can be celebrated, one must be clear in the articulation of three basic claims. The first is that the Bible itself is not God. The second is that patriarchal tendencies found in the Bible are not divinely inspired. A third and particularly helpful claim becomes this: texts and subsequent interpretations are not one and the same. Let us consider each claim in turn.

The Bible Is Not God

While the Bible is the word of God, in that it can mediate encounter with the living God, it is not God. It is written in human words by concrete-historical and socioculturally conditioned human beings, and must be interpreted as such. Far from being viewed as the final and sole word about God, the Bible should be treasured as the sacred text of a people, one that holds their story and vision. The Bible is a presentation of "the initiating presence and mystery of God in the course of human life."[13]

No sacred text, theological idea, or religious image ever captures the fullness of the sacred encounter between God and the human. To think otherwise turns human descriptions of this encounter, even those found in the Bible, into idols. God is forever ultimate mystery, and human language, however fine, is inadequate for speaking about this mystery. The best we humans can do is to speak of God in metaphors. Yet the assertion that scriptural language is metaphorical sometimes offends people, largely because the nature and function of metaphor is so poorly understood.

Metaphor touches on deep realities that elude literal expression. Biblical scholar Sandra Schneiders reminds us that there is "a simultaneous affirmation and negation of the likeness" between the two terms of a metaphor. The metaphor contains an "is" and an "is not," which must be held in irresolvable tension.[14] God is father, but not literally a father, because God is not a male sexual being. The Bible mediates the word of God, but is not literally *the word* of God, as it is written in human language by human authors. This understanding of metaphorical language concurs with a long tradition of "negative theology" within Christianity, which counters any tendency to hold God hostage to human thought or human constructs.

Patriarchy Is Not Divinely Inspired

The Bible's patriarchal patterns and male-dominant language should be of little surprise. The Bible reflects the ancient cultures in which it was written. As patriarchy existed well before the Bible, it can hardly be argued that patriarchy is part of God's "revelation." Patriarchy is a sociohistorical construct, not a biblical invention, and one with very long roots.[15]

Patriarchy can be described in broad terms as the visible expression, manifestation, and institutionalization of male dominance over women both in family and society. It includes the notion that men have held familial and societal positions of significant power over time. But it does not suggest that women have been entirely role-less without any rights or influence or resources. Patriarchy sanctions a division of reality into two worlds: the public world of men's affairs and the private world to which women largely have been confined. Because women in biblical times were relegated to private realms, women's voices are rarely heard in biblical texts.

It becomes imperative then, when reading the Bible as women, to discern what in a text reflects the limitations of a specific cultural matrix. What is *descriptive* of women in biblical times should not be interpreted as *prescriptive*, as indicative of how women should be treated now.

Texts and Interpretations

Biblical texts can be confused with subsequent interpretations of those texts. The bumper sticker that reads; "God said it; I believe it; that settles it," omits the key component: "according to what I interpret it to mean." The Bible is not self-interpreting; texts do not interpret themselves. However familiar the expression, "it says so right in the Bible," every text requires careful interpretation and few texts have only one interpretation. In fact, literary critics speak of texts having layers of meaning and multiple interpretations, with one seldom exhausting all of the text's meaning.

According to contemporary hermeneutical theory, an interpreter is always part of an interpretation. Interpreters have "social locations" (gender, race, class, ethnicity, sexuality, education, experience, upbringing, and the like) that shape (or misshape) how they understand a text. This realization becomes the basis for claiming "hermeneutic privilege." For example, those whose social location causes them suffering at the hands of political, social, and economic systems of oppression and exploitation will have a more immediate grasp of the Bible's message of liberation.[16] As a result, biblical interpretation and subsequent commentary need to come from a variety of social locations in order for us all to grapple better with the intent of biblical texts, particularly those that have been used to justify sexism, heterosexism, racism, colonialism, and the legitimation of war.[17]

With these three claims in place, it becomes possible to ask: How can knowledge of the Bible empower women?

The Bible as Revelatory Text

Revelation implies encounter in which there is a disclosure of God to the human. Like good conversation, revelation requires the attention and activity of two parties, both speaking and hearing. When there is active listening, and God's words are received, revelation occurs. Sandra Schneiders describes this occurrence as "the loving encounter of God and humans in which the self-disclosure of God invites the responding self-gift of the believer resulting in a shared life, a participation of the human being in the divine life of God as God has shared our life in Jesus."[18]

Schneiders, when developing her definition of revelation, reflects on language as self-expression. She notes that we humans speak, first and foremost, "to bring ourselves into the light."[19] Through language, claims Schneiders, persons are able to move beyond a superficial recognition to an actual sharing of "a common life born of communication."[20] She writes: "Speaking/hearing, especially that which takes place in intimate conversation, is not primarily the transfer of information but the mutual gift of selves."[21] The revelatory "word" invites and sustains an ever-deepening relationship with God.

Liberating the Bible and Empowering Women

One of the primary goals of feminist biblical hermeneutics is to "bring *women* into the light" through hermeneutics of retrieval and reconstruction. Another has been to move toward more inclusive translations of the Bible, especially as they so influence communal worship. Language, after all, is powerfully informative and our choices of words matter.

Translating Biblical Texts

When the Bible gets translated in a very literal fashion, taking its cues from the original language of the text, it can read in patriarchal ways showing androcentric bias. Sometimes translators do not stay true to the more inclusive intent apparent in the original biblical language, making matters worse by rendering texts in even more patriarchal fashion. One example of this is the muting of feminine metaphors for God that results when translators insert male pronouns for feminine references.

Readers today are fortunate to have access to a number of excellent commentaries and some very fine inclusive-language translations of the Bible. All efforts to render the Bible's language more gender-inclusive should be welcomed, as these are true to the justice intent of the Gospels. Recent translations like the New Revised Standard Version, the New American Bible, and the Contemporary English Version show marked improvement in this regard. And more broadly inclusive versions include The New Testament and Psalms: An Inclusive Version[22] and translations sponsored by the Priests for Equality: The Inclusive New Testament, The Inclusive Psalms, and The Inclusive Hebrew Scriptures.[23]

While biblical study continues to require the use of modern critical versions of scriptural texts that preserve the original patriarchal, androcentric language of the Bible, Christian communities would be well served to move toward inclusive adaptations of biblical texts in community worship.[24]

In addition to the issue of gender-inclusive language, other considerations regarding translations arise. Translation so impacts interpretation. The Genesis story of Adam and Eve provides an illustration of this. Too often, this story has been interpreted and used to justify women's subordination, based on man being created first and woman being derived from "Adam's rib." How this text gets translated matters greatly. Conscious of this, Phyllis Trible, in 1978, proposed a new reading of Genesis 2–3.

Rereading Adam and Eve

Beginning with the Hebrew word *ha'adam* in Genesis 2:7, Trible argues that the first use of *ha'adam* is translated better as "human" or "the earth creature" than "man," because not until the woman is created does sexuality enter into the picture. Only then does *ha'adam* refer to the male Adam. Before that, she argues, the reference is to all of humanity as it is in the first creation story of Genesis 1:26–27: "Then God said, 'Let us make humankind [*adam*] in our image, according to our likeness.' ... So God created humankind [*adam*] in his image, in the image of God he created them; male and female he created them" (NRSV).[25]

The NRSV does not translate Genesis 2:7 as Trible notes that it should, but the Inclusive Hebrew Scriptures does: "So our God fashioned an earth creature out of the clay of the earth, and blew into its nostrils the breath of life. And the earth creature became a living being." Male superiority based on being created first disappears.

Trible's translation of *ha'adam* is just one part of a complete rereading of Genesis 2–3 that overturns its traditionally male-biased interpretation. Her book *God and the Rhetoric of Sexuality* celebrates Eve and Adam as gifted by God with human sexuality.[26] The creation of Eve is not of Adam's doing (he is asleep) and the rib denotes not Eve's dependence on Adam but her solidarity and equality with him. He says of her: "bone of my bones; flesh of my flesh" (Gen. 2:23).

Selecting Biblical Texts

Just as the Bible does not self-interpret, it does not self-select. Choosing a biblical passage is an interpretive act. It matters who selects and when, where, how, and why certain biblical texts are quoted or studied, while others are not. In the New Testament some troubling texts for women get quoted and attributed unfairly to Paul, while genuine Pauline material suggesting women's equality in discipleship gets underrepresented. How is it that Pauline passages that affirm women's equality of discipleship get overlooked?

A New Testament passage that is not Pauline, one that proves particularly disturbing for what it claims about women, is 1 Timothy 2:11–14:

Let a woman learn in silence with full submission. I permit no woman to teach or
to have authority over a man; she is to keep silent. For Adam was formed first,
then Eve; and Adam was not deceived, but the woman was deceived and became
a transgressor. Yet she will be saved through childbearing, provided they continue
in faith and love and holiness, with modesty. (NRSV)

No translation can amend the problematic interpretation of the creation of
Adam and Eve that is found in this passage. Must a modern reader therefore
accept this flawed typology? Certainly not. The Bible, when taken as a whole,
serves to raise serious questions about this kind of claim.

New Testament texts that advocate women's submission to male authority
frequently reflect a cultural construct of antiquity known as the "household
code," which hierarchically orders the moral duties and responsibilities of husbands and wives, parents and children, masters and slaves. In Ephesians, for
example, one reads: "Wives, be subject to your husbands as you are to the Lord.
For the husband is the head of the wife just as Christ is the head of the church,
the body of which he is the Savior. Just as the church is subject to Christ, so also
wives ought to be, in everything, to their husbands" (5:22–24). Often, when this
passage is quoted, the line before those cited gets omitted. Ephesians 5:21 encourages mutual respect between women and men: "Be subject to one another
out of reverence for Christ." In her classic study *In Memory of Her,* Elisabeth
Schüssler Fiorenza views Ephesians 5:22–24 and others like it as contributing
to the overturning of the original equality of discipleship within the Jesus movement.[27] Indeed, one finds nothing remotely close to the sentiment expressed in
the oppressive Ephesians 5:22–24 appearing in the Gospel tradition.

In response to New Testament texts that advocate a Christianized version
of the "household code" (Col. 3:18–4:1; Eph. 5:22–6:9; 1 Pet. 2:13–3:7),
texts that disempower women, Schüssler Fiorenza points to the early baptismal
formula quoted in Paul's letter to the Galatians, something that clearly mandates
equality in discipleship: "For in Christ Jesus you are all children of God through
faith. As many of you as were baptized into Christ have clothed yourselves with
Christ. There is no longer Jew or Greek, there is no longer slave or free, there
is no longer male and female; for all of you are one in Christ Jesus" (3:26–28
NRSV). Why is it that the admonition "Wives, be subject to your husbands as
you are to the Lord" is recited often, whereas the message of Galatians 3:26–
28 is less heard? Surely the Pauline message of Galatians 3:26–28 is fully in
keeping with the heart of the Gospels. It fits with the story of Pentecost, in which
those gathered in the Upper Room, women and men, experienced together the
power of the Holy Spirit (Acts 2–12). And it is congruent with the mention of
the names of prominent women disciples that Paul provides identifying them as
friends and associates in the work of spreading the good news (Rom. 16:1–15).

Interpreting Biblical Texts

When women call attention to texts that are important correctives to sexism,
texts like Galatians 3:26–28 and Romans 16, they are practicing a *hermeneutics
of retrieval.* When they read the Bible with a keen awareness of the patriarchal

cultures that gave rise to the texts, they are practicing a *hermeneutics of suspicion*. Bringing an awareness of how one's own present *experiences* and *social location* influence one's reading of the text also becomes important. Biblical interpretation is thick with considerations, requiring not just Bible-knowledge, but self-knowledge. In trying to interpret a biblical text most adequately, we look to what is potentially informative, formative, and transformative. What did a text mean originally and what meaning could it have for us today?[28]

Feminist biblical interpretation has the potential to open up fresh understandings of the Bible in relation to women's experiences and concerns. As Hebrew Bible scholar Phyllis Bird states, a feminist reading will "make sense of women's experience, or 'ring true' for women readers."[29] As such, the whole people of God is enriched.

Good News for Women

Gospel means "good news," but traditional presentations of women in the Bible have not always proven to be good news for women. Examples of this abound. The portrayal of Mary Magdalene as a follower of Jesus is remarkably strong in all the Gospels and particularly striking in the Gospel of John. One has to wonder then how her role in tradition sadly and falsely became of a repentant whore, something without biblical warrant. The powerful promise found in Luke's story of Mary and Martha has been lost amid innocuous abstract commentary. And there is the matter of the genealogy of Jesus in Matthew, which appears to be all about men, though there is unexpected mention of *five women*, which continues to "perplex scholars." In each of these New Testament examples, the potential of women's leadership has been submerged. Feminist biblical interpretation seeks to recover the power of women's leadership.

Mary Magdalene (John 21) and Mary and Martha (Luke 10:38–42)

Mary Magdalene was a preeminent witness to the Resurrection, as attested to in all four Gospels, but her significant leadership has been muddied by a false presentation of her as a repentant prostitute — without a shred of textual evidence. John's Gospel has a particularly strong portrait of Mary as the first disciple to experience Jesus as the Risen Lord. He commissions her to tell his other disciples, and she becomes an apostle to the apostles. Fortunately this powerful portrait of Mary Magdalene as a primary witness to the Resurrection is being reclaimed and proclaimed in our time. Through a *hermeneutic of remembrance and reconstruction*, Mary Magdalene's status as a disciple of Jesus has been restored, fending off the popularization of her as romantically involved with Jesus, *Da Vinci Code* style, and thus once again identifying her with her sexuality rather than her leadership as a disciple of Jesus.[30]

In similar fashion, contemporary biblical scholarship has underscored the significance of Mary and Martha in ways that are important to women today. For centuries, Luke's story of Mary and Martha (10:38–42) stood as a lesson about contrasting religious lifestyles. Should one be like Mary, who sat quietly at the Lord's feet like a contemplative, or like Martha who, busy about many things, was reprimanded by Jesus for asking Mary to help? Does this mean that prayer is more important than feeding the hungry?

This is not a story about an older sister nagging her younger sister to help her in the kitchen, but rather, one that reflects an important change in women's leadership roles within the house-churches of early Christianity. The real question here is whether women should be restricted to serving the eucharistic bread (which kept women in their traditional roles of serving food) or whether they should also be instructed in order to be able to go out to preach the Word of God. Is Mary being taught by the Master himself so that she can preside over the breaking open of the Word? Are Mary and Martha "sisters" of Christian faith whose leadership roles are being reexamined and reconstituted? This story comes shortly after the sending out of the seventy-two in pairs, found in Luke 10:1–12, and in it readers are being invited to think about women as leaders alongside of men within the church.[31]

Rethinking Genealogy in Matthew's Gospel: A New Birth Ends Patriarchy

At first blush, the genealogy that introduces Matthew's Gospel seems to be all about men. Not far into the long list of male progenitors of Jesus, however, one finds the name of four women whose inclusion baffles biblical scholars. The genealogy lists male progenitors with each named twice, first as son, then as father. The opening line reads like a title: "An account of the genealogy of Jesus the Messiah, the son of David, the son of Abraham" (Matt. 1:1, NRSV). Then follow the rhythmic lines that tell of men "begetting" more men: "Abraham was the father of Isaac, and Isaac the father of Jacob, and Jacob the father of Judah and his brothers, and Judah the father of Perez and Zerah *by Tamar . . .* and Salmon the father of Boaz *by Rahab,* and Boaz the father of Obed *by Ruth,* and Obed the father of Jesse, and Jesse the father of King David. And David was the father of Solomon *by the wife of Uriah*" (Matt. 1:6).

The naming of women breaks the exclusivity of the patriarchal pattern. But New Testament inclusive versions add the names of known mothers as well to read "Abraham and Sarah were the parents of Isaac, and Isaac and Rebekah the parents of Jacob, and Jacob and Leah the parents of Judah." Even these versions appear to miss the punch line at the end: "And Jacob was the father of Joseph the husband of *Mary of whom Jesus was born,* who is called the Messiah." With the mention of Mary, males-begetting-males comes to an end. Jesus' birth breaks the patriarchal mold forever, opening the possibility of a whole new reality. Kinship is no longer based on blood relations but on common humanity with God as our Parent, referenced as Heavenly Father.

The four other women mentioned in the genealogy all have storied pasts. Tamar, twice-widowed and left childless with empty promises, seduced Judah, her father-in-law, and gave birth to twin boys. Rahab was a resourceful prostitute who helped the Israelites conquer Jericho. Ruth, another foreigner, traveled with her Israelite mother-in-law, Naomi, back to the homeland. Both were widowed but Ruth managed to secure their well-being by a carefully planned seduction of Boaz, a good but reticent relative. Finally, there is the story of Bathsheba, the wife of Uriah, whose beauty attracted King David, who, after making her pregnant, plots Uriah's death. Eventually her son, Solomon, inherits David's throne, in part through her timely intervention.

What perplexes scholars is the connection these four women have to Mary. One suggestion is that the four women foreshadow the Gentiles who join the Christian community — except Mary is Jewish. Viewing the women as sinners fails for the same reason. Another view is that the women's stories of sexual irregularities prepare for Matthew's story of Joseph learning Mary is pregnant.[32] But perhaps what connects all five women in the genealogy is the obvious. They are women and not men. Their existence is necessary, but biblical authors perceive their appearance as intrusive. Their own births are completely ignored in genealogies, as if they did not exist. And their absence in birth records as daughters is worsened by being counted only when they become mothers of *male* children. This kind of injustice to women is staggering in its effects and must be acknowledged and addressed. Replacing patriarchy with Matthew's vision of a new basis for kinship between women and men — our common humanity born of God — within our own church is one fine place to start.

Conclusion

There is ever more in the Bible than meets the eye, more to be understood and to be imagined. At its core the Bible reflects not only our thirst for God but, to our astonishment, God's everlasting desire to be with us — women and men alike. Women's marginalization has been legitimated by patriarchal texts and problematic interpretations of existing texts. It is this author's hope that with the aid of feminist biblical scholarship and more adequate and sensitive translations of Scripture, women the world over will remain able to draw spiritual strength from this "fount of spiritual life" and will respond with enthusiasm to the biblical invitation "Let those who thirst come."

Chapter 5

Sisters of Thecla

Knowledge, Power, and Change in the Church

FRANCINE CARDMAN

A N UNEXPECTED CONVERSATION reoriented me to questions of women and change in the church. Speaking with a woman who had been a student years ago, I was completely surprised when she told me that she had been among the nine women ordained priests in July 2005 on the St. Lawrence River. I knew of her many years in ministry, but not that she felt called to priesthood. It never occurred to me that, among the hundreds of women from Boston's theology and divinity schools that I have known, she would be the one to take this audacious step. Yet the more we talked, the more I understood how authentic her action was — how true to herself, to the decades of faithful, compassionate, and competent ministry she has shared with so many people, and how true to the God who calls her. Her courageous action, in the company of other faithful and empowered women, was also an act of fidelity to all of us and to the future of the church. I told her how moved I was by her story, and that it challenged me and gave me hope. I also told her that I was eager to tell people but that I would refrain until she was ready to make her story public.

Recalling that conversation now brings to mind other stories I have heard and read and told many times before, stories from the earliest days of the church and across the centuries, stories that have insistently demanded my attention as I have thought about women, knowledge, and power. Trying at the same time to think about concrete strategies for change in the church has heightened the cognitive and practical dissonance that I and so many others regularly experience as women in the Roman Catholic Church.

That dissonance makes itself known when I think about Thecla, for instance, who figures in early traditions about the preaching of the Gospel in Asia Minor.[1] It continues when I remember Teresa of Avila who, as a child, resolved with one of her brothers to embark on a missionary journey to the Moors in hopes of being martyred, and who as a nun instead prayed for the conversion of "Lutherans."[2] The dissonance increases when I consider Thérèse of Lisieux, whose desire to be a priest caused her great pain at the age of twenty-four — when young men were ordained — and who died before her next birthday.[3] It reached a new pitch when I first heard about Ludmila Javorova, who was secretly ordained a priest in 1970 for the underground Catholic Church in communist-controlled Czechoslovakia.[4] And, prior to that reorienting conversation, it escalated when I contemplated the small but growing number of Catholic women who have been ordained deacons, priests, and bishops.[5]

What does it all mean? I wonder how these insistently reappearing women, crossing so many centuries, could possibly come together and what they would have to say to each other and to us about strategies for reform in a church that does not want to change. Yet face to face with this unnamed woman priest, I began to see lines of connection as well as conflict in our past and present as women in the church. I began to see a possible way forward, a way beyond dissonance. In what follows I offer one thread of narrative meaning and strategy by looking more closely at the interaction of knowledge and power as revealed in the story of Thecla and in the story of contemporary women called to priesthood in the Roman Catholic Church. That thread, when joined with other threads of women's memory, knowledge, and diverse experiences of power, holds within itself the capacity for braiding an ever-stronger rope that can draw us toward a future of change and hope.

Knowledge and Power

In thinking about knowledge, power, history, and women, it is important to begin with some cautions and clarifications.

First, the connection between knowledge and power is not straightforward; it does not run in only one direction. Simply knowing more about women's history in the church will not in itself make us more powerful or transform us into agents of change. But *not* knowing that history is dangerous and keeps us in our place (as determined by those with power). As the historian Gerda Lerner maintains, "It is the nature of the relationship of women to history which explains the long duration of their subordination and the slow development of the rise of feminist consciousness." Reflecting on her breakthrough two-volume work, *Women and History*, she observes that, "The insight that religion was the primary arena in which women fought for hundreds of years for feminist consciousness was not one I previously had. It was won in work on Volume One; I listened to the voices of forgotten women and accepted what they told me."[6]

As women we need to be aware of the church's history and of our forgotten or erased place in it. We need to listen to the voices of women striving for a new consciousness. Lacking knowledge of our history and of how the church has changed throughout its history, we are captive to an ideology of church in which nothing *can* change because nothing (allegedly) *has* changed. Ignorance of history reinforces power relations whether they are visible or not, acknowledged or piously denied by those in positions of dominance. History can be a key to unveiling and renegotiating the relationship of knowledge and power. It is especially helpful in revealing the way in which particular knowledges (as the French theorist Michel Foucault puts it) are submerged in a more powerful and more "complete" knowledge that claims "objectivity" and "truth." Overpowered by the dominant discourse, these "subjugated knowledges" are lost to us, or at least deeply buried. The knowledge brokered by the powerful then becomes the story we learn to tell ourselves of "the way things are" and the necessity of their remaining so. The keepers of the dominant knowledge are the only ones who can judge who has the story right and what it really means. *If this sounds familiar — it ought to!* We collude in our own disempowerment, then — in the church and in social and political life — if we ignore Foucault's critical insight that power makes knowledge.[7]

Second, given the complex relationship of power and knowledge, it is not enough simply to retrieve the stories of women, "exceptional" or otherwise, from the history of the church, or to learn about what women have accomplished and how they managed it. Rather, we must also look at the shadow side of the picture, acknowledge the cost of their achievement, and recognize their unavoidable limitations. It is especially important to see how the space women create for exercising agency can be lost — contained, co-opted, marginalized, subverted, forgotten — and how this has happened over and over again throughout our history. We have as much to learn from the history of loss as we do from the history of achievement. The lessons of loss may, in fact, prove to be the more powerful and necessary ones.

Third, it is important to recognize that, however useful history can be, it can never offer perfect models for our present endeavors and desires. The contexts and constraints of women's lives in other eras are similar enough to ours to offer cautionary lessons, but different enough to make direct transfer of ideals or practices from their lives to ours difficult, even hazardous. Certainly the women of the church's history are our foremothers. Too often they have been lost to us, their memory dimmed or distorted. We must continue to reclaim them, for they show us how we have become who we are. They also show us who they were *not* able to become. Our knowledge of that loss must inform our reflection on who *we* are not yet able to become. We can be empowered by their knowledge, power, spiritualities, and stories. But we do not have to — indeed, we cannot — look to them to authorize our lives and actions. They are, at most, limited prototypes, the first in a long line of visions and revisions that we are called upon to continue, not repeat. We must claim our own subjugated knowledges and power and take our lives into our own hands.

There are multiple layers, then, to recounting the stories of women in the church's past and present history. The first level is simply reclaiming lost lives, lost histories. The second is connecting those histories to their contexts and cultures, examining the dynamics of power and loss. The third level is connecting their lives to ours, learning cautions and strategies, identifying differences, mourning losses, and imagining new or renewed possibilities. Telling their stories is an exercise in "telling tales," not in the sense of recounting tall tales or fairy tales, but in the sense of being "tattletales." In telling stories of women past and present we are "tattling" — transgressing the boundaries of politely contained, sanitized, and subjugated discourses, and revealing deeper and more complex stories of achievement and loss, privileged interests, and marginalized memories. In this respect, the tales themselves are also *telling.* They are revealing stories of the negotiations of power and knowledge that have shaped and continue to shape our lives as women in the church.

The first story I want to tell *is* a tale of sorts — the first-century story of Thecla, in part a legend, that for many women has become emblematic of possibility and loss, resistance and reaction. The second is a story made up of many stories: of Ludmila Javorova; of the unnamed woman who gave rise to this essay; and of all the latter-day sisters of Thecla who are claiming their vocation to Roman Catholic priesthood.

Thecla

Thecla's story is a tale with a long life and roots in reality.[8] That it arose at all and was preserved for so long — circulated orally and in writing, rewritten and subtly reinterpreted over time, mostly forgotten (at least in the West), and now resurgent — testifies to its power. Because it goes against later currents in Christian history, the persistence of the story points to its foundation in a particular knowledge, that of women's leadership and ministry in the early churches.[9] There may or may not have been a historical Thecla, but at the very least she represents women of that period who were apostles, teachers, and preachers.[10] Thecla's story was handed on orally before it became a written text, the *Acts of Thecla,* which circulated independently and may have had particular appeal to women. Because of her association with the apostle Paul, her story was incorporated into another text, the *Acts of Paul,* sometime in the second century. These and other "apocryphal" (extracanonical) Acts and Gospels are contemporary with and at times parallel to writings that came to be recognized as the canonical Christian Scriptures.

In outline, Thecla's story goes like this. As a young woman engaged to be married, Thecla is entranced by the preaching of Paul in her hometown of Iconium. After listening to him day and night, she resolves to follow his gospel of "continence and the resurrection." Angered by her decision, her fiancé, Thamyris, and her mother plot to have her arrested by the Roman authorities and urge them to "burn the lawless one, burn her that is no bride in the middle of the theater, that all women who have been taught by this man may be afraid." In the arena the fire is extinguished by a sudden downpour and does not touch her, and Thecla is released by the governor. She seeks out Paul, who has been expelled from the city, and asks him to baptize her, but he refuses. He grudgingly allows her to accompany him to Antioch, where she is assaulted by a leading citizen, Alexander, who offers Paul money and gifts in order to marry her. Paul disclaims any relationship to her and abandons her to his clutches. Struggling with Alexander, she rips his cloak and knocks a wreath from his head, making him a laughing-stock. She is brought before the governor and condemned to death, this time by wild beasts. Queen Tryphaena and the women of her household shelter Thecla as she awaits her death and accompany her to the arena on the appointed day. Paul is nowhere to be found. The lioness meant to kill her falls at her feet instead, and then kills a bear sent out to do the job. Thecla leaps into a pool of water occupied by "killer" seals, but a bolt of lightning strikes them dead, leaving her to seize the moment. "In the name of Jesus Christ I baptize myself on the last day!" she exclaims. Once released by the governor, she returns to Tryphaena's household, instructs her in God's word, and converts many of the women servants as well. Thecla again searches out Paul, who is amazed she is alive. She reports that she has been baptized with God's help and announces that she is going back to Iconium, to which he replies, "Go and teach the word of God." She teaches her mother and others there, and then departs for Seleucia, where she "enlighten[s] many with the word of God" and dies years later.

Thecla is transformed in the course of the story. She appears initially as an avid hearer of God's word as preached by Paul. She acts on that word when she abandons her fiancé, accompanies Paul to Antioch, and resists Alexander's assault. In the arenas of Iconium and Antioch she becomes a powerful and victorious witness (the original meaning of the Greek word *martus*), willing to die for her new faith. She is the agent of her own baptism. She teaches Tryphaena and her household, who become believers; although the story does not say so, it is likely that she also baptizes them. When she again finds Paul, it is not to follow him but to instruct him about what God has done for her and then to set out on her own as a preacher of the word. Paul's injunction to her to teach is not so much a commission as an acknowledgment of God's call. By the end of the story, Thecla is clearly an *apostle* — one sent by God to preach the Gospel.

A later addition to the story supplied answers to questions that readers and hearers no doubt asked: What happened next? How long did she live? How did she die?[11] In the "sequel" Thecla takes up residence in a mountain cave near Seleucia, suffers diabolical temptations, and triumphs over them. Women seek her out, she instructs them, and they form an ascetic community there. She works miracles and heals the sick. Local physicians, put out of business by her healings, plot to rid themselves of her by hiring young men to rape her. The youths force their way into her cave, seize her, but hold off while she prays for divine assistance. Aid comes in the form of an opening in the cave wall through which she flees as it closes behind her. This new ending to the story concludes with a recap of her life that fixes it for future memory: "Thus suffered that first martyr and apostle of God, the virgin Thecla, who came from Iconium at eighteen years of age; afterwards, partly in journeys and travels, partly in a monastic life in the cave, she lived seventy-two years, so that she was ninety years old when the Lord translated her."

The sequel's emphasis on Thecla's virginity is consonant with the gospel of "continence and the resurrection" in the earlier narrative. But her solitary life in the cave, the threat of the would-be rapists, and the women's monastery are all elements of an ongoing domestication of her image. The Thecla of the sequel conforms to roles that are comprehensible for women of later centuries: solitary ascetic; leader of a monastic community; miracle-worker within a very circumscribed environment. The image of Thecla as a martyr is comprehensible, too — so much so that later tradition tends to forget that she was not in fact martyred. She did witness to her faith and suffer for it in the arenas of Iconium and Antioch. She did resist assault and defend her virginity. She suffered, but she did not die from her sufferings; if anything, she became more powerful as a result of them. Yet in the Western churches she is remembered as "virgin and martyr"; in the Orthodox churches she is remembered as "protomartyr" (first martyr), the female counterpart to Stephen (Acts 7:54–60). There is no other "martyr" like her, and so we must wonder: Why the penchant for regarding her as good as dead, rather than alive and powerful?

We must also wonder: what happened to Thecla, "apostle of God" and *is-apostole,* "equal to the apostles," as later manuscripts and Orthodox churches even today title her? What happened to Thecla the itinerant preacher and teacher?[12] To Thecla the self-baptizer, whose ministry was authorized by God and by her own actions? What happened to Thecla the model of women's ministry and, if we can trust Tertullian's outraged complaint, the authorization claimed by second-century women who preached and baptized?[13] What happened to Thecla not only of blessed but of *dangerous* memory?[14]

The image of Thecla as martyr, ascetic, and healer is a strong representation of women's power and agency. But it is also relatively easily domesticated, constrained to match gender expectations and to support structures of male authority. The image of Thecla as apostle, equal to the apostles, teacher, and preacher is a far more volatile memory. *That* Thecla became an *endangered* memory[15] and then a buried one, another strand of subjugated knowledge. That image was relegated to safe obscurity, hidden in plain sight. But what happens when that subjugated knowledge rises again? What happens when it comes to mind and to power among women today?

Power and Knowledge

During the "second wave" of twentieth-century feminism, women began to rediscover a history of their own. They drew on emerging feminist theories, women's history, and women's studies, as well as other critical theories and scholarship that engaged the social realities of its contexts. They brought feminist insights and methods to the history of the church, too, helping to fuel a new interest in the study of neglected sources such as the *Acts of Thecla* and other texts that did not become part of the Christian biblical canon. They put movements previously deemed "heterodox" in a new light, viewing them as alternative Christianities that offered more scope to women and revealed much greater diversity in this early period than previously thought.

The rediscovery of women's history in the church coincided with the rapid expansion of feminist and liberation theologies critical of patriarchal social and religious structures. Movements for women's ordination in the Anglican and Roman Catholic churches arose at the same time, and there was a sharp increase in the number of ordained women ministers in Protestant churches. Roman Catholic women entered into this ferment, encouraged by the vistas of change that Vatican II had opened. They found new sources of knowledge and power in the memory of Thecla and her sisters. They studied Scripture anew, reread the sources, and rediscovered a tradition that was broader and deeper than Vatican I or the Council of Trent. And they read the signs of the times. They witnessed the valid but irregular ordinations in Philadelphia of eleven Episcopalian and Anglican women to priesthood in July 1974. (The ordinations were "regularized" in 1976.) They went themselves or observed over two thousand women and men gather in Detroit for the first Women's Ordination Conference in November 1975. They heard the stories of women missionaries and pastoral workers who, for nearly all practical purposes, were priests to their communities, especially in Latin America. They listened to each other, heard calls to ministry and priesthood, and claimed their spiritual agency.[16] Women were rising again, and subjugated knowledges were rising with them.

Roman Catholic women were claiming their power. The Vatican soon pushed back with power of its own. The Congregation for the Doctrine of the Faith (CDF) attempted to define and restrict knowledge about women, priesthood, and ordination in its *Declaration on the Admission of Women to the Ministerial Priesthood*. The document was quietly released in Latin in October 1976 but, mysteriously, an English translation did not appear until January 1977.[17] Although documents from Roman congregations were not typically known by their Latin titles, Roman officials referred to this one only as *Inter Insigniores* (from the first words of its Introduction, "Among the characteristics that mark our age"), an apparent effort to ratchet up its perceived authority. Quite atypically, the declaration also acquired its own official commentary.[18] Nevertheless, its arguments against the ordination of women stand or fall on their own strength, and they are not very strong.[19] My point here, however, is not to address its arguments, but to highlight the inescapable dynamics of power and timing in the appearance and claims of the *Declaration*.

The same dynamics are evident in John Paul II's apostolic letter, *Ordinatio Sacerdotalis (Priestly Ordination)*, of 1994, in which he declared the question of women's ordination closed and prohibited any further discussion of the matter.[20] In 1995, the pope presented the CDF with an interestingly contrived question, or *dubium*: "Whether the teaching that the church has no authority whatsoever to confer priestly ordination on women, which is presented in the apostolic letter *Ordinatio Sacerdotalis* to be held definitively, is to be understood as belonging to the deposit of the faith." Yes, came the reply from the congregation and its prefect, Cardinal Joseph Ratzinger, it is.[21] Here, too, it is not my purpose to debate the arguments of the letter, the meaning of ordinary magisterium, or the possibility of its infallible exercise; nor to distinguish the intricate degrees of authority that attach to documents from Vatican congregations or from popes themselves, except to note that the letter does not meet the criteria of infallibility.[22] Rather, my purpose is again to highlight the dynamics of power, knowledge, and timing. *Ordinatio Sacerdotalis* appeared near the twentieth anniversary of the Philadelphia ordinations of Episcopal women to the priesthood. The *Reply to the Dubium* was issued almost twenty years after the Detroit Women's Ordination Conference, when the twentieth anniversary of the *Declaration* was only a year away. Anniversaries are not insignificant for an institution built on tradition. They can be used to bolster institutional authority or to refute unacceptable precedents. It is no coincidence, either, that these documents followed the approval of women's priestly ordination by the Anglican provinces of South Africa, England, and Australia in 1992.[23]

Sisters of Thecla

Undeterred by the Roman documents, Catholic women continued to act on their calls to ministry and, for some, to priesthood. The growth and professionalization of lay ecclesial ministry since the 1980s, especially in the United States, meant that their vocations did not remain simply personal and interior, but received affirmation from the ecclesial communities and professional chaplaincies within which they ministered. For some the affirmation was of their call to lay ecclesial ministry as such; for others it was also an affirmation of their call to priesthood. For all, however, acceptance and recognition of their vocations by those they serve already constitutes real and significant recognition *by the church,* the gathered people of God. It is therefore not possible to deny the authenticity and the ecclesial nature of their vocations, which are manifest even without hierarchical approval and other institutional processes of approbation.

There are, of course, significant juridical issues regarding women's ordination to the ministerial priesthood in the Roman Catholic Church. The most important of these is canon 1024 of the 1983 Code of Canon Law, which states tersely that, "A baptized male alone receives sacred ordination validly."[24] Again my purpose is not to argue the issues as such, but to point out the problematics and possibilities in our present experience as women in the church. The crucial question about women's ordination is not finally canonical or even theological or doctrinal. Discipline, doctrine, theology, and law all develop and change. Rather, the crucial question is simpler and more essential. It is a question of discernment: Where is the Spirit leading the church as it seeks to carry out its mission of living toward the reign of God?

One way in which to discern the Spirit's leading, I suggest, is to look to the experience of women called to priesthood and to trust the angel's response to Mary: nothing will be impossible to God (Luke 1:37).[25] This process of discernment is itself a strategy for change in the church. Earlier in this essay I suggested one strategy: a faithfully resistant reading of the tradition that is cognizant of the dynamics of power and knowledge and sensitive to the presence of subjugated knowledges. Here I am suggesting a further strategy: that we take seriously the experience of women called to priesthood and solidify their stories by making them the subject of careful, critical, and prayerful reflection. We cannot allow our own fears of marginalization by association to prevent us from acknowledging their existence and their claim on us. Nor can we allow the power that produces knowledge to make them *desaparecidas.*

To take their experience seriously would involve telling the stories of women who minister within the structures of the church, aware of a call to priesthood and living patiently with its daily denial. It would involve, too, telling the stories of those whose consciences have called them to the margins of the institution or beyond it. They include Ludmila Javorova, ordained priest by Bishop

Felix Davidek of the hidden church in Czechoslovakia, and Dr. Magda Za-
horska, ordained deacon by a Slovakian bishop, whose ordinations have been
deemed invalid along with those of other priests and bishops of the hidden
church.[26] They include Mary Ramerman and Denise Donato, ordained in 2001
and 2003 by an Old Catholic bishop for a parish that had been expelled from
the Rochester, New York, diocese.[27] And they include Roman Catholic women
priests ordained in Europe and North America. Seven women were ordained
priests by Bishop Romulo A. Braschi on the Danube River in June 2002; six
were ordained deacons in June 2004; and four ordained priests on Lake Constance in Europe in June 2006.[28] Gisela Forster, Ida Raming, and Patricia Fresen
were ordained as bishops by several male bishops. On the St. Lawrence River
in July 2005 nine women were ordained priests following the Women's Ordination Worldwide Conference in Ottawa; eight were ordained priests and four
ordained deacons in July 2006 on the three rivers of Pittsburgh.[29] Aside from
Ludmila Javorova's story, much of the information about these women is available only online. Without the Internet we would know little about them, given
the economics of publishing and the tendency of church media to dismiss them
and newspapers to sensationalize them. We must follow the stories of all these
women's ministries, wherever and however they serve, and look for signs of the
Spirit's presence and gifts.

Now it is possible to acknowledge Jean Marchant, the no-longer name-
less woman priest who began this essay, and allow her to tell her own story.
She broke her silence in July 2006 and resigned her position as director of an
archdiocesan office in Boston.[30]

Although these ordained women stand outside the boundaries defined by
the institutional church, they remain deeply Roman Catholic by heritage and
affection. They have been formed by years of listening to the quiet and not so
quiet call to priesthood and by years of pastoral experience. They continue to
act, as Patricia Fresen puts it, out of "prophetic obedience."[31] They stand as
signs of contradiction and challenge, signs of change and possibility, signs of
hope. They stand, too, as sisters of Thecla, dangerously *present* memories. We
must remember them, listen to what they have to say to us, and consider what
it would mean for us to welcome them back into a changing church as Roman
Catholic women priests.

Chapter 6

Women within Church Law

Shifts, Expectations, and Strategies in Current Times

LYNN JARRELL

To set the context for this discussion of the duties and rights of women within the church a story told by Sue Benson in her book *Everyday Sacred: A Woman's Journey Home* offers us insights on the baggage of false perceptions and impatience about what is possible within the legal structure of the church in the twenty-first century. Benson tells a story about a woman rushing to fill a teacup as a way of trying to control the situation and force the information.[1]

The teacup of what we want to know could be empty, half-full, or overflowing. Our determination to force the shifts and expectations could be causing us to miss the reality and the nuances of what is. Our searching may have exhausted our energy and misdirected our strategies because we are searching for a precise answer.

The focus of this essay is to provide the reader with ways of measuring what shifts have occurred and continue to occur in the church's law concerning women and what expectations, as well as strategies, might assist women in exercising their full range of duties and rights as described within canon law. The essay will first present a thumbnail sketch of the changes in canon law that have occurred for women in the exercise of ministry within the church. Then the essay will discuss the equality of women with the other members of the church and any limitations that exist for women in specific ministerial roles. Finally, the essay will consider the challenges and strategies for women in the coming years.[2]

Changes in the Official Church's Position on Women

Since the later part of the twentieth century gradual shifts have occurred in canon law concerning women as members of the body of the Christian faithful and the duties and rights available to them. These gradual shifts in canon law have continued to be affirmed, to some degree, by church officials in various church documents, statements, and practices over the past forty years.

While the viewpoint that women are to be restricted in the exercise of official ministries continues today, there have been positive changes. Canon law now speaks of the equal dignity that each person, female and male, has from the act of baptism or the profession of faith within the church and the resulting duty and right to participate in the work of evangelization.[3]

To ascertain a sense of the shifts that have occurred in the last forty years in the official church's perspective on women it is necessary to compare the description of the 1917 Code of Canon Law to the current Code of Canon Law published in 1983.[4]

1917 Code of Canon Law's Position on Women[5]

In the text of the 1917 Code of Canon Law women were seen as having a limited role in the mission of the church. Since their role was limited, there was no need or possibility for them to have many duties and rights. They were described as having the right to receive the sacraments and the duty to obey church officials.[6] They were not part of the official ministry of the church's internal life; rather they were to bring the Gospel message to the secular world.[7]

In the 1917 Code of Canon Law women were considered equal to infants and the insane as far as the rights they possessed.[8] They received what rights they had through their spouses in marriage. As a result, the structures called for in the canons and in accompanying legal documents during much of the twentieth century continued the centuries-old perspective that women were not capable of holding an office or of exercising any decision-making role within the church.[9]

1983 Code of Canon Law's Position on Women[10]

The shifts in the 1983 Code about women are expressed, first, in the understanding of the equality that exists between the laity and the clergy, and second, in the possibility of the cooperation of laity in the exercise of jurisdiction within the church. In the 1983 Code the members of the church are called the people of God or the Christian faithful. All are recognized as equal by baptism both in dignity and in the foundational duties and rights of being a member of the church. From this equality flows a listing of the fundamental duties and rights of membership.[11]

In addition to this fundamental shift expressed in legal texts on the equality of the members of the Christian faithful, the laity are invited to cooperate with the clergy in the exercise of jurisdiction.[12] Concretely, the cooperation of the laity is made possible by the shift in the description of and requirements necessary for holding an ecclesiastical office.[13] In addition, the cooperation of the laity is to be sought by the clergy in carrying out pastoral care in parishes and dioceses.

The end result is that the distinction between male and female laity has been reduced to one area: women are not capable of petitioning for ordination and thus exercising the many roles in the church reserved to the ordained.[14] This distinction, while enormous, does not reduce the significant expansion presented in the canons and accompanying legal texts considering women equal to men in their fundamental duties and rights.

Duties and Rights of Women as Equal Members of the Christian Faithful

The fundamental duties and rights for women as for any member of the Christian faithful flow out of a two-step process: reception of a valid baptism and the ongoing choice exhibited by one's actions to remain in communion. Observance of these two steps is the source of the duties and rights for both women and men in the church, whether lay or ordained.

Reception of Baptism

By reception of baptism as described in the law "one is incorporated into the church of Christ and is constituted a person with the duties and rights which are proper to Christians in keeping with their condition."[15] This makes both male and female "sharers in their own way in Christ's priestly, prophetic, and royal function . . . to exercise the mission which God has entrusted to the church."[16]

The condition of the individual determines the possible functions the person may assume in the church. Condition is described as the capacity of the individual in light of background, health, talents, education, experiences, maturity, formation, and availability to take on a function. A function is a particular responsibility or role in the public life of the church. To assume a function one needs an appointment from the competent church official.[17] One's condition and function can change but not one's baptismal status.

Remaining in Communion

Being in communion is described as being "joined with Christ in its visible structure [the church] by the bonds of the profession of faith, the sacraments, and ecclesiastical authority."[18] This entails a responsibility of Christian obedience to that which the ecclesiastical authorities declare in their roles as teachers of the faith and administrators of the church.[19] Accountability to the competent authority in ministry as well as in one's public actions would be expected. To lose communion formally requires a public action in which the person knowingly intends to break communion and to give up active membership.

Ministry within the Public Life of the Church

Ministry within the Church

Ministry in canon law is equated to mission and is spoken of as "Christ's priestly, prophetic, and royal functions" or to "exercise the mission which God has entrusted to the Church to fulfill in the world."[20] The church's mission is rooted in its nature to be missionary and thus to evangelize so that "the divine message of salvation more and more reaches all people in every age and in every land."[21] Women, as members of the Christian faithful, are "bound . . . to imbue and perfect the temporal affairs with the spirit of the gospel and thus to give witness to Christ."[22]

Different Forms of Ministry[23]

Each of the three forms of ministry generally presumes baptism and being in communion with the church. Authorization to carry out the given form of ministry may be needed as well as specific qualifications named in the law.

Common Ministry

The first form of ministry named in the law is the duty and right proper to each member by baptism according to one's condition and the culture where one is living to exercise *common ministry*. This form involves such acts as (1) love of neighbor, (2) evangelization, (3) growth in one's spirituality, (4) transforming the temporal order, and (5) marriage and family life.[24] Examples of common ministry are the everyday acts that are part of an individual's personal, family, and professional life.

No formal appointment to exercise this form of ministry is necessary. However, while this type of ministry is essential for sharing the Gospel message, the individual has no authority to make specific decisions or handle certain responsibilities that may belong to others in the church. Historically, women have been and continue to be involved in the fullness of exercising common ministry within the church.

Public Ministry

The second form of ministry named in the law is rooted in the duties and rights of the baptized if one's condition, including culture, permits the exercise of it. This would mean the person needs to possess the skills specified by universal and/or diocesan norms necessary for filling roles that carry out (1) the *munus docendi* (teaching function), (2) the *munus sanctificandi* (sanctifying function), and (3) the *munus regendi* (governing function). Examples of public ministry are religion teachers, directors of religious education programs, eucharistic ministers, parish visitors of the sick or prisoners, parish council presidents.[25]

A confirmation (sometimes called a formal appointment) possibly conferred verbally or in a liturgical event or in a written document is necessary in order to assume a function in this category. However, instead of decision-making authority being attached to the ministry, the person is given the responsibility to handle certain actions while remaining directly accountable to a competent church authority. Historically, women have been and continue to be involved in public ministry in varying ways.

Jurisdictional Ministry

The third form of ministry named in the law is carried out by those members of the Christian faithful who are ordained or the laity in cooperation with the ordained. While functions entailing the full care of souls are restricted to the clergy, other functions named in the law can be filled by either the laity or the clergy. Examples of this type of ministry are: the offices of bishop, pastor, vicar general, judicial vicar, finance officer, judge, and superintendent of schools.[26]

A formal appointment is necessary and can be given only if the person has the condition and qualifications prescribed in the universal law.[27] The appointment bestows on the person the authority to make specific decisions. While there has been a significant shift in canon law in this third category, historically women have not been and continue not to be able to exercise most of the ministries of this type.[28] Instead, it is still the expectation in the law that functions involving jurisdiction over the care of souls are generally to be filled only by the clergy since jurisdictional ministry is frequently seen as linked closely to the sacrament of ordination.

Addressing Challenges in Our Times

The development of strategies for enhancing the role of women within the church in our times is limited by established practices or the perceptions attached to these practices. This essay proposes two ways in which the role of women within the church might be enhanced in light of what is stated in the law. Both are grounded in the position expressed in the 1983 Code that the foundational duties and rights of the Christian faithful are the same for men and women, laity and clergy.

Strategy One: Expansion of the Roles of Consultation and Cooperation

The Practices of the Faith Community (Custom and Culture)

A primary means for interpreting how to apply canon law is the lived experience of the people involved in a given situation.[29] The 1983 Code directs that custom is to be the tool used for adapting the law to fit the situation because "custom is the best interpreter of the law."[30] The only time that custom is not to be the means for determining how to act in a given situation is when it is interrupted by the competent authority.[31]

Custom can be understood in two ways. First, in the technical sense, it is a practice that has been formally approved by the competent authority. Second, and in the richer sense, based on the church's long legal tradition, it is what has been adopted by a given group of the Christian faithful from the range of possibilities allowed for in the law. In the latter, no approval of the competent authority is ever sought. In both understandings it is presumed that those practicing the custom have the intention both of remaining in communion and of establishing a practice that is to become normative for those persons who belong to the given community unless one is individually dispensed.

A major influence on the customs of a community is the culture within which the group finds itself, including all of the social conditions that are part of living with a given geographical area and the way the people living there handle their affairs. The particulars of the group's culture need to be absorbed and appreciated to help the faith life be vibrant. Enculturation requires that there be ample room for assessing the practices of a given area and for applying the legal norms in a manner that fits the people receiving them.[32]

Use of Exceptions and Options Permitted in the Law

The concept of custom is at the core of what it means to be at one with the culture or the circumstances in which human beings, who are part of a community, are living. In the true sense the law allows for mercy and compassion. It speaks of the need to be open to (a) the exercise of the practice of dispensation, or (b) the possibility of circumstances existing that the lawmaker never imagined.

One such cultural and current circumstance not taken into account in the universal law of the church is the recent rapid development of women in professional training, faith formation, lived experience, and secular roles and responsibilities within some cultures. This development indicates the readiness of women to assume positions of increased involvement and influence in ecclesiastical decision-making.

Action Needed: Expansion of the Roles of Consultation and Cooperation

The roles of consultation and cooperation of the Christian faithful in the exercise of jurisdiction are called for in the 1983 Code but have been opened only in a limited manner to women. Serving in either of these roles brings the participants into increased participation with the ecclesiastical decision-making process. Expanded involvement of women in these two roles follows from the principles of (1) *mutual relations,* long urged between bishops and consecrated religious, which is understood in the spirit of the law to include all the laity, and (2) understanding how all the baptized by baptism and communion are to have an active part in the *mission of Jesus.*

The strategy is to put a strong emphasis on the acceptance and integration of these two principles so competent ecclesiastical authority will grow in seeing women as essential for true consultation and cooperation. In the everyday life of a diocese or a parish, this would hopefully result in changes in structural practices concerning who holds church offices and who are part of the vehicles of advice. The law allows for bishops, who have the responsibility to provide appropriate pastoral care to the people in their dioceses, to make use of the dispensing power that comes with their office to appoint women with the prescribed capacity and qualifications to exercise roles of consultation and cooperation. While this has occurred in limited ways in some dioceses there is still much room for expansion of these two roles.

Strategy Two: Formation and Readiness of Women for Assuming Expanded Participation in Jurisdictional Ministry

Legal Expectations for the Formation of Christian Faithful

Foundational to being a member of the church and thus assuming any rights or obligations that follow from baptism is the principle that the person needs to be formed in the church's beliefs and rituals. Both the individual and the community bear the responsibility to seek and provide appropriate formation in what it means to be a member.

For the community the obligation in the formation process is to teach the individual about the sacraments and the Gospel as well as to provide to all the Christian faithful sufficient opportunities to receive the sacraments and hear the Gospel preached.[33] All of this needs to be done within the context of what is reasonable for the resources of the community.

For the individual the primary obligations are to retain communion and follow the authority of the church.[34] Since these obligations are fundamental to claiming the other aspects of membership, the individual needs to have the opportunity to be formed. This means there is to be no coercion in order to ensure freedom of conscience and freedom to choose one's state of life.[35] The formation process is to fit an individual's capacity allowing for necessary adjustments.

Formation for Being Part of the Public Life of the Church

Being part of the public life of the church and to be appointed to exercise official functions require that ministers take into account the common good of the church, the rights of others, and their own duties. The communal dimension will ask of the Christian faithful that they allow the competent ecclesiastical authority to determine how best to handle situations for the sake of the common good of the whole.[36]

At the same time the overall consideration of the mission of the church and its common good needs to allow the Christian faithful to give input and direction within their particular cultural setting and the unique movements of grace they are given. The laity, women and men, need to be respected and listened to when they make known to the ecclesiastical authority their needs, especially spiritual ones, and their desires. Also, the laity have the obligation and right to express their opinions on matters that pertain to the good of the church and to make their opinions known in the appropriate manner and place, attentive to the good of the whole and the dignity of persons.[37]

Beyond the foundational teaching the Christian faithful are to receive, laity who are willing and able to give their lives to special service in the church need to receive additional formation. The scope of this additional formation is to provide the individual with the competencies required for exercising particular public and jurisdictional functions.

Within canon law the competencies spoken of regarding the exercise of public and jurisdictional ministry cluster into three areas. The first of these areas of competencies is to have appropriate theological preparation. Theological preparation includes (1) basic Christian education, (2) comprehension of church doctrine, and (3) understanding and acceptance of church authority.[38]

The second of these areas of competencies is to have sufficient administrative skills. The law specifies the skills needed, while varying with different functions, include sufficient knowledge of (1) the purposes and uses of church property, (2) the processes governing contracts, alienation, and other acts of administration, and (3) the responsibilities of a church administrator.[39]

The third of these areas of competencies is reasonable appreciation of the communal nature of life in the church and its mission. This communal nature requires that individuals develop an understanding of how their ministries are part of the church's mission of carrying out works (1) of charity, especially for the needy, (2) of evangelization, and (3) of building up the life of the church primarily through worship and ministry.[40] It calls the laity to cooperate in the church's public and jurisdictional ministries. Thus, their ministries are carried out in the name of the church and are part of the church's public life.

Action Needed: Preparation of Women to Exercise Public and Jurisdictional Ministries

This strategy calls for the ongoing development of programs and funding that can assist women in being formed and educated so they are competent and ready to apply for or commit to holding particular functions in the church, especially as openings occur. Much wisdom for the development of such tools can be learned from the seminary and formational programs used in priestly and religious life preparation, especially from the formational personnel and written resources that guide these programs.[41]

Women need to be introduced to and educated about their foundational duties and rights in a balanced and comprehensive manner, grounding them in the theological nature of church and its teachings. At the root of the exercise of duties and rights is the common good of the life of the church. This means women need be formed in what is reasonable and what fits the reality of the culture and custom in which they are living while recognizing they are part of a worldwide church that is over two thousand years old. In addition, increased numbers of women need to see themselves as capable of being part of the public and jurisdictional ministries of the church. This capacity will require formation in the three areas described above within training centers approved by ecclesiastical authorities. All this will entail expenses that often women may not be able to afford without assistance and extended periods of time to absorb the commitment and skills involved in exercising jurisdictional ministry. If they are endowed with this level of education they will have one of the prescribed qualities in the universal or particular law for being eligible for ecclesiastical functions not ordinarily held by women.[42]

In Conclusion

The two strategies that will enable women to assume more fully their rightful place in the roles and functions of the church's life as well as to exercise their duties and rights from baptism depend on an expanded understanding and acceptance of the equality of women as members of the Christian faithful. Putting into place concrete objectives for carrying out these two strategies in the coming years will hopefully lead to further opening up of the possibilities already permitted to women in canon law. In particular, there needs to be increased participation in ecclesiastical jurisdiction through serving in roles of consultation and cooperation.

However, such expansion of possibilities for women will result only if ongoing formation and mentoring are provided to all the Christian faithful, clergy and laity alike. Only then will it become more acceptable to have women in public and jurisdictional roles without this change being perceived as a threat to either the nature of the church itself or to the ordained in particular.

All of this means moving through difficult legal choices facing the church. Or to return to the image of the overflowing teacup, it is only when expanded space is made within the understanding of the members and the structures of the church that the expectations about women can shift and openness can come. Without this movement to view and understand women in this expanded way, the common good of the church and the good of women individually could be unjustly harmed now and into the future.[43]

Chapter 7

Wise as Serpents, Innocent as Doves
Strategic Appropriation of Catholic Social Teaching
MARGARET R. PFEIL

"See, I am sending you out like sheep into the midst of wolves; so be wise as serpents and innocent as doves." (Matt. 10:16)

J ESUS' SENDING OF THE DISCIPLES on mission in wise innocence presupposes radical trust in divine power at work in their ministry, and his instructions bear an abiding resonance for his followers today. They provide a promising departure point for appropriating and applying Catholic social teaching, something contemporary figure Helen Prejean has demonstrated in her work to abolish the practice of capital punishment. In this essay I underscore the power of appropriating Catholic social teaching, using the moral epistemology of the option for the poor, by taking a close look at the praxis of Helen Prejean.

Three particular dimensions of Prejean's witness offer insight into strategic engagement of Catholic social teaching. First, she demonstrates the significance of social location for interpreting the signs of the times in light of the church's social doctrine, embracing the moral epistemology of the option for the poor to press for both ecclesial and civil rejection of the death penalty as a form of torture. Second, viewing social reality from the perspective of society's outcasts, she practices solidarity as a *specifically pneumatological* form of power available to those on the margins of dominant power structures. Finally, with the wise innocence of a prophet, Prejean has relied upon charisms imparted through baptism by the Holy Spirit to shepherd the church in tapping into the power of solidarity to shape its social teaching and, in turn, its witness in the world.

Strategic Appropriation and Social Location

Growing up in a white, Catholic family of comfortable means in Baton Rouge, Louisiana, Helen Prejean became steeped in the Catholic moral tradition at an early age, formed by the writings of the church fathers and mothers, as well as the documents of Catholic social teaching. Her early faith development, however, put her at some remove from strategic appropriation of the church's social doctrine, leading her to embrace instead a rather privatized conception of Christianity marked by "a personal relationship with God, inner peace, kindness to others, and heaven when this life was done," she remembers. "I didn't want to struggle with politics and economics."[1]

As a Sister of St. Joseph of Medaille, she chafed when the community decided in 1980 to make an explicit option for the poor. "We were nuns, after all, not social workers, and some realities in life were, for better or worse, rather fixed — like the gap between rich and poor."[2] Sr. Marie Augusta Neal, a sociologist, addressed her community that year, presenting compelling data that could not be ignored, noting, for example, that the United States consumed almost half of the world's resources, though it accounted for only 6 percent of the population. "She pointed out that to claim to be apolitical or neutral in the face of such injustices would be, in actuality, to uphold the status quo — a very political position to take, and on the side of the oppressors."[3]

That message seared Prejean's heart and sparked her imagination. As Vatican II's Pastoral Constitution on the Church in the Modern World (*Gaudium et spes)* had urged, she attended to the signs of the times and responded generously, a choice that led her to change her social location, the decisive movement of a genuine option for the poor. She began to live and work in solidarity with socioeconomically marginalized African Americans on affordable housing issues in New Orleans and, over time, to accompany prisoners on death row.

Through living according to the Catholic social teaching principle of the option for the poor, Prejean opened herself up to a particular way of knowing, the epistemology of society's outcasts. One's standpoint determines what one is able to perceive and therefore the sort of data that will inform one's moral vision. Those located at the center of social, economic, political, and cultural power structures will find it difficult to notice and understand the lived reality of those on the margins, and so they suffer from an epistemological disadvantage.[4] Changing her social location had the immediate effect of *decentering* Prejean's knowledge claims, allowing her to tap into a certain kind of power available on the periphery, the power of solidarity.

The Power of Solidarity

Having been sent on mission in wise innocence, Jesus' disciples carried with them his example of exercising power from the margins. As Rosita deAnn Mathews insightfully notes, Jesus "limited his involvement in the religious structure of his day and took a peripheral posture to the establishment. He did not sell his soul or give his allegiance to them. He maintained his character and call within a larger framework, . . . to bring the freedom and responsibility of the kingdom of God." She further notes that "by remaining on the periphery of the system, he was able to utilize his power to change the system and not perpetuate it."[5] Planting his feet on the edge, Jesus consciously chose to interpret lived reality from the perspective of the poor, calling attention to the transformative power of solidarity.

In his 1987 encyclical, *On Social Concern (Sollicitudo rei socialis)*, John Paul II identified solidarity as a virtue: It is "not a feeling of vague compassion or shallow distress at the misfortunes of so many people, both near and far. On the contrary, it is *a firm and persevering determination* to commit oneself to the *common good;* that is to say to the good of all and of each individual, because we are *all* really responsible *for all.*"[6] As an antidote to what he deemed the two most prominent signs of moral underdevelopment in the contemporary world — greedy desire for profit and insatiable thirst for power — he proposed solidarity, "a commitment to the good of one's neighbor with the readiness, in the gospel sense, to 'lose oneself' for the sake of the other instead of exploiting him, and to 'serve him' instead of oppressing him for one's own advantage (cf. Matt. 10:40–42; 20:25; Mark 10:42–45; Luke 22:25–27)."[7] Solidarity, this readiness to give not only one's possessions but even one's life on behalf of others, derives its power from God's gracious and passionate love for God's creation, especially the most vulnerable. It represents the power of wise innocence, capable of disarming the power of violent domination with love.

Solidarity as Pneumatological Power

Holding John Paul II's account in conversation with Prejean's witness, I suggest, highlights solidarity as a specifically *pneumatological* form of power, that is, one mediated by the Holy Spirit and therefore bearing distinctive marks. First, it appeals to human freedom and does not resort to coercion.[8] Second, it assigns value to self-sacrificial love rather than material possession. Third, it decenters knowledge as power, relying not upon the dominant influence of certain individuals or institutions, but rather working through each member of a community and all together to nurture the common good.

Marks of the Spirit in Prejean's Witness: Human Freedom and Love in Dialogue

Planting her feet on the margins afforded Prejean a radically different interpretive lens for reading Catholic social teaching. From that vantage point, she took notice of the disturbing truth that not only did Catholic social teaching number among the church's "best kept secrets,"[9] but its treatment of capital punishment stopped short of a clear condemnation of this practice. In his 1995 encyclical, *The Gospel of Life (Evangelium vitae)*, John Paul II recognized the theoretical legitimacy of state recourse to capital punishment to protect public order. But, he urged, the state should not resort to the practice of execution "except in cases of absolute necessity: in other words, when it would not be possible otherwise to defend society. Today however, as a result of steady improvements in the organization of the penal system, such cases are very rare, if not practically non-existent."[10]

To Prejean's dismay, prominent public figures such as the Catholic district attorney of New Orleans, Harry Connick, Sr., manipulated *Evangelium vitae* 56 to press for even more frequent imposition of capital punishment.[11] In light of such signs of the times, Prejean realized that in order to advocate the abolition of capital punishment in society she would first need to do some evangelizing within the church. So began, she said, "a long, patient, and unrelenting dialogue to help my church realign its teaching with the non-violent Gospel of Jesus."[12]

Her commitment to a dialogical model of ecclesial participation led Prejean to write to Pope John Paul II on January 1, 1997, the World Day of Peace, appealing to him to amend the church's teaching on capital punishment. Arguing from the power of her own experience in faithful witness on the margins, she wrote: "I have already accompanied three men to their deaths in Louisiana's electric chair, and I have 'seen with my eyes and touched with my hands' the suffering face of Christ in the 'least of these' as they went to their deaths. I have seen the practice of the death penalty close up and have no doubt that it is the practice of torture."[13]

Having studied *Evangelium vitae* closely, Prejean insisted to the pope that the practice of capital punishment represents a cruel affront to the "gospel of life." "Pro-life," she noted, usually means "pro innocent life, not guilty life."[14] In addition, those sentenced to die are almost always socioeconomically poor, and 85 percent of them have been convicted of killing whites.[15] Alluding to Connick's misappropriation of Catholic social teaching to support more frequent recourse to the death penalty, Prejean gently but firmly asserted that *Evangelium vitae* 56 as well as the *Catechism of the Catholic Church* had left a "loophole" prone to exploitation by those wielding coercive social power: "How can any government, vulnerable to undue influence of the rich and powerful and subject to every kind of prejudice, have the purity and integrity to select certain of its citizens for punishment by death?"[16]

Less than a month after receiving Prejean's letter, the Vatican announced that the section of the *Catechism* pertaining to capital punishment would be revised. The change promulgated on September 8, 1997, to paragraph 2266 acknowledged the state's right and duty to impose punishment "proportionate to the gravity of the offense" but eliminated the specification, "not excluding, in cases of extreme gravity, the death penalty."[17]

Prejean seems to have played a part in what is now acknowledged even in the Vatican as a development of doctrine in process regarding capital punishment, a movement toward a "quasi-abolitionist" position.[18] In wise innocence, Prejean has appropriated Catholic social teaching using the moral epistemology of the option for the poor, thereby embracing a way of knowing capable of unleashing the power of solidarity.

Following the *Catechism* revision, she remarked that "the long, hard work of changing hearts and minds of 'people in the pews' can now be undertaken."[19] Her commitment to solidarity has led her to evangelize both the church and society, traveling continuously across the country, giving passionate public lectures designed to form consciences in light of developing Catholic social teaching on capital punishment. "It is the vocation of the prophet," Walter Brueggemann writes, "to keep alive the ministry of imagination, to keep on conjuring and proposing futures alternative to the single one the king wants to urge as the only thinkable one."[20] In the tradition of the prophets brought to fullness in Jesus' ministry, Prejean engages in the twofold task of denouncing "the culture of death" while stoking imaginations to envision a commonweal in which *all* life is held sacred, one oriented toward the energizing love of God's reign.[21]

When asked by John Dear where she experiences the presence of God in her advocacy for the abolition of capital punishment, Prejean replied:

> You get found by God more than you find God. You get taken over, you know you
> are in the presence of God.... The energy and the commitment within myself, this
> passion that won't stop in me, that's God, too.... The energy just keeps unleashing
> itself inside of you, and you know this commitment in you is not going to die.
> That's divine love, that won't quit, that keeps us going. God is a life force, a love
> force, that's strong and unrelenting.[22]

Those who have heard Prejean speak in the public arena against the death penalty readily testify to the energy of love moving through her, filling the room and contagiously inspiring those present to share her prophetic vision of a society that strives toward fulfilling the common good without resorting to capital punishment.

Charism, Power, and Catholic Social Teaching

The Dogmatic Constitution on the Church (*Lumen gentium*) promulgated at Vatican II offers rich insight into Prejean's extraordinarily dedicated ministry, employing the theological category of charism to offer an account of the church's mission:

> It is not only through the sacraments ... that the Holy Spirit makes holy the People,
> leads them and enriches them with his virtues. Allotting his gifts according as he
> wills..., he also distributes special graces among the faithful of every rank. By
> these gifts he makes them fit and ready to undertake various tasks and offices for
> the renewal and building up of the Church, as it is written, "the manifestation of
> the Spirit is given to everyone for profit" (1 Cor. 12:7).[23]

Lumen gentium relies on Paul's description of the diverse gifts freely given by the Holy Spirit for service to the church. They may accent and coincide with natural abilities, but they are distinguished precisely as charisms by their essential direction toward the common good of the ecclesial community.[24]

Prejean, responding full-heartedly to her baptismal call to discipleship, has used the charisms given to her by the Holy Spirit to serve the church not only in its mission in the world — upholding all life as sacred — but also in its effort to offer credible witness through its own institutional practices. By drawing on the pneumatological power of solidarity, she demonstrates a valuable strategy for appropriating the wisdom of Catholic social teaching without falling into the lacunae regarding power dynamics that mark both the content of those texts and the process of their formulation.

Power as a Missing Subject in Catholic Social Teaching

Catholic social teaching documents have generally promoted a vision of harmonious social change, giving little consideration to entrenched disparities of social power that institutionalize systemic injustice. Since those wielding power to serve oppression tend not to cede it without some catalyzing impetus, this tendency in the church's social teaching has often led to tacit affirmation of a societal status quo that relies on the coercive power of institutionalized violence to maintain order.

In *Sollicitudo rei socialis,* mindful of the popular struggle waged in the name of solidarity in his Polish homeland as well as in other regions of the world, particularly Latin America, John Paul II acknowledged economic, political, and social structures of sin that seem to function "almost automatically" (16), but he did not address the corresponding ethical implication: societal institutions, including the church, would need to transform those power dynamics that render them complicit in structural sin.

As Michel Foucault noted, power relations always meet with resistances, and like power, these can be strategically negotiated.[25] By neglecting the ethical obligation to resist coercive power dynamics, *Sollicitudo rei socialis* missed this opportunity for strategic engagement. Donal Dorr's assessment of this particular encyclical also applies to the broader corpus of Catholic social teaching in general: "What is lacking is a social analysis which would take more seriously the causes of the class structure in society and which could then go on to examine ways in which tensions between the different classes can be overcome or lessened."[26]

Lacking an explicit account of power to guide its ethical evaluations, the church's social teaching becomes vulnerable to misappropriation in support of oppression, and its potential as a means of evangelization in service of the church's mission is vitiated, even for those firmly grounded in the faith, as Prejean's experience shows. Her troubling memory of becoming aware of her own complicity in broader systems of injustice might, unfortunately, find wide resonance among white Catholics in the United States: Prejean's well-catechized, white, Catholic family of privilege treated blacks charitably but never questioned the structures of race and class that enforced segregation as a function of oppressive white power. Looking back, she reflects, "It would take me a long time to understand how systems inflict pain and hardship in people's lives and to learn that being kind in an unjust system is not enough."[27]

Strategically appropriating Catholic social teaching using the tools of social analysis from the margins, she gradually came to realize that resistance to unjust exercises of power involves thoughtful attention to the relationship between charity and justice: "On this path I have learned that love, far from being passive in the face of injustice, is a vibrant force that resists and takes bold action to 'build a new society within the shell of the old,' as Dorothy Day used to say."[28]

The pneumatological power of solidarity, she discovered, uses love strategically to disarm coercive forms of power. This insight has held true even when her path has taken her beyond the moral wisdom available in Catholic social teaching. Where the texts themselves have fallen short of providing lucid ethical guidance regarding unjust power dynamics, she has proceeded in wise innocence to forge an uncharted course of pursuing justice sustained by charity, providing prophetic witness to both the church and society.

Formulation of Catholic Social Teaching as an Object of Power

The textual neglect of power issues in Catholic social teaching may have its roots in the institutional practices guiding the formulation of these documents. Charles Curran has argued that a shift toward a historically conscious anthropology in the first century of Catholic social teaching resulted in a move from a more deductive to a more inductive methodology within the texts themselves.[29] In theory, an inductive textual method has the potential to draw from a greater diversity of human experience. In practice, even if one accepts Curran's account, the fact remains that the vast majority of Catholic social teaching documents have born the scars of what might be called "patriarchal creeping hierarchism," i.e., the reservation of critical ministries to ordained clergy, even when the proper fulfillment of these ministries does not require ordination. Up to this point in history, women have played virtually no formal part in the process of drafting Catholic social teaching texts. Barbara Ward's invitation to offer expert advice in the preparation of Paul VI's encyclical *On the Development of Peoples* (*Populorum progressio,* 1967) represented a groundbreaking exception to the rule.[30]

So, while the textual methodology of Catholic social teaching may have become more inductive over time, the practice of limiting the key decision-making roles in the drafting process almost exclusively to clerics means that the interpretive lens used to discern the signs of the times and analyze the data has reflected a relatively narrow band of human experience. The charisms of others gifted by the Holy Spirit to contribute to the formulation of the church's social teaching have not been tapped to fulfill this ministerial need. Perhaps cognizant of the tremendous loss this unnecessarily constraining institutional practice represents for the life of the church, Pope Benedict XVI mused in a question-and-answer session with the priests of the diocese of Rome, "In any case, it is right to wonder if even in ministerial service . . . more room and more positions of responsibility might be offered to women."[31]

The church would do well to consider this issue on ethical and theological grounds. Ethically, it is a matter of justice, as the world's bishops articulated in *Justice in the World* (*Justitia in mundo,* 1971): in order to preach the Gospel with credibility, the church must endeavor to apply the same standards of justice to itself that it advocates for the world. Theologically, Benedict XVI's remark begs the question: given the church's theology of charism articulated at Vatican II, is the challenge at hand "to offer" more roles of responsibility to women, or is it rather a matter of transforming institutional practices that risk obstructing the work of the Holy Spirit among the People of God?

Since their inception following Vatican II, many national episcopal conferences have begun to attend to such concerns by adopting more participatory approaches to the formulation of Catholic social teaching. In the United States, the dialogical, public consultation model adopted by the bishops in drafting the pastoral letters *The Challenge of Peace* (1983) and *Economic Justice for All* (1986) provided the opportunity for greater lay input. At the regional level, the Appalachian bishops' texts *This Land Is Home to Me* (1975) and *At Home in the Web of Life* (1995), as well as the Pacific Northwest bishops' *Columbia River Pastoral Letter* (2002) transparently and explicitly acknowledged the direct role of lay collaborators in the drafting process, bearing witness to a model of ecclesial power sufficiently supple to attend to the dynamism of charism at work in the formulation of Catholic social teaching.

Conclusion

Given the church's struggle to offer an explicit ethical account of power in its Catholic social teaching texts and a corresponding witness through the institutional practices guiding the formulation of these documents, Helen Prejean's strategic appropriation of Catholic social teaching appears all the more remarkable. Using the charisms imparted to her by the Holy Spirit in baptism, she has taken up Jesus' call to discipleship in wise innocence, drawing upon the pneumatological power of solidarity. From the vantage point of the societal margins, she has used her knowledge of ecclesial tradition to press for a more prophetic rejection of the practice of capital punishment, both within Catholic social teaching and in the church's witness to society. In so doing, she has invited the church to imagine into being not only a commonweal that holds all life sacred, but also a way of life together as an ecclesial community that dares to counter the coercive power of violent domination with the pneumatological power of solidarity, drawing strength from God's love enlivening each and all of the faithful through the charisms of the Holy Spirit.

Part Three

INSISTENCE ON DIALOGUE

Chapter 8

Unknowing in the Place
of Understanding

The Theological Fruits of Dialogue

Jeannine Hill Fletcher

Just then a lawyer stood up to test Jesus. "Teacher," he said, "what must I do to inherit eternal life?" Jesus said to him, "What is written in the law? What do you read there?" The lawyer answered, "You shall love the Lord your God with all your heart, and with all your soul, and with all your strength, and with all your mind; and your neighbor as yourself." And Jesus said to him, "You have given the right answer; do this, and you will live."   (Luke 10:25–28)

I F THE MISSION OF THE CHURCH is to carry on Christ's witness in the world, the future of the church will be found in the way that it helps people to love God and neighbor. But what this looks like in our current context requires the Gospel story to continue as we place ourselves within the narrative to ask, "And who is my neighbor?" (Luke 10:29). Seeking an answer through the prism of globalization, the bewildering complexity of religious difference comes into view. Thus, for the church in the twenty-first century to live out Christ's commands it will be necessary to engage our neighbors of diverse faiths. Interreligious dialogue is, therefore, key. And, while such dialogue is not without its difficulties, it has the potential to enhance the Christian path to salvation. For just as the neighbor whom Jesus presents challenges those who hear him, our neighbors today might challenge us to witness the Christian message anew.

Dialogue and Its Difficulties

Since Vatican II, Catholic Christians have increasingly had opportunities for interreligious dialogue to be part of their faith practice.[1] Yet formal dialogue opportunities remain inconsistent and, for many, inadequate to afford authentic interreligious understanding. The former may be the result of ideological resistance and bears witness to the difficulties of getting to dialogue. The latter is more intimately linked to the challenges within dialogue itself. Genuine dialogue takes time, organization, and effort, both on the part of those who will provide the resources to make the event a reality and also on the part of those who participate. Real understanding of another faith tradition is a very long (indeed lifelong) process. The difficulties of understanding across religious

74

difference need to be illuminated in order to reassess the theological possibilities in dialogue.

Imagine a group whose aim is to get to know the religious traditions of their particular multifaith locale. A dialogue is set up where members of different religious traditions gather to talk about their religious outlooks, practices, or beliefs. The organizers have chosen a particular topic for members to discuss from out of their particular faith tradition. Dialogue partners begin by offering the key terms that form the central vision of their religion. As Miroslav Volf describes, "Such dialogues can range from boring to exhilarating. They are boring when both parties repeat predictable lines; they are exhilarating when each, without betraying its own identity, opens itself up to the adventure of the encounter with the other."[2] In our imagined dialogue, our ideal participants are indeed open to the adventure of encounter with the other. But, as they begin their explanations, each word uttered by conversation partners raises as many questions as it does answers. This is because each word is linked not only to a particular idea but to an interconnected life-world of sacred stories, ritual remembrances, and religious practices. As Sallie King describes,

> Living in the Buddhist world, one lives in the world of the serenely smiling Buddha; a world whose vista embraces lifetime after lifetime of countless rebirths held in tension with an invitation to complete selflessness; a world in which one strives to remove all "thought coverings," to erase everything and plunge again and again into vast emptiness; a world in which one feels one's connectedness with all things and has compassion for all beings, the insect as well as the human. Say "Buddha Nature" and all this is implicit.[3]

Thus, as the Buddhist participant begins by affirming that all who are gathered share in "Buddha Nature," her hearers are bewildered by the many ideas that are connected and require further explanation. Is the "complete selflessness" of Buddha Nature what Jesus had in giving himself over to the will of God? How does "vast emptiness" compare with the Christian view of heaven? Do I really need to have compassion for insects? What are "thought coverings" and is "rebirth" real? The many questions knotted within the interglossing set of Buddhist references reminds us that the adventure of dialogue is one that is open to ongoing, indeed lifelong possibilities. Aware of the positive possibilities, proponents of dialogue often encourage such exchanges with the enticing benefit of "mutual understanding."[4] But such a goal is out of reach for most persons. The cultural-linguistic theory of religion proposed by George Lindbeck helps to explain why.

First, to understand the religious outlook of my neighbor of another faith, I must be conversant with his or her sacred Scripture. For Lindbeck, Scripture provides the essential landscape of the life-world religious persons inhabit. Indeed, the many terms and ideas that are central to a religious outlook are often found precisely in the sacred text. But Lindbeck illumines that the text is more than a mere reference book presenting ideas. His cultural-linguistic theory proposes that the canonized text of a religion functions as a conceptual paradigm that shapes the way people experience the world itself. Believers see the world imaginatively through scriptural lenses as the structure of the sacred narrative absorbs and organizes the sensory stimuli of the world.[5] The Buddhist sees "Buddha Nature" in herself and the other because she has been shaped by the story of the Buddha to be able to recognize that reality in the world. Extending beyond the individual, religious communities are "story-shaped"[6] and "canons function to help construct communities"[7] by similarly shaping experiences. This means that persons within a given tradition see and experience the world in similar ways, but in a way different from persons not shaped by the same Scripture. As King articulates it, "The world looks one way within one language and quite different within another. Languages are not really mutually translatable. They are not interchangeable. Something is always lost in translation.... These worlds [of differing religions] overlap, but they are not the same. They are two life-worlds, two languages. On some points they can understand each other deeply; on other points they elude each other."[8]

Embracing cultural-linguistic theory and witnessing the way the sacred texts of my conversation partner will shape his experience of the world, our imagined dialogue might follow Volf's suggestion to "put the scripture at the center of the dialogue."[9] Yet in this alternative approach to an imagined dialogue we do not easily overcome the difficulties recognized by King and illuminated by Lindbeck. This is because the sacred stories are given further meaning through the ritual practices, worship experiences, and communal life that extends from them. Thus, for example, while a Christian may be conversant with the Hebrew Scriptures of his Jewish dialogue partner, the former is not a practicing member of the latter's community, so he will miss the rich Jewish understandings that emerge not merely from reading Torah but from embodying it in ritual practice. As Judith Plaskow explains, the critical moments of Jewish religious history recorded in the Bible are not merely past record or source of information, but shape Jewish memory and consciousness. This happens through "the liturgical reenactment and celebration of formative events." She writes, "The weekly renewal of creation with the inauguration of the Sabbath, the entry of the High Priest into the Holy of Holies on the Day of Atonement, the Exodus of Israel from Egypt every Passover — these are remembered not just verbally but through the body and thus doubly imprinted on Jewish consciousness."[10] Following through on Lindbeck's cultural-linguistic theory, one recognizes that genuine understanding across religious difference requires not merely conversation or study, but full participation in the life of the community. To understand a religious outlook one needs to be steeped not only in its language, but also in its "culture." Although not impossible, this level of engagement is a practical impossibility for all but the most sophisticated of scholars or committed practitioners of dual religious traditions.[11]

In recognizing the comprehensiveness of the sacred story in shaping the outlook of my conversation partner and accepting that the meaning within her religious life-world is communicated also through ritual practice, I relinquish the naïve hope of arriving at genuine understanding. Mutual understanding is not the primary theological fruit of interreligious dialogue. In the words of Lindbeck,

The gravest objection to the [cultural-linguistic] approach we are adopting is that it makes interreligious dialogue more difficult. Conversation between religions is pluralized or balkanized when they are seen as mutually untranslatable. Not only do they no longer share a common theme such as salvation, but the shared universe of discourse forged to discuss that theme disintegrates. There are ways of getting around this obstacle such as bilingualism... but genuine bilingualism (not to mention the mastery of many religious languages) is so rare and difficult as to leave basically intact the barrier to extramural communication posed by untranslatability in religious matters. Those for whom conversation is the key to solving interreligious problems are likely to be disappointed.[12]

Adopting the cultural-linguistic understanding of religious difference, as I am encouraging, I affirm with Lindbeck the genuine difficulties of dialogue. Yet while dialogue *is* difficult, it remains a crucial strategy for the future of the church in the way that it affords the opportunity for Christians to follow through on the great commandment to love God and neighbor. If the goal of "understanding" cannot be attained as the first fruits of interreligious dialogue, perhaps reclaiming the theological fruits of "unknowing" is the strategy our dialogues must take in the future. Through unknowing, the church might follow through on the command to love God as we are stirred by wonder. As we are drawn into ongoing relationship, this dialogue might sustain the love of neighbor envisioned in the Gospel story.

Love of God and Neighbor through Dialogue

Precisely in its difficulties, dialogue can be a practice that fosters a love of God rooted in wonder. To understand this, we must reclaim what the Catholic Christian tradition has affirmed of God's nature as mystery. In biblical tradition, God's ways are beyond the reach of human understanding (e.g., Rom. 11:33–34; Luke 10:21; Matt. 11:25). In the philosophical development of this tradition, the incomprehensibility of God is rooted in God's very being as infinite. In the classic articulation of Thomas Aquinas, "Every thing is knowable according to its actuality. But God, Whose being is infinite ... is infinitely knowable. Now no created intellect can know God infinitely. . . . Hence it is impossible that [any created intellect] should comprehend God."[13] In Christian theological tradition, the human experience of God is constituted by "unknowing" in the presence of an infinite and overabundant reality. As Teresa of Avila images the encounter, just as a sponge becomes saturated with water, the soul overflows with divinity when face to face with the mystery of God.[14] Or as Karl Rahner explains,

The incomprehensibility of God should not then be regarded as a distant reality, for it increases rather than diminishes in the vision of God, in which alone it becomes an inescapable event. It does not describe the remnants of something which, sadly, remains unknown, but rather points to the immediate object of the experience of God in heaven, an object which is present in the mind overflowing with the fullness of God's self-communication.[15]

For Rahner, following Aquinas, the human response to the mystery of God is not to leave the mystery unexamined, but to strive always to know more and to experience the mystery ever more fully. Rooted in God's infinite knowability, the process of coming to know God is one that never ends.

For Aquinas, the process of coming to know God is ultimately fulfilling for human beings. What there is to know of God is infinitely overabundant and God's reality never-endingly sustains the human process of exploration. This pursuit is fulfilling not only within this lifetime, but even beyond the bounds of time and space. The inability to fully know God is not the source of eternal frustration, but rather, the experience of eternal contemplation is fulfilling in itself. As Aquinas describes,

> Nothing can be wearisome that is wonderful to him that looks on it, because as long as we wonder at it, it still moves our desire. Now the created intellect always looks with wonder on the divine substance, since no created intellect can comprehend it. Therefore, the intellectual substance cannot possibly become weary of that vision.[16]

The human intellect cannot comprehend God, and the appropriate posture toward God, then, is wonder.

The fundamental affirmation of the church is that God is a reality beyond any human comprehension or control. If wonder, not certainty, and unknowing instead of understanding constitute the human response to God, interreligious encounter might remind us of all that we do not know of God's mystery. An awareness of religious realities that one does not understand, if approached in the posture of wonder, can stir the recognition of the infinite incomprehensibility of God.

As an example of what I am proposing as new fruits in interreligious encounter, I offer a snapshot from my experience. When my Muslim neighbor unfolds his prayer rug in the space of my daily commute, I am disoriented by his presence. I pause to wonder at his practice. While I may attempt to draw connections with my own posture toward the divine, I do not know what fruits he experiences through a devotion to God through five daily prayers (at times necessarily a public witness to his faith). My experience of being human has not been organized by the pillars that structure the framework of Islam, and so understanding his experience is beyond me. Having only read portions of his holy book, I cannot tell you precisely how the world looks when seen through the lines of the Quran. Being moved to awe and wonder at the posture of his prayer, my mind is stirred to the infinite reality of God that must sustain this life of faith. In the complex life of my Muslim neighbor and its persistent alterity, I glimpse the God who surpasses all understanding. Capturing the spirit of this encounter, the posture of wonder might encourage an appreciation of religious differences for the way they open us up to the incomprehensible mystery of God. Interreligious dialogue might provide an opportunity to commit oneself anew to loving God with one's whole heart, soul, mind, and strength.

While stirred in wonder by the theological outlooks and worship relationships of persons of other faiths, dialogue also affords the opportunity to know and therefore better love our neighbors. For while I cannot tell you what my neighbor anticipates in the unrolling of his prayer rug because I do not inhabit that world and its practices, I can tell you something about his job, his family, his home, his school system, and his local community because elements of those worlds I do inhabit. Our lives are joined by economic, political, social, and geographical realities, while our religious lives separate us. The cultural-linguistic approach to interreligious encounter reminds us of all that we do not know of our conversation partner's religious outlook and experience, but it overlooks the fact that these same encounters provide opportunities for connection and recognition of where our complex humanity overlaps. This is because we each are shaped not only by the story of our religious tradition, but many other stories as well. And while we many not come to the dialogue sharing the sacred story of our conversation partner, we may share other stories through which we pursue the connections and commitment to love of neighbor. Here, the recognition of "hybridity" is essential to the functioning of dialogue.

Hybrid Identities Shaping Dialogical Encounters

In the interreligious encounter of dialogue, participants can see that they come to the discussion not simply with their religious identity, but with a web of identity. As feminist theorist Morwenna Griffiths describes, the self is "intricate, entangled and interlaced, with each part connected to other parts."[17] We come to the encounter not simply as a "Christian," "Muslim," or "Jew," but with a web of identity. Thus, the religious outlook of my conversation partner is interlaced with other outlooks that I *may* share.

The infinite internal diversity of any given religious community derives from hybrid identities that can foster connections outside any one particular grouping. This is possible because each strand of the web of identity is formed relationally through engagement with other communities. Although I have been shaped, in part, by my affiliation with a religious community, my identity has also been fostered in conversation with other communities — the community of my family, my generation, my profession, my nationality, my gender. And as Martha Minnow suggests, "No one identity category, sexual orientation, gender, ethnicity, class, family status captures [an individual's] world. These very differences afford chances for connection."[18] The Christian, then, can be in conversation with other Christians, but the multiple facets of his or her identity and the web of identity itself allow him or her to forge innumerable solidarities by virtue of association in multiple communities. It is our internal diversity as a Christian community that affords an infinite number of possible sites for fostering conversations and forging solidarities beyond our given religious category.

In her study of women's engagement in interfaith dialogue, Helene Egnell witnesses the way making space for hybrid identities shifts the center of dialogical concerns. She reflects, "The women brought different questions to the conferences.... Their questions were how to survive in male-dominated religious traditions, but also the survival of humanity and the planet in a world of war and injustice."[19] Our hybrid identities allow us to bring to the theological

exchange shared concerns for human well-being in light of all that threatens
and dehumanizes us. Where theological investigations of the issues of religious
difference have centered on the question of salvation in the abstract, the pursuit of interreligious dialogue through the impetus of love of God and neighbor
requires that we see salvation in the concrete. But the shift of dialogical center from eschatological to material salvation is not too far from the biblical
vision witnessed in our story from Luke. In this exchange the words placed
on the lips of Jesus link eternal life to the love of God and neighbor. While
the question posed to him was framed in terms of eschatological salvation,
he responds with a present-centered vision: "Do this and you will live." Hybrid identities in dialogical encounter allow us to share concerns in a vision of
integral salvation.[20]

As we foster relationships and forge solidarities through interreligious dialogue, we might search the Scriptures again to give texture to the love of God
and neighbor that Christians are called to witness. What the Gospel of Luke
adds to these essential commandments through the story of the good Samaritan (Luke 10:29–37) provides specific content for the love of neighbor in the
form of self-giving service. A further dimension for the future of the church
is evident. If the church is to carry on Christ's witness in the world, it must
be rooted in the love of God and neighbor that takes the form of self-giving
service. Here another aspect of dialogue emerges. In order to serve the needs
of our neighbors, we must understand those needs. Interreligious dialogue provides the opportunities for the church to hear the needs of the neighbor and in a
practice patterned on the life of Jesus to commit to serving those needs toward
the wholeness that is salvation.

A Strategy for Dialogue

In this essay, I am proposing that dialogue is a strategy for renewing the church's
mission of loving God and neighbor. But what strategies will encourage dialogue? While embracing the difficulties of dialogue from a cultural-linguistic
perspective, one concrete strategy is to encourage interfaith programming in
our parishes. Interfaith programming can provide sites for both relationship
and wonder as we overlap with the complex and hybrid identities of our neighbors of other faiths. Like the imagined dialogues of my earlier discussion, parish
programming might include public lectures on interfaith issues or informal
dialogue circles. Yet even these simple programs come with the challenge of
creating a safe and sacred space in which persons of different religions can interact. In too many of our global locations, distrust precedes any invitation to
dialogue — and, too often, with just cause. Christian houses of worship are
experienced as exclusive enclaves, not welcoming respites for the stranger. The
theologies of the Catholic tradition and the vision promoted in Catholic magisterial teaching do not often dispel the fears of our neighbors. Moving forward
with strategies for the future of the church, we cannot evade the question of
Kwok Pui-lan as she forces us to ask, "How do we deal with the fact that Western Christian theological discourse about religious difference is constructed in

such a way as to justify a hierarchical ordering of religious traditions, which always puts Christianity on top?"[21] The promotion of interfaith dialogue will require reform of our self-understandings and our theologies as we attempt to open ourselves to the other.

The revision of Christian theological self-understanding carries with it also the imperative that Kwok illumines from a postcolonial perspective, namely, that theological, hierarchical orderings have had material impact that renders our encounter with the religious other often one of inequality. In idealized writings on dialogue, conversation partners are envisioned as coming to the table "as equals."[22] While the theological concept is a valuable one, the reality is that we come to the table under conditions of inequality, power, and domination. Keeping dialogue from mere lip-service, it must aim also at redressing those inequalities through which Christians may find themselves in positions of privilege over and against their neighbors of other faiths. This too can come only through the commitment of dialogue. Only by knowing the other is one able to stand and speak on behalf of the marginalized other. But speaking on behalf of the other must not be a patronizing gesture. Rather, it must be understood instead in the way that Homi Bhabha envisions, where speaking on behalf means being willing to "half" oneself, to restructure one's interests and privileges in solidarity with the other.[23]

Hearing the particular story of the other and his or her experience, one is reminded of all that one does not know of the incomprehensible mystery of God. Hearing the experience of the other, one can see more clearly how one's own religious outlook or practice may negatively impinge on the other. Dialogue is a strategy that can reform Christian relationships with other faiths. But the benefits of interfaith dialogue may also aid other areas of reform in our church. From an internal perspective, voicing our story forces Christians to recall the heart of the Gospel — Jesus' own disdain for power and prestige, the critique of religious authoritarianism, Jesus' vision of human wholeness, and the call to a discipleship of equals.[24] Speaking the truth of the faith reminds one of the importance of living it. Further, in the sacred spaces of dialogue, one entrusts oneself to a renewed and mature understanding of the faith. When speaking aloud "what my religion believes," one is forced to bring critical reason to the faith so that one can communicate with clarity. Importantly, in the process, we often experience the cognitive dissonance that forces us to articulate not merely "what my religion believes" but "what *I* believe." That is to say, in attempting to explain our faith we often encounter things that simply don't make sense. Dialogue forces one to clarify one's own position, testing received tradition with experience and making conscious choices in a mature affirmation of the faith.

A strategy for the future of the church includes interfaith programming that offers the fruits of interreligious encounter. Realistically, most people will not have the expertise to arrive at genuine understanding of the religious other. Even further, many people will not have the leisure, the resources of time, or the opportunity to participate in the structured interfaith dialogues that might be sponsored by our religious communities. And yet "dialogue" happens all the time in our globalized world when people of different faiths meet one another in the messy complexity of our everyday world. In everyday encounters, the "Muslim" and "Christian" do not compare notes on religious abstractions. Instead, Muslim and Christian co-workers might collaborate on a project that requires accommodation for a Friday mosque visit. Or the Hindu, Jewish, and Christian caregivers share snacks at their child's playgroup and embarrassingly realize the food cannot be eaten by some members of the group. These imagined encounters take diverse forms around the globe. In the messy complexity of the everyday world, individuals with multiple sites of identity encounter each other with a broad range of stories from which to make possible connections. How might the church respond to these interreligious encounters as parallel "dialogues" that open us to love of God and neighbor?

In a cultural-linguistic approach to religion, sacred texts and ritual embodiments shape human outlooks on the world. In liturgical spaces, we hear the stories that shape us. Strategies for the future of dialogue must enter into this liturgical space. Implications of the Gospel for interreligious encounter need to be preached in our churches. In addition to reading Christian Scriptures anew with the reality of religious difference in mind, the lives and concerns of our neighbors of other faiths ought to be woven into Christian liturgy. Inclusion of the concerns of our neighbors of other faiths within Catholic worship can remind us of our commitment to love the neighbor and to share in the struggles of the marginalized, and exposure to the diverse practices of other faith communities can underscore in a theologically fruitful way the incomprehensibility of God.

The reality of religious difference deserves to be celebrated as central to the Christian commitment to live out Christ's commands. It is through relationships of solidarity with our neighbors of other faiths that we will live more freely the command to love our neighbor. And it is through the disorienting encounter of interreligious dialogue that we stand ready to be stirred anew in the wonder and love of God.

Chapter 9

The Dialogical Imperative

Listening to Concerned and Engaged African Women

TERESIA M. HINGA

AS I BEGAN THIS ESSAY, stories of women and their quest for sustainable peace in Africa flooded my consciousness.[1] One was the story of genocide in Rwanda in 1994, a story that was reanimated for me after watching the Hollywood rendition of these events in the movie *Hotel Rwanda*. The movie chronicled the events that constituted this nightmare and the reckless killing of close to eight hundred thousand people. Many of these were women and children. The media explained this as part of the so-called "tribal" animosity between two "tribes": the Tutsi and Hutu.

This horror movie reminded me of the terror that women and children face in situations of war, or "hot violence," what analysts refer to as violence inflicted through various weapons like bombs, spears, guns, or, in this case, machetes. Women in situations of hot violence frequently experience double jeopardy when rape and sexual assault on the "enemy" side become a military strategy of choice by combatants. The specific intimate terror that women faced in Rwanda will probably never be comprehended. Many, no doubt, preferred outright death to such torture.[2]

As I further contemplated stories to include in this essay, I took a break and surfed the Internet, drifting momentarily to the website of the *East African Standard,* one of the Kenyan dailies. The headlines screamed back at me. Thirty people killed in clan violence in northern Kenya as rival clans clashed! I looked at the demographics of those who were killed. Most were women and children. Some had survived the orgy and escaped with wounds. But for how long? There were no health facilities where their wounds could be treated. For lack of a mortuary facility and cold storage, the dead were housed in a toilet under construction. Indignity haunts the poor even after they are dead.

The story of deadly violence in northern Kenya reminded me that hot violence often is occasioned or compounded by what has been dubbed "cold violence," the pain and suffering caused by poverty. I was reminded too that cold violence kills as surely and as painfully as hot violence and that in many impoverished third world countries, death and massive loss of life are daily routines. The question is "What will get you first?" Will it be the bomb, the random sniper's gun, the machete, or will it be cholera, untreated malaria, dysentery, tuberculosis, malnutrition, AIDS, and other diseases of poverty?

It is this kind of headline news of violence, both hot and cold, that led a team of us, faculty and staff from a U.S. university, to travel to Kenya in December 2004. Our goal was to explore ways in which the university we came from could participate in the quest for social justice in Kenya. I was privileged to be part of that delegation and determined to witness the desperate situations that we had heard about in the media. In this exploratory journey, we visited several contexts characterized by poverty, where cold violence prevails. The plight of people living in places like Kibera and Kariobangi, some of the largest slums in Nairobi, left many in our delegation in shock several months later. Having visited and spoken with many caught up in indigence and poverty traps, we confirmed that indeed cold violence kills as painfully and as certainly as hot violence.

The story of the likes of Njeri, a woman afflicted by HIV/AIDS whom we visited, hauntingly floats to the forefront of my reflections and demands to be told. On the day that we visited her, Njeri had not had a meal, and there were no signs of her getting one. Neither were the opportunistic diseases manifested in her properly diagnosed, and she had no prospect of being treated. The nearest health-care facility was some twenty miles away. The closest she came to nursing care beyond that offered by her mother out of her meager resources was by a volunteer untrained nurse from the local Catholic church, who did her daily rounds of visitation with the sick and disabled in the village armed with nothing but her compassion, words of encouragement, and a listening ear. Njeri spoke of losing hope. She had lost her only child to the disease and her husband had also died. Her husband's family blamed her for his death and had kicked her out of her marital home.

Njeri was twenty years old. HIV had made her a spectacle of sorts. She lived in partial seclusion in a cold and ill-ventilated dark room emerging only to greet visitors when they showed up, like we did, witnessing her emaciated condition. For Njeri, the violence of hunger and the pain of disease was compounded and multiplied by stigma, a condition that I refer to here as social violence. Long before Njeri dies from whatever gets her first, the malnutrition or the common cold hitting her when her immunity is lowest, she suffers the anguish of social death occasioned by *social-psychological violence* through stigmatization, rejection, and maybe even guilt. For surely they were right, were they not, about her being responsible for her husband's death or even that of her child? Social death kills her spirit even as AIDS attacks her physically. In the case of Njeri and many others in similar circumstances, social death compounds the pain and violence of disease and poverty that she endures.

Despite this background of despair, however, and against many odds, stories of hope and courage also shine through from the continent. One such story competed for my attention as I sifted through pieces to include in this essay. It was the story of Professor Wangari Maathai, who had just been awarded the Nobel Peace Prize for her sustained efforts to reclaim forest cover for Kenya, through the Green Belt movement. My heart glowed with pride at the news of the peace prize for Professor Maathai and for women like her for their "never say die" attitude and perseverance in applying their moral agency to change things for the better in Africa and beyond.

It has not been a rosy road for Wangari Maathai. Her story has been one of courage and endurance. She sometimes faced imprisonment and torture for believing in herself and for believing that change was possible, necessary, and doable, even, or perhaps particularly, by women.[3]

Some people thought that Wangari Maathai's prize was misplaced. What had trees got to do with peace? Maathai spoke for many African women when she reminded those who construe peace as mere absence of war that there is an organic connection between justice and peace. She reminded us that there could neither be justice nor peace unless we heeded the imperative to conserve and reclaim rapidly diminishing natural resources and learned to distribute them more humanely.

Many in Africa are killed or maimed in desperate struggles for survival as people scramble for resources like land and water, which are becoming more and more scarce. Many are also killed because the few resources that are there are unjustly distributed, with the moneyed elite grabbing the lion's share and hoarding, particularly land, even when they do not need it.[4] Professor Maathai celebrated the fact that the international community was finally beginning to see the link between injustice and lack of peace in Africa and indeed in the world. Responding to the award, she appreciatively commented:

> The Nobel Prize has presented me with extraordinary opportunities.... [However] the biggest challenge [since getting the award] has been how to respond to the countless requests to visit and see, celebrate, encourage and empower the huge constituency that felt honored by the prize.... The environmental movement, those who work for women and gender issues, human rights activists, those advocating for good governance and the peace movement. *This interest was partly due to the connection the Norwegian Nobel Committee had made between peace, sustainable management of resources and good governance.* This was the first time such a link had been forged.... It was also the first time the Nobel Peace Prize committee had decided to *recognize the* importance [of the link] by awarding a Nobel Peace Prize to somebody who had worked in these areas for decades.... *As we had said for many years, humanity needs to rethink peace and security and work towards a culture of peace by governing more democratically, respecting human rights, deliberately and consciously promoting justice and equity as well as managing resources responsibly....* (emphasis added)[5]

The story that I finally chose to elaborate on in this essay is one of hope in the midst of desperate situations. It is the story of the Circle of Concerned African Women Theologians (hereafter the Circle) and their concerted efforts toward justice and peace. The women who constitute the Circle have chosen to present a sustained critique of religions and cultures in Africa. They seek to unmask ways in which religions and cultures nurture injustices and therefore non-peace and also to unveil ways in which religions and cultures can be resources for freedom, peace, and justice.

In telling the story of the Circle, I will highlight proposals and practices that not only name, but model what African women who form the Circle hope for, namely, a peace with justice and the dialogue that is its necessary prologue and catalyst. Specifically, I will highlight the socially transformative dialogue that these women engage in when interacting with one another and that they champion as a vital precondition and ingredient for the quest for sustainable peace in Africa and beyond. Before discussing the centrality of dialogue, its various dimensions, and its rationale in the thought and praxis of the Circle, it is important to contextualize the Circle and identify its goals.

The Circle and Its Goals

Professor Maathai made the connection between environmental justice and peace, and her vision is also that of many other African women. There is indeed a wider-based initiative by African women to transcend their victim status and to bring their collective moral agency to bear in the quest for lasting solutions to the multiple and crisscrossing crises that make Africa a continent where peace is marked largely by its absence. Whereas this movement of African women is not all faith-based, or even exclusively concerned with the link between religion and justice, I focus in this essay on one example of a community of women working systematically and in solidarity to unmask injustices, particularly that of sexism, and to make strides toward sustainable peace.

The Circle of Concerned African Women Theologians was founded in 1989 under the agency of Mercy Amba Oduyoye, an Akan woman from Ghana who was then one of the deputy secretaries of the World Council of Churches.[6] The primary goal of the Circle has been to examine how religion and culture in Africa have promoted injustice, particularly sexism, and alternatively to examine ways in which religious beliefs and practices could facilitate peace, justice, and other freedoms that define and enhance *Ubuntu*,[7] true humanity.

Noting that religion and culture are pivotal in shaping women's lives for good or ill, and proceeding with what feminists elsewhere have called the "hermeneutics of suspicion," the women in the Circle embarked on a seven-year cycle (later reduced to five) of sustained analysis of religion and culture with several specific objectives in mind:

1. To encourage and empower the critical study of the practice of religion in Africa.
2. To publish theological literature written by African women with special focus on religion and culture.
3. To undertake research that unveils (and names) both positive and negative religio-cultural factors, beliefs, and myths, which affect, influence, or hamper women development.
4. To promote a dialogical approach to religious and cultural tensions in Africa and beyond.
5. To strive for the inclusion of women's studies in religion and culture in academic research institutions in Africa.
6. To empower African women to contribute to the cross-cultural discourse on women's issues through engagement in critical cultural hermeneutics.
7. To promote ecumenism and cultural pluralism.[8]

After suitable deliberation and consultation, the group designated itself "the Circle of Concerned African Women Theologians," and for the last two or so decades it has sought to fulfill the objectives identified above. Since 1989 the Circle has published a number of monographs from their five yearly Pan-African conferences. These include *The Will to Arise* (Maryknoll, N.Y.: Orbis, 1992), an anthology of papers presented in the 1989 inaugural Pan-African conference. The list also includes *Transforming Power: Women in the Household of God* (Accra-North, Ghana: Samwoode, 1997), which constitutes the proceedings of their second Pan-African conference in Nairobi in 1996. Several books including *African Women, HIV/AIDS and Faith Communities* (Pietermaritzburg, South Africa: Cluster, 2003) were published as outcomes of one week of deliberations on the theme of "African Women, Religion, AIDS and the Problem of Stigma," during the Circle's third Pan-African conference in 2002 in Addis Ababa, Ethiopia.[9] Circle research and publication is also expected at the national level where local chapters are encouraged to write and publish on issues germane to their specific regions. Thus, the Kenyan chapter of the Circle published an anthology of essays entitled *Violence against Women* (Nairobi: Acton, 1996), while the Nigerian chapter published an anthology entitled *African Culture and the Quest for Women's Rights* (Ibadan, Nigeria: Sefer Books, 2001).

The Circle has identified critical hermeneutics of culture and religion as integral to the overall quest for sustainable solutions to issues of peace and justice. It has also identified dialogue as a major means to the hoped-for goal of just-peace. In their research, in their writing, and in their praxis as a community of scholars, these women embody what they envision, namely, a more humane, just, inclusive, and pluralistic society both in Africa and globally. I turn now to an exploration of insights offered by the Circle, particularly those pertaining to the integral role of dialogue.

Just-Peace, Circle Praxis, and the Promise of Transformative Dialogue

The above list of goals and objectives reveals a two-pronged Circle project, namely, the eradication of injustices, particularly those based on sexism among other systems of domination, as well as the quest for a radical pluralism without which peace and justice are simply moot. The goals therefore cohere with each other, and as I will show in the following segments, the internal coherence of the Circle project revolves around and is shaped by a dialogical imperative that the women embrace and champion. I will discuss the implications of this dialogical imperative as embodied in the Circle by looking at women's will to arise, their responses to the problem of denial, and their efforts to model pluralism, challenge hierarchies, and move toward solidarity across borders through conscientization and transformation of consciousness.

The Will to Arise: Women Overcoming Enforced Silence, Exclusion, and Misrepresentation

The Circle was inaugurated partly in response to the efforts by the World Council of Churches to be in solidarity with women and to begin to engage them as dialogue partners. During the inauguration of the Circle, Mercy Oduyoye observed that a major obstacle for women seeking justice was the failure in church and society to give heed to the voice of women as moral agents who were capable of working toward justice. The women attributed this silencing and marginalization to the cumulative and multiplicative impact of sexism, racism, and other systems of domination, particularly colonialism in the African context. For African women caught up in these multiple systems, there has been a multidimensional jeopardy. Even when there has been an attempt to listen to African voices, the voice of women is still unheard since it is assumed to be included in that of men. It is this marginalization and enforced silencing that led Oduyoye to lament: "As long as men and western strangers continue to write exclusively about Africa, African women will continue to be represented as if they were dead."[10]

In this context of enforced silence, the Circle women's covenant to "research, write, and publish their perspectives on religion and culture" in Africa has meant several things in the quest for justice. First, it serves as these women's way of protesting being marginalized and silenced. To put it more positively, it is their way of asserting their right to speak on their own behalf as full-fledged citizens of church and society. Second, since the women are acutely aware that years of enforced silence may have made them apathetic and seemingly acquiescent with various oppressions, their writings further serve as a wake-up call to each other to rise and fight such oppression and injustice. Through their writings the women engage in dialogue among themselves, challenging and encouraging each other to speak up. It is hardly surprising, then, that they deliberately and appropriately named their first book *The Will to Arise*. Oduyoye, introducing this work, described it as "the voice of African women theologians grounded in the challenge of Scripture and resulting from a new wave of change." She noted further: "God's call for them [African women] is compelling and compulsory. . . . It is a call to action and wholeness that challenges their (women's) will and their intellect."[11]

For these women, breaking the silence, overcoming enforced muteness through mutual dialogue, and encouraging each other to speak out in a persistent way has become a compelling strategy that is integral to their quest for justice. Through their writings they also demand transformative dialogue within church and society on crucial issues of concern to women. Such dialogue within church and society becomes a major ingredient in the overall quest for justice and peace on the continent. It is to a further discussion of women's naming of crucial issues about which they demand transformative dialogue and consequent transformative action that we shall now turn.

Transformative Dialogue and Women's Power of Naming: Circle Responses to the Problem of Denial

One of the major obstacles toward attaining sustainable peace in Africa or anywhere is denial that the painful realities that constitute injustice and non-peace exist. Denial thrives on deliberate or cultivated ignorance, and it is often used by perpetrators to save face amid atrocities. It is in this context, for example, that African women have been accused of "crying wolf," by claiming that they are "victims" of cultural sexism, where there allegedly has been no wolf to speak about. Other times they have been accused of exposing too much of the seamy side of Afro-religions and cultures. African women, however, realize that such denial and trivialization of their concerns is not only frustrating and demeaning; it can be and often is lethal.

The deadly impact of silence and denial has been particularly palpable in the case of global responses to the crisis of AIDS where denial, myths, and misrepresentation of the facts about AIDS have robbed humanity of crucial time in which to seek urgently needed and sustainable solutions. For African women, this has been compounded by the failure or refusal to acknowledge the multiplier effect of cultural and other forms of sexism, which has made many like Njeri disproportionately more vulnerable to HIV/AIDS. By responding to the deadly effect of denial regarding the HIV crisis, and insisting that saving face must yield to saving lives, the Circle women have deliberately embraced what they call "engendered critical cultural hermeneutics" and engaged in research and publication that exposes the cultural sexism (and other forms of domination in Africa) that has robbed thousands of women of their lives through HIV and allied "viruses."[12]

Addressing HIV/AIDS and the multiplier effect of religio-cultural sexism became the focus when the Circle convened its fourth Pan-African conference, which had as its theme "Sex, Stigma, and HIV/AIDS: African Women Challenging Religion, Culture, and Social Practices." This conference was designed to provide a safe and collegial space where the women could learn in-depth about the challenges that HIV/AIDS posed to them within the African religio-cultural and social context and where they could present to each other research about religio-cultural factors pertaining to HIV/AIDS. Such learning and sharing enabled them collectively and in solidarity to break the silence and debunk deadly myths and denial that ferment stigma and social death for women like Njeri, who are infected or affected by HIV/AIDS.

A second area in which denial and misrepresentation have taken a toll on African women pertains to gender-based violence against them. In an effort to deal with issues of sexual violence, a violence that brings not only pain and death but also shame and embarrassment, and out of interest in saving women's lives instead of merely saving face as has been the inclination even for some victims of such violence, Circle women have collectively embraced the moral obligation to name gender violence for what it is.[13] In their analysis, African women have exposed sexual violence and the subtle ways in which it is denied or trivialized. They also have rejected the preferred simplistic and dismissive description of sexual violence in the family as domestic violence. Instead, they have insisted on naming the violent rape and sexual assault that women and girl children suffer in their families for what it is: criminal assault and battery. They lament the fact that for too long, the phrase "domestic violence" has served as a deadly euphemism, camouflaging the intimate terror and sexual assault that women have suffered in their families.

When women thus expose and name the issues of life and death in their lives, they are often accused of "washing society's dirty linen" in public. Undeterred by this criticism, however, Circle women stand in agreement with Mercy Oduyoye's rejoinder that instead of worrying that our dirty linen is going to be washed in public, we should worry about why and how the linen got dirty in the first place! For her, as for the women of the Circle, the answer never lies in denial that there is dirty linen. Rather, the answer lies in owning up to our dirty linen and therefore undertaking to wash it or, better still, to devise ways of keeping the linen clean in the first place. The Circle women insist therefore that religio-cultural dirty linen, which nurtures the violence of sexism, is an obstacle to justice and peace. Thus, they feel compelled to speak and to name these issues, hoping that such voicing fosters lifesaving social transformation. They fully concur with Oduyoye, who, in her book *Daughters of Anowa*, writes:

> Any strategy to achieve greater power for women must be *accompanied by voicing*.... For if we do not deliberately attempt to *break the silence* about our [painful] situation as African women, others will continue to maintain it.... We must not let our voices grow quiet, for simultaneously with our cries for change, a vigorous campaign is being waged against change by *both men and women*.[14]

Oduyoye speaks for the Circle women when she reminds us that such naming and voicing become socially transformative only if women are listened to and their naming gets taken seriously. Failure to listen to women, or worse, silencing them as they attempt to name and address the deadly structural violence against them is simply not acceptable. Through their work, Circle women address church and society demanding that as a matter of justice, society listens and responds to women by acknowledging and engaging them in their project of humanizing society in Africa and beyond. In Oduyoye's words:

> Dealing justly with African women must begin by taking seriously women's questions and concerns about their status. *Trivializing women's concerns does more harm than good....* [Instead], *women's voices should be listened to when they speak about the God-given dignity of every person* and the consequent need for each person for respect. *To expect women to uphold all that which is humanizing in African culture and yet deny them participation in the politics of the family and the nation is like asking them to make bricks without straw....* We must acknowledge that women are not merely symbols of morality but are also human. Perhaps then we can remove the obstacles in women's paths to self-actualization ... and continue on our path to democratization based on *the full participation of all women and men*.[15] (emphasis added)

Thus, Circle women insist that there is transformative power in naming and acknowledging social injustices. Demanding transformative dialogue as prelude to transformative action in church and society is a legitimate strategy for African women, as exemplified by the work of the Circle in the last three decades. One hopes that the world is listening to them as they assert their agency and work toward life-serving social change.

Living the Dialogue by Embracing Pluralism: The Dialogical Imperative

A third obstacle to peace in Africa and beyond is the mishandling of the fact of diversity, which characterizes humanity today. In Africa, for example, much violence and pain is occasioned by failure to come to terms with and appropriately respond to the reality of religio-cultural, ethnic, gender, and other forms of difference. More often than not, racial, ethnic, and gender chauvinism prevail. Such chauvinism is manifest directly in the exclusion, rejection, and often violence against those who are seen as "different." Ethnic chauvinism in its extreme manifestation has led to frequent violent ethnic clashes and even, in the case of Rwanda, genocide. Racial chauvinism has furthered the exploitation of black people and their resources for centuries under colonialism, with apartheid in South Africa being a painful example of racism gone wild. Sexism, a gender-based chauvinism, has also led to violence against women and loss of life for thousands of them.

Chauvinism also is manifest more subtly in a conditional tolerance and inclusion of the "different other" that carries the provision that the "other" should change in the direction dictated by those with power. This kind of chauvinism is exemplified in Africa in the coercive proselytization projects of dominant religions, with proselytizers sometimes using "charity" and other alleged benefits of affiliating with the dominant traditions as "bait" for such conversion. Other times chauvinism against each other has been nurtured among indigenous peoples by outsiders who insist that their religion or denomination is superior. Consequently, conflicts among Christians and Muslims and even among Christian denominations in Africa have been fanned by outsiders, all fighting for a greater share of Africa as a "spiritual territory."

It is against this background that Circle women, realizing that religio-cultural and other forms of diversity are a major "given" in Africa, and realizing that many tensions and conflicts are due to chauvinism and a gross mishandling of difference, made a covenant in their work to "promote a dialogical approach to religious-cultural and other tensions in Africa." Beyond promoting the idea of dialogue as a means to pluralism, however, Circle women have adopted pluralism and a radical inclusivism in their practice, thus living the dialogue rather than just speaking about it. For example, recognizing religio-cultural diversity as a given and honoring their covenant to embrace pluralism and dialogue, the Circle opened its membership to all women regardless of faith tradition, whether that faith is Islam, Christianity (in its multiple forms), Hinduism, or Judaism. Furthermore, despite the Christianized background of most of the founding members, the Circle includes women who practice the Indigenous African religions undeterred by many years of propaganda against these. While this openness to all traditions does not necessarily guarantee that Circle members are themselves beyond chauvinism, it does signify their commitment to practice rather than merely speak about dialogue and pluralism. Though not an

easy course to follow, especially since some of the Christianized women rather
uncritically accept the alleged superiority of imported Euro-Christianity, the
commitment by the Circle to embrace women from all faiths has been viewed
by members as a challenge and opportunity for women to understand both
each other and the various faiths with which they affiliate.[16] Moreover, having
members from the various faith traditions allows for a collective and insider's
critique of sexism and other injustices, as these are manifest in and through
the various faith traditions. It also allows women to detect and reject misrep-
resentations and caricatures of each other's faith as they explain to each other
the beliefs and practices of the respective faiths in an atmosphere of mutual
respect. Armed with a better understanding of each other and how their respective faith traditions shape their experiences as women, they are better placed to
launch a more *credible religio-cultural critique* and thus pave the way for social
transformation.

Women in the Circle also recognize that there are differences among them
and that there is no such a thing as a generic African woman. In particular,
they recognize the problem arising out of elitist attitudes among women themselves. For this reason, the Circle deliberately names and rejects classism and
elitism. Consequently, membership to the Circle is not pegged on membership
dues (at least so far). Nor is a university degree necessary for membership. The
necessary and sufficient condition of membership becomes one's willingness
and commitment to work in dialogue and sisterly solidarity with other women
across Africa's many borders, both physical and metaphorical. Membership
further calls for commitment to a radical inclusivism that is embodied in practice.[17] Through such a practice of pluralism and inclusivism, the Circle does not
just talk about dialogue but *walks the talk*. The Circle is therefore an example
of a living, dialogical community where women from diverse backgrounds feel
affirmed and are in communication with each other for mutual enrichment and
empowerment.

Circle Thinking Transforming Power: Overcoming Systems of Domination and Dualistic Hierarchies

Yet another obstacle toward attainment of peace in Africa is the mishandling of
power. Elisabeth Schüssler-Fiorenza has named the multiple systems of domination that thrive on the exercise of power as dominion, a power over others
rather than power for or with others. She identifies dominion as a root cause
of much of the suffering in the world today and refers to various systems of
domination as "Kyriarchies."[18] These include sexism, the domination of one
gender over another; classism, the domination of the poor by the rich; racism,
the domination of one race over another; and colonialism, the domination of
one nation over another.

Recognizing the mishandling of power as a major issue that shapes the des-
tinies of women in Africa, the Circle of women dedicated their 1996 Pan-African

conference to a discussion of the theme: "Transforming Power: Women in the Household of God." The women theologians worked with broad definitions of power, particularly political power and women's access to it or lack of it. The title of the conference was also indicative of African women's awareness of the need to transform power and its use, so that it could be more beneficial and transformative for women, many of whom have been victims of abuse of power.

Circle women are also aware that frequently oppressed peoples, fed up with their erstwhile oppressors, desire to overturn things and reverse their situations. Many coups in Africa are based on this principle. Unfortunately the liberators of today often become the dictators of tomorrow, since what has been sought has been the mere reversal of the oppressive situation. The idea of transforming systems of domination is hardly ever given enough thought, and, therefore, the notion of power as dominion or as power-over others remains unchallenged.

In critical response to this situation, women in Africa, like many of their sisters across the world, are beginning to rethink questions of power and have begun to practice alternative ways of wielding power and authority. The emphasis among many feminist analysts, at least *de jure* if not entirely in practice, is to nurture the idea of "power for" and "power with" other women.[19] It is in this context that we begin to understand the symbolic significance of the fact that the African women theologians deliberately chose to call themselves "Circle" of Concerned Women.

The term "Circle" signifies women's intentions to overcome a hierarchical thinking that supports and facilitates the use of power as domination. To actualize their goal of overcoming hierarchical thought and practices, Circle members decided that their leadership would consist of a steering committee. It was decided not to use terms that suggest hierarchy such as "president" and "chairman." Moreover, leaders would serve the Circle on a voluntary basis and for a specific time and then rotate off. The overall coordinator of Circle activities was and remains designated "Circle Coordinator."

By deliberately replacing hierarchical, dualistic, and pyramidal thinking with Circle thinking, dialogue, and practice, the women have indeed made significant steps in the direction of transforming power, at least within the context of their particular community of scholars.[20] Such Circle thinking and practice is recommended as a significant ingredient in the quest for peace and justice. By embracing such thinking and practice, African women come to embody and model what they long for, a transforming power that is in the service of *Ubuntu*, human dignity instead of exploitation and vandalization of humanity.

To Grow Peace with Justice: Dialogue, Conscientization, and the Transformation of Consciousness

One of the greatest insights by feminist analysts of culture and society in the face of sexism is that one is not born a woman or a man; rather one becomes a woman or a man. In other words, notions of manhood and womanhood are learned rather than innate. The insight that gender is socially constructed implies that there is no such a thing as a generic woman or a generic man. Gender essentialism is therefore a fallacy. This implies also that much of the behavior that is manifest as sexism and gender violence is learned behavior, acquired through the various strategies by which society transmits its notions of manhood and womanhood. If sexism is not innate but learned, it can be unlearned. The same processes of socialization that are used to ingrain sexist views of men and women in society, concerned women argue, can and should be reclaimed and rechanneled to help people unlearn negative and destructive thought patterns and practices.

Against this background, women in Africa as elsewhere have realized that dealing adequately with social injustices demands conscientization, the awakening of awareness of such problematic mind-sets in society as well as awakening the desire to do something about them. Such awakening and transformation of consciousness is necessary since no amount of calling for justice, preaching peace, or sending troops to keep peace will work until we begin to learn the practice of peace and to own up to factors like internalized sexism and racism that make it difficult to practice peace.

Women themselves have had to unlearn internalized sexism and socialized self-depreciation and have made great efforts in transforming their own consciousness in order to deal with the enemy within that is an obstacle to their path to freedom and justice. As Adekunbi, a Circle member from Nigeria, aptly puts it:

> The African woman's line of thinking and her perceptions of life have been subtly directed against her by the society to such an extent that in her mind's eye she tends to see everything about her existence as subordinate to that of her male counterpart.... The African woman has to discard the negative beliefs about life and about herself which she has been made to live with.[21]

Women also are calling for similar unlearning of hateful and violent mind-sets in others, mind-sets that breed hateful and violent behavior in church and society. They are also reclaiming their roles as formatters and nurturers of consciousness through their role as educators of their children. For them, rethinking socialization and its potential for transforming society toward justice and peace is a key piece of the puzzle. Adekunbi continues:

> Most times, women complain about the behaviors and attitudes of men and yet they raised their sons.... If we want men who are kind, loving, and in touch with their feminine side, then it is up to us to raise them that way.... What is it you want in a man? In a husband? Teach your son to be that way.... His wife will love you for it.... The female child should be encouraged and must not be made to feel inferior to her brothers because of her sex.[22]

In this context, it is noteworthy that the Circle doubles as a major forum for women's mutual education, consciousness raising, and positive resocialization, through mutual dialogue toward freedom. The Circle, through sustained and focused research, is also a forum for identifying culturally conditioned areas of human consciousness that nurture violence. Specifically Circle women have

applied critical cultural hermeneutics in examining the role of myth and ritual (particularly rites of passage) and the construction of gendered roles and
identities in Africa. They have named specific problems in what has been the
construction of men and women through socially and culturally sanctioned out-
lets. For this reason, too, and in an effort further to expand the dialogical table,
the most recent Pan-African conference (September 4, 2007) was constructed
as a forum for the mutual education of women, including women from outside
Africa, and most, importantly, of men.[23]

Toward Global Justice:
Dialogue as Prologue for Solidarity across Borders

One of the most significant of the Pan-African Circle conferences was held in
August 2001, at the Talitha Qumi center in Ghana. The theme of this meeting
was "Overcoming Violence: Women of Faith Speak." As a participant in this
meeting, I was impressed by the Circle women's ability to identify the complex
and interlocking issues that go under the name of violence. The women spoke
loudly and clearly against multiple manifestations of violence rendered against
women in contemporary African contexts. They denounced domestic violence,
witchcraft accusations, enslavement in the name of religion, and female genital
mutilations as manifestations of physical violence. They also discussed the root
causes of such violence, examining, for example, its historical roots and its
entanglement with poverty, racism, and sexism.

As the title of the conference indicates, the women theologians were concerned about identifying ways of overcoming violence rather than merely
denouncing it or complaining about it. Consequently they challenged each
other proactively to tackle root causes of such violence and to provide practical
responses to the issues. They spoke of the need for advocacy and creating nonviolence through education and resocialization, particularly of the youth. Most
importantly, members from the various regions of Africa developed a platform
for action to take home with them to address violence against women.

By developing such platforms for action, the women affirmed their understanding of feminist theology as applied scholarship. Such scholarship demands
but is not satisfied by mere naming or denouncing of injustices. These women
challenged each other from their specific local contexts to devise practical ways
of dealing with specific injustices. Their conversations and dialogue during
the Pan-African conference became a suitable prologue for women to generate
transformative action.

While encouraging analysis and action at the local level, the Circle also encourages analysis, action, and solidarity across Africa's many (often arbitrary)
borders, both physical and ideological. The periodic Pan-African conferences
provide a forum for such cross-border analysis and action on issues, as women
come from various African countries each with their own distinctive matters
to tackle and to share. The Pan-African forum for analysis is demanded by the

very nature of the problems, many of which transcend borders in their genesis and in their effects. The consequences of the various regional conflicts are
rarely contained within the borders where the conflict arises. And problems
across borders, in their genesis and effects, often are triggered by events and
decisions made far beyond the continent. The trans-border, even global nature
of the problems in Africa therefore demands awareness of underlying causative
factors and ethical issues in order to respond in more radical and appropriate
ways. The periodic Pan-African conferences are forums where women, through
mutual dialogue, become aware of the trans-border nature of the issues that
they face.

    While African women, like their sisters elsewhere, have developed a theology
that responds in practical ways to their specific local circumstances, they also
have come to realize that effective responses to these complex injustices demand
the collective efforts not only of women but of all people of goodwill. This realization led the Circle to participate as co-conveners in a 1999 joint conference
with other theological networks on the continent including EATWOT, AACC,
and OAIC.[24] This conference allowed members of various theological organizations to share their insights and visions with each other. The forum allowed
concerned African women theologians to partner with other collectivities of
similarly concerned theologians to construct a common platform for action to
address the interlocking and shocking crises facing the continent. Responding
to the imperative of dialogue and solidarity demanded by these circumstances,
the participants drafted a joint communiqué naming common areas of concern,
including the poverty crisis, challenges of globalization, violent conflicts, and
the crisis of HIV/AIDS.

    Finally, African women theologians also realize that we are living in an
increasingly intimate global village where the ripple effects of an event in seemingly remote corners of the world are experienced on the other side of the globe
in quite unexpected ways. Such a globalized context demands that women be
aware of the global perspectives and dynamics, particularly the political, economic, and ethical ramifications of globalization. In recognition of the intimate
world in which we live today, African women theologians along with other
concerned African theologians have vowed to work together to address the
challenges of globalization. What is needed, they have agreed, is collective *action* and mutual support from all people of goodwill, even beyond the continent
itself. The dialogical imperative is therefore central in the quest for just and sustainable peace and is a prologue to the much needed solidarity within and across
borders. Injustice anywhere is a threat to justice elsewhere, African women collectively adopt the dialogical imperative as a vital strategy that energizes and
enriches their prophetic call for global justice.

Chapter 10

Asian Women and Dialogue

Gemma T. Cruz

A SIA COULD BE REGARDED as a continent of superlatives. First and fore-most, it is the world's largest continent. It encompasses one-third of the land area of the world, spanning Turkey in the west to Japan and Indonesia in the east. Asia is also the world's most populated continent. It is home to almost 60 percent of humanity, many of whom live in about twenty Asian mega-cities that have populations of some 5 to 20 million.[1] Moreover, Asia has at least seven major linguistic zones, which is more than any other continent can claim.

Asia, however, is also a continent of contradiction. It is home to the world's second largest economy, that is, Japan, and to some of the world's dynamic economies, like Singapore, Malaysia, South Korea, China, and India, but it is also home to more than half of the world's poor. It is the birthplace of Christianity, yet, to this day, Christians remain a minority (around 3 percent), despite centuries of Christian missionary activities. The vast majority of Asians are Hindus, Buddhists, Taoists or Confucianists, and Muslims. These facts coupled with Asia's rich cultural plurality are what the Federation of Asian Bishops' Conferences has taken seriously in its adoption of dialogue as the new way of being church in Asia.

The Federation of Asian Bishops' Conferences construes dialogue in a threefold fashion, as pertaining to liberation, inculturation, and interreligious understanding. This construal of dialogue is at the very heart of Asian women's employment of dialogue as a strategy for reform. Hence an exposition on dialogue as a transformative strategy will not be complete without some elaboration of the Federation of Asian Bishops' Conferences' vision and praxis of dialogue.

Dialogue in Three Directions:
Inculturation, Interreligious Understanding, and Liberation

What is the rationale and exhortation for this triple dialogue? According to the Federation of Asian Bishops' Conferences, the "essential mode" in which evangelization should be carried out in Asia today ought to be one of dialogue, more precisely through a resolute, creative, and yet truly discerning and responsible inculturation; through interreligious dialogue undertaken in all seriousness; and through solidarity and sharing with the poor and the advocacy of human rights.

With regard to dialogue as inculturation, the Asian bishops are convinced that the dialogical encounter between the local churches and Asia's living traditions and cultures is critical in building a church *of* Asia and not so much a church *in* Asia. The bishops reckon that an inculturated church "seeks to share in whatever truly belongs to the people: its meanings and its values, its aspirations, its thoughts, and its language, its songs and its artistry."[2] They maintain that *true* inculturation, far from being a means for the propagation of the faith, "belongs to the very core of evangelization, for it is the continuation in time and space of the dialogue of salvation initiated by God and brought to a culmination when he uttered his Word in a very concrete historical situation."[3]

This stance is firmly rooted in the Federation of Asian Bishops' Conferences recognition of the gifts and richness that Asia's diverse cultures have to offer. And this is the same attitude that the Asian bishops have assumed in relation to Asia's various religions. Noted Indian Jesuit theologian Sebastian Painadath, in his exposition of the Federation of Asian Bishops' Conferences' theology of dialogue, underscores the bishops' fundamental commitment to interreligious dialogue, drawing attention to the promise that they made in their first meeting in Manila in 1970: "We pledge to an open, sincere and continuing dialogue with our brothers and sisters of other great religions of Asia that we may learn from one another how to enrich ourselves spiritually and how to work more effectively together on our common task of human development."[4] The pledge suggests that the work of human development depends upon a sustained commitment to dialogue.

Dialogue as liberation, in the meantime, is of the conviction that Christ is calling the churches of Asia to address the material deprivation of poor people.[5] The Federation of Asian Bishops' Conferences believes that because millions in Asia are poor, "the Church in Asia must be the Church of the poor."[6] The practice of justice is a commitment that was made very explicit during the bishops' sixth plenary assembly, which centered on the theme "Christian Discipleship in Asia Today: Service to Life." The bishops asserted:

> Like Jesus, we have to "pitch our tents" in the midst of all humanity building a better world, but especially among the suffering and the poor, the marginalized and the downtrodden of Asia. In profound "solidarity with suffering humanity" and led by the Spirit of life, we need to immerse ourselves in Asia's cultures of poverty and deprivation, from whose depths the aspirations for love and life are the most poignant and compelling. Serving life demands communion with every woman and man seeking and struggling for life, in the way of Jesus' solidarity with humanity.[7]

In the mind of the bishops, this dialogue with the poor toward liberation addresses one crucial goal of the Asian church, that is, "total human development" or "integral human development." Noted Asian American theologian Peter Phan, who has written a trilogy of books that address the Asian bishops' concept of triple dialogue, bolsters this point with the following observation: "One point repeatedly stressed by the Federation of Asian Bishops' Conferences' is that human development and progress in all its aspects — political, social, economic, technological, and cultural — is an intrinsic and constitutive dimension of the church's evangelizing mission."[8] This integral human development, also expressed by the Federation of Asian Bishops' Conferences in terms of "holistic life," should go hand in hand with the other two components of the Asian concept of dialogue: namely, inculturation and interreligious understanding.

Indeed, the three realms of dialogue are closely linked, with dialogue as liberation often making up the hub. Drawing from the bishops' thoughts, Sebastian Painadath asserts:

> Hence, when believers of various religions work together to bring about integral human liberation and environmental harmony, they discover the creative and redemptive forces in each religion and articulate the liberative and unifying potential of each religion.... Concern for the poor, therefore, is the meeting point of religions; compassion is the hallmark of a religious person.[9]

Commentators like Painadath and Phan commend this inseparable linkage between liberation, inculturation, and interreligious dialogue, identifying it as part of the originality and depth of the Federation of Asian Bishops' Conferences. Phan, in particular, highlights the importance of making interreligious dialogue and inculturation necessary phases of the church's work for liberation, avoiding possible distortions of a one-sided emphasis on the material and political aspects of salvation. Phan states that by combining these three aspects of the church's ministry, the Federation of Asian Bishops' Conferences has improved upon papal teachings on human development and most Western theologies of inculturation and interreligious dialogue.[10]

Dialogue and Asian Women

Next to children, women are the poorest of the poor in Asian society and are an oppressed faction. Even the Federation of Asian Bishops' Conferences admits that, too often, Asian society views women as inferior. The 2006 report on the "State of the World's Mothers" sees most Asian countries faring dismally. In a survey of 125 countries, Japan — a highly developed country — ranked only 12th in its treatment of women. China and Thailand ranked 39th, Malaysia 52nd, Philippines 63rd, Indonesia and Sri Lanka 69th, India 93rd, Laos 94th, Bangladesh 106th, Cambodia, Nepal, and Pakistan 107th.[11]

The bishops themselves acknowledged in 1982 how they and their communities have been indifferent and hesitant too often, taking little action against the "oppression and degradation of women."[12] The movement toward inclusive language in the Federation of Asian Bishops' Conferences' documents has been slow and gradual. And it was only in the last plenary assembly in 2005 in Korea that women who were not directly involved with the Federation of Asian Bishops' Conferences were included as observers. As it turned out, the assembly included a contentious discussion on feminism.

This deeply entrenched patriarchy in the Asian continent has impinged on women's self-esteem and development for centuries. As former and first woman dean of a theological school in the Philippines, Amelia Vasquez writes: "In Asia, women in general still need to be drawn out, to be educated to come to self-awareness. They need to overcome their timidity and fears and inertia; they must come out of the corners which have given them security through habit and familiarity. They must take risks, even if it means challenging unjust structures and practices."[13] This is not to say, however, that there have been no efforts by women in the past to break the fortress of Asian patriarchy.

Slowly Asian women are rising out of their invisibility. They are beginning to break their silence, to chart their own destiny and work toward their own liberation. Today, for example, the women's movement is vibrant in the Catholic-dominated Philippines. Here women have worked to secure paternity leaves and to change the legal definition of rape from being a crime against chastity to a crime against persons. Women-led initiatives are having transformative impacts in other Asian countries as well, even in countries that have been considered to be bastions of male privilege, like India and China. In India, dowry deaths and rape continue to ignite the praxis of the women's movement. In Malaysia the Women's Voice, a group of Catholic women based in Kuala Lumpur working for women's empowerment, has contributed significantly toward the greater participation of women in the Malaysian Catholic Church.[14]

I have met countless women's groups across Asia that stand at the forefront of women's struggles for liberation. These include women from parishes in Indonesia who arrange sessions on violence against women, women workers in Hong Kong who organize themselves in fighting against the injustices rendered against them as migrants and domestic workers, and groups of women religious in southeastern Thailand who network to provide help for young women victimized by the sexual exploitation found in Thailand's thriving tourism industry.

One very notable pan-Asian effort by Asian women themselves toward greater participation in the Asian church is the formation of the EWA, or Ecclesia of Women in Asia. This is an association of Asian Catholic women entering into dialogue doing theology on the academic, pastoral, or grassroots level.[15] The EWA started in 2002, after the glaring absence of Asian Catholic women theologians was noted by the four (out of forty) Asian women participants in an Asian theologians' conference held in India on the synodal document *Ecclesia in Asia*. EWA's first gathering, in Thailand, brought together about fifty-five women theologians from seventeen Asian countries and has, in its succeeding meetings, drawn members from usually underrepresented places like Myanmar and Mongolia.

The formation of the Ecclesia of Women in Asia as a movement has been critical, as Asian women have been and continue to be marginalized in the theological enterprise.[16] Theological education is still mainly done in seminaries, where priests and male religious teachers are a priority; jobs are harder to come by for women theologians. Women theology teachers too frequently become the recipients of unsavory, and even sexist, comments, particularly when they assume roles in the seminary contexts. In a conference in Thailand, designed to evaluate the curricula and teaching of theology in Asia, a lay male professor noted some of the remarks that he has heard from Filipino seminarians regarding women teachers that he suspected would not have been made about their male teachers: "She's too old to be our teacher," "She's decently dressed today," "Is she married or not?" "She talks like a singing bird," "We call her 'Miss' [not 'Doctor']," and "She's a woman; women are compassionate and generous, so she will not give us failing marks."[17] Such comments sadly are heard in Catholic seminaries and theological schools all across Asia.

Asian women theologians have to hurdle obstacles not just with the hierarchy but with male counterparts in the theological field.[18] Mary John Mananzan, in a session titled "Gender Dialogue in EATWOT [Ecumenical Association of Third World Theologians]: An Asian Perspective," speaks about efforts by Filipino women theologians to engage their male counterparts in a dialogue leading toward greater understanding of women's experience and more incorporation of women's perspectives in male theologians' theological reflections. While the endeavor has not been a smashing success, as pointed out by Mananzan, women's efforts to engage in dialogue deserve much praise.[19] The pioneering effort of Virginia Fabella, for example, a Filipina Maryknoll sister who was actually the sole woman staff member of EATWOT even before its inception in 1976, deserves specific mention.[20]

Today, many Asian women are blazing a trail in the area of interreligious dialogue. In a conference held in Thailand that was organized by the Federation of Asian Bishops' Conferences–Office of Ecumenical and Interreligious Affairs, the initiatives of women were highlighted. The efforts of FIRE (Fostering Interreligious Encounters) in Malaysia,[21] for example, received mention, as did the curricular innovations in peace education by the Sisters of Notre Dame in their basic schools in Mindanao, the southern Philippine island that has been ravaged by a conflict rooted in historically strained relations between Muslims and Christians.

Diane D'Souza sheds light on the critical work by Asian women in the area of interreligious dialogue found in the project known as "Women's Interfaith Journey."[22] D'Souza claims that one strength that women bring to the interreligious dialogue table is their tendency to operate from a worldview where personal relationships are central. Quoting a participant in the "Women's Interfaith Journey" project, D'Souza maintains that women, in meeting and conversing, form relationships on a more personal level than is found in so-called "objective" dialogue. D'Souza comments: "Relationships bring with them a sense of *connectedness* to one another within the relationship.... Women *take time* to be with other women and to know one another as persons in a holistic way, not merely as bearers of a particular faith or ideology."[23] D'Souza asserts that a different level of interaction is apparent between women when women engage in interreligious dialogue. The focus is on more than learning about each other's belief systems.

Interreligious dialogue is especially important for Asian Christian women, not only because of the religious plurality and minority status that they deal with on a daily basis, but because in Asia Christianity in the view of many non-Christians is sadly associated with colonialists and neo-colonialists. Mary John Mananzan and Sun Ai Lee Park ask: "As Christian women, can we condone all the structural and systemic evils Christian civilization has brought, and concentrate only on securing privileged posts in a rotten structure?"[24] Mananzan and Park offer their response: "While it is important to fight for power positions when one is discriminated against for being a woman, it is as important to be committed to bringing about radically new values that are people-oriented, concerned for life and for a truly humane community."[25]

Strong valuing of and experience with interreligious dialogue is considered to be one of the contributions of the Asian church and, particularly, a contribution of Asian women to the global church. Asian Christians have more experience living with people of other religions than the rest of the world.[26] And Asian women have known firsthand the challenges inherent within this pluralism. In this day and age when the world is grappling with cultural and religious diversity, the Asian experience provides a fertile ground for reflecting upon what unity means in Christian community and what the unity of humankind means. The Asian notion of harmony, which is a driving force (among Asians) for dialogue, serves as an important resource for a theology that imagines the whole.[27]

In the area of inculturation, women of Asia are rediscovering their history and are finding the women leaders, heroines, and saints of their specific traditions who can serve as role models for the journey and inspirations amid struggle.[28] Closer scrutiny of Asian women's initiatives toward dialogue reveals attention to the three central realms of liberation, inculturation, and interreligious dialogue. Asian women know the significance of these realms. They know these to be crucial in transforming the Asian church into a community of equals. What is at stake, after all, is not only more equality for women in the church. What is at stake is the future of the church itself.[29]

Asian women have come a long way in their journey from invisibility to engagement in the strategic use of dialogue. An attitude of critical listening, which has roots in the well-known Asian tradition of contemplation, plays a major role in Asian women's strategy. Critical listening is part and parcel of contemplation. It helps one to be more attuned to hidden dynamics and assumptions, and also to the wisdom embedded in things. Critical listening is the only kind of listening that promises to make a real difference. If we hope for genuine dialogue with the Asian poor, then we must first listen. It is in this spirit that I claim: In the beginning is listening.

Chapter 11

Feeling through the Limits of Conversation

MICHELE SARACINO

W HAT DID JESUS TALK ABOUT when he ate with "sinners"?[1] What type of conversation did he hope for at a banquet with "the poor, the crippled, the lame, and the blind"?[2] Was having the right voice tone, gesture, and affect important to him as he offered hospitality to those who were different or *other?* While few would expect to find this sort of information in the Bible, these are the kinds of questions that Christians engaging in table fellowship are faced with today. Whereas Scripture mainly focuses on the act of inviting others to the table, engendering table fellowship demands even more, namely, a way of speaking with one another that respects every guest's particular identity. In today's world of hybrid identity and globalization, persons encounter difference at every turn. As the world has flattened, Christians struggle not just to welcome others to the table, but to create an atmosphere that nourishes everyone's hunger for a place in the conversation.[3]

Within the Christian traditions, conversation takes various forms, including interreligious, ecumenical, intertextual, and interpersonal dialogue. In what follows, I begin to examine the corporeal complexity of dialogue in interpersonal and interreligious relationships. Beyond the commonsense meaning of dialogue as talking with one another, I offer an interpretation of dialogue as a type of trespass, a process where we are called to cross affectively charged boundaries in order to maintain and even build relationships with those who are different from us in terms of gender, class, race, ethnicity, religion, age, sexual orientation, ability, and so on.

Conceptualizing Dialogue as Trespass

In our dialogical encounters with others, we leave our closed, safe worlds behind and trespass into unfamiliar worlds, and in doing so we reveal that we have desires that cannot be fulfilled in isolation. Unsure of how our words and gestures will be received, we put ourselves at great risk and expose our vulnerability. As our dialogues pass into the unknown, our words acquire the potential to become sacred. In our willingness to relinquish the security and privilege of our worlds and worldviews in order to engage those of others, we imitate

God's generosity to humanity through creation, the incarnation, and the continuing work of the Spirit. Incarnating dialogue as trespass reveals our "sacred vulnerability." Insofar as we are aware of this sacred vulnerability in the act of conversing, human relationships can become the site of God's presence.[4]

Not all trespass ends well, and at times dialogue can emerge as a sign of injustice rather than of sacred vulnerability. The raw differences that are uncovered in dialogue may result in uncomfortable feelings, some of which may cause the parties involved to act aggressively toward one another. Unchecked, a negative situation quickly develops, turning dialogue into violence. In interpersonal relations and dialogue there are no signs stating, NO TRESPASSING or BEWARE OF DOG, as there are with respect to personal property. One must take great care not to disrespect the other's needs and desires. Without clear limits, we often are forced to rely on emotive cues and bodily gestures to make sense of ambiguous interpersonal territory.

Filling in the discursive gaps in interpersonal communication is not easily done, since most of us are not practiced at dealing with corporeality in dialogue. Over twenty years ago, linguistic scholar Deborah Tannen gained notoriety by explaining how even with the best intentions, our communication is often ineffective.[5] Although people may use the same terms, conflict arises in dialogue through discontinuities in style, phrasing, voice tone, pitch, affect, and gesture, creating tense conversations with our partners, family, friends, and colleagues, in which we are noticed not for what we say, but how we say it.

Well known for her work in French feminism and psychoanalysis, Luce Irigaray also problematizes communication, asserting that all language, even scientific discourse, is "never neutral."[6] Irigaray extends her analysis to gender oppression and argues that obstacles to dialogue are rooted in the different grammars men and women use to express their identities. Rejecting what she deems phallocentric discourse, Irigaray calls for a language for women built on excess, affectively charged, and even carnal.[7] Words cannot always capture the totality of our intentions; rather, Tannen and Irigaray reveal that the emotions, gestures, and even power dynamics that materialize in our conversations often evade verbal communication. When words fall short, all that remains are what post-Shoah thinker Emmanuel Levinas calls "affective disturbances," or sensual traces of our fragile relationships with one another that cannot be captured by linguistic discourse.[8]

When Dialogue Turns Violent

For some, attempting to put the affective disturbances that accompany human relationships into words does more harm than good, turning the trespass of dialogue into something unjust and violent. Jean-François Lyotard argues along these lines, maintaining that dialogue has the potential to turn into an oppressive monologue in which one party's needs are squelched violently by another's, or even those of a third party who is attempting to negotiate between the two.[9] The violence here is not physical in nature, but a psychic and coercive control over discourse. With contentious debates regarding revisionist history and the Shoah in mind, Lyotard laments our investment in linguistic "sign-systems," including the ways in which we divinize them and imagine them as privileged places of knowledge and reality.[10] Taking account of Lyotard's insights, it is arguable that any mentality that assumes the possibility of dialogue without the negative effects of trespass reinforces unjust power differentials and rationalizes violence.

To illustrate the potential of discourse to become violent, it may help to turn from theory to film. In Sofia Coppola's *Lost in Translation,* we are invited into the brief, intense, and unconsummated affair between a young married women named Charlotte, who feels ignored by her husband, and a lonely, Hollywood star named Bob Harris on a commercial shoot in Japan.[11] At the end of the shoot, Bob says goodbye to Charlotte, whispering something in her ear. The audience's desire to hear Bob's message is thwarted as the characters recede into the larger landscape of Tokyo and away from the viewers' gaze. It is as if whatever Bob says could never capture the longing between them, and any attempt to signify it would be futile. Neither sex nor logos could represent what they shared — all would have been lost in translation.

Maybe it is the case that her father, Francis Ford Coppola, trained her in the art of attempting to communicate the incommunicable. Near the end of his *Godfather, Part III,* the audience watches as the head of the mafia family, Michael Corleone, witnesses his daughter being shot dead in front of the opera house in Palermo, Sicily, where the Don's son just performed.[12] Both the audience and the characters in the scene look to Michael to piece this traumatic event together, for a clue about what to think, act, and feel. Coppola resists the audience's desire for a resolution by focusing the camera on the father's screaming face, while muting his voice. The silent scream epitomizes the way in which communication sometimes is doomed to failure. There is no discourse that could account for Michael's predicament. Both films challenge the audience to grapple with the limits of discourse. What could Bob ever say to Charlotte that would satisfy the viewers? How loud and long would Michael Corleone have to scream to express his overwhelming grief? It seems that any words would fall short and render the intended communication violent and damaging rather than sacred.

Speaking about language as somehow being violent often puzzles people, even making them uncomfortable. How could a pivotal process in human development, such as language, be connected to, even embedded in violence? When babies make their first sounds and when toddlers start speaking sentences, parents are overjoyed that their children have begun to master language, specifically that they can communicate with one another. Still, for some, there is a sadness that accompanies the development of language: that in the process of rigidly categorizing the world through words and narrative, we risk destroying the ambiguity of feeling, which is critical to making meaning in our interpersonal relationships.

To say that dialogue can lead to violence, conversely, neither means that dialogue inevitably leads to aggression, nor that understanding one another is impossible. We have all sorts of interactions with people in our everyday experiences — in shopping centers, hospitals, schools, and at home — where effective communication occurs.[13] The theoretical lenses of Tannen, Irigaray, and Lyotard, and the artistic lenses of the Coppolas serve to demonstrate that in our excitement to make connections with others, we frequently forget or overlook the possibility that, in initiating dialogue, a complex drama involving affect and power unfolds. Framing dialogue as trespass accentuates the unfinished quality of our dramatic, even operatic communication with others, underscoring that there is something, namely, affect, that resists being captured in language, and more importantly, complicates our being at the table with those who are different from us. In order for dialogue to emerge as sacramental rather than profane, this affectively charged drama needs to be embraced.

Interreligious Dialogue and the Canonization of Edith Stein

Already I have alluded to the complexity of dialogue on the interpersonal level, and now I want to stretch that line of reasoning to the communal level, particularly to the relationship between Catholic and Jewish communities. Pope John Paul II's beatification (1987) and then canonization (1998) of Sister Teresa (Teresia) Benedicta of the Cross, born as Edith Stein, brings to the table the affective dissonance and ambiguity of dialogue as trespass. Stein was raised in a culturally assimilated German, Jewish family, and then as an adult studied philosophy under Edmund Husserl. After converting to Roman Catholicism, she became a Carmelite nun. Stein fled from Germany to Holland after Christians of Jewish descent were threatened; however, she was unable to avoid the wrath of the Nazi regime, and in August of 1942 she was murdered in Auschwitz.[14]

For some, Stein's canonization honors not only Stein, but also her work in creating a bridge between Catholicism and Judaism. From this perspective, in exalting her, the church commemorates the enmeshed histories and overlapping borders of these two sacred religions. Moreover, Stein's canonization demonstrates the church's refusal to be isolated from other religions and validates reaching out to one another in hope of friendship. One might consider that the canonization of Stein represents the sacramental type of trespass in which one leaves his or her closed, safe world to cross to that of another. This trespass refuses to merely tolerate Stein or her background, but rather makes a public commitment to set a privileged place for her at the table and paves the way for continued friendship and conversation between Catholics and Jews.

For others, Stein's canonization represents the unjust kind of trespass, the type that masquerades as an offer of dialogue with another, but instead erases the particular identity of that other. In canonizing Stein, it is arguable that the church narcissistically refused to respect its limits by appropriating the Shoah for it own use, without considering how Jewish communities continue to struggle with the trauma of Auschwitz.[15] As John Paul II declared, "Edith

Stein died at the Auschwitz extermination camp, the daughter of a martyred people.... This was the cause of the martyrdom suffered by Sister Teresa Benedicta a Cruce," many people were left wondering how exactly she serves as a martyr, as well as how declaring her a martyr overshadows the 6 million Jews who died at the hands of the Nazi murderers for no imaginable, communicable purpose.[16] Naming her a martyr, and thus providing a rationale for her death, avoids dealing with the affective, untranslatable disturbances that arise in conversations about the Shoah. By including Catholics in the portrait of Auschwitz, it has been suggested that the church is attempting to control the dialogue about the Shoah by Christianizing it.

Even though a more sustained and rigorous analysis of Stein's life, conversion, and canonization is necessary to make any definitive conclusions about what type of trespass has occurred, there are some relevant and important lessons we can learn.[17] First, the outcome of dialogue is not always or immediately obvious. Sometimes dialogue is an invitation for relationship, attempting to connect with one another through word and gesture. Dialogue in this sense can be framed as sacramental, for in taking leave of our safe worlds and reaching out toward another, we celebrate the sacred working within our diverse relationships. Even so, at other times, dialogue can squelch any hope for relationship, especially when the emotional needs of the other in the conversation are not met. More often than not, as in the case of Stein, both types of trespass seem to be present. Such ambiguity and overlap need to be expected when we encounter persons or worlds radically different from our own.

A second lesson is that dialogue is not always as simple as two parties speaking with one another and both being understood. Emotions are involved, making dialogue a highly corporeal process. The emotional turmoil caused by Stein's canonization signals that in the increased relations between Catholics and Jews, there are issues and reactions that escape concrete linguistic norms. In many ways, Stein presents Catholic and Jewish communities with what Lyotard calls a *differend*, a conflict that cannot be resolved with discourse.[18] What is the Christian response then? Maybe the affective overflow surrounding the canonization of Stein has shown Catholics and Jews that they are "beyond dialogue."[19]

In suggesting that we are beyond dialogue, I am emphasizing the need to be affectively vigilant about what divides us, whether that is gender, race, religion, story, culture, trauma, and so on. We need to feel our way beyond the limits of our discourse. We need to be mindful to not only invite others to the banquet, but to make sure they are comfortable there, and also to be honest and forthcoming when they are not. Edith Stein's legacy illustrates how relating to one another through dialogue involves an ambiguity of trespass. This ambiguity is not cause to opt out of conversations, but a call to interact with them with integrity and awareness. If we are serious about embracing others, we need to be attentive to how affect creates ambiguity in our embraces. By setting a place at the table for another, we also are challenged to foster their safety.

The Role of Trauma Theory in Dialogue

Throughout this essay, I have argued that for life-giving dialogue to occur, Christians must acknowledge the trespass associated with affective being. We need to stretch ourselves beyond merely tolerating affect to welcoming it, not only the positive feelings of joy and love, but also the more unpleasant emotions of sadness and hate that surface in relationships. Some may want to assert that women have the advantage here, in that they have been programmed either biologically or socially to be more comfortable with their feelings. While this may be the case with some women, such generalizations are unhelpful, since grappling with dialogue as trespass is not just a concern for one's own emotional well-being, but more importantly for that of another. The quest for detecting and embracing affect reflects a more universal struggle of how to be human with others.

Likewise, some may want to argue that Christians may have an easier time dealing with the mysterious quality of affect, as they celebrate the power and movement of the Spirit in their everyday life. Additionally, others may claim that Catholics share a particular affinity for affect, as their aesthetics and spirituality are overdetermined with body and feeling, allowing for a distinctive imagination or sensibility to develop.[20] Celebrating porous boundaries between creator and creation certainly is comparable to embracing the ambiguous feelings that seep out of neat discursive phrasing. Still, it would be shortsighted to end there with the assumption that Christians have one up on everyone else in dealing with the affective messiness that dialogue brings, since many Christian traditions continue to deal with old and new versions of dualism. Pushing dialogue to reflect the whole human being — mind and body together — involves more than being a certain gender or religion; it takes work.

In contemporary treatment of trauma survivors, techniques are used to embrace the role that body and affect play in organizing one's life and relationships.[21] In what follows, I raise the question of whether tactics used in treating trauma might help us think, or better yet, *feel* through the affective overflow of dialogue in everyday life. While I in no way presume that our interpersonal interactions with one another mirror the predicament of a person presenting with a complex history of trauma, I am questioning whether techniques employed by clinicians in treating trauma survivors can help ordinary people become more vigilant about noticing how emotions impact their communication and, of course, their relationships.

Trauma in a strict sense refers to the psychological cost a person pays after living through an event or series of events, such as chronic physical or sexual abuse, neglect, serious accidents, war, terrorism, natural disasters, or chronic illness, which cannot be easily put into words.[22] Bessel A. van der Kolk, a leading clinician and researcher in the area of posttraumatic stress, claims that for the average person, "ordinary events generally are not relived as images, smells, physical sensations, or sounds associated with that event. Ordinarily, the remembered aspects of experience coalesce into a story that captures the essence of what has happened. As people remember and tell others about an event, the *narrative* gradually changes with time and telling."[23] However, when patients present with posttraumatic stress disorder (PTSD), they are unable to integrate or contextualize the traumatic event into a coherent self-narrative; instead, the event remains fixed in the original moment. Victims of trauma sense the exact sounds, tastes, and feelings of the original event, probably because they are "too hyper- or hypo-aroused to be able to 'process' and communicate what they are experiencing. . . . The person may feel, see, or hear the sensory elements of the traumatic experience, but he or she may be psychologically prevented from being able to translate this experience into communicable language."[24] When reminded of the event, they return to it sensually and emotively and usually do not even know they are doing so. As one might imagine, this has an impact on a person's development and social relations, since the senses and feelings associated with the event intrude on other everyday experiences and activities.

Traditional treatment of trauma has focused on helping patients attach meaning to the event in question, so they can gain perspective and control over it. Such treatment privileges the discursive in that it is the patients' verbal connections that give the event meaning and context. Although narrative therapies may be useful in treating persons experiencing acute trauma, such as someone who has been raped or has witnessed a violent event, people with complex histories of trauma, such as children who have been abused over long periods of time, may not be helped primarily with talking therapies. Instead, body-based, holistic therapies, which are attentive to irregularities in affect might work better "to help survivors tolerate the sensory reminders of the trauma."[25] In being attentive to the response of the body to the event, as well as to the emotional impact of the trauma, clinicians are able to help the patient regulate his or her emotions, while also enhancing the quality of his or her interpersonal relations, which undoubtedly suffer in cases of trauma. It might prove useful to evaluate whether the goals set for trauma patients are beneficial to Christians who want to embrace the affective overflow of dialogue, the trespass that cannot be put into words.

Everyday Practices for Feeling Dialogue[26]

One of the therapeutic goals for people suffering from trauma is to create a safe environment in which intense emotions can unfold and be maintained, to provide an outlet for the unregulated affect, the sadness, rage, grief, shame, etc. that often accompanies trauma reactions. Analogously, there are emotions that interrupt our dialoguing with others in our ordinary life, feelings that often are connected to old hurts. As already suggested, communication between family members breaks down from time to time because of incommunicable emotions. Also as we have seen, dialogue between religions can unravel because of affective disturbances. In transitioning from a clinical situation to everyday life, our first goal in communication is to locate places that can serve as safe environments to express our unruly emotions to one another. These sanctuaries need to allow all frustrations to be heard, yet not necessarily reconciled. In families, there could be time set for venting frustrations, with the assurance that anything expressed would *not* be used against anyone either then or at a later time. Within the larger community, parishes, synagogues, or other institutions, such as schools, hospitals, and social service organizations, could hold workshops in which one would feel free to discuss the institutional issues that create affective disturbances. In such safe places, conflicting feelings related to religious intolerance, racism, sexism, or even homophobia might be addressed.

After revealing one's feelings in a safe environment, the second goal is to be able to label these feelings in order to gain perspective on them. In a family meeting, the emotions that fester beneath the issues would need to be articulated, and so for example, a son might say, "I am feeling angry because of x." Within the community, one group might label what they are feeling as frustration as a result of not being heard in regard to a specific issue. The process of labeling integrates affective and cognitive processes, creating the potential for rich, corporeal dialogue.

Once feelings are labeled, the next goal is to be able to recognize how affect is building in one's body before it becomes debilitating. This requires paying attention to changes in the body's responses to situations, such as a tightening in one's throat or profuse perspiration. In addition to promoting a dialogue that is more body-conscious, becoming aware of the connection between body and emotion empowers persons to have more control of their situation, preventing him/her from easily falling into the same emotional patterns.[27] When persons or groups publicly process or explain the physiological changes occurring within their bodies to another who has never recognized these, the limits of discursive dialogue become evident to everyone involved. Avoiding the pain of the other at your table is easier when you have only heard about it; when its physical manifestations become readily apparent, avoiding it seems irresponsible, unjust, and inhospitable.

The last goal is to grapple with the fear of intimacy with others in relationships, because, as clinicians point out, this fear can cause an inability to deal with the emotions of others. Acknowledgment of our fear of intimacy demands that we ask the difficult questions: Why we are petrified of appearing vulnerable to others in dialogue? Why does it seem necessary to be right or have the last word? Such inquiries require some honest talk in both interpersonal and communal contexts. In family systems, this might mean that parents would have to admit that they need their children as much as their children need them and own up to how that need scares them to the point of feeling like they are out of control. Regarding the emotional tumult over the canonization of Edith Stein, dealing with a fear of intimacy might mean that both parties would have to admit how their sacred stories are enmeshed with one another. It might also require reflection on whether it is helpful or hurtful to a relationship to hold on to the idea that one person or group has suffered more than another. Building intimacy in the dialogue over Stein would involve both parties, Catholics and Jews, relinquishing any attachment to being a victim, as that stigma often prevents people from embracing the connections between one another.

Creating a safe place for emotional encounter, labeling feelings, paying attention to physiological changes, and learning intimacy are strategies for enhancing the corporeal dimension of dialogue and creating a place for otherness at the table. I am in no way implying that any of these are performed easily, or are feasible in every context; moreover, one can never be certain what these practices will reveal. One thing is for sure. Until Christians embrace the role of affect in dialogue, they run the risk of alienating someone at the table.

Part Four

POLITICS OF
THE HEARTH

Chapter 12

For the Sins of the Parents

Roman Catholic Ethics and the Politics of Family

CRISTINA TRAINA

"FAMILY VALUES" HAVE OCCUPIED center stage in domestic politics for over twenty years. But most items that make their way to the top of the family values grocery list fail to address the basic economic flourishing of the children in whose name they are enacted. Worse, broad initiatives aimed at their parents under other labels often disregard and even jeopardize children's basic welfare.[1]

Only widely shared, perhaps unspoken fears and aims can allow us to eclipse so fundamental a concern. Roman Catholics rely on the Roman Catholic social justice tradition (rearticulated in the 2005 *Compendium of the Social Doctrine of the Church*)[2] for the prophetic leverage to refocus the political conversation on children. I will argue that in certain cases, like immigration and welfare, the tradition largely succeeds, but that in others, particularly the debate over gay and lesbian marriage, its tendency to adopt the language and assumptions of the political debate actually implicates it in the continuing compromise of children's basic welfare. An insistent feminist-liberationist focus on the least powerful can cure what ails the ecclesiastical conversation, but not without radicalizing our interpretation of social teaching.

Political Assumptions

At heart, political family values are not about children's good directly but about parents' rights to have children and exercise power over them. In political parlance "family" implies nuclear family: a married couple with minor children. A related assumption, common to the whole political spectrum and reinforced by developmental theory[3] and the pop culture celebrity pregnancy and adoption boom, is that parenting is a necessary condition for leading a rewarding adult life. From this perspective making a family becomes a natural and universal need. This reasoning leads to a third nearly universal conviction, that parenting is a right that society cannot deny (indeed, for most people becoming a parent requires less certification than driving a car or buying a beer), and a fourth, that children are possessions that adults have a "right" to own and care for as they see fit.[4] The rhetoric of rights and ownership is as common on the left as on the right: arguments for adoption by gay and lesbian couples often employ it, for example.

Our social agreement that "family values" includes the right to parent is so strong that we barely restrict this right. But it does not imply absolute support of parents. First, social consensus around the right to *assistance in becoming a parent* extends only to married heterosexual couples. Second, social consensus around the right to *support in parenting* extends only to working, legally resident, married couples and single parents. Finally, the consensus hints that with rights come responsibilities: people ought not to bear children for whom they cannot care without assistance. Like mortgages and car loans, children imply ongoing obligations; if parents take on more than they can afford, they must deal with the consequences themselves.

All three tacit agreements are more interested in delineating adults' rights to parent than in guaranteeing children's rights to be parented. Three contemporary political issues with profound implications for children's basic welfare demonstrate this point and provide some hints about why children's welfare, which should be the focus of any social debate over parenting, is so easily elided. They also demonstrate the strength and limits of contemporary Catholic social justice teaching for child welfare.

Three Contemporary Political Debates

Informed by the assumptions outlined above, American law and policy commonly put children at risk by making it more difficult for parents of whom society disapproves to care for them. That is, society forces children to suffer for the purported sins of their parents.

Children on Welfare

Our underfunded welfare policy is one of the most obvious and uncontroversial cases of children suffering because their parents are being punished. The original purpose of the old welfare program, Aid to Families with Dependent Children (AFDC), was to promote young children's welfare by enabling mothers to stay at home to care for them. Fears about hereditary welfare dependency and the antimarriage implications of AFDC, combined with a growing conviction that parents should earn their benefits and should be discouraged from bearing additional children, altered the course of welfare. AFDC's 1996 replacement, Temporary Assistance to Needy Families (TANF), aims to get adults and their children, including young children, off the rolls as quickly as possible. The strategy is that short-term pressure exerted by a sixty-month lifetime benefit limit, combined with enticements like job training and child care, will urge adult recipients toward work, and that they and their children will then enjoy the long-term benefits of permanent economic independence.

TANF opened with a period of relative success. But the economic downturn of 2000–2004 revealed the weaknesses of the reforms and the ineffectiveness of tying children's welfare to parents' employment. The number of children in deep poverty (income below one-half the poverty line) increased by more than three-quarters of a million, and 1.4 million additional children fell into poverty. By 2004, in an average month 1 million single mothers were neither working nor on welfare. They — and 2 million of their children, an increase of 66 percent since 1996 — were completely without income. The percentage of families qualifying for assistance that actually received it fell from 86 percent in 1992 (under AFDC) to 48 percent in 2002, the last year for which data were available. The percentage of poor children receiving assistance dropped from 58 percent in 1996 to just 31 percent in 2003.[5]

Two distinct failures underlie this horrific neglect of child welfare. First, the legislation: mandates are underfunded. States receive lump sums for welfare assistance, regardless of the number of needy households,[6] with no adjustment for the rising cost of living; their real value by 2011 will be just 70 percent of the original 1996 value.[7] At the initiation of welfare reform, Congress cut back low-income programs, SSI, Food Stamps, and Medicaid, by $55 billion over six years, cutting off many recipients and failing to keep up with inflation for others. The Deficit Reduction Act reduced childcare support; between 2000 and 2011 there will be a 26 percent decline in the number of children whose parents can take advantage of childcare to pursue education and employment.[8]

In addition, the legislation withdraws funding from states whose rolls do not meet strict compliance and work participation thresholds, forcing the states into a dilemma: maintain funding by restricting participation radically, or lose funding entirely.[9] Among the most often dropped from the rolls, because they have the hardest time complying with meetings and work and paperwork requirements, are the disabled, the mentally ill, and those who care for them.[10] Children are doubly vulnerable if a parent is disabled or mentally ill, or must provide difficult and time-consuming care for another person. Such parents may be both without work income and without benefits. In addition, modified job-training programs for the disabled and stand-alone ESL programs do not count as work participation, posing a clear difficulty for the children of disabled or non-English-speaking parents.[11] As a last resort, states are permitted to fund the children of parents whose benefits have run out but, because these households count as "nonworking families," states often drop the children's benefits anyway.[12] In sum, the federal block grant squeeze forces states to punish parents for noncompliance, which in turn endangers children.

Second, the social, physical, and economic infrastructure that work participation assumes is nonexistent in many places, further disadvantaging the children of poor adults. For example, in poor and working-class urban Massachusetts, community-based nonprofit organizations are increasingly focusing on individual behavior and compliance to the detriment of neighborhood development and community politics. Welfare reform is eroding the places, institutions, and spare time in which people formerly collaborated in order to build viable local economic and social opportunities.[13] In addition, entry-level jobs are often distant from low-income housing and from public transportation. In 1998, 45 percent of the entry-level jobs in high-growth North Waltham could not be reached within two hours from central city Boston.[14] A parent could easily spend eight hours away from children to earn $30 doing four hours' worth of work. Chicago women, regretfully returning to welfare after working, reported that their low wages and unstable jobs often netted them lower pay with fewer benefits than TANF gave them,[15] not to mention taking them away from their children. Similar problems plague rural households.[16]

TANF holds adults accountable for work within an economy that does not guarantee them a living wage, but without providing a viable safety net. The anxiety that drives the legislation is that undeserving adults must not "freeload" indefinitely at taxpayers' expense. But cost of this assurance, apparently less widely feared, is that a staggering number of American children go underfed, badly clothed, and inadequately housed as a result, even when their parents are employed.

What prophetic inspiration can we glean from the social justice tradition? The United States Conference of Catholic Bishops responded resoundingly in their 2002 pastoral reflection *A Place at the Table*. First, the most vulnerable among us deserve our solidarity.[17] Child poverty features prominently in the document, which holds that poor children deserve solidarity regardless of their parents' marital or employment status. By arguing for support for all good parents, single and married,[18] the bishops also imply that children's poverty should be overcome by elevating their families' incomes, that children deserve intimate care within families rather than institutional care outside them. They further imply that raising children is a vocation. Thus our obligation to children is part of our obligation to parents: we must not put inadequate wages or impossible TANF requirements in the way of parents' calling to care for their children.

Second, solidarity implies multipronged action based in the principle of subsidiarity, which levels criticisms at all of the people and institutions that collaborate to encourage child poverty. Children's needs should be provided for within their households, but higher levels of social organization must supply structures and safety nets. For instance, in order to provide wisely for their children, parents need support from "community organizations and faith-based institutions" both for short-term practical assistance and for long-term political transformation of unjust social and economic structures. Corporations and other influential citizens of the marketplace are responsible for ensuring that work is "an escape from poverty, not another version of it." And finally, "government must act" "to address problems beyond the reach of individual and community efforts."[19] The American assumption that parents are solely responsible for raising all the children whom they bear or who otherwise end up in their care is false.

Yet the bishops have not gained perfect prophetic distance from the terms of political welfare debate. The bishops argue correctly that the "personal virtue" of single and married parents' good choices and self-sacrifice are indispensable to the eradication of child poverty and should be rewarded by "public policy and all our institutions."[20] This position intimates that children deserve help only if parents are well behaved. The bishops do not explain what constitutes personal virtue or wise choice in a system that still punishes rather than rewards work and marriage, how to protect children whose parents make poor choices, or how to support such parents. Given patterns of child custody, more

of these ambiguous choices seem likely to fall to mothers than to fathers. Without a living wage, stable employment, health insurance, and adequate daycare,
is a mother's decision to stop work and return to TANF unwise? When un-
employment is high and a husband represents an increased economic liability,
both absolutely and with respect to TANF work participation requirements for
couples, is a woman's refusal to marry her children's father really selfish and
shortsighted?[21] The bishops' vision of family values and of the scope of parental
responsibility in such circumstances is unclear.

Children of Undocumented Immigrants

Today 5 million children live with at least one undocumented immigrant parent.
Studies indicate that 72 percent of these children are low-income.[22] About one-
third of the children with at least one undocumented parent are undocumented
themselves, but two-thirds are citizens.[23]

What are the special vulnerabilities of children of undocumented parents?
Parents can be deported even if their children are citizens or legal residents, and
the whole family can be deported if they are not. The pall of this fear shades
every dimension of family life. Ordinary daily activities — working, driving
a car, renting an apartment, buying a home, getting medical care, registering
children in school, handling money — require either false documents, the risk of
getting caught without documents, or under-the-table alternatives that require
no documents. For example, employers of undocumented workers often pay
low or even sub-minimum cash wages, train employees inadequately, ignore
OSHA regulations, and provide no reimbursement or sick pay when workers
are injured. Household workers face a likelihood of unpaid overtime and even
near slavery. The problems of undocumented migrant workers and sweatshop
employees are likewise well known.

The cumulative results of these overlapping problems are startling. Low-
income young children of immigrants are about half as likely as low-income
children of natives to participate in TANF, Medicaid, or housing assistance
programs. In 2002 young children of immigrants were more than twice as likely
to be in fair or poor health than children of natives, and almost three times as
likely to have no reliable, steady source of health care.[24]

For undocumented children, who include nearly half of noncitizen children
under six years old,[25] and about 1.8 million children overall, life is even more
challenging than for their citizen counterparts. They arrive as minor children
with parents or relatives (in addition, nearly eight thousand per year are detained entering alone).[26] They are normally ineligible for all benefits except
emergency Medicaid. They become undocumented adults, unable to get education loans or find regular employment. In sum, children of immigrants, and
undocumented children of undocumented immigrants most of all, do not and
often cannot fall back even on the meager safety net that child welfare programs
provide.

Bishops of the United States and Mexico have applied the social justice principles elucidated above to immigration. They have called for solidarity with
migrants, declaring them to be among "the most vulnerable."[27] Family integrity,

in particular between parents and children, ranks high on their list of concerns. They lament U.S. immigration and deportation policies, pointing to families "kept apart," "children left alone when parents are removed from them," and the impossible choice between honoring "moral commitment to family" by risking undocumented immigration to follow spouses or parents and facing "indefinite separation from loved ones."[28]

Second, the bishops update the century-plus-old doctrine of subsidiarity. It, like solidarity, must go global. Finding "the economic, political, and social opportunities to live in dignity and achieve a full life" in one's own homeland is a basic human right; other countries must collaborate to relieve the political, economic, and other pressures that stand in the way of this goal.[29] In the meantime, one has the "right to find work elsewhere in order to survive," to take one's family along, and to be treated with justice and hospitality.[30] Nations with relatively robust economies are obligated to provide hospitality and justice to immigrant workers, to help workers preserve their families intact, and to assist other nations with job development. We can describe all of this as a consequence of our obligation to children: parents need economic and health and political security for themselves in order to provide for and raise their own children, regardless of citizenship and residence.

Children of Gay and Lesbian Partners

Partly because of underreporting, reliable data on children of gay and lesbian couples are difficult to discover. The most conservative estimate (based on 2000 U.S. census data) counted over 600,000 gay and lesbian couples in the U.S., about 180,000 of whom were raising over 415,000 of their own children under the age of eighteen.[31]

The numbers are low, but the legal and economic vulnerabilities are high. Children of gay and lesbian couples experience a secondary vulnerability much like that of children of undocumented immigrants. Unlike heterosexual couples, gay and lesbian partners barred from marriage or civil union do not automatically inherit from each other; they are not protected from liability or testimony in lawsuits against their partners; and they may not be able to extend employer benefits to their partners or children. These partners also cannot make critical medical decisions for each other, potentially excluding them and their children from care for and contact with an ill partner. Some state laws do provide these advantages through civil unions, but they are null if parents move to a state that does not.[32]

Adoption law is a much more severe problem. Children usually enter gay and lesbian families, whether by adoption or by birth, through only one parent. If only that parent has legal custody, only that parent can authorize educational and medical decisions and provide insurance and social benefits. Traveling between states, and especially out of the country, with the second parent is problematic.[33] If the custodial parent dies or becomes incompetent, the child is often placed with the custodial parent's relatives or in foster care. If the parents split up, children have no presumptive right to visits, continued contact with, or support from the second parent. Only ten states and the District of

Columbia formally permit second-parent adoption, that is, permit the second partner also to adopt the children without temporarily terminating the custodial parent's rights.[34]

It is possible for savvy parents to circumvent some of these problems. The ideal gay or lesbian couple protects their children by moving to a state that recognizes gay and lesbian marriage or civil unions and second-parent adoption, hires a lawyer to ensure that protections equivalent to marriage are in place for their children, and leaves that state only for states where these arrangements will be recognized. But this strategy hardly guarantees the basic welfare of children whose parents do not make such arrangements, and the gay/lesbian-partnered households with incomes under $30,000 (over 22 percent in 2000) probably could not afford them anyway.[35] Children of gay and lesbian couples need a nationally recognized institution that secures the same rights and duties of parents toward children, and the same rights of children toward parents, for gay and lesbian couples as marriage does. Otherwise they are unfairly exposed and, through no fault of their own, denied "the financial and social benefits and privileges available to children in heterosexual households."[36] Gay and lesbian marriage laws are in the interests of the children whom gay and lesbian couples are already raising.

In this case, Roman Catholic teaching condemns both unmarried hetero-sexual and gay and lesbian partnerships for setting mortal sexual sin up as a good; both are "forms of cohabitation which, by their very nature, deserve nei-ther the name nor the status of family [and therefore do not imply the right to parent]."[37] Yet because homosexual partnerships do not involve the "com-plementarities of the two persons, father and mother"[38] they are seen as even more injurious to children than common-law marriages;[39] the state should nei-ther permit children to enter their households nor grant them even analogous family status. Here the church puts the moral and sacramental status of parents before the basic, material welfare of their children.[40]

Assessment

The Roman Catholic social justice tradition contains a prophetic critique of the parental rights–based American politics of parenthood. Solidarity insists on the care and nurture of the vulnerable, especially children, whose basic human dignity demands that they be raised in stable, loving families with adequate re-sources. Subsidiarity insists that children's families are called to nurture them, with support from government and society at all levels. Neither makes a par-ticular family configuration the condition of support. Both the Vatican and the American bishops reinforce these commitments consistently when they speak of social welfare, wage, trade, and immigration policies.

But the church's radically different treatment of gay and lesbian marriage points out two pieces of unfinished business. First, the church's public witness on family is inconsistent and confusing. On one hand, it argues for living wages, welfare benefits, and other means of securing children's livelihood without re-gard for their parents' marital status or sexual orientation. When immigration and basic welfare are at stake, the church's choices rank providing for children's survival through nurture by a relatively stable configuration of loving adults above the gender, number, or status of their parents. And that is a good thing, because the children in the 45 percent of American households that do not adhere to the Roman Catholic ideals of celibacy and marriage[41] live through no fault of their own outside the bounds of the ideal Catholic family.

On the other hand, the church teaches that "the natural society founded on marriage" is the true family, clearly demarcated from "all other forms of cohabitation which, by their very nature, deserve neither the name nor the status of family"[42] and should not receive the same privileges from civil society. Here children's immediate need for survival and stability take second place to their need for married parents of complementary genders.

This inconsistency leads to the second concern: contemporary sacramental theology has muddled social justice reasoning. Sacraments are signs and sites of grace in concrete earthly life. Yet the language the church uses to describe sacramental marriage is eschatological and abstract: "the union of two sexually different persons [in which the partners] can achieve perfection in a synthesis of unity and mutual psychophysical completion."[43] Male and female are eternal, essential, complementary forces with no definite content, united on the transcendent plane, detached from kin, society, work, and politics.[44] We read about *the* mother, *the* father, *the* child, and *the* family, as if they were static archetypes.

Social justice, on the other hand, is about figuring out how to give to dignified sons and daughters of God their due through the limited and imperfect mechanisms of a sinful world. Social justice documents like *A Place at the Table* nod realistically to families as imperfect but nonetheless essential mechanisms. For children receive the intimate care that enables them to mature in good health and character in concretely existing social households and kin networks. Functional families thus have a political, economic, developmental role that is distinct from any sacramental character they may also possess. Properly expressed in the plural rather than the singular, they take on various sizes and shapes in different cultures and circumstances, even in the same household over time. The authoritative *Compendium* melds the sacramental and the functional in defiance of these distinctions: "*the family* has a completely original and irreplaceable role *in raising children*,"[45] and "the unborn child *must be guaranteed* the best possible conditions of existence through the stability of a family founded on marriage, through the complementarities of the two persons, father and mother."[46] These quotations imply that children have an absolute moral and legal right to be born or at least adopted only into sacramental families, and in turn only adults in sacramental unions have the moral and legal right to be parents and to have their parenting supported by society. The languages of sacrament, social justice, and political rights are uncritically merged. But functional families are rarely archetypal sacramental families. They are larger or smaller or differently configured, and sacramental marriages may or may not be at their hearts. Especially if the church is serious about opposing abortion, it cannot afford to say that nonsacramental families are not "true" families.

Catholic speaking needs more precision. An argument for social justice for children in a variety of family structures is not reducible to sacramental theology or to parental merit. Whether gay and lesbian unions are sacramental or poor parents' decisions are always wise is beside the point. Not all families are, or ever will be, sacramental, nor will all parents be wise. As Catholic treatment of immigration demonstrates, we owe it to children to ensure simply that as many functional families as possible have the wherewithal to be places of love and nurture for the vulnerable children whom they shelter.

Chapter 13

Children and the Common Good

Protection and Participation

MARY M. DOYLE ROCHE

IN A TIME WHEN THE POLITICS of the home and hearth are as divisive as ever, with hot-button issues like norms for marriage and parenting occupying more and more space in the public debate, often to the exclusion of other urgent issues, a movement is emerging to reinvigorate a conversation on the common good of society and its place in political decision making.[1] For example, Catholics in Alliance for the Common Good has formed as a grassroots effort that builds on the insights of the U.S. bishops' publication *Faithful Citizenship*.[2] When Catholics, whether they be voters or running for elected office, negotiate the political and electoral process, the concept of the common good provides a framework for sifting through the many urgent questions our communities face and for uncovering some issues that may be obscured during a campaign season.

This renewed attention to the common good is an important development for the church and has the potential to make a meaningful contribution to public discourse. The tradition on which it draws is long in the church and is being carried into the twenty-first century by theologians and ethicists in a variety of contexts.[3] One area in which there is room for further development is precisely in our understanding of the meaning and goals of family life. In particular, thinking more explicitly about how children receive the fruits of our common good and how they participate in the building up of that good is especially urgent.[4]

In order to arrive at specific strategies for securing the well-being and flourishing of children, however modest they may be, we must start with an assessment of the very real situations children face, especially poor children. The response of the world community to the plight of children has been to articulate a position on children's rights that could provide a benchmark with which to measure the concrete well-being of children. Though such an approach has its liabilities, the language of children's rights remains a crucial tool for child advocates. When rights language is employed in the broader context of a commitment to the common good, it avoids the distortion of children's rights that emerges from an excessively individualistic perspective. Taking children's rights seriously will also allow us to sketch a vision of the common good that includes children as full and vital members. In many ways, such a project will challenge many of our cultural assumptions about who children are, what they need from their communities, and what they have to offer. Then we will be in a position to highlight existing programs that are informed by a richer image of children and childhood and to suggest where attention to these strategies might lead us. The focus in this essay will be on initiatives in Catholic education and their potential to serve as models of resistance to and transformation of a highly commercialized, consumer culture (gone global) that exploits children.

Reading the Signs of the Times for Children

The concept of the common good is a key element in contemporary Catholic social teaching, and as such it begins with, and takes seriously, human experience.[5] Consideration of the common good as it relates to children begins with an exploration of the concrete situations many children face, both here in the Unites States and across the globe. Because the vision of the common good advanced here is shaped by the preferential option for the poor, we begin first and foremost with the experiences of poor and marginalized children. That is no small task, and sources to which we could turn are numerous; we will catch only a glimpse of the many realities that must be kept in mind.

In the United States, we consider information gathered by the Children's Defense Fund (CDF). Data provided on their website in February of 2007 claims that each day in America: one mother dies in childbirth; four children are killed by abuse or neglect; five children or teens commit suicide; eight children or teens are killed by firearms; 33 children or teens die in accidents; 77 infants die before their first birthday; 192 children are arrested for violent crimes; 383 are arrested for drug-related crime; 906 infants are born with low birth weight; 1,153 infants are born to teenaged mothers (in many ways, children themselves); 1,879 infants are born without health insurance; 2,411 infants are born into poverty; and the list goes on.[6] Statistics, of course are only a part of the overall picture. Advocates for children like Jonathan Kozol provide the complex narratives behind the numbers.[7] Elsewhere in this volume, Cristina Traina has focused on what we know about children living in poor homes, often headed by one parent (and that parent is often a woman), about children of immigrant families, and children being parented by gay and lesbian men and women.[8]

Globally, the picture for poor children is even bleaker. The United Nations Children's Fund, UNICEF, provides a helpful resource. According to UNICEF's fact sheet, nearly 115 million children worldwide do not attend school; more than 1 million children are trafficked each year; approximately 1.8 million children are exploited in the global sex trade; at any given time, 250,000 children are involved in armed conflict; 143 million children are orphans; 246 million children are engaged in child labor (of these, 117 million are working in "hazardous" conditions and approximately 8.4 million in "horrific circumstances"). Child mortality rates and the causes of death, many of which are easily avoided in wealthier nations, are tragic to say the least.[9] UNICEF's publication *The State of the World's Children 2007: The Double Dividend of Gender Inequality* paints a startling portrait of the lives of the world's poor children, revealing that in many ways girls are the poorest of the poor.[10] How are the world community and the church to respond to these concrete realities of oppression and exploitation?

Children's Rights and the Common Good

Catholic traditions of Christianity, particularly those that contribute to the development of Catholic social teaching, have articulated a commitment to human rights, rooted in intrinsic human dignity and the sanctity of the human person across the entire lifespan. The *Compendium of the Social Doctrine of the Church* notes, "The movement toward the identification and proclamation of human rights is one of the most significant attempts to respond effectively to the inescapable demands of human dignity." It goes further to claim that the *Universal Declaration of Human Rights* is a "true milestone on the path of humanity's moral progress."[11]

Notions of human dignity and human rights in Catholic social teaching are however, understood within the context of the radically social and interdependent nature of the human person who is oriented toward relationships, community, and the common good of society. So, like other strands of religious reflection on rights, Catholicism considers rights to be inextricably linked to responsibilities. The full inclusion of children in the common good of society will require transformations in rights and responsibilities and in relationships with and between adults. Discerning children's role in the common good in the Catholic tradition is then aided by two other concepts: subsidiarity and the option for the poor, without which the common good can be easily misunderstood as a form of utilitarian thinking or collectivism that could further marginalize children and fail to recognize the legitimate roles many institutions play in securing children's well-being.

The common good in this tradition is understood to be the sum total of the conditions of social living, which enhance the flourishing of individuals and communities. The individual is not lost or obscured, but rather receives the goods of our life together and participates in the development of those goods. The common good encourages the pursuit of goods and goals beyond one's own (particularly the goals of the poor and marginalized) and secures an environment in which solidarity of this sort is a real possibility for all members.

As full, interdependent members of the many overlapping communities of which they are a part (familial, neighborhood, ecclesial, educational, health care, economic, national, international), children claim the fruits of our common life together and are called to ever increasing participation in that life. In this common good framework, children's rights serve as a "tool of critical analysis" by which we measure children's concrete well-being.[12] This involves meeting their basic needs for food, clothing, shelter, education, recreation, health care, and crucial relationships with adults. It also demands that we assess children's ability to participate in social life and have a voice in decisions on issues that affect them (and we are hard pressed to think of an issue that doesn't).

According to the U.S. bishops' pastoral *Economic Justice for All,* "Basic justice demands the establishment of minimum levels of participation in the life of the human community for *all persons.*"[13]

The language of children's rights loses this critical edge when both advocates and opponents of such rights use the term rhetorically without linking rights to specific responsibilities.[14] We hear claims like "children have a right to a childhood" or to "an open future." Opponents claim then that we have "abandoned children to their rights" and that asserting rights for children is tantamount to a form of neglect.[15] This characterization of rights fails to capture the intentions of the United Nations' *Convention on the Rights of the Child* and distorts its claims about the responsibility, shared by all levels of society, to ensure children's economic and political rights.

What then is the Catholic Church's record on the rights of children, both in its rhetoric and its praxis? The documentary heritage of Catholic social teaching has demonstrated support for children's rights, though with important reservations. While the Vatican has ratified the *UN Convention on the Rights of the Child,* we see at the outset of a 2000 document, *Children: The Springtime of the Family and Society,* developed at the Third World Meeting of the Holy Father with Families, this claim, "We appeal first of all with insistence to the public authorities, both national and international to not transform children into abstract, isolated, windowless, and doorless 'monads' whose rights have no relation to their real situation of dependence and need for protection."[16]

A conflictual model of rights, that pits the rights and needs of children against the claims of adults, strains against the church's images of the patriarchal family and its assumptions that such a family is headed, of course, by a benevolent patriarch.[17] The Catholic tradition has tended to make more robust claims for the rights of the family as the institution best suited to guaranteeing the well-being of children.[18] According to the 1983 *Vatican Charter on the Rights of the Family,*

> The rights of the person, even though they are expressed as rights of the individual, have a fundamental social dimension which finds innate and vital expression in the family.... The family, a natural society, exists prior to the State or any other community, and possess inherent rights which are inalienable.

Furthermore,

> The family is the place where different generations come together and help one another to grow in human wisdom and to harmonize the rights of individuals with other demands of social life.... The family and society, which are mutually linked by vital and organic bonds, have a complementary function in the defense and advancement of the good of every person and of humanity.[19]

Families should have the crucial social supports they need in order to exercise their responsibilities toward children, which include securing their material, physical, emotional welfare, the freedom to educate children and pass along religious and cultural values, and the freedom to associate with other families and organizations to facilitate participation in the wider society.

At several points in the Vatican *Charter,* particular reference is made to what children themselves can claim from their communities. Before and after birth, children "have the right to special protection and assistance, as do their mothers," and this protection and assistance extends to all children, including children born out of wedlock, orphaned children, children with disabilities, and children of immigrants.[20]

Nevertheless, recourse to the language of rights with respect to children appears more often in the context of a right to life (in which the focus is on abortion, rather than on meeting the basic needs of born children) and a right to be born of a man and a woman in marriage (which may speak both to recent debates about same-sex unions and parenting, and the possibilities for human cloning). The *Compendium* states, "The first right of the child is 'to be born in a real family,' a right that has not always been respected and that today is subject to new violations because of developments in genetic technology."[21]

Still reeling from the multiple implications of the sex abuse scandal, the emphasis now is on the protection of children from those who would harm them — though there remains disagreement on exactly what and who pose the greatest threat to children's concrete well-being (for example, neither the CDF or UNICEF highlight any potential harm to children parented by homosexual men and women as an urgent issue). So, claims about the "right to a real family" also fall victim to the rhetorical trap that fails to focus rights language on concrete well-being. What is a real family? How do we secure such a right? Who is obligated to provide it? The challenge that is before us, when we consider children's rights in the context of the common good, is to protect in ways that do not lead to the further marginalization of some children, especially those who do not find themselves in "real" families or who are without families altogether, or to the exclusion of children's participation (a situation that only increases the vulnerability of all children).

The common good tradition, with its insistence on distributive justice *and* participation, both guided by the principle of subsidiarity and the option for the poor, can provide the grounds for a rigorous defense of children's rights and can help us to nuance the anthropology at their foundation so that it reflects the profoundly social and interdependent reality of children's lives. Children need justice and care, participation and protection. Moreover, such an approach to children's rights and responsibilities highlights the need for the involvement of institutions beyond the family to ensure the conditions of social living that allow children to flourish. Subsidiarity calls us to recognize the family as an institution with unique authority and autonomy; the state should not assume the tasks in child rearing that a family is best suited to carry out. At the same time, the state, together with the many institutions of civil society, has a moral obligation to aid families in carrying out these obligations and to step in when parents and families are unable to secure the conditions necessary for children's flourishing on their own or when the family environment itself undermines the well-being of its individual members.

Yes, children are members of families — all kinds of families. But they are not only members of families; they are members of many communities and they are also individuals whose well-being must be attended to and measured along a number of different axes. We may not always assume that children's interests and the interests of their families are the same. The potential for this conflation of interests can be a danger in the church's family-centered approach.

The notion of the common good is also shaped in important ways by the option for the poor. When we think of the common good simply as "what's good for everyone," we may miss the insight that progress toward the common good will require sacrifice on the part of some so that others may enjoy even the minimum conditions for well-being. Without embracing an option for the poor, the reality and the burden of sacrifice continues to fall on the same groups — the poor — and children are the poorest of the poor — and girls are the poorest of these.

What, then, does the tradition of the common good have to offer the wider conversation on children's rights? To see what fruit such an approach could bear let us proceed to some considerations of children's rights and responsibilities in the economic life of their families and communities. If economic participation is constitutive of the common good for persons, as claimed in *Economic Justice for All,* then it will be for children as well. How should that participation be shaped? Children's rights, informed by elements of the common good tradition, will assist us in avoiding two dangerous extremes: (1) the toleration of exploitative and dehumanizing working conditions for poor children (this includes factory wage labor, domestic service, agricultural work, sex work, and soldiering); and (2) the self-interested consumer child who is targeted by powerful corporations. In situations of poverty and gender inequality, children's work is exploited and comes at the expense of their individual health and education. In a highly individualistic consumer culture, rights rhetoric is easily distorted (children have rights to advertising and unlimited choices) and the sense that even children and young people might pursue goods and goals beyond their own is diminished.

Attempts at eliminating all child labor have failed and sometimes meet with resistance on the part of communities in which they take place. Rights activists may fail to take into account the crucial role children's income plays in the family's economic life, or the sense in many cultures that children have concrete obligations to their families. Parents are not always convinced that education will make a real difference in their children's lives.[22] Yet acknowledging these realities need not imply that all forms of work are acceptable. In the ideal, breadwinners should earn a family living wage that would allow children to pursue education and continue to live faithfully in their family relationships in ways that do not threaten their life and health.

The Cristo Rey Center for the Working Child in Peru gives us an example of children's rights and the common good in action at the grass roots. Founded in 1986, the center's mission is to "dignify and defend the working child by promoting and defending the rights of children and youth." Their website states, "While the center does not encourage child labor, we must respond to the social and economic reality which forces children to work in order to survive."[23] The center provides service to three hundred children: an alternative school, job skills training, nutrition, health care, counseling, a shelter, family outreach, and pastoral care. The reality that these children face, in all of its complexity, is taken seriously and *they* are taken seriously, as people who have much to contribute, but who need increased support and protection from the negative effects of child labor. The situation these children face has root causes; we may find these roots growing in our own backyards.

In my own culture and community, the sense of children's participation is less clear, and destructive in its own way. What children often "give" or "provide" is emotional gratification for their parents, who invest considerable resources to secure, not just flourishing, but *advantage*. Children's participation might be limited to soccer games and piano recitals. My husband and I strive to create Bonnie Miller-McLemore's "pitch-in family" in our home, with less than spectacular success.[24] When we, as a community, and even as a church, fail to clearly articulate the nature of children's participation and our relationships and responsibilities, there are others eager to fill the void. Major corporations are acutely aware of the role that children can play in the family and in the global economy, particularly in their spending of the family's financial resources. Advertisers, corporations like Disney and Nickelodeon (more frequent visitors to my home than I would like to admit) hunger for children's participation. They will take children and their needs (which are often actually desires that have been shaped by the industry) "seriously" and respond enthusiastically, giving children avenues by which to exercise their "right" to consume.[25] Children participate by spending, and when they do work, upper-middle-class children often work for a new iPod or some other personal pleasure. The child remains an individual consumer. No connection is made between patterns of consumption in one place and exploitative child labor in another. Surely, even wealthy children must have another role to play in the economic life of families and communities.[26]

Children's rights considered in the context of the common good alert us to these dangerous poles and may allow us to sketch a vision of children's protection and participation that makes room for some child work and discourages intensive marketing to children and an individualistic sense of self. Children's rights need not be articulated in a way that views the rights bearer as a radically autonomous individual with no responsibility to family and community. Children are full, interdependent members of all of the many communities of which they are a part. They have a claim on our resources to be sure, but also a right to our solidarity and commitment to building with them an environment that welcomes their meaningful participation in community.

Participation and Protection: Strategies for the Church

The church in recent years has rightly been concerned with elaborating policies and procedures that ensure the safety of children in ecclesial institutions and environments.[27] This attention to children's well-being is long overdue. Yet, as has been maintained here, protection is only one piece of the puzzle. Any notion of the common good that includes children must also sketch a vision of their participation in our common life. We have already mentioned the Cristo Rey Center for the Working Child as one example.

The Cristo Rey network of schools in the United States also illustrates a richer notion of children and young people that emerges from a common good perspective.[28] In Cristo Rey schools, the academic program is supplemented by work experience. This distinctive element has several aims. It gives young people who, by virtue of their socioeconomic background, do not have the social capital needed to secure internship experiences an opportunity to do so. Students are introduced to industries and careers that might otherwise be closed to them. The corporations involved pay to be a part of the program, and this in turn helps to maintain the financial stability of the school. Children served by Cristo Rey would not otherwise be able to afford a Catholic high school education. The dynamic is different from working after school and contributing to tuition expenses. Individual students work for the well-being of the school community as a whole. They pursue goods and goals beyond their own, though these goods surely redound to them as unique individuals. The individual child is not lost or obscured, hardly. Students are valued as interdependent members of a community that owes its existence to their full participation.

The possibilities for children's participation in the common good and their protection from exploitation come clearly into relief. The young people attending Cristo Rey schools do need protection from the effects of poverty and violence in our communities. The academic program opens up new possibilities for work and further education. They also participate in the school community with a sense of ownership. The students are not simply drawing on the community's resources; they are building them up.

This example is not without ambiguity. We must be alert to the ways in which we support work on the part of poor children as vital to their well-being, and even "character building" without feeling the same is necessary for wealthier children. Our often unacknowledged assumptions about poor children (that they are more mature or street savvy) must be challenged.

Nevertheless, Cristo Rey and other educational initiatives like the Nativity/ Miguel Network provide models of resistance to an individualistic and consumer-driven culture that suggest several priorities for the church.[29] First, churches and religious institutions (higher education and health care) should support these creative initiatives in whatever way possible, be that financial support, interning opportunities, or providing mentoring and tutoring programs. Second, in keeping with the U.S. bishops' document on Catholic education, *Renewing Our Commitment*, churches must call for increased access to Catholic education and demand that the burden of providing such an education fall more evenly across communities rather than having parishes with schools (especially in inner-city and rural areas) bearing a heavier load. Third, the churches should also be vigorous and outspoken supporters of an adequate, and dare we say outstanding, public school system. Fourth, private Catholic schools should resist becoming "gated communities." Rising tuition costs, highly competitive admissions policies, practices of exclusion, marketing strategies (religious schools are increasingly vulnerable to having a market metaphor shape the institution's goals), and school closings must be carefully scrutinized using a common good/option for the poor framework.

Children are full, interdependent members of the many communities, beyond home and hearth, of which they are a part. The church's commitment to children's inclusion in the common good of society must recognize them as vulnerable recipients of the fruits of that life and as valued participants in its creation.

Chapter 14

When Pregnancy Hits Home

Recognizing the Need for
Familial and Ecclesial Solidarity

ANGELA SENANDER

WHEN PARENTS LEARN FROM THEIR CHILD that they are grandparents, this is often a source of joy. However, if this child is not married, whether a teenager or young adult, the parents' response might include disappointment, fear about their child and grandchild's future, and concern about the judgments of others. In the midst of such feelings, parents do well to recognize this news as an invitation into solidarity with their child and grandchild, an invitation that many parents in the United States do not receive because of the way in which U.S. abortion laws and rhetoric foster a culture of isolated, "lone rights-bearers"[1] among young women. While the politics of abortion in the United States emphasizes the individual rights of the pregnant woman or the unborn, often at the expense of the other and to the exclusion of the woman's partner and their parents, a politics of the hearth invites reflection on the familial and spiritual homes in which a pregnant young woman and her partner might find solidarity or rejection.[2] This solidarity not only takes seriously the social nature of the human person by embracing interdependence and communal responsibility, but also respects human dignity by valuing mutuality and participation as the young people respond to the pregnancy.

Reflecting the pragmatic American spirit, families and parishes might be tempted to move quickly into a problem-solving mode when they learn about a teenage or young adult pregnancy before marriage. A move to action without adequate understanding of the young person's experience, however, threatens the efficacy of the "solution." By listening, one can grow in understanding of and solidarity with them. From the Catholic Church's ministries of listening to those who have experienced crisis pregnancies and abortions,[3] one learns about the need for familial solidarity and structural changes in institutions to support pregnant young women, and indirectly learns about the perspectives of parents and partners.

As a spiritual home for a young pregnant woman, her partner, and their families, the Catholic community needs to grow in its capacity to (1) listen to the stories of these young people, (2) model solidarity with them through structural changes in Catholic organizations, and (3) provide pastoral care to those troubled by the news they are grandparents. Allowing the Gospel story of the woman at the well to shed light on young people's experiences of pregnancy and the Catholic community's responses, we will learn from the perspectives of young pregnant women who have been accompanied through a Catholic ministry of listening and then consider strategies for broadening and deepening this ministry of listening. Based on this foundational activity for ecclesial solidarity, we will identify the need for and strategies for Catholic organizations to evaluate how their structures manifest solidarity with these young people, whether they are students or employees. Following this focus on the Catholic Church's response to young people becoming parents earlier than expected, we will turn to a potential church response to their parents who are becoming grandparents earlier than expected. The Emmaus story will illuminate an approach to pastoral care for the grandparents that will promote familial solidarity. We now turn to the story of the woman at the well as a lens for considering the experience of and ecclesial response to teen and young adult pregnancy.

Solidarity and Alienation in a Spiritual Home

As a community of disciples, the church continues to learn from the practices of Jesus. In the story of the Samaritan woman at the well (John 4:1–30),[4] Jesus does not let either community expectations or the woman's personal history prevent him from entering into solidarity with her. As part of a people who Jews considered unfaithful to the covenant and rejected on account of their worship practices, this Samaritan was surprised to interact with Jesus, a Jew. Not only was her lack of adherence to Jewish ritual practices a potential basis for alienation in this situation, but so too was her gender. The disciples were attentive to community expectations about interactions between men and women and were surprised to find Jesus and a lone woman engaged in conversation. The disciples would have been even more surprised had they heard her personal history. She had had five husbands, and she was not married to the man that she was living with. Her sexual practices did not conform to Jewish religious law. Not only is this story about Jesus sharing the good news of God's love with this woman as she is, but it is also the story of this woman evangelizing her community.

Women and men who have experienced crisis pregnancies and those who have chosen abortion might be like this woman in various ways. Often their sexual practices have not reflected the values of the Catholic community. Those who fear, and often experience judgment by members of the Catholic Church might be surprised to find Catholics, in imitation of Jesus, reaching out to enter into solidarity with them through ministries of listening, such as crisis pregnancy counseling and postabortion ministries. While these ministries provide important expressions of ecclesial solidarity and identify the need for familial solidarity, ecclesial solidarity needs to expand beyond these particular ministries to be a significant characteristic of the community as a whole. The Catholic Church, as a community of disciples, needs to grow in its capacity to share the good news of God's love with those whose choices might be contrary to

Catholic teaching and to recognize the ways in which these women's and men's encounters with Christ might lead them to evangelize the Catholic community. Let us look at developments and areas for growth in the Catholic community's response to teens and young adults who are becoming parents earlier than expected.

Young, Pregnant, and Alone?

Undoubtedly, the challenges of teenage and young adult pregnancy predate the changes in abortion laws in the United States. Yet the changes of the late 1960s and early 1970s raised awareness about circumstances in which women need support to carry a pregnancy to term and, at the same time, created a context in which abortion more readily served as a substitute for that support. One response to this situation was the development of crisis pregnancy centers, offering emotional and material support to pregnant women in need. From their earliest "Pastoral Plan for Pro-life Activities," the U.S. Catholic bishops have supported and encouraged this type of pastoral care for pregnant women, whether provided by a church-sponsored agency or in collaboration with another organization.[5] At its best, this ministry of listening provides support through solidarity that empowers a woman to choose life for herself and her unborn child and helps her address the challenges that she faces.

Whether by intent or circumstances, crisis pregnancy centers serve primarily, if not exclusively, pregnant women, and there is much for the church to learn from these women. As we listen to these women's stories, the differences in their backgrounds and needs emerge. They are racially, ethnically, and religiously diverse. These women are typically young and single; many are finishing their education and others are beginning their careers. For students, their educational levels range from junior high school to graduate school, and the economic background of their families of origin ranges from welfare to wealthy. The needs of these women vary greatly: from medical care they cannot afford because of a lack of health insurance to employment that pays a living wage, from educational accommodations to alternative housing, to name a few. Some turn to crisis pregnancy centers because of the pressure they face from parents or partner to abort. Others come from families who would respond with support if only they knew about the pregnancy. Their partners, parents, and partners' parents offer different degrees of support and exercise different levels of influence in their considerations about the future.

Not only do we need to listen to the stories of pregnant women, but we also need to offer a ministry of listening to their partners. Since the partner's perspective is often heard only indirectly at crisis pregnancy centers, the Catholic community needs to be more intentional about offering a ministry of listening to young men who learn that they are fathers. These young men might learn that expectations about their role in the child's future are greater or less than they would desire. Those who are students could face financial responsibilities that are daunting. This might call into question their ability to pursue their career plans. These young men also face the question of how they envision their future relationship with the child's mother. Just as there is a need to be in solidarity with young women who experience the burden of facing a challenging pregnancy, so too is there a need to be in solidarity with young men in these situations. Because the political rhetoric and legal environment insist that women alone have the right to make decisions about pregnancy, some men think that they must be silent about their concerns. An intentional ministry of listening for young, single fathers would challenge this, and it could help them discern ways to contribute to the decision-making process and create a space for them to share their experiences.

When young people share the news of pregnancy with parents, they may be inviting a ministry of listening from their familial homes. In this case, parents have the opportunity to exercise solidarity or alienation in relationship to their child and their child's partner. When the home becomes a place of listening and support in the process of discernment about the future, parents begin the process of offering life-giving solidarity to both their child and grandchild. From these conversations, a variety of concerns will emerge that they can address together, whether more immediate questions like housing, medical expenses, employment, or continuation of education, or long-term questions such as who will raise the child after birth.[6] When parents refuse to enter into solidarity with the young pregnant woman and her partner, the young people face greater challenges in carrying the pregnancy to term.

A lack of solidarity in the familial home during pregnancy characterizes the stories of many postabortive women who turn to ministries of listening, such as Project Rachel and Rachel's Vineyard.[7] Theresa Burke, the founder of Rachel's Vineyard, recounts such a story in her first chapter of *Forbidden Grief: The Unspoken Pain of Abortion*. Gina shared:

> I came home from college on a Friday to tell them about the pregnancy and what we were planning to do. . . . My dad hit the roof. He wanted to know what he ever did to deserve this. Dad took my boyfriend into the kitchen to have a man-to-man talk. They would not let me in. Dad tried to pressure him to convince me that abortion was the best thing.[8]

Despite Gina's protests insisting that she did not want an abortion, her mother took her to the abortion clinic. Her parents feared that she would not finish school and would raise a child in poverty without the support of her boyfriend, who failed to provide financial support for the child he already had. Gina's father was not open to listening to the plan his daughter and her partner developed in light of her pregnancy. He was concerned that her pregnancy would reflect negatively on him and did not want others to know about it. Her father wanted to control the situation by using abortion to return her life to the way it was before the pregnancy, not realizing that a true return to the past is not possible. Like Gina's mother, he wanted her to continue her education and feared the future that she and her child might have. Gina's story of lacking familial solidarity is not an isolated occurrence, as stories shared by other women suggest.[9]

When the Catholic community enters into solidarity with young women like Gina, by loving them as they are and empowering them to make life-giving choices, the church evangelizes like Jesus did at the well. Often though, members of the community act more like the disciples, who avoid interaction because of community expectations regarding sexuality. In contrast, women who have experienced solidarity from the church through crisis pregnancy centers and later desire to enter into solidarity with pregnant women teach the church powerfully through this solidarity, just as the woman at the well evangelized her community.

How might the church grow in its capacity to listen and respond to the needs of young pregnant women and their partners? Given the pastoral plan's understanding of this activity in terms of pastoral care, the Catholic community would do well to develop a diocesan ministerial formation and interdisciplinary training program to prepare crisis pregnancy center volunteers, as well as others, for some of the complex situations that they will encounter. A ministerial formation program would provide a foundation for understanding this work as part of a response to a call to discipleship. The interdisciplinary training program could draw on the expertise of doctors, nurses, psychologists, spiritual directors, educators, and attorneys with expertise in welfare and employment law, to name a few. The presentations and cases would prepare people to consider factors, such as those mentioned above, influencing the perspectives of the young pregnant woman, her partner, and their parents. Through their presentations and evaluations of both representative cases and extremely challenging cases, these experts could provide the stimulus for crisis pregnancy center volunteers to become more effective ministers.

Not only could this program serve those preparing to work in crisis pregnancy centers but it could also be a form of continuing education for Catholic educators, youth ministers, and young adult ministers, so that more Catholic ministers could become prepared to engage in a ministry of listening with young people affected by a crisis pregnancy.[10] As those ministering to young people gain experience in this form of service, they would benefit from gathering for theological reflection about their ministry, which could both deepen their ministerial engagement and inform the wider Catholic community about social justice issues that arise from their ministries. This theological reflection could lead the church to foster familial solidarity proactively, particularly when a young person sought support during a crisis pregnancy from a teacher, youth minister, or crisis pregnancy center before a parent.

Structured as a Pro-Life Church?

The Catholic Church's response to crisis pregnancies often focuses on pastoral care for individuals, including both material and emotional support. This pastoral care needs to be complemented by communal self-reflection and transformation to create conditions that support life through structural change. Since continuation of education and employment are primary concerns for pregnant teens and young adults, we will consider how a structural approach might lead to change in each instance. Some of the considerations affect men and women alike. Others are uniquely focused on the pregnant woman, who is more likely to face discrimination and other challenges because of her physical condition.

Surprising as it might sound, Catholic high schools and colleges should be suspicious if they do not have visibly pregnant students on campus. Whether students resort to abortion or leave school to carry a pregnancy to term, the absence of visibly pregnant students invites reflection on improving the school's structures to encourage students to continue their education while pregnant. Even if the school's policy allows a pregnant student to continue her education as the bishops' pastoral plan calls for,[11] she might face marginalization because of student culture and policies restricting full participation in the community's life.

At times, Catholic high schools expect the pregnant student to continue her education at home while pregnant. This often reflects the fear of administrators and teachers that the presence of a pregnant student at school will undermine their efforts to communicate Catholic teaching about marriage and sexuality. Such actions, however, undermine Catholic pro-life teaching. In order to embody this teaching, schools need to structure themselves in such a way as to encourage pregnant students to continue to attend classes and participate in the life of the school while they carry their pregnancies to term. By listening to students, especially those who have been pregnant, the school can discern concrete changes it might need to make, ranging from attendance policies to the size of desks.

Catholic colleges and universities also face this challenge of identifying policies and practices that are obstacles for pregnant students. For residential students, the school's housing policy needs to be considered to ensure that students can live in the residence hall while pregnant (or return to a residence hall after a leave of absence). University health services need to evaluate billing policies in terms of confidentiality so that students do not have reason to fear parents learning of a pregnancy test from a bill. Student health insurance policies need to provide maternity coverage and make coverage for dependents available. These are just a few examples of structural changes that might result from an institutional self-examination. The participation of students who are aware of challenges at their own institution will enhance the self-evaluation of institutional structures and policies.[12] By giving witness to the significance of structural changes, the church will be able to advocate with credibility for similar changes in other educational institutions in society.

The Catholic Church's pro-life witness and advocacy for pregnant students needs to be complemented by witness and advocacy for single, pregnant employees. The Catholic Church struggles with giving this type of witness. Given the church's teaching about marriage and sexuality, a church employee's pregnancy outside of marriage potentially threatens an aspect of the Catholic institution's mission, as the case of Michelle McCusker and St. Rose of Lima School illustrates.[13] Because her pregnancy as a single, Catholic woman did not embody church teaching about marriage and sexual ethics, the school fired this Catholic grade school teacher so that her presence would not undermine one of the values that the school was trying to teach. This action, however, undermined another value that the school was presumably trying to teach, that is, the importance of supporting and respecting life. McCusker has reminded the Catholic community that firing a single, pregnant woman who is carrying her pregnancy to term fails to embody the church's pro-life teaching. In this case, the school needs to think creatively about how to teach both about marriage as the context for pregnancy and about the need to be in solidarity with, rather than cause economic hardship for, one carrying a pregnancy to term.

Recognizing the need for greater ecclesial solidarity with young pregnant students and professionals through systemic change as well as the need for familial solidarity made evident through the sharing of women who have experienced crisis pregnancies and abortions, we turn to the experience of those who learn they are going to be grandparents earlier than expected and consider how the Emmaus story might help the church offer them pastoral care.

Disappointment and Fear in the Familial Home

In the story of the disciples traveling to Emmaus (Luke 24:1–35), one encounters disciples whose expectations about the future have been shattered by Jesus' death on the cross. They had hoped he would redeem Israel, but his death appeared to prevent that from being possible. While they had heard the proclamation that Jesus Christ is alive from the women who had been at the tomb, they could not believe what they heard. They needed someone to walk with them and interpret these events in light of their traditional Jewish faith in the Scriptures. This experience touched their hearts, and they invited the stranger to share a meal with them. In the midst of offering hospitality, they recognized the presence of Christ in their midst.[14]

This story might offer a paradigm for pastoral care of parents whose expectations about the future have been shattered by the news of their teenage or young adult child's pregnancy. Like Christ, the church needs to walk with these grandparents, allowing them to share their disappointment and fears about the future. This ministry would allow the church to hear directly what is often heard only indirectly.

Parents often hope that their child will live the "American dream" by being more successful than they are. In some cases this means finishing high school or college; in other cases it means becoming a doctor or a lawyer. Whether this success is defined in terms of level of education, income, or prestige of occupation, parents often have either a general or specific vision of their child's future work. They might also have a vision of the type of person they hope their child will marry and the age their child will be when he or she has a child. Parents' hopes for their child's future with regard to work and family set the stage for disappointment when they learn from their teenager or young adult that they are going to be grandparents. Disappointment is a natural response to learning that a dream about the future seems less likely to be realized. However, an intense focus on the future that might not be or on a past action that cannot be changed endangers solidarity with their child in the present situation.

Not only do parents often have to confront the disappointment of shattered dreams, but they also have a legitimate basis for some fears about their child and grandchild's economic future. As the church more effectively witnesses through and advocates for structural changes that support pregnant students and employees, as discussed in the previous section, the church's actions begin to address some of these fears. Even as structures change, though, the church will need to accompany parents whose fears might prevent them from seeing possibilities that would allow their child and grandchild to flourish. These might involve marriage, adoption, or the extended family participating in raising the child, depending on the circumstances. The parents do not need to propose a solution in response to their fears but support their child and their child's partner in their discernment about the future.

After hearing their disappointments and fears, the church needs to invite the parents to interpret the events in light of faith by looking for ways in which Christ is present in the midst of their shattered dreams. A pastoral minister or volunteer could facilitate a faith-sharing group for these parents at different stages on the journey. This could provide an opportunity to reflect on the activity of God in their lives as well as in their child's and grandchild's lives. Those who have just learned the news could receive the gift of hope from others who have gone through the experience. This ecclesial solidarity with the new grandparents could support them in offering hospitality and solidarity in the familial home.

Conclusion

As the Catholic Church reflects on strategies for being pro-life that are attentive to the experience of pregnancy hitting home, the community as a whole is challenged to both learn from and participate in ministries of listening to those affected by crisis pregnancies. This listening often reveals the need for greater familial and ecclesial solidarity. The church can express this solidarity not only through pastoral care but also through continued reflection on possible structural changes to be more pro-life as an institution. Structural changes regarding education and employment policies and practices in Catholic institutions will empower the church's pro-life witness. This will also provide credibility for the church to engage in pro-life advocacy in society on these issues. This witness and advocacy express solidarity not only with the pregnant woman and her partner but also with the larger familial context in which her parents and her partner's parents might fear for their child and grandchild's future. The fears and disappointments of those becoming grandparents earlier than expected are rarely heard in the ecclesial community, and the church needs to provide pastoral care for them as they face the challenge of offering solidarity to their child and grandchild.

Chapter 15

Fostering the Next Generation
of Faithful Women

Jane E. Regan

I REMEMBER ONE OF THE FIRST TIMES that my daughter and I went grocery shopping, not long after she had arrived from Russia at the age of four. The color and wonder of the gumball and candy machines lining the store's entryway attracted her attention, and she darted toward them. Catching up with her as she gazed at the glass containers with their enticing gums and trinkets, I leaned down, placed my arm around her shoulders, and said, "Oh, Natalya, you know what? Regans don't get gum from gum machines." As we turned away, she looked up at me solemnly and nodded. Though her English language was limited, she'd gotten the message; she received the tradition that this was something Regans just didn't do.

Over the next several shopping trips, we repeated the interchange and soon we walked right past the once attractive machines; after awhile I doubt she even noticed them. But the depth of her internalization of the Regan worldview was made clear about a year later when her sister arrived from Russia at the age of two and a half.

Again, one of our first excursions as a family of three was to the grocery store. Before Catie could even take in the wonders of the gumball machine, Natalya took her by the hand, walked her over to the machines, stooped down next to her, and proclaimed the truth that she had received: "Regans don't get gum from gum machines." I remember reflecting on the incident that day and thinking many more times about it in the days and years that followed. If only we could pass on all of our beliefs and practices so easily to our daughters! And if only all of our beliefs and practices could be so clearly articulated as simple statements of fact.

On "Handing On" Faith

The theme for this essay as it was first proposed to me was "Handing On the Faith to Our Daughters." The importance of this topic to the broader conversation reflected in this collection of essays seemed clear to me: as Catholic women strategize about the church, articulating hopes for its future, our thoughts naturally turn to the women who will follow us, expecting that things will be better for them. This topic also resonated with my work as a religious educator; I am convinced that the perspective offered by the Christian faith, and specifically by the Catholic tradition, is worth embodying myself and sharing with others. And, as the single mother of two teen-aged daughters, this topic is dear to my heart as I strive to provide them with the guidance and resources they need to be and become strong women of faith.

As I began working on the essay, however, problematic implications of the title surfaced. "Handing On the Faith to Our Daughters" proves too static to express the deep concerns and dynamic commitments I share with many others as Catholic women and as parents. "Handing on" sounds too much like we are dealing with a carefully tied package that we place neatly in unbroken form into the next person's hands, hoping that she[1] will hand it on complete and intact, and possibly even unopened, to the next. In this context "the Faith" became that tied package. Comprising beliefs, prayers, moral practices, or sacred texts, the term "the faith" implies a singular completeness that runs counter to the vision and vibrancy that I hope for my daughters. And this is not just my hope for "Our Daughters" but for all of the women — friends, sisters, mentors, teachers — who form and transform our daughters into the women they are and are becoming. And so, in this essay I seek to examine the foundations and strategies for fostering the next generation of faithful women.

I begin with an exploration of faith itself and a consideration of the faithful women that we are intending to nurture in faith. Drawing on the work of developmental theorists, I examine the dynamics of faith and the movements of faith from adolescence into adulthood. In light of this discussion of faith I suggest what it means to be faithful women, freeing the word "faithful" from any narrowly limited connotations. I conclude then with the proposal of some strategies that support all of us as we strive to be and become the church of our deepest hopes.

Faith That Is Beyond Belief

A contemporary theorist who looks at the way in which faith develops or changes over a person's life is James Fowler. Influenced by Paul Tillich and Richard Niebuhr, Fowler understands faith as a universal human concern, or as Tillich would say, "that which is of ultimate concern."[2] Working out of the developmental frameworks of Jean Piaget and Lawrence Kohlberg, Fowler posits a sequential, hierarchical, generally invariant schema through which the person passes in her faith development. We can examine each of these two dimensions of Fowler's theory in turn.[3]

Faith as Human Meaning Making

In *Stages of Faith* Fowler expresses the fundamental role of faith within the quintessential human activity of meaning making: "Faith is a person's or group's way of moving into the force field of life. It is our way of finding coherence in and giving meaning to the multiple forces and relations that make up our lives. Faith is a person's way of seeing him- or herself in relation to others against a background of shared meaning and purpose."[4] Faith, according to Fowler, "has to do with the making, maintenance and transformation of human meaning."[5] Used in this sense, faith differs from belief.

"Belief" refers to the categorical expression of that toward which the individual expresses or experiences faith. "Faith" refers to the basic orientation of the person, the way in which she knows the world and engages in the activity of meaning making. As such, faith is not necessarily theistic or even religious. The "object" of her faith — the ultimate environment in which the centers of value have meaning and unity — provides the context for the constitutive meaning-making activity that we understand as human knowing. In this sense, faith is not so much focused on beliefs or moral practices or church membership. It has more to do with our mode of engaging with self, world, and the transcendent as well as with the commitments that give life meaning.

Within this understanding of faith, the heart of the task of fostering (and being) faithful women becomes developing an awareness and connection with what is most important to us, what gives meaning to our lives. Where does our passion rest? That is where we can connect most deeply to the source of meaning in our lives — to our faith. We will return to this idea of naming our passion when we consider some strategies for fostering faithful women.

Faith in Transition

Considering the framework of Fowler's understanding of faith, we turn now to look at his presentation of the stages of faith,[6] focusing upon the adult stages. Keep in mind that we understand each stage of faith not as a single entity but as a unified syndrome of ways in which persons engage with the world and with their ultimate center of meaning and value.

The first three stages of Fowler's schema — numbered Zero through Two — describe the faith perspective of childhood and correlate with the movement of intellectual development articulated by Jean Piaget. At the conclusion of these stages, the child has moved into what might best be described as a socialized faith. She has taken on the ways of making meaning that she has received from her parents, her teachers, and, finally, her peer group. Fowler designates this as "Stage Three: Synthetic-Conventional Faith," which generally coalesces around the ages of twelve and thirteen and can serve as an adequate faith perspective into adulthood, as it does for many their whole lives.

As the title of the stage indicates, the focus here is on creating a system or structure for meaning making within which the stories, images, and values learned or experienced during childhood can be worked together into a useable whole. This synthesis takes place and is defined in relationship to a group. While the reference group is larger than in the earlier stages — from parent, to family, to beyond the family — there is nonetheless a perspective of faith in which what "we" do and what "we" believe is important. This "we" can become increasingly sophisticated over time as the focal point of the defining convention moves from local parish to wider church and beyond. Within Stage Three there is a growing ability to recognize what is central to one's reference group and what is not. The growing sophistication of conventional faith as it is expressed in adulthood is nonetheless shaped by what "we" believe and the values that "we" hold. These serve as the framework for how a girl or young woman in Stage Three makes meaning of her life, coming to understand herself, to grow in her awareness of the world around her, and to shape her relationship to God.

In Stage Three the worldview that has formed and been formed by the person's primary reference groups is synthesized and internalized. The process of taking in (assimilation) and actively interpreting and making meaning (accommodation) of new experiences introduced through the developing child's and adolescent's intellectual capacity and his or her expanding social world takes place within the established frame of meaning of the dominant reference groups. This process of socialization leads to a faith that can sustain a person over a lifetime.

But what if the coherent framework for meaning making and faith knowing amalgamated in Stage Three comes under challenge by disagreement or contradiction within the primary reference groups? What happens when valued authority sources — the defining agents of what "we" believe — begin to disagree among themselves? What happens when the person's expanding world introduces her to people with differing beliefs and ways of life; when "they" are recognized as worthy of admiration and emulation; when "they" offer a viable and attractive alternative to what "we" believe? And what happens when the belief system and the image of God, which were received in this process of socialization, are inadequate for dealing with the challenges of life? These are all factors that initiate the transition into "Stage Four: Individuated-Reflective Faith."

Often coalescing in the early twenties, though for many it does not emerge until the mid-thirties or beyond, Stage Four is, in effect, a leaving home, leaving the often tacitly held worldview that has been received and moving into one's own explicit worldview. With this comes a reinterpretation of one's self-identity; whereas previously it had been shaped as a compilation of the variety of roles one maintained in relationships within the significant reference groups, now one begins to define the self as identifiable beyond that context. For the established Stage Four faith, I am first myself and then part of the group. "Self (identity) and outlook (worldview) are differentiated from those of others and become acknowledged factors in the reactions, interpretations and judgments one makes on the actions of the self and others."[7] With this comes "an interruption of reliance on external sources of authority."[8] While influenced by the views of others, the final arbiter of decision making is the internal conviction and personally appropriated values and commitments that form the individual's frame of meaning.

An essential element of the move into Stage Four is a "demythologizing" of the symbols, myths, and rituals of the tradition. The emphasis on articulating a personally coherent, internally consistent framework of meaning leads the person living out of Stage Four to value the symbolic as meaningful if it can be translated into propositions or conceptual formulations. The symbols have lost their power to serve as a point of entry into the transcendent. It is often this foundational "accomplishment" of Stage Four that serves as the platform for the transition into Stage Five. Fowler describes it this way:

> Stories, symbols, myths and paradoxes from one's own or other traditions may insist on breaking in upon the neatness of the previous faith. Disillusionment with one's compromises and recognition that life is more complex than Stage Four's logic of clear distinctions and abstract concepts can comprehend, press one toward a more dialectical and multileveled approach to life truth.[9]

Stage Five, "Conjunctive Faith," is characterized by a postcritical reappropriation of the symbols of one's own tradition and of the power of symbols to be transformative of human consciousness. One is able to suspend one's critical perspective and engage again with the symbols, myths, and rituals of one's tradition.[10] There is a reinterpretation and reintegration of the richness of aspects of faith from earlier stages and a willingness to live with the ambiguity that such a reintegration generates. One is able again to be overwhelmed by the power of the first fire of Easter while still being able, at a later time, to step back and critique the liturgical event in light of aesthetics or even ritual theory.

Fowler describes the person at Stage Five as engaging in dialogical knowing: "In dialogical knowing the multiplex structure of the world is invited to disclose itself. In a mutual 'speaking' and 'hearing,' knower and known converse in an I-Thou relationship. The knower seeks to accommodate her or his knowing to the structure of that which is being known before imposing her or his own categories upon it."[11] This renewed openness to one's own tradition, the ability to engage and live with ambiguity, and the mode of dialogical knowing contribute to one's perspective on truth. Where once "truth" was defined within the confines of the "we" (Stage Three) or circumscribed by the individual's personally appropriated framework (Stage Four), the person at Stage Five recognizes the multilayered thickness of truth. This contributes to the apperception that each articulation of truth is only partial and always in need of being complemented by the insights of other traditions. As Fowler points out, the relativity of the various traditions is not only in relationship to one another but in their common relativity to that which they are attempting to mediate.[12]

As with the other stages, the seeds of the transition to "Stage Six: Universalizing Faith" are found in the characteristics of Stage Five. The genuine awareness and openness to the other and the appreciation of the symbols and myths of other traditions that are part of Stage Five serve as a prerequisite for the movement to Stage Six. While recognizing the possibility of an inclusive community, a person embodying Stage Five lives between an untransformed world and a potentially transforming vision. The person with Stage Six faith works to give expression to the most inclusive of ultimate environments both in her own person and in the structures of society that oppress. While rare, the impact of those people whom Fowler names as Stage Six is significant: Martin Luther King Jr., Dag Hammarskjöld, Gandhi.[13] Their significant contribution to the transformation of world without regard for the preservation of self is unquestionable.

Faithfully Faithful

This consideration of Fowler's understanding of faith and its development across women's lives casts an important light on what the term "faithful women" might mean. A dictionary definition of "faithful" includes strong, positive words such as "trustworthy," "steadfast," "firm in resolve," "conscientious," "loyal." And yet there is a shadow there, cast perhaps by our ecclesial history, where "faithful," particularly "*the* faithful," implies a blind or uncritical fidelity, childish or careless trust, and loyalty that is too easily given. But I believe that the perspective on faith that we are examining here allows us to see faithful-ness not simply in terms of relationship to authority. Rather, it challenges us to see faithful-ness as fidelity in our own meaning-making journey.

A woman's movement across these stages, from Three to Four to Five, represents both a movement out toward expansion and a turning inward. Across these stages, there is a moving out from her world; her awareness of others and the ability to take the perspective of others is an enlarging movement. At the same time, there is a turning inward to claim an authority in her own wisdom as it is read within the wisdom of her community. There is a returning to reembrace the richness of symbols and myths that have shaped her childhood faith.

The movement across these adolescent and adult stages can be thought of as a fundamental shift that begins with being "faithful to" and moves toward being "faithful in." The essence of Stage Three is one's connection with and allegiance to primary reference groups. For the person in Stage Three the task is to be *faithful to* the teachings, way of life, and sense of identity held by the group. This is often most clearly expressed as being faithful to designated authority sources. The transition from Stage Three to Stage Four is instigated by a questioning or a challenging of that to which one has been faithful. The reestablishing of equilibrium in the meaning-making process then involves a shift in what it means to be faithful. The locus of one's faithfulness moves from received teachings, defined identity, and external authority toward creating meaning within personally appropriated teaching, self-identity, and internal authority.

Note that I use the term "shift *toward*" rather than "shift *to*"; it's in these prepositions that the key to our renewed understanding of "faithful" might be found. While the dynamics of a socialized faith (through Stage Three) can be characterized as being faithful to received and generally externally held tradition, identity, and authority, moving beyond this signals an entering into an ongoing process of meaning making. And we are called to be faithful *in* our engagement with that process.

The apparently minor nature of these word shifts must not cause us to miss the significance of their meaning. To claim this shift is to understand faithful women not as women faithful to the church, but women who are faithful in the process of being and becoming the church. Such faithful women give neither their fidelity naively nor their loyalty too easily. Rather, they are steadfast in their commitment to the always challenging, often uncertain, and at times confrontational process of coming to faith in today's church.

Strategies for Fostering Faithful Women

How do we support the next generation of faithful women as well as one another in this work? Here I propose three strategies: naming where our passions rest, talking with our daughters about what gives us hope, and acknowledging the challenges in being faithful women.

Strategy One: Naming Our Passions

Flight attendants offer us a reminder each time that we prepare for take off: put on your own oxygen mask before you try to assist anyone else. This advice surely applies here: as we strive to foster faithfulness in others, we begin by considering our own ways of being faithful women. I pointed out earlier that the understanding of faith and faithfulness is not concerned with belief claims or allegiance to authority. To be faithful entails developing an awareness and connection with what is most important to us regarding God, self, others, and the world, what gives meaning to our lives. We ask ourselves where our passions rest because it is there that we can connect most deeply to the source of meaning in our lives — to our faith.

In the midst of our lives we are challenged to carve out time and space to ask ourselves those questions that bring our passions and commitments into focus: Where do I invest my time and myself? What gives me joy? What relationships warrant my full presence and engagement? Where does my hope rest?

As we think about these questions let's note that the Catholic tradition offers some long-standing practices that can be helpful to this process: *lectio divina,* contemplative prayer, the Spiritual Exercises of Ignatius, the daily *examen,* and spiritual direction. We are called to be faithful in practicing these traditions.

Strategy Two: Conveying What Gives Hope

A friend recounted to me that it was in the months following the sudden death of her husband that she realized how seldom she had spoken with her now grown children about her faith. Convinced that "actions speak louder than words," as her children were growing up, my friend had left unspoken her understanding of God's enduring presence and her confidence in God's grace in her life. "So," she said, "after Jim's death, when I tried to express my sense of hope in the midst of sorrow, the kids had a hard time hearing it as anything other than holy platitudes. I really think that if I had talked with them about my faith and the source of my hope in more day-to-day events, they might have been able to hear it better when they were dealing with their dad's death." I'm not sure if it would have made a difference to her children's experience, but I am convinced that talking about our faith, taking about that which matters to us is important for us as faithful women.

I am convinced that adults learn best about their faith through being in sustained, critical conversation with others about things that matter.[14] This is true for several reasons:

- Conversation provides us the opportunity to practice articulating our faith. We get practice in naming where our passion rests, in giving "an accounting for the hope that is within us" (1 Pet. 3:15). In the process *we* come to further clarity.

◆ Conversation helps us to learn to attend with care to the faith expressions of others. The rules of conversation — speak from your own experience; speak with the intention of being clear, not of convincing the other; listen with openness and in a way that expresses mutual respect — are important precepts in supporting one another in our journey of faith and fostering the next generation of faithful women.

◆ Conversation serves as a context for recognizing pluralism within our community. Sustained conversation brings us beyond the first level of discourse, where the lines of agreement and disagreement are fairly clearly drawn. In sustained conversation we recognize the variances in the perspectives of those whom we thought agreed with us and the shared views of those who seemed to disagree. In either case, we come to a deeper recognition of the complexity of our faith and an appreciation for the faith lives of others.

◆ Conversation serves as a context for our assisting one another in living our faith. As adults gather for conversation about things that matter, we inevitably move to the most important of faith questions: "So what?" So what does my faith mean for my life, for how I make decisions, raise my children, spend my money, and so forth? It is in sustained conversation that we support one another in being and becoming faithful women.

Strategy Three: Acknowledging Areas of Challenge in Being Faithful

Being and becoming faithful women is not easy. Much of the world that forms us and that we form militates against such faithfulness. We live in and are part of a consumerist culture that values what we have or how much we earn over who we are and what we care about. We are a militaristic country that believes (or acts like it believes) that might makes right and the ends justify the means, and we live in social contexts in which working and producing take precedence over consciousness and reflection. And we live in a media-saturated setting that prizes the superstar and the scandalous and that is, at best, ambiguous about the place of sexuality and the image of women. Ours is a human-centric world that is slowly (and belatedly) coming to recognize the devastation caused by human consumption and that is only now moving toward solutions because of the recognition of the threat to human existence. And if that weren't enough, we are being and becoming faithful women in a sinful church that must grapple with all of these challenges as well as some of its own.

Taking the time to be aware of these cultural, social, and ecclesial dynamics and understanding their effect on women in particular and on the ways in which both women and men make meaning of their world is paramount. By engaging in sustained conversation with our daughters and with other women about our experiences of and perspectives on culture, society, world, and church, we will be more able to work together for transformation.

In fostering the next generation of faithful women, we must reclaim an important element of our tradition: *Catholic realism.* Embodying the Catholic predilection to select both/and rather than either/or, we can refuse the dichotomies drawn between saints and sinners, good and evil, sacred and secular. Rooted in a strong theology of the incarnation, Catholic realism invites neither a naïve optimism nor a doomed pessimism. It calls us to face fully into things as they really are — including the pervasive expressions of sin and evil — without losing track of the present offer of grace.

Where does this leave us in our work of fostering the next generation of faithful women? In a word: *hopeful.* We are not ignorant regarding sinful aspects of church and society, and we will not allow the darkness to overshadow the light. As we strive to be and become faithful women, we affirm that *this* is the faith that we are handing on to our daughters, and to our daughters' daughters.

Part Five

FEMINIST ASCETICAL
PRACTICES

Chapter 16

Making Room for Beauty

Susan A. Ross

I T MAY SEEM STRANGE AT FIRST to be talking about beauty in a section on
feminist *ascetical* practices. For one thing, asceticism is usually associated
with giving something up, with *not* having. And since beauty is of necessity
tied to material reality — we have to see, hear, touch, taste, smell, in order to
experience something as beautiful — it would seem that asceticism would mean
giving up beauty. Aren't ascetical practices a means of distancing oneself from
the world? And haven't feminists worked hard to show that appreciation for
the world and for the body is a good thing? Moreover, feminists have been
highly critical of the ways that beauty is used as a measure of women's worth.
To "make room for beauty" might be understood to mean taking more time
for makeup, clothes shopping, and home decoration, and, if so, doesn't this
mean doing all of those things that feminists have fought so hard to move
beyond?

As art critics, philosophers, and theologians have written, and as some have
lamented, beauty has lost its luster in the contemporary world. We are suspicious of beauty, presuming that it invites a focusing on the superficial, on
appearance rather than inner reality. The modern art world then wants to see
reality, rather than an air-brushed picture of romantic or bourgeois ideas of
beauty. The arts, some argue, ought to shock rather than comfort, ought to
make us confront reality rather than putting a pretty face on it. Further influencing our perceptions of beauty are unrealistic standards of body size that
continue to exert a powerful and negative influence, particularly on women.
Beauty has certainly been the object of much misunderstanding.[1]

In response to these assumptions and presumptions regarding "the beautiful," there are voices in the contemporary church calling for a "return to
beauty." Some of these voices long for a return to the days of elegant Latin
liturgies,[2] a model of womanhood based in the quiet and humble Virgin Mary,[3]
and a hierarchically ordered church where clergy and laity know their proper
places.[4] These images of the church, they argue, are beautiful: in them one finds
order, symmetry, and an intimation of the heavenly future. Such portrayals of
beauty suggest that women ought to remain in the background of the church —
even relegated to the rear, in some traditions — making their presence unob-
trusive and even invisible. The ideal picture of the liturgy, in this portrayal, is
devoid of women in any visible place at the altar. Feminist and activist Catholic
women, from this perspective, are perceived as coarsening the church, ruining

150

its beautiful, elegant language with their calls for "inclusivity" and with their pleas that the traditional, hierarchical church become more democratic. In response to this picture, a feminist might ask: Who needs beauty? Don't we need justice?

Well, we need both. And I am not alone in arguing for the linkage of beauty and justice: a number of contemporary U.S. Hispanic theologians suggest that the two be joined.[5] In this essay, I make a case for women's practices of beauty that are also practices of justice. I suggest that women (as well as men and children) can make the church and the world not only a better place, but a more beautiful place, and that these two goals, beauty and justice, need not be in conflict: indeed, they work together beautifully! I will describe practices of beauty that can contribute to a more just life, particularly for women in the U.S. Catholic Church. These suggested practices arise out of conscious attention to the diverse experiences of women and out of concern to retrieve a sense of beauty that is mindful of the ways that women have been excluded from its creation and recognition.

I first wish to examine what we mean by "asceticism" and how it relates to beauty. What is a "feminist ascetical practice of beauty"? Second, I will look at how women have been excluded from beauty or isolated in a narrow conception of it. Third, I will suggest some "practices of beauty," drawing some conclusions as to how practicing these "virtues of beauty" might open ways for women, children, and men to make the church and the world a more beautiful place, and in so doing, render it also a more just place.

An Ascetical Example of Beauty

The purpose of *askesis* has traditionally been one of discipline and training. Genuine asceticism is not a goal in and of itself; rather, it is directed toward something larger. The goal of fasting, for example, is not to make oneself thin or to develop a distaste for food. To the contrary, it is to develop an appreciation for the goodness and beauty of food, to become more aware of our dependence on it, and to give us pause for reflection on its role in our lives. If we never think about what we eat and simply do it mindlessly, as we so often do — eating whatever is most readily accessible at a fast food restaurant, popping a frozen dinner in the microwave — we lose our appreciation for what food truly is: sustenance, taste, nourishment.[6]

The film *Babette's Feast* offers a wonderful picture of the difference between true and false asceticism in relation to food. The film's heroine, after fleeing from Paris to Denmark for political refuge, finds herself working for two elderly sisters whose late father had founded an ascetical sect. They live very simply, and Babette, a celebrated chef, accommodates herself to the sisters' lives, cooking simple meals of salted cod and potato soup. When she wins the French lottery (her nephew had been buying tickets for her since her departure), she decides to use her winnings to prepare a feast for the one hundredth anniversary of the founder's birth. Over the protests of the two sisters, both of whom had given up the possibility of marriage to continue their father's mission, Babette prepares a sumptuous feast for the tiny remnant of the sect, with course after course of gourmet food, including turtle soup, quail, and the finest French Champagne. The meal becomes a transformative experience for them as their petty quarrels fade away in the extravagant and celebratory feast. When the meal is over and the guests have gone home, the two sisters say goodbye to Babette, assuming that she will leave now that she is a wealthy woman. But Babette tells them that she has in fact spent every penny of her winnings on the feast and will remain with them as their servant.

Babette knew what it meant to live ascetically. Before she won the lottery, she purchased food for the sisters, herself, and the poor they assisted with care, taking time for the simplest meals, and appreciating the small pleasures of her life. I think that even when Babette lived in Paris as a chef, her approach to food would not have been qualitatively different. To be sure, she would have had good food every night, not just on the birthday of someone important. But her deliberate attention to using every part of the ingredients she had, her delight in a small glass of wine, her attention to the details of the table, indicate that this was not only how she cooked, but also how she lived.

The sisters, although they lived an ascetic life on the surface, were sparing in their attention to beauty in their lives. They focused on how little they could use, not how much they could enjoy the little they had. When Babette proposed the feast, they were at first aghast at the idea, and the expense, and only relented as a favor to Babette. At the dinner, they instructed the members of their sect to say "nothing about the food." But when the old suitor of one of the sisters came as a surprise guest to the feast, he could not help but exclaim over the exquisite repast. Only then did the other guests reluctantly taste the wine and begin to savor the meal. The beauty of the food and the feast opened the hearts of the members of the sect. In their increasing delight and appreciation for the generous food, they became more generous with each other, moving beyond hurts and arguments that had festered for too long toward reconciliation.

Babette showed all of them what a true asceticism of beauty is: an approach to life that uses resources mindfully, appreciates the beauty that is made available to us, and shares it without counting the cost. She saw how beautiful food and thoughtful preparation could be an occasion not only of beauty but also of generosity. Babette was grateful for her lottery winnings but saw them as an opportunity to bring beauty and joy to her adopted community. She truly knew what asceticism for the sake of the Kin-dom of God was and is: a preparation for living in the beauty and joy of life with God here and in the hereafter.

This is what I mean by "ascetical practices of beauty": ways that we can live with the fullness of God's love for and joy in creation in our everyday lives. These practices are meant to offer a sort of "training" in how to live in this fullness here and now. The theologians who write of the need to retrieve a sense of God's beauty are right. But they are not always right, as I see it, in their suggestions regarding how human beings can best do this.

Women and Beauty

One need not look far in church documents to see concerns expressed about the negative implications of the presence of women or of problems with notions of women's beauty.[7] Warnings about women's dress and behavior in church go back to the earliest Fathers of the Church. Women have been relegated to the backs of churches, assigned to separate spaces within churches, ordered to cover their heads in churches, and forbidden to sing in churches. The voices of young boys — or, in the late Renaissance, the castrati — were preferred to the potentially seductive voices of women. In the church's liturgy and sacred spaces — the times and places where beauty has been given center stage, in soaring cathedrals, in exquisite works of art, in angelic music — women's presence has been carefully circumscribed since the beginning of the church's worship practices. Even in the more "enlightened" present, where women serve in pastoral and educational capacities, women are still seen as interlopers. While official church language and teaching about women no longer blame women for the sin of our first parents nor regard women as "misbegotten males," nevertheless the language and teaching continues to maintain the distinct or "special" identity of women, usually to be found in some form of biological or spiritual maternity. And prohibitions of women in the presence of the sacred still abound. For example, women cannot officially be installed as lectors or eucharistic ministers; they can, however, fill these offices as "extraordinary" ministers, when suitable males are not available.

In recent years, the growing popularity of Hans Urs von Balthasar's theological aesthetics has given much greater attention to the role of beauty in theology and liturgy. Yet Balthasar's theology, as Elizabeth Johnson has observed, is a theology that celebrates "the Eternal Feminine," an image of women that projects a quiet, maternal, and comforting image. This is more the projection of ideas of women by celibate males than something reflective of women's real experiences. Johnson argues that this image is in the long run a dead end, particularly when it comes to the place of women or "the feminine" in theological ideas.[8] Such an image is an idealized one of women that poses no threat to the traditional order of things.

Conceptions of beauty such as Balthasar's also stress the contemplative and spiritual dimensions of the perception of beauty, not its creation. Beauty is seen as eternal, more in line with the Enlightenment philosopher Immanuel Kant's version of the "sublime," which views "mere beauty" as tied to (lower) physical and concrete things and the "sublime" (a higher category than beauty) as spiritual, and eternal.[9] In this way of seeing, beauty is something that transcends the day-to-day existence we labor in and is evidence of the much higher, unearthly realms to which we are destined. Such ideas of beauty focus much less on the everyday beauty we may encounter in nature, in the earthly, and more on the transcendent beauty of the Eternal Divine. Within this casting, the most beautiful woman is the Virgin Mary, whose purity stands in opposition to the experiences of the vast majority of women who are sexually active and many of whom (but not enough of whom) find in sexual relations beauty of desire and joy.

In short, women's beauty has been — and often continues to be — viewed as a threat to the beauty of God and to the seriousness and holiness of proper religious expression in music, iconography, and dress. Male definitions of beauty, which emphasize unrealistic ideas of women and the spiritual over the material, often find the beauty of real women to be dangerous.

Feminist Ascetical Practices of Beauty

As I have suggested elsewhere, women have not been the major thinkers about beauty.[10] Women's approaches to beauty have historically tended to be more practical: in quilts, needlework, pots, fabrics, clothing. Women were actively discouraged from formal education in the arts and if they demonstrated any talent, they were encouraged to use it in the home or for their families. No doubt women's needlework has graced many churches. But it is almost always anonymous. By the same token, women historically have not spent much time reflecting on what "true beauty" really is. They have been busy making themselves and their homes beautiful (if they have had the resources). For many male thinkers about beauty, women have been seen as icons of beauty, or models for male artists to paint or draw, if they have not been in the kitchens and laundry rooms preparing food and washing the clothes of male artists. Women and men alike have been taught to see beauty in the same way, with the "male gaze" as something that both women and men adopt.

It is time to reclaim beauty as something more than what is in the pages of fashion or home decorating magazines, more than unrealistic expectations of body size or never-ending youthfulness. Women's historic and present practices of beauty do indeed have much to offer the church and the world, but women — as well as men and children — need to come to appreciate beauty in ways that our consumer culture does not. So I suggest here some practical ways of "making room for beauty" in our lives, and in so doing, making the world a better place.

Taking Time for Beauty

It seems that time is the most precious commodity for many people today. We are all busy, all overcommitted, and we struggle to get to work, the gym, the store, to daycare on time. Taking time for beauty might seem to be an impossible ideal — a great idea in theory, but who has the time?

My suggestions for "taking time for beauty" are actually very small steps that anyone can choose to open oneself up to beauty. One first step is to allow silent time during the day to enable ourselves to appreciate the beauty that we may pass by but barely notice. Something as small as turning off the radio or the CD player while driving can allow us to be more attentive to the world around us. Who are these people waiting for buses, driving alongside us, pushing a stroller? Who are these children walking home from school, the young boy with the dog, the old woman with the grocery cart? What are their hopes and dreams? What is it about the gray of a snowy February day that can inspire one to think about beauty? This practice is contemplative: it offers one the small space of time to take in what is going on around us.

Another initial step for allowing oneself to be more open to beauty is to consider how time too often spent in front of the television might be better used. Reading, needlework, playing or listening to music are all other ways of taking "down time" that we so often need in order to relax. While I enjoy television as much as anyone else (probably more than many!), I realize how television watching can alter my vision of what is beautiful. Margaret Miles, a historical theologian who has written much about women and beauty in the history of the church, suggests that the old practice of "custody of the eyes" might be a relevant practice to revive in the present.[11]

"Custody of the eyes" may seem antiquarian at first: it is the practice of being careful of what one sees, how one uses one's eyes. Religious orders counseled "custody of the eyes" when someone walked into a room, or when walking along a corridor. The idea was that one's thoughts were to be on God, not on getting distracted by others. A contemporary retrieval of this practice doesn't mean that we should walk around with downcast eyes, not looking at others as we walk by. It can mean, rather, paying attention to what we see, and how we use our senses. There is much that we cannot help but see, and much that we really need to see: injustice in the world, necessary knowledge for ourselves, our families, our work. But there is much that we do not need to see: countless television commercials, stores offering more and more clothes that we have no room for in overcrowded closets.

Recently I received an iPod as a Christmas gift and began using it when I walked our dogs. But I found that I was paying less attention to what the dogs were sniffing at. I stopped looking for the hawk that lives in our neighborhood and was not attending to the changing of the seasons: how the trees were beginning to bud, how the light was different at the same time of day. I still use my iPod, but I think carefully about what I listen to, and whether or not I am making the best use of my senses for the time that I am taking.

One practice that has received much media attention is group knitting, which is growing in popularity in women's circles. More and more women are getting together to learn how to knit, to share patterns and lives as they sit together. Knitting is basically a contemplative practice (if the pattern one is using is not too difficult). While women's needlework has hardly received the kind of attention that it deserves, such needlework is also a way for women (and children and men) to enjoy the feel of various yarns in one's fingers, to see something grow out of a ball of yarn, to enjoy presenting someone with a gift of something that one has knit. The "prayer shawl" ministry is one practice that joins knitting with prayer, as one knits a shawl for someone who is ill, or as a gift.[12]

My intention in naming these various practices is to suggest that there is beauty all around us, but we are usually too busy to notice it. Practices of beauty do not need to be large-scale. Opening oneself to beauty opens the heart at the same time. In her book *On Beauty and Being Just,* Elaine Scarry writes that beauty "greets" us, welcomes us.[13] Yet I wonder if we are able to pay attention to beauty's greeting.

There is also a great deal of ugliness around us. The South African theologian John de Gruchy has written about the disconnection between art and ethics, as art has come to be seen as ornamental and has lost its former social role. He quotes the philosopher Theodor Adorno, who says that the beautiful "needs the ugly as a negation through which to actualize itself."[14] The ugly, in the various forms it takes — injustice, careless use of resources, lack of respect for humanity — calls out for beauty as a corrective. It is for good reason that social scientists talk about the role of "broken windows" in slum areas, where the lack of care for the environment leads to a sense of despair and hopelessness. Ivone Gebara writes about how the poor in the Brazilian slums see the ugliness of their surroundings as indicative of the lack of care they receive from others.[15] "Attentiveness to what surrounds us is the first step to seeing the beauty that does exist and the need for beauty that might exist but does not."

Sharing in God's Beauty in Ritual

Women have typically been the ones who have made churches places of beauty. To be sure, the architects and builders have been the ones who have constructed the churches, but it has been the altar societies and ladies' groups that have worked to make sure that there are fresh flowers, cushions on the seats or kneelers, freshly washed linens, clean floors, pews, and windows. Women have sewn and mended vestments, polished altar vessels (although they are technically forbidden to clean them, according to recent regulations). These are important ministries, and they have not received the respect and attention that they deserve.[16]

The beauty of the liturgy, as I suggest above, has traditionally excluded women from visible contributions. The reasons for this are complex and, as I have suggested elsewhere, have deep social and psychological roots.[17] But women (and children and men) do not need to limit ritual and symbolic expression of beauty to official liturgical contexts. To be sure, there does need to be more participation by women in ministries of the Word: reading and preaching.[18] But there is much official resistance to such practices, especially women's preaching. Preaching is a rhetorical art that ought to incorporate beauty — most of us are well aware of how little thought goes into the preaching of too many presiders — and there is precious little of the beauty of women's voices to be heard. So women need to make opportunities to read and preach.

Women's ritual groups have been meeting for many years: my first experience of one was in 1972. At the time, we all felt as if we were being subversive, and we were. But as the years have gone by, these ritual groups have taken on lives of their own. There is an increasing number of books on the subject, and organizations such as WATER (Women's Alliance for Theology, Ethics, and Ritual) have both publications and online resources available. In the pre–Vatican II church, there were many practices of spirituality for which women were responsible: sodalities, prayer breakfasts, altar societies. I am not suggesting a return to those days, when these groups were under the supervision of the parish and

"Father" usually came at the beginning to offer a prayer (and then usually left). But I do think that it is time to reclaim and reinvent some of these practices that did not and do not require priestly leadership. The Vatican II document on liturgy, *Sacrosanctum Concilium,* declared that the Eucharist is the fount and summit of the church's liturgical life,[19] but the practical consequence has been that it has become virtually the *only* liturgical practice of the church. And all too often, the Eucharist is the priest-presider's personal performance, while the congregation is reduced to spectator status.

Human beings have a deep need for ritual, and women's exclusion from official church rituals has driven many women from the church to other traditions that are more welcoming. For those of us who remain in the church, with all of our anger, frustration, and love mixed together, ritual need not — and ought not — be seen as the sacred preserve of the clergy, but as an opportunity for all of us to practice beauty in creative ways.

Making the World More Beautiful

Beauty has increasingly come to be seen as a private possession — as we see in decorating magazines, fashion magazines, TV shows, and so on. It seems that all one needs to have is enough money to buy beauty: a physical or fashion makeover, new decor, a new house or car. And our very practices of making ourselves and our homes beautiful can also be harmful to the earth. It is not only possible but imperative that we link our desire for beauty in our lives with the desire to make the world around us more beautiful. How can we incorporate practices that hold these two desires together in our lives?

There is an old saying: "Beauty is as beauty does." The depth of beauty is not measured by sensual appeal only but by its effects in one's life and in the world. There are some very practical ways that one can commit oneself to making the world we live in a more beautiful place. I have been inspired by the work of 2005 Nobel Peace Prize winner Wangari Maathai, who has worked to reforest East Africa and to fight against the forces of industrialization that take little or no account of the ecological needs of communities.[20] In this way, she also has dedicated herself to working on behalf of women: by showing how the desertification of Africa has had a disproportionate impact on women and children and by increasing the educational possibilities for women and children.

Most of us work on a much smaller scale than Maathai, but it is possible for women in the church today to join with her and others around the world to make it more sustainable, and more beautiful at the same time. As Margaret Pfeil has suggested, ecology can become a practice of "liturgical askesis" as we see how our daily lives can make the body of Christ come alive in the world.[21]

We have numerous opportunities to make our lives more ecologically responsible. As Al Gore's documentary, *An Inconvenient Truth,* and a host of scientific reports have shown, we are at a tipping point regarding how the earth will be affected by our human activity. In response, there are practices of caring for the earth that are possible: ecologically sensitive gardening, household recycling, mindfulness of actions that are harmful to the environment. Taking up the challenge that Pfeil poses, we can bring ecologically sound practices to our church and consider together how a congregation can incorporate them as part of its commitment to the beauty of the world.

Conclusion

Beauty needs to be rescued from the cosmetic counters and the fashion shows, the home decorating magazines and the department stores.[22] Beauty is necessary for life, but we have forgotten what real beauty is: the beauty of the lines and wrinkles of a woman's well-lived life, the beauty of silence and of the outdoors experienced without electronic interruptions, the beauty of the earth with more attention to the way greenhouse gases are interfering with our climate. We need to give beauty room, as crowding it out leads to impoverished lives and a lack of care for God's good creation.

By its very nature beauty will promote generosity. Catholic women, with our long traditions of women's activities of beauty, can be strong catalysts for making our lives and our churches more beautiful, and at the same time, more generous.

Chapter 17

Insistent Inclusion

Intersections of Race, Class, and Gender

DIANA HAYES

> *Sometimes I feel like a motherless child,*
> *Sometimes I feel like a motherless child,*
> *Sometimes I feel like a motherless child,*
> *A long way from home,*
> *A long, long way from home,*
> *True believer, true believer,*
> *A long way from home.*
>
> — Negro Spiritual

THE WORDS OF THIS SPIRITUAL, sung in the dark hours before dawn and after dusk by many of my ancestors who were caught up in the holocaust that was slavery in the United States, continue to ring true for many African American women today. Born into a world and society that speaks highly of women if they know and stay in their socially appointed places, and hemmed in by oppressive religious values that claim to be based on the teachings of Jesus Christ, black women (and women as a whole) continue today to seek a "space" for themselves in which to be free. They are assaulted physically, spiritually, and emotionally on a daily basis by those whom they thought were friends and allies, the men in their lives as well as other women, and by the racism and sexism apparent in the societies in which they live. African American women too often are valued not for their intelligence or their strength, but for their weight or lack thereof, the lightness or darkness of their skin, the size and prominence of their breasts and hips, and the texture of their hair. These are all superficial standards that seek to squeeze them into shapes and forms that inhibit and restrict. Never part of the myth of "True Womanhood," which placed white women on pedestals that were equally restrictive, African American women historically were never "good enough" and still today fail to reach the acceptable standards of contemporary society. Those who attempt to break out and stand on their own are labeled and demonized by church and society as "unfit mothers" and "unnatural women." Commenting on the social construction of African American women, Margaret Hunter writes:

> The sexual and racial images of African American women as oversexed or whorish are also a direct reaction to the cult of white womanhood. Because black women were deliberately dehumanized, they were denied even a basic identity as women. When enslaved, they were forced to work alongside men in physically strenuous

tasks, for long hours. They were not seen as pristine, dependent, passive, fragile, or as having any of the traits that defined white womanhood. Instead, African American women were used as workhorses who were forced to be always sexually available to white men. Black women were "de-feminized" because they occupied a gendered space for which there was no clear gender identity. They were wives and mothers, but they were also (unlike many white women) workers, independent from men, and strong. This combination of traits left black women in a non-gendered space where they did not have access to the rights of men, nor did they share in the female protections of patriarchy.[1]

Why, in the twenty-first century, do African American women, as well as women of other races and ethnicities, still find themselves hemmed in by the constraints of race and gender constructed centuries ago, constructions that attempt to define and by so doing confine all of humanity, male and female? What is the origin of these constructions and why does their impact still reverberate down countless centuries to the present day? What role has religion, and Christianity in particular, played in the development and perpetuation of these definitional constraints?

This is an inquiry at the heart of womanist theology.[2] Womanist theologians seek to break the chains of societal "isms" that constrain and restrain women's rights to work in nondomestic roles, to live independent lives, and to speak for and about themselves in words of their own choosing. They seek to do this, not alone or just for themselves, but in order to build and rebuild the black community and all communities threatened with destruction due to an onslaught of values that counter those that historically kept us strong. Parochial values such as individualism, materialism, consumerism divide rather than unite, tearing down rather than building up community. Womanist theologians seek to speak not for but in solidarity with their black sisters throughout the African Diaspora, asking what it means to be a black woman in the twenty-first century, especially a Christian black woman.

Why must women, regardless of race or ethnicity, continue to fight for inclusion into worlds of which they have always been a significant but overlooked part? Women make up more than half of the world's population yet still find it necessary to struggle to express themselves in meaningful ways without being constrained by the men in their lives. When they succeed in doing so, they are labeled unnatural and unfeminine.

In this essay, I seek to bring the voices and experiences of U.S. women of African descent to the forefront of the dialogue now taking place between the Christian churches and U.S. society. Black women's voices are ones that have not, historically, been included, despite the inroads that feminist thought has made in academia. Most black women are not feminists, and those who are still struggle against the latent and often unconscious but egregious racism that persists in the feminist movement. Black women's lives have been defined by very different experiences, including the lingering impact of slavery and its virulent offspring, racism, sexism, and classism. They struggle to defend a faith that is theirs in Roman Catholic and Protestant Christian churches of which they have been a viable part since their beginnings. They are stretched painfully by the tension that persists between black women and men, a tension rooted in part in slavery but aggravated by the ways in which black men and women have consistently been pitted against one another in American society. Black women are torn by the pain of loved ones, the increase in women and children afflicted with HIV/AIDS, and the increasingly blatant and phobic heterosexism manifested in the leading churches of the black community by their ministers.

Black Women Today

Black women today find themselves in a familiar situation, caught between "a rock and a hard place," with seemingly all exits barred. This sadly is a situation they had to deal with in slavery when they were worked like oxen and bred like cattle. It is the situation they knew in the post-Reconstruction era, when they were slandered as black women of loose morals, perceived to be negative influences on their husbands and sons. And it is one experienced in the civil rights and black power movements, when women activists, with graduate degrees and years of experience, were relegated to roles behind the scenes as secretaries and "comfort" women.

Delores Williams speaks of this experience in her discussion of the story of Hagar, found in the book of Genesis. Hagar, like many slave women, was forced to have sexual intercourse with her master, and then she was beaten by her mistress when she successfully became pregnant. Yet when she ran away, she was sent back into slavery by God only to be finally expelled from her community with her son, Ishmael, with little hope of survival. She was given the same promise by God that God gave to Abram, that her descendants would be many, her line would not run dry (Gen. 16:1–15; 20:10–20).

The story of Hagar, as Williams notes, provides insight into why womanists emphasize "survival" over "liberation" as invoked by most black male theologians. While womanists acknowledge that "liberation" is important and that those enslaved must act with God's assistance to free themselves, it does not prove enough. What good is freedom if it only leads to the death of oneself and one's family, as a result of homelessness, disease, and eventual starvation? Liberation is viable only after one has learned to survive and to provide for oneself and those around oneself a quality of life that ensures the survival of liberation. Williams comments on this, referencing Hagar:

> Like African American people, Hagar and her child are alone without resources for survival. Hagar must try to make a living in the wide, wide world for herself and her child. This was also the task of many African American women and the entire community of black people freed when emancipation came.[3]

Williams continues:

> The post-bellum notion of wilderness (with Hagar and child as its content) emphasized black women's and the black community's negative experience of poverty and social displacement.... This post-bellum African American symbolic sense of wilderness, with Hagar at its center, makes the female figure symbolic of the entire black community's history of brutalization during slavery; of fierce survival

struggle and servitude after liberation; of children being cheated out of their inheritance by oppressors; of threat to the life and well-being of the family; of the continuing search for a positive, productive quality of life for women and men under God's care.[4]

This was the situation in which blacks found themselves at the end of the Civil War and after the end of the short-lived period of hope called Reconstruction. Like Hagar, they found it necessary to return, many of them, to the very plantations on which they had been enslaved and to accept a life of subservience known as sharecropping. They did this while working diligently and also furtively to gain the skills that would enable them or their children or their children's children to escape and forge new lives out of the wilderness of Jim Crow's *de jure* form of slavery that persisted well beyond the 1960s and was not limited to only the southern states as most assume.

It is from within this context, as a descendant of slaves, sharecroppers, farmers, and domestics, that I speak as a womanist theologian today. I am a first-generation college-educated African American woman, a convert in my adulthood from the historically black African American Methodist Episcopal Zion (AMEZion) church to the Roman Catholic Church, seen as a predominantly white church but one that both historically and today is made up predominantly of persons of color. An attorney, and now a theologian, I have spent most of my life grappling with issues that assault the very core of my being, not just the usual question of "who I am," but as others have repeatedly asked "what I am." Having been born into working-class poverty yet now, because of my educational achievements and professional status, a part of the upper middle class, my journey has exposed me to class, race, and gender discrimination. I have fought to achieve my goals of higher education while having to defend constantly my presence and existence as a black woman of intelligence. Patricia Hill Collins describes my experience and that of other black women intellectuals very well:

> The exclusion of black women's ideas from mainstream academic discourse and the curious placement of African American women intellectuals in both feminist and black social and political thought has meant that black women intellectuals have remained outsiders within in all three communities. The assumptions on which full group membership are based — whiteness for feminist thought, maleness for black social and political thought, and the combination for mainstream scholarship ... all negate a black female reality. Prevented from becoming full insiders in any of these areas of inquiry, black women remain outsiders within, individuals whose marginality provides a distinctive angle of vision on the theories put forth by such intellectual communities.[5]

Just as most people are born into a religion, that of their parents or grandparents usually, and remain there all of their lives, we are born into our skins and our sexualities. No one decides in the womb what race, sex, or class they will be; it is an act of God and the random mixing of our parents' genetic contributions. These are most certainly not choices.

But church and society have established an elaborate set of attributes and responsibilities based allegedly on scientific "facts" that serve to designate supposed proper roles for men and women, blacks and whites. Similar "facts," with Scripture used to support them, were used to condone the infamy and horror of slavery in the Americas. Have we learned anything from that experience? It seems not.

The Social Construction of Persons

The world we live in today is increasingly complex while, at the same time, incredibly diverse. People from cultures with very different traditions find themselves praying and celebrating the Eucharist together, sharing histories and stories in classrooms and working together in the business world. The shifting demographics of the United States are reflected in our daily encounters and force us to recognize changes needed and changes that will come, welcomed or unwelcomed. We no longer live in a naive world leading simple lives, if ever we did. It is incumbent upon all of us — not just the poor or immigrants or persons of color, but white men, who still occupy most of the positions of leadership in U.S. society and its churches, and white women as well, who share in the rewards of white privilege — to begin to acknowledge the ways in which our lives have been socially constructed and to work to eliminate the harmful impact of these constructions.

All of us, not just a few, are affected when persons of intellectual ability are restricted in the quality of education they receive or in their access to higher education, because of race, gender, class, or sexual orientation. Those in positions of leadership and power (often the kind of power passed on from father to son and friend to friend) have defined how the terms "race," "class," and "gender" are to be lived. Upon these human constructions towering edifices have been built that hem in and constrain rather than allow persons to explore and expand the myriad possibilities of their being. The results have been disastrous for too many.

Ironically, it is often people who have experienced oppression or marginalization, and who, having been liberated and having achieved positions of authority, turn around and restrict, restrain, or "punish" others of whom they do not approve. We have seen this happen over and over in history yet still refuse to learn from it. The conquered vanquish their conquerors and then become as oppressive as those who oppressed them. A rare and refreshing shift from this pattern has been South Africa, which has fought and struggled to heal the wounds of its painful apartheid past without making martyrs of those who for so long a time martyred them.

The Catholic Church has seemingly not learned the lessons of its two-thousand-year-long history. Although the Vatican uncategorically denounced slavery in any and all forms in 1965, a brief forty-plus years ago, the church still persists in upholding degrading and exclusive structures that the rest of the world has long forgotten. As a divine and human institution, the church should attempt to learn from the history that is very much its own and repent of its sins. As Pope John made clear at the opening of the Second Vatican Council, the church is not perfect but is seeking perfection. It will thrive in its fullest form as the people of God, which means all of the faithful and not just a few with particular titles who are ordained. We are all called to be priests in the fullest understanding of ministry, in and through baptism, and that calling demands respect for the basic dignity of all human beings, as created in the image and likeness of God, regardless of race, class, sexuality, or sexual orientation. People are to be respected and seen as an aspect of God's grace.[6]

On Whiteness and Blackness

Whiteness, blackness, or any aspect of color used to divide and separate can be traced back to the laws that the United States established in the seventeenth century as a means of designating who was intended (allegedly) by God to be free (whites) and who was intended to be a slave (blacks). The arbitrariness of this designation can be seen in myriad laws that have followed in the wake of the initial designation, laws that were required to decide who could claim "whiteness" with all of the benefits of white privilege and who could not. The understanding of "whiteness" has shifted many times. It has included and excluded Native Americans, Asians, Arabs, and Latinos/as as well as many ethnic groups today considered white but who were not so designated when they first migrated to this country, such as Italians, Irish, and Jews. Results of court decisions regarding "whiteness" have led to suicides, to internments, and to various forms of apartheid that continue to haunt us to the present day. The reasoning behind these shifts in designation is deeply rooted in the proof-texting of Scripture, though the main undergirding factor has been economic: how to obtain the greatest number of laborers at the least expense.

Whiteness historically and to a great extent today exists only in the presence of blackness, a reality that has bound up the United States in a binary construct that continues to ignore the presence of others who are neither black nor white. Patricia Hill Collins comments:

> Based on the struggle for power in society, racial categories are manipulated and transformed to guarantee one segment of the population, whites, the largest portion of resources. Consequently the boundaries of the races are always changing and who is included in which category changes with politics, economics, and the historical moment.[7]

Critical consciousness of how racial categories function is sorely needed in our time.

The Intersection of Race, Class, and Gender in the Aftermath of Hurricane Katrina

Recently we witnessed in the United States a horrific example of the ways in which race, class, and gender can intersect to the detriment of thousands. I am referring to the chaos that ensued on the Gulf Coast and in the city of New Orleans as a result of Hurricanes Katrina and Rita. These hurricanes revealed the racism coupled with poverty that still persists in the United States, and they exposed the feminization of poverty. The face of Katrina's devastation that was flashed around the world on television, newspapers, computer screens, and journal covers was that of a distraught, half-drowned black woman clutching one or more children to her breast. This is the face of America in the twenty-first century. As Loretta Ross notes:

> Poverty in America is not only racialized but it is also gendered. The aftermath of Katrina must be examined through a gender lens that identifies the myriad of violations experienced by women. A disaster like Katrina is a violation against the entire community, but when threats to women's lives are not recognized, and steps are not taken to ensure that they are, women become doubly victimized — by the disaster and by the response to it.[8]

The hurricane and the subsequent flooding highlighted the particular vulnerability of women, children, the elderly, and the disabled, underscoring the complex intersections of race, class, gender, ability, and life expectancy. Ross continues: "Many people could not escape not only because of poverty, but because they were not physically able to punch through rooftops, perch on top of buildings, or climb trees to survive."[9]

Incredibly, the media and government at every level sought to place blame on those who died for making incorrect or poor choices. The truth, however, is that a majority of those who died did so in their attics and living rooms, or found themselves abandoned in the Superdome without food, water, or medicines, or dumped and left stranded on Interstate 10 in blazing heat for more than four days because they *had no choices.* They were left to the mercy of others who should have taken the responsibility to ensure their safety but who, like Pontius Pilate (Matt. 27:15–26), washed their hands of that responsibility and thereby washed away thousands, claiming that these people had to use their own initiative to escape the rising waters.

Some religious commentators placed blame on single black mothers for their plight, asserting that if they had married the father of their children, they would have been at a higher economic status and would therefore not have suffered as they did. Such comments obviously ignore the fact that many of those who were married and with children in New Orleans lived below the poverty line and had no access to a car or any other form of private transportation.

How did this come about? Quite simply because those in positions of leadership, who speak all of the right words — "love thy neighbor, care for the widow and the orphan," ensure the health and prosperity of all — do not live the message they preach. What we, in fact, have seen take place in the United States is the abandonment of the "least among us," the removal of any and all "safety nets," and the denial of basic human rights owed to all human beings because of their creation by God.

And What about the Church?

The situation in the Catholic Church is similar, albeit not as blatant. Women are denied positions of leadership based on "man"-made laws; gay priests and seminarians are being forced to deny their vocations because of the refusal to recognize that pedophilia and homosexuality have nothing in common and that celibacy is viable for them just as for heterosexuals. The church has become a bully toward those who are "the least among us" while claiming to protect them. The long Catholic social justice tradition shows how the church has spoken and at times acted with a "preferential option for the poor," but we also have seen how we have stomped on the rights and humanity of those who dare to speak in ways that, while still clearly a part of our tradition, don't fit the narrow and often untheological thinking of those in positions of authority. Rather than opening up to dialogue, some in positions of power within the institutional church find it simpler to condemn, silence, withdraw privileges, close down, shut down, deny, or excommunicate. Why does the church, which is of God, fear God's word coming from the mouths of others who, like the children Jesus blessed, speak a wisdom grounded in generations of a deep and abiding faith? The church denies that it changes, but anyone with eyes to see and ears to hear can see that it does and has repeatedly over the course of two thousand years. Some of these changes have been very beneficial, but today many shifts are simply reactionary responses to the "signs of the times," not in the least what the church fathers (and mothers although not allowed to speak in public) had in mind when writing the challenging words of *Gaudium et spes*.

A Spiritual Practice of Insistent Inclusion

It is the faith-filled who are the people of God and who are speaking out in the church today. They are seeking to remind it of its humble origins and calling it to return to its roots in Africa and the Middle East, albeit not the Africa of today, tied up in contradiction and restriction as a result of colonialism and its failures, nor the Middle East of today, caught up in a life-and-death struggle between peoples who claim to believe in and follow the same God. A return is called for and it is a return to the early church, which was a persecuted church before it became entangled in the imperial webs of Rome and Christendom. In other words, it was a church of the poor, of slaves, and of women.

It is to this church and the man Jesus that my ancestors turned when they found themselves "way down yonder" by themselves, unable to hear anybody pray. Their belief was in a wonder-working God who helped them to get over the obstacles and traps that others set before them. Their God was a stern and righteous God yes, but also a God of love and justice who sought to make a way out of no way for those in dire need. Jesus was to them a companion and a friend, a helpless infant and a lover, a brother and a sister, a mother and a father, a liberator who came "to set the captives free" and not entangle them in so many rules and restrictions that God Godself was lost sight of.

"Neither Jew nor Greek, neither slave nor free, neither male nor female, we are all one in Christ Jesus" (Gal. 3:26–28). This is the vision of church that we should be seeking to fulfill in our world today. Women and men are different biologically, yes, but those biological differences do not make one superior to the other in any way. We each have been given particular gifts and charisms, sprinkled by God across all of humanity regardless of gender, race, class, or sexual orientation: to preach, to proclaim, to exhort, to teach, to comfort, and to heal. These are found in men and women, gay and straight, of every race and nation, speaking every tongue as those who followed Jesus, including his mother Mary, Mary of Magdala known as the Great Apostle, and many other women and men, named and unnamed. Jesus gave his mandate to proclaim the good news, the Gospel message of his resurrection, to a woman, Mary of Magdala, calumnied much too long by a church apparently fearful of the powers of women.

Today we must teach, preach, pray, and proclaim that good news far and wide while recognizing the equal legitimacy of its proclamation in every language and by every people. No one nation or ethnic group has proprietary rights to Jesus, except perhaps the Jews of whom he was born. All the rest of us gentiles came to him late and had to learn of his ways.

As I understand the Christian message, we are sent to preach the Gospel to people as they are rather than to force them to become something or someone else. Insistent inclusion means continuing to fight for the rights of all, both in church and society. All are welcome, regardless of race, class, gender, sexual orientation, physical or mental ability, culture or ethnicity, or native tongue. Jesus came to the people as they were; should not the church and our societies, allegedly based on the vision of Jesus Christ, do the same?

We betray our calling as the people of God who make up this pilgrim church when we seek to restrict its membership or inhibit the actions and thoughts of its members in ways that Jesus never demanded. We must recognize the limitation of the human-made laws that restrict us and, as Martin Luther King Jr. affirmed, acknowledge God's natural law while recognizing our own subjectivity. The church is not just European; it is and has always been African and Asian, and it is increasingly South and Central American, Eastern European, and of course North American.

Where would Christianity be without the women who led its first humble home churches and passed down the teachings to the children? Where would it be without the faithful poor, of every race and ethnicity, who believed God would help them in their direst straits, even if only by listening to their cries? Where would it be without the many who maintained and sustained it, who suffered martyrdom for their faith, who passed it on despite all that was done to them? Where would our church be? Perhaps where it is today, floundering in a morass of shame and denial with the spectacle of the hierarchy scandalizing the faithful rather than allegedly heretical theologians doing so. The motherless children are reclaiming their church and insisting that their presence and contributions be not just welcomed and affirmed but also included in the history, traditions, and teachings of the church today.

Chapter 18

Practicing Justice with Spirit

Mary Jo Leddy

THERE ARE TIMES when I long for the clarity of certain theologies of justice in which the line between right and wrong, us and them, seems clear and definite. Even theologies that address the inevitable failures in the work for justice seem, somehow, noble. In practice, however, the work of justice becomes slippery and perilous. You can suffer the loss of your own soul in struggling for justice.

For more than thirty years I have been engaged in a variety of actions for justice and peace. Some of my efforts have been focused on the situation of women in the Catholic Church but more relate to working for peace, advocating for the rights of refugees, writing in solidarity with imprisoned authors, organizing local neighborhood development, and lobbying for changes in political legislation.

Along the way, I have grappled with the underside of practicing justice. Still, insights have impressed themselves upon me. There is, as Augustine wrote, the "pressure" of the times which, like an olive press, produces rich insights that may flow through further reflection.[1] In the pages that follow, I share some of these insights born of the pressures of practicing justice and suggest some spiritual practices that can provide a way of doing justice with spirit. Anyone committed to justice for the long haul inevitably experiences the shadow sides of that commitment. The need for a practical spirituality becomes all the more intensely felt.

The Pressure of the Practice of Justice

Powerlessness Corrupts

In fighting the good fight, it is easy to become more discouraged by one's allies than one's opponents. I still wince recalling peace rallies at which someone forgot the microphone, making it difficult to hear what the speakers had to say, and instances in which someone put the wrong date on the flyer and consequentially no one showed up for the protest. The heated rhetoric of some peace groups often was matched by a noticeably tepid commitment to the actual organizational work of peacemaking. Why? I wondered.

Michael Lerner, a U.S. leader in alternative politics, writes about being struck by the apparent "will to lose" in peace and justice groups. He coins the phrase "surplus powerlessness"[2] to describe what he sees as a sense of powerlessness that is not appropriate to the situation and an accompanying lack of conviction about the possibility of winning the struggle that had been articulated as so necessary. He names what I have come to know in an inarticulate way.

Some persons involved in justice and peace struggles are very articulate about issues of power, but they do not have a deep confidence in their own personal power. They remain unconvinced that what they do or say matters. Thus, securing a microphone to amplify words for change does not seem of great importance. Sadly, this sense of powerlessness tends to become a self-fulfilling prophecy.[3]

There are very real structures that indeed render us more powerless, but, Lerner notes, we tend to feel more powerless than we actually are. Our sense of victimization can become so generalized that we lose sight of who the powerless victims really are.

One possible reason for this feeling of surplus powerlessness is the sense of ambiguity that many good people feel about the exercise of power. Persons can associate power with control and domination, and they sometimes have learned from experience that the exercise of power for change inevitably involves mistakes. As a result, persons sometimes prefer what they think is innocence and thus remain powerless. When this happens the struggle for justice can become intensely moralistic: faced with the realities of evil one is constantly proving one's innocence and goodness; one must claim rights on the basis of having been wronged. In a rather perverse way the wrong must be perpetuated in order for the rights to be legitimated.

This kind of moralism is ineffective and exhausting. Canadian feminist writer Margaret Atwood wryly observes, about women's struggle for justice in particular, that equality for women should not mean that women have to be "gooder" than men.[4] This moralism is, in my experience, the kiss of death for many justice groups. The burden of being "gooder" makes it difficult to see how we wrong each other. Eventually our analysis becomes rigid and unrealistic. The grim moralism of the good prevails.

Difficulty Drawing the Line

There are situations in which standing in the middle is very demanding. I think of what has been the Irish conflict, and what continues as the Palestinian and Israeli conflict in which those who are in the middle, who are seeking peace with justice, are the greatest threat to extremists. In these contexts, the people in the middle pay a severe price for moderation.

Some of the most critical issues with which I have been involved, however, have been those in which the middle ground has disappeared. In the heat of the cold war, when nuclear weapons were poised to destroy not only millions of innocent people but also the earth itself, it was impossible to remain neutral. Either you were against the nuclear arms race or you were for it. Doing nothing or saying nothing was not a moral option. The Bystander was always an Accomplice in such situations.

In situations of acute injustice, such as Central America in the 1980s and 1990s, there was no middle ground between the rich and the poor. If you were not actively in solidarity with the poor then you were giving comfort to the rich and strength to the status quo. This was the lesson learned by Archbishop Oscar Romero and by thousands of other church workers at the time.

In many struggles, there is no middle to muddle through. Taking sides is imperative, choices must be made, and there is a high price for doing so. This is the context of political and social holiness, of martyrdom and heroic witness.

Discernment is required to differentiate between situations in which there is no middle ground and situations in which the middle is the radical option. The Gospel response in one context will not be that demanded in another. There are no recipes for justice; one size does not fit all.

Nevertheless, I have learned that there is a particular temptation when one is involved in the kind of struggle where there is no middle ground. It is a temptation as old as the church that showed itself early on in the form of Manichean dualism. It is the temptation to see the world as divided into two equal and unrelated powers, one good and the other evil. It is a worldview perpetuated by politicians today who see themselves on the side of a good empire in the struggle against an evil empire or "the axis of evil." This is a worldview in which *us* and *them* have nothing in common.

In ancient and orthodox Catholic belief there is no good without its shadow side and no evil that does not hold some possibility of redemption. By implication, the line between good and evil, while it may be clear in some contexts, is not absolute. And more importantly, the line between good and evil is not only out there; it also runs through the middle of each of us. To forget this is to run the risk of demonizing those whom we oppose and idealizing those for whom and with whom we struggle. Real life inevitably presents enough exceptions to jiggle this rigid worldview.

Becoming Like That Which You Are Fighting Against

From a distance it is easy to wax eloquently about small groups struggling for justice: "the alternative communities," "the Abrahamic minorities," etc. Up close and personal, though, it is distressing to see the amount of violence in peace groups, the racism in antiracist groups, the dogmatism in feminist groups.

It is easy for us all to become like that which we are fighting against. We actually start to mirror the patterns we have observed so carefully *out there, in them*. We don't see how they are *in here, in me and us*.

I have learned that there is all the difference in the world between being *for* peace and *against* violence. If we are only against violence we will probably replicate the patterns of violence within ourselves and within the group with which we are identified. If we are only against injustice we will probably generate our own different forms of injustice.

Defaced by Systems

In struggles for social change, one rarely gets to see or talk to those who supposedly are responsible for an injustice. One gets shunted from office to office until one meets someone who is supposedly responsible, and that person wrings his or her hands and shrugs that there is little that can be done because of "the economy" or "global realities" or "the tradition of the church." This person begins to sound like yet another helpless victim of the status quo. This person remains as faceless as the many victims who are defaced by the system, reduced to a number and filed away. Sinful social structures deface.

There is something demonic in this situation; it is not the officials in the system but rather the system itself. The political thinker Hannah Arendt describes the ways in which ordinary people doing a good job sometimes contribute to evil of great consequence without ever knowing it or willing it. This is because systems frequently act as a buffer between their intentions and the consequences of their actions. Bureaucracies, according to Arendt's analysis, are structured so that it seems as if nobody is responsible for the terrible consequences of cumulative action — not those on the top, who never see the people affected by their decisions, and not those on the bottom who see the people but experience themselves as helpless victims. Those on top can argue that they never really killed anyone while those on the bottom can say that they were only following orders.[5]

In the various systems which hold the power of life and death over real people, it often seems that *nobody* is responsible. Poor people, refugees, and the elderly know what happens when *nobody* is responsible. *Nobody* can kill you just as anybody or somebody could do so.

In working to change these systems, all concerned must be summoned to face themselves. Systems have been created by human beings and therefore can be changed by human beings. Systems must be changed so that human beings can face each other and face the consequences of their actions.

Blinded by the Ideologies of Empire

We live in the midst of an empire that, at the moment and perhaps for a little while longer, is the center of political and military power in the world. The cultural bias in this imperial situation is to take what is *here* and what is *now* very seriously as a point of reference.[6] We begin to assume that we are responsible for the good in the world, and that we have a manifest destiny to enlighten and civilize, to spread the values of democracy and freedom. Such is the exhausting burden and myth of imperial consciousness.

Increased information about suffering and injustice actually contributes to the burden of imperial consciousness. We are more aware about what is wrong at local, national, regional, and global levels and begin to feel vaguely guilty and responsible for all of it — and therefore powerless. The vagueness of these feelings can become crippling. Guilt that is specific, responsibility that relates to real names and places, has a much better chance of being transforming and motivating.

It is astonishing how many North Americans feel both vaguely guilty and powerless about the state of the world. This sense of powerlessness manifests itself in paralysis, both personal and political, and causes people more often than not to work on changes "in general" rather than on significant change. It becomes altogether important for all of us to pick a few struggles and to concentrate on them.

On Things Being Different Though Not Altogether Better

Most struggles for justice begin with an awareness of the acute suffering caused by present realities and a correlative dream of an alternative way. Embedded in a culture of consumerism as we are, we falsely assume that the struggle to realize the dream will be painful but brief. We are more geared to the instant, the short term rather than to the long haul over generations. Little wonder that we are so quickly and easily discouraged.

Those of us who have internalized the Western myth of progress are convinced that, by working hard enough and thinking smart enough, things will get better. After a while, however, we come to realize that even though we have worked hard and thought smart, even though we have called in consultants and developed new mission statements, things aren't getting better. Such is the long-term labor for justice.

In the midst of long labor, it becomes easy to rant or to whine. We start to blame others for not doing enough. We wonder whether we should quit or continue to continue. We long for the fruits of the spirit — charity, joy, peace, patience, goodness, long-suffering.

Spiritual Practices for the Journey

Considering these harder dimensions of practicing justice, what are practices that can sustain us in very worthy struggles? Resources from our Catholic tradition prove suggestive. They serve to jump-start our imaginations as we continue the struggle for justice. Such practices include regular gathering with like-spirited people, an ongoing practice of forgiveness, recitation of the Credo, contemplation of the face, practice of the works of mercy, keeping holy the Sabbath, and simple acts of consecration.

Gathering with Like-Spirited People

Struggles for justice depend on the capacity of people to generate a sense of energy and power for change. By gathering together with others who are not so much like-minded (sharing the same analysis of a situation) as like-hearted and like-spirited, we can renew our focus and our energy. Finding community proves more challenging than it sounds, however, because despite our rhetoric regarding its importance, we live in a culture of radical individualism that prizes autonomy above all else. The number of culturally established ways of practicing community remain few.

Our formation as Catholics reminds us that our lived faith is never solitary. It is to be shared, and we come to flourish in community. In the experience of community, desired habits of the heart deepen and expand.

An Ongoing Practice of Forgiveness

Justice gets practiced with others — sometimes through one event but more often than not through communal processes of talking together, worshiping together, strategizing together. If we are committed to developing a sense of power through interaction, we must also stand committed to practices of forgiveness. The practice of forgiveness needs to be entered regularly and with reference to a divine forgiveness, so that emerging futures are not determined by the past.

Rituals of forgiveness are particularly important for women working for church reform. To keep struggling to address wrongs wrought by the institutional church, we must also find ways of acknowledging wrongs done to each other in the process of righting those wrongs. It becomes essential to find spaces to be both self-critical and forgiving in the work of justice.

Recitation of the Credo

One of the most ancient practices of the church has been the recitation of the Credo, "I believe." It is relatively easy to define oneself in terms of who or what one is against. The larger challenge by far is to shape our lives in terms of who or what we believe in.

Our credo goes beyond and beneath convictions about particular issues or projects. We need to know who or what we are willing to die for, and this will give us a sense of who or what we are living for. We want to be able to name the source of our being. It is our Credo, ultimately, that concentrates our lives and makes them whole, providing the longer and deeper narrative within which to situate our particular small story. And a shared Credo enables people to summon one another to be self-giving. The "we believe" that is held in common becomes authoritative in the practice of justice.

We learn what we believe, in large part, from the modeling of others. *Who* we believe is as important as *what* we believe. We can choose to imitate violent, unjust, and sexist people, or we can choose to imitate those who are just and joyful, patient and passionate for peace.

Within Catholic tradition there exists a practice of the "Imitation of Christ." Historically, there have been some gruesome and irretrievable aspects to this practice, but the basic wisdom of learning through imitation that is held within it is as pertinent today as it was for our historical predecessors. Sadly our contemporary consumer culture socializes us to want to imitate the young and the restless, the rich and the famous, the so-called smart and sophisticated. Practicing the imitation of Christ offers a corrective here, along with a possibility for forming a profoundly countercultural value system.

Women today, who seek more inclusionary practices of church, benefit greatly from finding other faith-filled women who are worthy of imitation. Feminist theories and critical theologies are significant, but they run the risk of becoming abstractions unless there are embodied examples to imitate. We must be able to point to women, past and present, who have lived with integrity in the intricacies of the church, on the margins of society, and outside of the boxes created by ideologies and theories.

Contemplation of the Face

Systems deface and so do all the "big ideas" that serve to categorize and define the particularities of human affections and afflictions. It is very easy for those engaged in social change to become removed from real people when using general terms like "globalization," "the environment," "the economy." But big ideas that lose sight of the particularities of peoples and places inevitably become bad ideas. So how can we balance a wider and more inclusive consciousness without losing the particularity of faces and the specificity of places?

Within the Eastern Christian tradition there is a profound devotion involving "face to face" prayer, that prayer which places persons in the presence of an icon of Jesus, of Mary, of the saints. In this practice people recall the holiness of the face and find within themselves spiritual sources for resisting the desecration of the divine face in the human. The practice of contemplating an icon is not only about seeing the holy face but also about seeing ourselves as we are seen. Faced by Christ, we find the sacredness of our own face. We place ourselves in the gaze of grace and we are addressed, summoned.

Practice of the Works of Mercy

To see through and beyond the blindness of the imperial ideologies of our church and nation we must choose to stand at the foot of the cross. The most important insights of our tradition are found through the crucified ones. We see most clearly when we see through their eyes and hear through their ears. We are not really revolted by injustice until we become friends with someone who is poor and marginalized, until we see abuse through the eyes of a victimized child.

Where we live determines what we see, and the people we listen to affect what we hear. Loving our neighbor has to mean more than caring for those we happen to be beside. It means making options that place us in proximity to the crucified ones, the ones who see through the ideologies of empire — even if they remain inarticulate about its injustices. Thus, the very concrete "Works of Mercy" become essential practices for anyone engaged in the work of justice. They forever put us near those who are hungry and thirsty, homeless and in prison.

Keeping Holy the Sabbath

It is easy to be busy, running on the spot, getting ahead while falling behind. We consume time and are consumed by it. What more pertinent spiritual practice is there than the ancient one of keeping holy the Sabbath? To set aside twenty-four hours, to not "work" in the usual way, can be profoundly reorienting; the Sabbath can serve as a time in which to recognize that the work for justice is not just our work but also part of God's desire for the earth.

Keeping Sabbath reminds us that what began as God's desire for justice and peace in the moment of creation will be accomplished in a new creation. The Sabbath is an opportunity to relax into the awareness that our desire for the equality of women, for example, which is also God's desire, will be accomplished. It may take a lifetime, longer than a lifetime, but it will be accomplished. Much work will be left to another generation of women in the church, but it will be accomplished. Much depends on us, and this we know during the bulk of our week; but much doesn't depend on us, and this is the liberating insight that comes when we take time to be like the lilies, the sparrows, in the joy of the Sabbath.

Acts of Consecration

We are engaged not only in work for justice but in a journey toward holiness. Given the fragmentation of our lives and the ways in which our spiritual energies are sapped, a helpful spiritual practice is that of "concentrating" our lives to make them more whole. The concentration of our energy becomes a new form of consecration.

In this time and in this place, in this church as it is and in this world, *what am I called to do?* Until we live out this question, bear with it, we cannot concentrate our lives in an effort to make them more whole. We must say "yes" to something or someone and then say "no" to everything else. The choice to limit our lives and focus them becomes a rich form of holiness and prophetic witness in our time. The choice begins with a single act of consecration:

> *I concentrate this day*
> *In You.*
> *All that I have*
> *All that I am*
> *I give with You*
> *Unto this day.*
>
> *I consecrate this day*
> *To You, with You.*
> *I trust with You*
> *I can give*
> *And not be consumed*
> *I can receive*
> *And be satisfied.*
> *In You, for You*
> *Let this day begin.*
> *Amen.*

Chapter 19

Claiming and Imagining

Practices of Public Engagement

ROSEMARY P. CARBINE

O VER TWENTY-FIVE YEARS AGO, Martin Marty coined the term "the public church," which has significantly influenced U.S. Christian theological discourse and practice regarding religious engagement in the public/political sphere. Challenging the privatization of religion to personal, spiritual, or moral matters, the public church illuminates a long-standing tradition in Christian thought and practice regarding the mutual interplay between religion and public life, which Marty defined as "the *res publica,* the public order that surrounds and includes people of faith."[1] Religion contributes to the cultivation of the U.S. political order, which is identified not with the state but with civil society — with a democratic assembly of citizens who collectively deliberate and decide their common life via civic debate.[2] Theological understandings of the public church are grounded in this deliberative model of democracy, in which the church's participation in public/political life takes place via rational argument and debate about socially significant issues.

Who speaks for the public church is mainly constituted by institutional church leaders alongside leading (often male and ordained) church spokespersons. When public engagement is limited to discursive practices of rational argument by official church leaders, the institutional church may not be well equipped, as pointed out by Margaret Farley and Mary Hines, to engage in and reshape rigorous civic debate in contemporary U.S. public life.[3] The institutional church damaged its credibility in the priest sexual abuse scandals that centered around the Archdiocese of Boston in 2002–3, and tried to regain that credibility, in part, through its sociopolitical engagement around sexual values in the 2004 U.S. presidential election. The so-called non-negotiable moral guidelines for Catholic voters supported by some U.S. Catholic bishops in the 2004 U.S. presidential election served to separate moral and social justice issues, as well as to downplay the institutional church's role as a prophetic witness on a broad range of social issues. Furthermore, the credibility of the institutional church's civic discourse about the protection of human dignity and rights, especially the right to political participation, is undermined through an increasing magisterial control of ecclesial, theological, and moral discourse, on the one hand, and through patriarchal church structures that lead to a less than fully inclusive and collaborative church, on the other hand. Thus, when church leaders and their representatives function as a controlling vision of the public church in the U.S. context, not only does the institutional church lack public credibility of late, but also, and more importantly, women as well as some men are unable to express and embody the "public church," diminishing their religio-political agency.

To state, then, my guiding question for this essay: How do everyday church members, particularly women, reclaim the public church as well as reimagine the church's critical and credible witness in U.S. public life?[4] In response to this question, this essay argues that looking beyond civic debate and its practices of rational argument reveals a rich diversity of effective practices of public engagement, what I will call rhetorical, symbolic, and prophetic practices. As my examples of Christian social justice activism, particularly from the Plowshares movement, will demonstrate, these practices help to reshape and revitalize theological notions of political subjectivity and agency. Moreover, these practices challenge our common understandings of what constitutes U.S. public life and thereby open up a space to imagine and seek to enact an alternative and more emancipatory form of common life. Effective public engagement, in my view, has less to do with statements of institutional church representatives that get press and other media attention to shape civic debate; rather, effective public engagement has more to do with practices of the whole people of God that create community[5] — that critically transform our public life so as to embrace and enhance our common earthly life together. Women have played and continue to play a significant role in shaping such notions of political agency and public life; thus, this essay thinks through these practices — both theologically and from the perspective of women in religio-political movements — to regenerate the public church in our time.

U.S. Public Engagement: All About Argument

Christian theological reflection about what constitutes public engagement is often controlled and prescribed by the field of public theology.[6] Public theology in our time addresses the role of religion in an increasingly pluralistic international public order. Some leading figures in U.S. public theology (e.g., David Tracy, Francis Fiorenza, Ronald Thiemann, Jeffrey Stout) describe public engagement in U.S. political life through discursive practices. For these theologians and ethicists, the public/political order is considered a democratic assembly of citizens who collectively decide their shared common life through civic debate; participation in the public order takes place via shared norms and practices of rational argument, i.e., the giving and exchanging of reasons in a deliberative democracy.

When public engagement is primarily characterized via discursive practices, religious claims are introduced and expressed in a widely intelligible way by following shared norms of rational civic discourse. The goals of such public engagement are to apply theological perspectives to contemporary issues and public policies through reasoned argument, to cultivate lively civic debate and to build an emerging consensus about such issues and policies.

Public engagement through reasoned debate certainly stakes out a legitimate place for religious arguments in public life, provided they follow accepted political norms and procedures of rational argument. Moreover, for some theologians, religious traditions equip persons for such public engagement. The church constitutes a community of inquiry and interpretation regarding, among other things, the good life, which inculcates in its members certain civic virtues and skills for political participation. However, public engagement is still premised on gaining access to political forums of rational argument and decision making, while contemporary democracy more often reflects an alienating and exclusionary rather than fully participatory political life. According to feminist theorists and theologians, public theology resonates with a political idealism that insufficiently criticizes the institutionalization of ideologies within democracy. It presumes political participation in a discursive public and its practices of rational discourse and debate, and does not deal sufficiently with persons excluded from public life, i.e., with the lack of political access, representation, voice, and power to effect change that many feel.

Lack of political access and power carries grave theological and political implications. Theologically, any denial of full public/political participation undermines the common good, or the totality of conditions that enable the full humanity of all citizens. It amounts to a denial of full humanity both individually and socially; human beings, after all, are created in and for sociality — a relational life with others — which includes political life.[7] Politically, the effectiveness of public engagement is mainly gauged on discursive terms — e.g., gaining media attention; influencing congressional debate, legislation, and votes; shaping and sustaining wider civic conversation; empowering citizens for the political process (i.e., writing to representatives and political leaders) — which basically runs the risk of leaving unchallenged a rationalist and often exclusionary understanding of the public order.[8]

In sum, public theology with its focus on the rational ordering of public debate narrowly circumscribes practices of U.S. public engagement; it neither attends to other practices of political participation nor imagines their potential efficacy in U.S. common life. To reach for a more theologically adequate understanding of public engagement that can better account for a plurality of democratic practices and their purpose, I propose a constructive public theology that (1) goes beyond political participation via discursive practices of rational argument, and, in so doing, (2) opens up theological space to explore other modes of democratic practice that foster participation in as well as transformation of U.S. public life.

Beyond Argument:
Alternative Practices of Public Engagement

A participatory democracy that stresses building consensus through interactive debate should build on and create an inclusive community. However, when public engagement is construed as civic discourse, it can alienate, silence, and outright obscure a wide range of citizens, rendering them nonpolitical subjects in our everyday political discussions. Nonetheless, a lack of political access, voice, representation, and decision-making power in everyday public debate does not mean a lack of public engagement or political efficacy. As the late feminist political philosopher Iris Marion Young observed, marginalized and disenfranchised groups that lack access to discursive political arenas utilize alternative practices, such as narrative, visual, and symbolic media, and protest politics, to reclaim and regain meaningful forms of political participation.[9] Moreover, what makes such alternative political actions effective, especially from a theological perspective, is their capacity for what Roger Gottlieb calls "world-making," that is, their ability to imagine and at least partly incarnate a more emancipatory future vision of our public life. Effective religious practices of public engagement critically disrupt an at times oppressive U.S. public order, not to altogether undermine it, but to critically remake and reconstruct it in light of a more just, more emancipatory, alternative yet intrahistorical (or this-worldly) future. Faith-based social justice movements utilize practices of public engagement to criticize as well as seek to transform U.S. public life in light of an alternative future.[10]

A more adequate public theology, then, redefines public engagement beyond a shared community of rational discourse, and instead highlights multiple forms of democratic practice beyond debate that aim to reshape our common life. Practices, according to Craig Dykstra and Dorothy Bass, are "things Christian people do together over time to address fundamental human needs in response to and in the light of God's active presence for the life of the world."[11] Drawing on this definition, faith-based practices of public engagement emerge from a Christian response to the current sociopolitical situation in light of the Gospel and God's ongoing presence in the world. Thus, a more adequate public theology emphasizes alternative practices of sociopolitical engagement and likewise shows the significance of religion in contesting and remaking a more meaningful U.S. public life. Here, I identify and elaborate on three such alternative ways of public engagement, namely, rhetorical, symbolic, and prophetic practices.

Rhetorical Practices

Rhetorical practices focus on introducing theological claims into the public square in a variety of genres (e.g., speech, poetry, literature, music) that give voice to, gain recognition for, and urge solidarity with marginalized peoples often denied political subjectivity and agency. As thematized by Rebecca Chopp, one genre, testimony, holds much theological potential to reconfigure the shared "narrative identity" that presently underwrites U.S. common life, or our common assumptions about who contributes to public life, what can be spoken or said in public discourse, and how that discourse is articulated, regulated, and judged on legal and juridical terms.[12] Testimony, in Chopp's view, involves remembering and retelling narratives of suffering and of hope from marginalized peoples; it aims to reclaim a voice and place for such peoples in public life and to question predominant stories that structure and shape our often oppressive common life. The purpose of testimony is to enlarge our narrative identity, or our self-understanding of common life, as well as to imagine more emancipatory possibilities for it.[13] To accomplish this purpose, testimony presents an ethical summons to end suffering and to imagine a more transformative vision of common life, based on what Chopp calls "an ethos of cultivating compassion" that leads to collective action.[14] Thus, testimony takes on theological significance: "Testimony in public discourse narrates a story, a story that allows the transcendent, the possibility of the new, to break in and open us to change and transformation."[15] Testimony breaks open a counterpublic space for empathy, for solidarity with suffering, and for a collective and active hope in the possibility of creating a future flourishing common life.[16]

One example of testimony as a form of political participation is illustrated by Martin Luther King Jr. in his 1963 "Letter from a Birmingham Jail." In this acclaimed letter from prison, King responded to several allegations of southern clergymen against the civil rights movement. In so doing, King recounted the brutal realities of African American life under legalized segregation to elicit empathy, appealed to both constitutional and Christian principles of universal human dignity to garner broad public solidarity for an end to institutionalized racism, and legitimated collective action, especially civil disobedience (i.e., sit-downs, sit-ins, marches, rallies), as a means to realize both a fully participatory democracy and the theological notion of the beloved community.[17]

Symbolic Practices

Symbolic practices, according to Michael and Kenneth Himes, entail rethinking central religious symbols for their sociopolitical implications.[18] Rather than support a sociopolitical order or sacralize a theocratic state, religious symbols can criticize U.S. common life and engender a more emancipatory alternative vision of it on theological grounds. Religious symbols help craft a shared moral framework or a so-called "moral compass" for public life,[19] and thereby serve to construct a shared political space of moral discourse and practice regarding the meaning of human being and the mutual obligations of human beings to one another and to society. Linell Cady outlines a theological method for such symbolic practice called extensional theology, in which religious symbols are mined to furnish an alternative moral basis for public life. Extensional theology thematizes a religious tradition in its totality through its organizing symbols, for example of God, and then extends that tradition to develop and formulate shared moral rights and responsibilities for our common life.[20] Resembling a theological double vision, it looks back at theological symbols to address contemporary sociopolitical realities, and it looks forward through those symbols toward instantiating a more just public life.

One example of symbolic practice as a form of political participation appears in the 1986 U.S. Catholic bishops' pastoral letter *Economic Justice for All.* In this letter, the bishops defined economic justice as the rights to life, food, clothing, housing, rest, health care, education, and meaningful work — which included full employment, fair wages, safe and stable working conditions, and collective action via unions.[21] God-talk, which illuminates the intrinsic worth and interdependence of all earthly life,[22] provided a theological basis for articulating and promoting these rights, especially the theological symbol of the human person made in the image of God and made for participating in community.[23] Creation in the image and likeness of God establishes universal human dignity, while various legal, political, and social means assure and actualize that dignity. Such symbols do not directly correspond with a certain political order, translate into a formal legal code or theory of human rights, or discount religious and cultural pluralism.[24] Rather, such symbols contribute to a normative account of human nature, which then contributes to a faith-based critical social theory that critically assesses our current economic systems and that informs political advocacy for economic justice.

Prophetic Practices

Building on scriptural studies of prophetic traditions, prophetic practices, according to Walter Brueggemann, "criticize" an existing unjust sociopolitical order and simultaneously "energize" or imagine and engage in a lived hope in a more just, more emancipatory alternative vision of that order.[25] Such practices rest firmly on theological grounds. Remembering a fundamental relationship with God trumps an oppressive sociopolitical order and simultaneously sparks an imagined and lived alternative to it.[26] Prophetic practices in the Christian tradition often draw on christology as a *locus theologicus* to critically engage with and to constructively reshape U.S. public life. According to Mark Taylor, imitating Jesus is a Christological praxis, or "a Christian theatrics," that is, a present-day parody of the countercultural life, ministry, and death of Jesus.[27] Just as Jesus wielded the cross for the purpose of life rather than for imperial Roman purposes of punishment, repression, and death, so too, Christian protest movements imitate the way that Jesus "steals the show" or subverts a state-backed culture of oppression, violence, and death.

Prophetic practices confront the prevalent sociopolitical order and also attempt to partly actualize an alternative possibility to it through collective action, through nonviolent civil disobedience (strikes, picket-lines, marches, rallies, demonstrations). Such collective action raises public awareness about and aims to express solidarity with suffering peoples. One example of prophetic practice as a form of political participation occurred during the U.S. immigrant civil rights movement in 2005–6, which peaked in nationwide rallies and marches on May 1, 2006, designated as a national day of action to protest then pending anti-immigration legislation. At a subsequent rally in Boston Common on May 17, 2006, some of the five hundred protesters carried crosses.[28] In my view, these crosses critically denounced an existing U.S. public/political order that disregarded the sufferings of undocumented immigrants at and within its borders, and at the same time these crosses constructively announced and embodied an alternative U.S. public/political order based on solidarity rather than alienation, border fences, and so on.

In sum, rhetorical practices involve reclaiming a public voice and space to reimagine public life anew. Symbolic practices refer to locating moral grounds for a more flourishing public life within religious symbols, without coercing any conformity to a Christian theological imaginary. And prophetic practices involve taking nonviolent collective action to edge our U.S. political order toward a more inclusive and just quality of life. Taken together, these distinct but interrelated practices of public engagement urge us and U.S. common life toward a more fully just and participatory public life.[29] They help to cultivate an eschatological pull toward an alternative vision of our sociopolitical order, and in so doing begin to prefigure that order.[30] Effective religio-political engagement takes place through a rich array of these practices, which are reflected in the following interpretation of the Plowshares movement, both in its inaugural and more recent actions. As we will see, women within the Plowshares movement play significant roles in reshaping such practices and common conceptions of U.S. public life.

Plowshares: Inaugural and Recent Actions

Philip Berrigan (1923–2002), a World War II veteran, a former Josephite priest, and a leading U.S. Catholic peace activist, engaged in over one hundred nonviolent antiwar protest actions of the Plowshares movement, which he co-founded to confront and contest the conjunction of militarism, racism, and poverty during and beyond the Vietnam War.[31] The Plowshares movement inaugurated its nonviolent direct actions of nuclear disarmament on September 9, 1980, when the Plowshares Eight walked into General Electric in King of Prussia, Pennsylvania, and hammered and poured blood on nuclear missiles to dismantle and disarm such state symbols of violence, death, and war.[32]

Since the Plowshares Eight in 1980, almost eighty Plowshares protest and disarmament actions have taken place at weapons facilities around the globe, leading to trials, fines, and often lengthy jail sentences.[33] In one Plowshares action, on October 6, 2002, three Dominican nuns, Carol Gilbert, Jackie Hudson, and Ardeth Platte, broke into a missile silo in northeast Colorado, at which recently reactivated first-strike nuclear missiles lay beneath thousands of miles of farmland. Dressed in white hazmat suits, the nuns cut through the gates, poured blood in the shape of crosses around the silo, and hammered on its entrance. They called their symbolic disarmament action Sacred Earth and Space Plowshares to show, according to Gilbert, that nuclear weapons kill people and Mother Earth herself, that is, all living things. Moreover, as Platte observed, we are "all part of a loving nonviolent circle, the family of God. We are one body, one blood, and we must learn how to live on Planet Earth together."[34] As indicated by this action, Plowshares activists break into military facilities, hammer and pour their own blood on nuclear and other weapons, and risk jail along with fines (between two and a half and three and a half years for the nuns along with over $3,000 in fines) to expose the all-too-often invisible immorality and illegality of nuclear war and to witness to an alternative political reality — to the in-breaking of an alternative world without war.[35]

During their trials for trespassing on and damaging federal property with intent to obstruct the national defense, Plowshares activists relied on rhetorical practices, such as courtroom testimony, to interrupt a prevailing irrational civic discourse of war[36] and to reassert religio-political resistance actions as a legitimate form of political participation beyond prevailing legalistic forms of abstract argument.[37] Plowshares activists incorporated a broad range of defenses for their disarmament actions, relying on historical, legal, and religious defenses. On historical grounds, at the trial of the Catonsville Nine, Phil Berrigan situated nonviolent direct action within a long-standing U.S. democratic tradition of gaining public voice through protest politics.[38] On legal grounds, they argued a necessity defense, which basically elaborates the responsibilities of any citizen to prevent any imminent harm to human life.[39] On religious grounds, Elizabeth McAlister at the trial of the Griffiss Plowshares labeled nuclearism (nuclear weapons and their associated military and other structures) an established civil religion, which not only bordered on idolatry but also infringed upon constitutional rights to free exercise and disestablishment of religion.[40]

Combining both legal and religious defenses, Plowshares activists repeatedly confronted and resisted the law of the state, which authorizes and legitimates violence, with the law of Christ, which promotes nonviolence, love, and justice.[41] Thus, courtroom testimony afforded Berrigan and Plowshares activists a rhetorical vehicle to give voice to suffering peoples as well as to critically engage in and reshape public discourse about war. While most trial judges disregarded or placed extensive gag rules on such defenses as in the trial of the three nuns, testimony enabled Plowshares activists to educate about the atrocities of war and their faith-based reasons for participating in antiwar actions — thereby creating and enacting, even if briefly, a counter-rhetoric and counter-public to a militarist political order.

Religious symbols added an explicitly theological dimension to Plowshares practices of public engagement. Berrigan and other activists turned to symbolic practices to provide a theological basis of nonviolent direct action, of their active interference with U.S. militarist industry and society. A Plowshares theology of political activism rests on reinterpreting major Christian symbols, especially hammers and blood. Plowshares actions take their religious directive to disarm and destroy weapons of warmaking from Isaiah 2:2–4 "to beat swords into plowshares."[42] The blood signifies the death-dealing purposes of the weapons as well as a sharp contrast between militarist societies and the new society, the new family of God initiated in the life-ministry, death, and resurrection of Jesus. Pushing this symbol beyond solely antiwar protest, Sacred Earth and Space Plowshares underscored that militarism means the end of all earthly life. In resistance to nuclear war and its impending ecological disaster, the nuns used blood to resignify the missile silo and the surrounding farmland as a site for sustaining rather than annihilating full earthly flourishing. Sacred Earth and Space Plowshares thus enabled an imitation of Christ and emulated the purpose of Jesus' life and ministry — to establish a more interdependent, interconnected sense of community with all of life.

The Plowshares movement centers on nonviolent direct actions of civil disobedience that reflect the dynamic of criticism and imagination within prophetic practices. Plowshares actions denounce an oppressive war-making state on the one hand, and announce and prefigure an alternative possibility to it on the other hand. Nonviolent direct action enacts both "divine disobedience" to a militarist state and divine obedience to a gospel of life, epitomized in the resurrection of Jesus, that provides "a vision of life by which to interpret and to confront the works of death."[43] Nonviolent direct action provides a major "means for making this vision real" and for "recreat[ing] the political order."[44] In other words, Plowshares protest actions embody prophetic practices because they engender and enact an alternative possibility for common life, that is, a more just counterpublic to a militarist society.[45]

Reinterpretation of Christian symbols informed and influenced Plowshares prophetic practices in that the movement relied on religious symbols to criticize the predominant sociopolitical order as well as to propel collective action that imagined and attempted to actualize a more just, more peaceful this-worldly order. Philip Berrigan connected Plowshares protest actions to an imitation of a revolutionary Christ, a Christ who used subversive public acts (such as living among the outcast and oppressed, overturning the moneychangers' tables, dying a criminal's death on the cross) to confront and confound forms of domination.[46] For example, the Good Friday Plowshares of Holy Week 1995 in Washington, D.C.[47] politically reenacted Christ's last days during Holy Thursday, Good Friday, and Holy Saturday, pouring blood at the World Bank and Pentagon as well as staging symbolic sanctions on Iraq at the White House, to signify that Christ confronted Roman imperialism, colonialism, and militarism with nonviolence.

To envision and enflesh a counterspace to a militarist society that is bent on sustaining rather than destroying life, Berrigan drew on theological symbols from Christian eschatology to articulate in theological terms an alternative pacifist vision of the good society that rests on love, justice, equality, and peace, or what Phil called the "kin-dom" of God.[48] Lacking its original imperialist meanings, the kin-dom of God, much like the theological image of the body of Christ (1 Cor. 12) invoked by the Dominican nuns, underscores the interrelation and interdependence of all life in the reality of God. Plowshares actions get a this-worldly glimpse of this good society, so that the kin-dom of God might become an intrahistorical reality — especially with regard to women and to the earth.[49]

In sum, my analysis of Plowshares actions has held these practices of public engagement in dynamic tension — without reifying or drawing sharp distinctions among them — to demonstrate multiple ways in which religious resources propel participation in and transformation of U.S. public life. Berrigan and Plowshares activists gave testimony and engaged in protest politics to educate in both word and deed about an alternative sociopolitical order. They articulated and attempted to live out a Christian symbol of the good society, the kin-dom of God. By seeking to realize the kin-dom of God, they did not coerce conformity to Christian morality and thereby eschew religious pluralism. Rather, they rethought central Christian symbols for their political meanings, in order to reshape, reconfigure, and remake a more just, more emancipatory body politic, which includes the body of the earth.

To conclude, we can invoke these practices for their theological potential to redefine the public church. What makes a practice "public" entails more than an interjection of religious claims into civic debate; what makes a practice "public" consists in its ability to create community. As strategies of renewal and reform, rhetorical, symbolic, and prophetic practices shed new light on a praxis of imagining and creating community. They point toward a more just sociopolitical order and offer us a theological horizon in which to reconsider how practices of public engagement integrate with and bring to birth new possibilities for our common life. Let us be about the task of actively imagining and engaging in such practices in ways that proclaim the church's critical witness and healing presence in our fraught and fractured world.[50]

Part Six

ATTENDING TO
EMERGING DISCOURSES

Chapter 20

Through the Leaven of Popular Catholic Practices

Women Transforming Church

Nancy Pineda-Madrid

I N HER CONTRIBUTION to the 2002 volume *The Church Women Want,*
Miriam Therese Winter wrote,

> My vision of the Church in the twenty-first century is one that is shared by
> a growing number of American Catholic women, and it is decisively, radically
> feminist.... To be *radical* means to be rooted, deeply rooted, in the spirit of the liv-
> ing God.... To be *feminist* ... means to be fully committed to the liberation of all
> peoples ... [and] to be in the struggle for ... the unequivocal inclusion of women
> in all decision-making and celebrational roles in the Roman Catholic Church.[1]

Her statement resonates. In surveying our current ecclesial landscape, we
quickly and easily recognize that a widening chasm separates the church we
have from the one we long for — a deeply painful realization for many of
us. We ask ourselves, what strategies will sustain us during this time? What
strategies will till the soil of reform?

Popular religious practices bear emancipatory possibilities. Just as a small
bit of leaven can be worked through a large volume of dough causing it to rise,
to become light, so popular religious practices can release their own form of gas
and lighten our ecclesial load. They can bring new life to our souls, transforming
our experience of the divine and transforming our experience of church. We,
in turn, become leaven. Being leaven is exactly what we are called to be (Luke
13:21), and as Paul reminds us, even a little leaven has wide impact (1 Cor.
5:6). Emancipatory popular religious practices enable women to reclaim their
" 'birthright' of being Church, fully gifted and responsible members of the 'body
of Christ.' "[2]

While in many cases popular religious practices have been undeniably designed to maintain and solidify an ossified form of Catholicism, nonetheless, as
a strategy, they are malleable and potent, and as such they can offer life-giving
possibilities for Catholic women. When popular religious practices reflect not
only an expansive imagination but also an emancipatory commitment, they
hold open the possibility of transforming our understanding of church.

In order to defend such a claim, we first need to explain what popular religious practices are, why so many women have understandably regarded them

with ambivalence, and why, nevertheless, they can be empowering for women and subversive of the kyriarchal church.[3] This clarity, then, will allow us to explore in greater depth a particular instance of a popular religious practice with attention to its dynamism. Finally, the examination of this particular instance will elucidate how popular religious practices not only offer welcome food for the soul but also invite conversion. They invite conversion on personal and communal levels. Popular religious practices can offer leaven for our lives, transforming us so that we become leaven for the church, leaven for society.

Popular Religious Practices — Life Giving?

Within the discourse of theology one can find various definitions of Christian practices in general as well as of popular religious practices in particular. For our purpose, Dorothy Bass offers a description of Christian practices that broadly and helpfully orients what I am calling popular religious practices. Along with Craig Dykstra, Bass identifies Christian practices as "things Christian people do together over time to address fundamental human needs in response to and in the light of God's active presence for the life of the world."[4] Further, practices and reflection on practices can "contribute to building up ways of life that are abundant . . . in love, justice and mercy."[5] Practices may be distinguished by the following characteristics:

> First, as meaningful clusters of human activity (including the activity of thinking) that require and engender knowledge on the part of practitioners, *practices re-sist the separation of thinking from acting,* and thus of Christian doctrine from Christian life. Second, *practices are social, belonging to groups of people across generations* — a feature that undergirds the communal quality of the Christian life. Third, *practices are rooted in the past but are also constantly adapting to changing circumstances,* including new cultural settings. Fourth, *practices articulate wisdom that is in the keeping of practitioners who do not think of themselves as theologians.*[6]

This general description of Christian practices highlights several points pertinent to women looking for spiritual sustenance. This description assumes that there is a link between basic human needs and God's action in the world; that there is a link between thinking and acting; that there is a link between traditions of the past and the pressing questions of our own time; that there is a link between the social practices of our generation of believers and generations of the distant past and far future; and, finally, that practices express a wisdom that intends human flourishing. Practices understood as such offer an effective strategy because they deepen women's relationship to themselves, to the larger human community, to the living God — all the while affirming women's desire for life abundant. This general description lays an excellent foundation.

Yet this description does not situate Christian practices in the context of the Roman Catholic Church. Here the experience of U.S. Latina/o Catholics is instructive for clarifying this aspect of "popular religious practices." The term "popular" does not refer to common, widespread, en vogue, and the like. "Popular" means that the "symbols, practices and narratives are *of the people.*"[7]

"Popular religion is 'popular'...because its creators and practitioners are the people, and more concretely, the marginalized people in society (i.e., those social sectors *pushed* against their will to the dispensable or disposable margins of society)."[8] Even a cursory reading of the history of Latinas/os in the U.S. Roman Catholic Church reveals a long narrative of exclusion and disregard by church officials.[9] For centuries, popular religious practices have remained important among communities of Latina/o believers who want to appropriate their Catholic beliefs. Through these practices, this distinctive group of Catholic believers have held on to beliefs that, while different, are not necessarily in opposition to "official" or "institutional" church teaching and practice. Latina/o Catholic believers understand their own beliefs as dialectically linked to those of the ecclesial elites, yet different.[10] This description of popular religious practices, while based on the experience of Latinas/os Catholics, offers a vision and a strategy to Catholic women and others who find their experience of the institutional church either too circumscribed or too foreign or too disconnected, such that it is no longer life-giving.

Many Catholic women find themselves unwilling to consider practices as a potential font of spiritual nourishment and an effective discipline for furthering constructive change. Too many women have experience with well-meaning church leaders, family members, and friends who have encouraged religious practices as a way to "deepen" faith. However, these "practices" have turned out to be ossified rather than life-giving. These practices are ones that have become stale and have embodied a rigid traditionalism rather than a flourishing tradition. For example, various Marian devotions have often been used to keep women in subordinate positions. Such practices have been designed to hold up the Virgin Mary as the ideal model for women; however, "with all her glory she is always obedient, she is not 'ordained,' she is the busy but submissive, patient and suffering auxiliary who can intercede but not decide."[11] The idealization of this portrayal of Mary has lead to a widening rift between women's lives and faith, and to an increasingly dulled sense of God's presence in our lives. Among Latinas, Marian practices have been used, at times, to further the ideology of marianismo. Marianismo, which is grounded in a traditional understanding of Christianity, encourages women to follow the "example" set by Mary, that is, to model "self-sacrifice, self-effacement, and self-subordination"[12] and, by so doing, to become "spiritually superior." "Superiority" is achieved through "submission and invisibility."[13] In the end, marianismo promotes the "noble sacrifice of the self," and erodes women's self-esteem.[14] Obviously, such limited and limiting practices are not what I intend by "popular religious practices."

María Pilar Aquino has pointed out that popular religiosity (and therefore popular religious practices) remains an ambiguous arena for women. Too often practices bear the stain of the patriarchal worldviews out of which they emerge. And, problematically, not much work has been done on popular religiosity from the perspective of women.[15] She observes, "Although popular devotions express liberating impulses that have helped the poor masses in their struggle to survive, especially when they are expressed in the language of resistance, it is also true that this same popular religiosity contains elements that legitimate submission to the oppressor. Because this environment has been basically patri-archal and *machista,* it is not surprising that women's religious expression also contains these elements."[16] All of this suggests that popular religious practices are complex and fraught with slippery slopes. Even so they can be a powerful and crucial tool along the road to transformation.

If Catholic women seek effective strategies for renewing the church, then those strategies must embody ways for women to express their power, partic-ularly their power to act on and practice their own account of their Catholic faith. Recall that "power is the ability to take one's place in whatever discourse is essential to action and the right to have one's part matter."[17] It is only when women actively take on roles in which they publicly generate and express their account of their Catholic faith that the process of transformation can begin. Failing this, women will remain alienated from their own experience of faith, cut off from what can be a life-giving experience of the Catholic faith, short-changed in the graces of human flourishing. Popular religious practices can be one effective strategy.

Such practices can allow women's emancipation to move to the fore through the use of religious symbols, language, and actions that offer not only an inter-pretation of women's experience of oppression but also make visible women's hopes and actions in search of their own liberation. For example, women in many Latina/o cultures have a tradition of creating home altars and displaying on them pictures of deceased family members and close friends, some of whom likely knew suffering from oppression. Often these pictures are placed along-side pictures of the young, the coming generation who symbolize hope for a brighter tomorrow — and alongside pictures of special saints, often a Marian image and one of Jesus. In creating a link between past suffering, future hope, and the presence of the sacred, women "name" sacred space and time. Women choose which family members and religious icons will be placed on the altar and which ones will be left aside. The very act of naming sacred space and time is in itself an expression of power. Whether the women who build altars realize it or not, the act of creating an altar is a form of speaking, of refusing to be silenced, of resisting assimilation into someone else's definition of what consti-tutes sacred space and time. And as Elisabeth Schüssler Fiorenza has observed, along with many, many others, there is power in the act of naming.[18]

Moreover, popular religious practices, such as the building of altars, can affirm an elastic understanding of the Christian faith. Again drawing from the experience of Latinas, popular religion has roots in "pre-Reformation, sixteenth-century Christianity of southern Spain" as well as "the religious be-liefs and rituals of African and Amerindian cultures."[19] These two major roots afford popular religion the ability to mediate in a credible way an experience of the divine as known through traditional Christian symbols while taking seri-ously God's active presence in the midst of non-Christian peoples. The elasticity of popular religious practices has allowed the vitality of Catholicism to thrive among Latinas even when the institutional church has ignored them or of-fered few resources.[20] And while this account is particular to the experience of Latinas, the principle here bears wider significance. Because popular religious practices can be said to thrive in the borderlands of the Catholic faith, similar to any borderland experience they hold open the possibility of fresh, invigorating interpretations of the faith. This, of course, is complicated. When does a popular religious practice cease to be Catholic? When does it go too far? While these questions are of vital importance, engaging them would take us far afield from the task of this chapter.

I would caution, however, against quick judgments about their validity as Catholic practices. Popular religious practices intend a tangible manifestation of, in Catholic parlance, the sacramental principle. The Catholic tradition "has long held a reverential place for the concrete ways in which God can be manifest through the material. . . . According to the sacramental principle, human beings find God not by leaving or denying the world, but by becoming immersed more deeply in it."[21] Ideally, popular religious practices enable their practitioners to do exactly that, namely, to find God by becoming more deeply immersed in the world. So, when women create and engage in such practices, they inherently recognize the larger truth of the sacramental principle.

Just as leaven expands bread dough, good practices can expand our imaginations. The best of them ground us in our multifaceted experience (they engage our minds, our bodies, our emotions, our imaginations, our moral vision), enabling us to enter into our experience, consider it, and come to understand it some new ways. This kind of practice generates life.

An Expansive Imagination, an Emancipatory Commitment

To appreciate fully why popular religious practices can sustain women spiritually and over time transform the church, we need to understand the dynamism that the best of practices embody. We will explore this dynamism through an analysis of an extended example below. In brief, effective practices invite participants to enter into their personal and communal experience more deeply, to expand their religious imagination, and to commit collectively to seek the vision of abundant life that Jesus promised (John 10:10).

A Story of Forgiveness and Healing

The following example illustrates well that popular religious practices can not only stretch the ways we think about God but also create an experience wherein the presence of God is felt and known deeply.

Some years ago I worked in the chancery of the Archdiocese of Seattle and represented the archbishop among many ethnic communities. During this time I was invited to take part in a Native American sweat on an area reservation. Most Native Americans who participated were Catholics attempting to make sense of their Catholic faith in light of their Native American traditions and vice versa.

For the purpose of the sweat, some members of the community gathered the day before to build the sweat lodge. They found a nice clearing in the middle of the forest, found long and sturdy cedar bows, bent each bow into an arc and secured each end into the dirt. Many bows were used to form the frame of a domed structure. Next, several large, impenetrable tarps were placed over the domed structure and secured such that utterly no light could enter. At the center of this circular sweat lodge a small round pit was dug and the earth from it removed and placed in a mound not far from the entry to the sweat lodge. Quite early the morning of the sweat the "firekeeper" arrived, built a fire, and placed several medium sized rocks in the midst of the fire. The firekeeper kept vigil for hours before and throughout the sweat, ensuring the availability of red-hot rocks. The sweat lodge represented the womb of mother earth and the absence of light within signified death to the destructive patterns of life and a place of gestation before a new life. In addition, the sweat lodge represented a kind of confessional.

Shortly before the sweat was to begin about seventeen of us gathered outside and then entered the lodge in silence through a small flap of tarp left free for this purpose. Our leader, a middle-aged woman, entered last. We all sat down two deep along the perimeter of the lodge. We spanned the age spectrum from about seven to seventy-five years of age — both men and women. Almost all of us were dressed in bathing suits except for the elders, who entered with only a towel to cover themselves. Our sparse clothing was certainly practical, but it was more. It represented that we were bringing nothing but ourselves to this prayer, and that we were symbolically going back into the original womb of all creation. We left behind all the trappings of our lives.

Once we were all inside the lodge our leader began our prayer by reminding us that the great religious traditions, the Native way and the Catholic way (among others), had rituals to encourage us to face our sins and failings. She then directed the firekeeper to bring in four or five red-hot stones, place them in the small center pit, and pour water over them. He left. With the small flap of an opening securely closed, we all sat in utter darkness. We began to sweat. She spoke of the generations of Native peoples, many of whom had adopted the Catholic way, who had entered the sweat lodge, recognized their failings — personal and collective — and sought forgiveness. In her prayers she reminded us of our fervent desire to live in relationship with ourselves, with each other, with the whole of creation and with God. She repeatedly invited us to offer our prayers. She spoke of the ways in which a mother's body sustains the life she carries within. So too the earth who is like our mother was here to sustain and support us as we died to our destructive patterns and recommitted ourselves to a more abundant life. We continued to sweat. Various participants offered prayers acknowledging the ways in which we have betrayed ourselves, one another, our community, creation, and ultimately, God. At one point our leader invited those of us who wished to do so to publicly acknowledge our sins and to seek forgiveness from God in the presence of those gathered, who represented the larger human community. The cover of darkness made confessions somehow easier. Many of us spoke of our sins, and many of us prayed for each other's healing. After each prayer we responded with the refrain, "to all our relations," signifying the inherent social nature of our humanity.

As the sweat progressed through three different time periods my heartbeat quickened, my breathing became slower and more shallow. The physiological changes we experienced during the sweat enabled us to listen more attentively to each other's prayers. When the sweat ended, we all emerged reborn from the womb of the earth and from the sustaining love of God. The toxins we carry in our bodies had been drawn out, leaving us internally purified. We felt physically transformed and noticeably more healthy.

Entering into Our Experience

The practice of the Native American sweat encouraged each of us to enter into various facets of our experience and to do so deeply. We experienced physical transformation as we sweated out the impurities within our bodies; emotional transformation as we heard, received, and forgave one another's failings; and spiritual transformation as we prayed to God to forgive our sins and enable us to live a more righteous life. Our physical, emotional, and spiritual transformation worked together in synergistic fashion to create a cumulative effect greater than the sum of its parts. In sum, we experienced our "confession" more fully precisely because the practice attended to experience in a multifaceted fashion.

Our leader, a woman, created a ritual that foregrounded symbols associated with female humanity and represented them as sacred. She spoke of the earth as a mother who supports our journey to wholeness. She compared the earth to our mother's womb, which sustained our lives when they were most vulnerable, and she represented the earth as a metaphor for God — a radical notion. She invited each of us present to actively take part in furthering the wholeness of one another as well as seeking wholeness in our own journey. We were invited to share, to hear, to receive, and to actively pray for one another. This invitation reflected a high regard for the social, interrelated character of the human community and challenged the prevailing metaphor for God as mighty warrior or sovereign king.

We entered into our experience understood as not only our personal journey, not only our collective journey, but also our ecological journey. The practice emphasized that we are part and parcel of creation, an insight increasingly brought to the fore in the work of eco-feminist theologians. For example, Elizabeth Johnson describes a vision of the Creator Spirit as "enfolding and unfolding a reconciled human community and a healed, living earth, [that overcomes] sexist disparagement of the female in the three basic relationships of human beings among each other, with the earth, and with God, and [that thereby serves] the future of life itself."[22] Emancipatory practices are those that on the level of physical embodiment situate human persons as part of creation and not as a group that stands over against creation or somehow apart from it.

Through the use of religious rituals and symbols, this practice honored the complexity of what it means to be both a committed feminist and a faithful Roman Catholic. These two commitments often live uneasily together. Yet, arguably, the practice of the sweat attempted to respect both.

Susan Ross uses the phrase "expressive ambiguity" to describe the dynamism of this kind of practice. It manifests a worldview that clashes with univocal modes of religious understanding and instead necessitates that participants become aware of a multiplicity of meanings that shape their religious experience. When participants become aware of the multiplicity of meanings, they concurrently open themselves to the possibility of a transformed self-understanding.[23] Indeed, effective strategies such as these will of necessity take us to the borderlands of our Catholic tradition.

Imagination, Emancipation

The practice of the sweat expanded our imaginations by weaving our personal and collective stories together with the Christian story as well as with stories drawn from Native traditions. When the leader invited participants to pray, some offered prayers to Jesus, others to the Creator, and still others to Grandmother and Grandfather Spirit. All these ways of naming God facilitated in each of us a new appreciation for the inexhaustibility of the mystery we call God. Moreover, in prayer many expressed an expansive understanding of community. Some acknowledged that we stand *in community* with our brother the sun, others, our sister the moon, and still others, the spirit of the owl, the bear, the deer, the running water. For the participants who were largely Native American and Catholic this strategy responded to their deepest yearnings.

While our leader did not explicitly refer to the Catholic understanding of our common priesthood symbolized by baptism, she did lead our prayer in a way that made manifest this dimension of our Catholic faith. In her prayers she reminded us how interrelated we are, how each of us has something to contribute that someone else present needs, and then she invited each of us to actively contribute for the good of all. We were encouraged again and again to recognize the common lot of humanity and the whole of the created order, particularly when we responded to each other with the words, "to all our relations." Through this practice, we participated in a common priesthood rooted in a vision consonant with a "discipleship of equals."[24]

Further, the practice of the sweat offered an opportunity for our leader to reclaim for women "the same imaginative freedom, popular creativity, and ritual powers" afforded to the patriarchal church's "founding fathers."[25] As a constructive endeavor it embodied a critique of the patriarchal church in light of a commitment to foster a more emancipatory church. As Elisabeth Schüssler Fiorenza rightly reminds us, only when Catholic women reclaim our own "religious imagination and our sacred powers of naming" can we then transform and invigorate the church with new dreams and a new vision.[26] Through this process of reclaiming, we can become the leaven that transforms the church from a patriarchal institution into a living body that values the liberation of all.

Life-giving practices such as the Native American sweat carry formative power. In such practices, as in all ritual and liturgy, we express our convictions about who we understand ourselves to be and what we intend in our understanding. Popular religious practices refashion, reshape our relation to God. In the process, they form us. This insight is captured in the age-old saying *lex orandi, lex credendi;* that is, that the way in which we pray not only expresses our beliefs but it also shapes our beliefs. Thus a strategy for reform is one that reshapes the ways in which we pray.

In the practice of the sweat, we prayed with our whole selves (mind, body, spirit) and in explicit connection with other community members and with the earth. We were invited to imagine ourselves in a world more acutely aware of its interrelatedness. We heard each others' prayers and knew each others' painful struggles and heartfelt desires for wholeness and healing. This was not an abstraction but was quite real in the stories heard and shared, and in the physiological experience we had in common. Our common experience expanded our understanding of confession and deepened our appreciation of the wisdom of the confession practice within the Catholic tradition. This popular religious practice offered us a strategy, a way of viewing the core tenants of our faith anew and of gaining a radical appreciation for their life-giving intent.

Leaven for Our Lives, Leaven for the Church

When popular religious practices grow out of the experience of a marginalized community and reflect a thoughtful commitment to appropriate the Catholic faith, then the faith can be named and claimed anew in ways more deeply rooted in the spirit of the living God. This happening extends our imaginations.[27] Further, when practices support women's roles in ritual leadership, then women take their place in public, sacred space and that role matters not only for the leader herself but for all participants, men as well as women. Susan Ross reminds us: "For Roman Catholic women who have been socialized in a church that has excluded women not only from ritual leadership but also from ritual space, *claiming a ritual role is an empowering act.*"[28]

Effective popular religious practices offer a vital strategy that demands our conversion. The best practices thoughtfully and vigorously support another consciousness, one in which we are no longer objects of our Catholic faith but become subjects of this wondrous tradition. The ecclesial vision that informs effective practices has been identified by Schüssler Fiorenza. She calls it *ekklēsia*. It is a model of church that strives "to make women visible as active participants and leaders in the Church, to underline women's contributions and suffering throughout Church history, and to safeguard women's autonomy and freedom from spiritual-theological patriarchal controls."[29] While this model necessarily involves critique it likewise entails a constructive vision of church. *Ekklēsia* signifies a "gathering of free and fully responsible "citizens."[30] We are called to be subjects.

As Catholics we do not have a choice about being "leaven." The Gospels tell us — we are to be leaven in a loaf of bread (Luke 13:21), salt of the earth (Matt. 5:13) and light of the world (Matt. 5:14–15). We are to make a difference in this world now. When we create and participate in life-giving practices we become leaven. We are changed in the process. As we are changed, the church is changed and our society is changed as well.

Chapter 21

Catholic Sexual Ethics
in the Twenty-First Century

Patricia Beattie Jung

M Y GOAL IN THIS ESSAY is to identify what I think will be two of the
topics at center stage in Catholic sexual ethics in the twenty-first century.
Undoubtedly, the official prohibition of contraception, the prophylactic use of
condoms that can be used to prevent the spread of STDs, including HIV and
AIDS, and the prohibition of faithful homosexual relationships will continue
to be disputed by faithful Catholic laypeople and moral theologians. As long
as the magisterial ban on these practices continues to shape public policy and
the work of relief agencies across the globe, these will remain important moral
questions. Still, the broad parameters of the debates will not change much from
what was first sketched in the twentieth century, though the pastoral dilemmas
that fuel them will probably intensify. In that sense, I do not think there will be
"new" conversations about these matters in the church.

However, I do think that conversations about both priestly celibacy and
gender complementarity will take new turns in the decades to come. Concerns
about priestly celibacy will shift from pastoral and pragmatic arguments to a
close examination of the claim to spiritual superiority made about celibacy. It is
the *idealization* of this practice that has reinforced its status as mandatory for
most priests in the Latin rite. Celibate persons make a permanent commitment
to abstain from marriage and sexual intimacy "for the sake of the kingdom of
heaven." While few question the value per se of such a consecrated life, many
question whether such a style of discipleship is inherently superior to marriage
or the (nonconsecrated) single life. Consequently, they do not see it as inherently
more suitable for those in church leadership positions.

Similarly, new scientific information about the truly diverse pattern of human
sexual differentiation is raising questions about the notion of heterosexual
gender complementarity. If human sexuality is more accurately thought of as
polymorphic, rather than dimorphic, then the interpersonal complementarity
that sexuality energizes should not be restricted to a rigid, binary heterosexual
model, even if that is its most common form.

The Idealization of Celibacy Reconsidered

At the Second Vatican Council in the mid-1960s the bishops of the Catholic Church proclaimed that the Christian call to perfection was universal. All Christians, they declared — whether lay or religious, single, married, or celibate alike — were called to bear witness to God in and through their specific sexual vocations. Nothing about marriage was identified as second class, as love was discerned to be at its very heart. In essence, marriage was defined as an exclusive, permanent, intimate partnership of both life and love. Additionally the Second Vatican Council affirmed the importance of lay witness in the world and of the domestic church.

Ever since, questions about the traditional claim to *superiority* associated with celibacy and the necessity of requiring celibacy as a prerequisite for ordination to the priesthood have flooded the church. Not coincidentally, the number of vocations to "religious life" among women and men alike, especially but not exclusively within countries that border the North Atlantic, has plummeted. While a powerful case for the ongoing value of celibacy can and undoubtedly will be made, its *idealization* in the tradition has come under steady fire.

Traditionally, the church has taught that while marriage was good, celibacy was even better. Indeed, nearly from the beginning of the Common Era, sexual lifestyles were ranked in church teaching according to their "sexual purity." Virginity was seen as best, then perpetual celibacy, followed by widowhood, temporary continence within marriage, and finally procreativity within marriage. Even the Protestant Reformer Martin Luther affirmed this ranking in theory. While he did indeed argue that like most of the faithful, clergy should marry, it was *not* because he had a higher view of sex or a lesser view of celibacy than his contemporaries.[1]

Despite the Second Vatican Council's several challenges to a two-tiered notion of discipleship, in an apostolic letter "On the Dignity and Vocation of Women" delivered near the turn of the century, Pope John Paul II described celibacy as an evangelical ideal. He proclaimed the superiority of virginity over marriage to be "a constant teaching of the church."[2] Like his predecessor, Pope Benedict XVI sees consecrated celibacy as a "radical" expression of "exclusive devotion to Christ" and "an objective sign and foreshadowing of the 'wedding feast of the Lamb' (Rev. 19:7–9)."[3] Still, the theological foundation for that claim and its corollary — the requirement of celibacy for the priesthood — seem to be increasingly unstable. In order to understand the parameters of the deliberation before us, it is important to understand its historical backdrop. The idealization of celibacy is rooted in the church's traditional overemphasis on sexual purity and its correspondingly asexual vision of resurrected life.

Historical Background

There is tension between these teachings and much of the rest of the Christian tradition about embodiment. Christians have always given great value and status to the human body. Because of their convictions about the goodness of Creation, the Incarnation of God in Jesus of Nazareth, the Resurrection of Christ, and the promised resurrection of the body in the life of the world to come, Christians traditionally honor the body, treating it as a "temple of the Holy Spirit" (1 Cor. 6:19–20). This contrasts sharply with the views of embodiment that prevailed in much of the rest of the ancient, first-century Mediterranean world. The body is part and parcel of the glorious life to come; the anthropological conception of persons as an integral unity of body and soul is rightly considered distinctively Christian. The story of why human sexuality was not woven into this integral vision of embodied persons is complex. It has biblical, philosophical — especially Stoic — and theological roots.

The biblical testimony about sexuality in general, and celibacy in particular, is complex. Though tradition has long held that Jesus died a virgin, the Christian Scriptures are clear: Jesus spoke of celibacy as given only to some, and he began his public ministry celebrating at a wedding feast. While at times he denounced the "family first" mentality typical of antiquity, Jesus encourages his disciples to welcome children and never speaks disparagingly of intimate friendships, sexual or not. Repeatedly in the Gospels Jesus is portrayed as challenging the primacy of family ties, structures, and duties (even one as "sacred" as burying the dead); however, his target is clearly not marriage and family life per se, but is rather a concern about the temptation to give it too much priority.

We don't know whether the apostle Paul was widowed or divorced, but we do know that at least after his conversion, he was celibate. Through his celibacy, Paul aimed to free himself from the anxieties he associated with having a spouse and children. In comparison to some of his disciples in Corinth — who apparently believed that the "singleness of heart" (Acts 2:46; Col. 3:22) required by discipleship could only be achieved by dissolving their households — Paul's views of marriage and celibacy seem comparatively moderate. Paul worried that marriage might divide the heart and thus prove to distract the faithful from God. But because he believed the end time was near, he suggested that those who were married should simply remain so. (Paul also saw marriage as a licit "remedy" for sexual desire and commended it to all those who might be overwhelmed by lust.) To singles not likely to be overwhelmed by their sexual desires, Paul commended celibacy over marriage. He preferred celibacy because he thought it would leave the faithful disciple free from the worrisome distractions that accompany family life.

Once it became clear in the second century of the Common Era that Paul had been mistaken about the imminent arrival of the end time, Christians set about trying to discern how best to witness to the life of the world to come over the course of a lifetime. As noted above, discipleship entails orienting the whole self toward God. In the earliest centuries, the threat of martyrdom offered Christians a clear, if terrifying, way to offer themselves — body and soul — to God. After the Emperor Constantine's conversion ended persecution in the fourth century of the Common Era, celibacy offered another dramatic form of witness. This "bloodless" form of martyrdom built upon the Pauline suspicion of sexual "distractions."

Early church fathers interpreted the remark attributed to Jesus in the Gospel of Matthew (12:25) — that in heaven people will neither marry nor be given in marriage — to mean that there would be no sex in heaven. Thus, celibacy would embody a clearer witness to the life of the world to come. It would best enable believers to witness here and now to the asexual purity and singleness of heart that would characterize heaven. In contrast, because they were seen as "entangling" us with others, many church fathers perceived sexual desires as obstacles to such undivided devotion to God. Thus, in the early church, most people thought celibacy was the best way to imitate the Risen Christ.[4]

In view of the expectation that everything — including the body — would be gloriously transformed in the life of the world to come, many Christian theologians of this era argued that in this new creation the body would be "spiritualized." They thought the body would be gutted of all its "impure," visceral — especially venereal — emotions. Sexual desire was conflated with lust. For much of its history, the church *misidentified* sexual desire per se as morally pathological and held all desire for sexual pleasure (even in marriage) to be morally suspect.

Even the comparatively moderate views of the late fourth-century church father St. Augustine of Hippo basically reflect this viewpoint. He presumed that marriage — along with sexual differentiation and reproductive activities (though they were conceived of as devoid of desire) — were part of God's original blessing in Paradise.[5] Nevertheless, Augustine believed these dimensions of sexuality, along with the passion and pleasure he associated exclusively with "the Fall," would have no place in the new creation.

An account of how the distinction between lustful and graceful experiences of sexual desire became blurred in Christianity must also include the Christian adoption of Stoic ideals. Within the various dualistic worldviews that pervaded the ancient Mediterranean world, the material world — including the body and its sexual passions and reproductive functions — was frequently thought to be a threat to reason and freedom. The realities of marriage in the ancient world confirmed this. Marriage at that time frequently involved older men marrying very young women for economic, political, or procreative purposes. Wealth, power, and pleasure — even a sense of immortality — were often tied to and transferred through marriage and kinship systems.[6] In such a context, sexual continence vividly signaled the renunciation of such worldly pursuits. The idealization of virginity, celibacy, and widowhood signaled the refusal to prioritize such concerns. (Of course, its "mere" endorsement would have done the same.)

Additionally marriage in the ancient Mediterranean world was marked by high maternal and infant mortality rates. Stoic prescriptions frowned upon not only the involuntary "intemperance" of most sexual passions, but also upon even the tender affections sometimes shared by lovers. Along with indifference and control, emotional detachment and autonomy were admired and commended as morally ideal within Stoicism.[7]

This overemphasis on sexual purity coupled with the Stoic distortion of both emotional intimacy and deep attachments clouded the church's theological imagination. In the eschatological visions of the new heaven and new earth that prevailed in the early church, everything associated with human sexuality was absent. As I shall discuss in the second half of this essay, in most accounts, even sexual differentiation disappeared. Since the task of the moral life on earth is to embody insofar as is realistic the "new creation" God inaugurated in Christ, this vision of heaven sanctified the idealization of celibacy. Ultimately, the absence of human sexuality in eschatological conceptions of Risen Life underlies arguments for priestly celibacy in the Roman church (and for celibate bishops among Orthodox Christians). In the twenty-first century Catholic moral theologians will want to reconsider the place given to human sexuality in Christian visions of heaven.[8] What follows is a taste of what such arguments may look like.

Sex in Heaven?

There are three reasons for affirming that there will be sex in heaven. The first is theological: God is a God of desire and delight. The second is anthropological: our resurrection destiny is bodily and communal; sexuality is the source of our capacity for relationship. The third is hermeneutical: it is not unbiblical to envision sex in heaven as glorious. So, the case can be made for explicitly and deeply theological reasons that consecrated celibacy and matrimony have an equal potential to bear witness to the shape of life in the world to come. Consequently both ways of life should find expression in church leadership.

What we know about God is that the love revealed in the Trinity is passionate. This divine mutual indwelling erupted into and continues providentially to spill over into creation. God's delight is creative. God desires to be in a wild and warm communion with all that is. So desirous is God of such communion that God's love pours out into redemption. Our Lover-God is the "hound of heaven." The life and death of Jesus was fueled by God's desire for intimacy with us. The Cross was not about the denial of passion, but was its very expression on earth. Divine love reveals that ultimately what we ought to do cannot be split from that to which we are deeply drawn. There is a happy collaboration between what is good and what is beautiful.

Creation is made precisely for this fiery dance! Desire and delight are grounded in — and image — God. They come from God to us as grace. Far from an obstacle to love, passion fuels desire and delight and is supplied so that we may hunger for and enjoy each other and God. Through desire's grace, we can literally taste the communion that we were made for and know ourselves to be intimately loved. The ache of loneliness, the attraction of desire, the heat of arousal, and the joys of genital pleasure and friendship are good and gracious gifts.

Who we are is mediated to ourselves, to others, and even to God through our bodies. Only through our bodies can we transcend ourselves and relate to what is other/Other. To believe in the resurrection of the body is to believe that the communion with God and the cosmos for which we have been designed will be both mystically immediate and, in some transformed sense, embodied and mediated as well. Because passion and pleasure fuel the communion that

glorifies and delights God, conjugal union can sometimes be a sacrament of
Christ's love for the church, indeed of God's love for all that is.

It was profoundly mistaken to have thought of human loves as "distracting"
us from God, as if God were simply another possible object for our affections
alongside and competing with human lovers, particular friends and children,
for our loyalty and affections. God is the Ground of all that is and can be loved
precisely through such relationships. The church has long taught that sexual
activity within marriage could be viewed as a positive source for mutual sancti-
fication (as well as a concession to lust).[9] At the council at least some recognized
that sharing sexual pleasure could be lovemaking, in proportion to what we extend as gift. This is why most theologians recognize sexual intercourse as the
primary symbol of sacramental marriages.[10]

Jesus himself suggested that friendship is an important overarching paradigm
for our calling to embrace one another. What is unique about marital friendship
is that spouses vow to devote themselves to each other in a way that is total
and lifelong in scope. They promise to weave together their spiritual, familial,
economic, medical, sexual, productive, and reproductive histories. Tradition
recognizes that matrimony (like celibacy) can be for Christians consecrated to
the Reign of God. Conjugal love can be sacramental.

While there appear to be some biblical rationales for the widespread belief
that the life of the world to come will be asexual, these texts may be faithfully
interpreted in quite different ways. Consider for example Jesus' remark about
the absence of marriage in heaven. All interpreters of this text recognize that
in his reply to the Sadducees, Jesus is stressing the discontinuity between the
present age and our life to come. He is clear that the promise of bodily resurrection implies much more than the mere resuscitation mockingly insinuated
by the Sadducees. Unquestionably, risen life — and our experience of sexuality
in it — will be vastly different from what we now know.

But beyond this point, reasonable interpretations may vary tremendously.
Some, as noted above, conclude that there will be no sex in heaven. As they
envision it, celibacy is the only true full model of the life to come. Yet consecrated celibacy gives an embodied, indeed dramatically sexual, witness to our
common calling to love God wholeheartedly. Those few called to vowed, celibate religious life give bold witness through their celibacy to this invitation by
excluding from their life other significant commitments, such as to a spouse,
children, or even a particular ministry. Undoubtedly, as the Reign of God forms
in our midst, consecrated celibacy witnesses in a wonderful way to the dynamics of that eschatological community, wherein we will delight in loving the Lord
with all our heart, soul, strength, and mind.

However, as that Reign unfolds in our midst, we are also called to delight in
loving our neighbor as ourselves. Conjugal unions, especially as they witness to
our gracious capacity to become "one flesh," can also bear witness to the Reign
of God. The church has long taught that in heaven our union with God will
not be a private, solitary relationship, an encounter between "God and me,"
no matter how personally intense and intimate. In Christ we all stand together
as children of God, brothers and sisters, united as friends.

Elizabeth Stuart notes that there may be no marriage in heaven because on earth it institutionalizes preferential and exclusive (and in many cases, patriarchal) forms of love.[11] Since the Christian belief in the resurrection of the body is communal in scope, all systems of preference, privilege, and exclusion — including those rooted in biological and sexual relationships — will be overcome in the End. But for Stuart this does not necessarily mean that there will be no sex in heaven. We may enjoy being drawn by God into ever-fuller relationships with an ever-widening circle of friends. Since our transfigured body-selves will no longer be restricted by limitations of the life of the flesh and our commitments may be perpetual, there need be nothing promiscuous about such love. Faithfulness is essentially about long-standing and total devotion, and only accidentally — in the earthly city — about exclusivity. Consider again the almost defiantly "promiscuous" love of God for all that is. Similarly, Ronald Long argues that sex in heaven will have both the intensity of one-to-one relationships in which on earth three's a crowd, as well as the vast scope of an orgy in which no one is left out or receives less love than they deserve.[12] If God loves us with both such interpersonal intensity and unabashed expansiveness, then it is perhaps most appropriate to presume it is into such a communion that we are being drawn.

In resurrected life we will become increasingly creatures of desire and delight, ever growing in our capacity for intimacy with and the enjoyment of God, each other, and all that is. Together marriage and consecrated celibacy bear witness to this future. Therefore, the church should welcome into leadership all those whose sexual lives are so consecrated to the Reign of God, whether married or celibate.

Gender Dimorphism Reconsidered

In the coming century, Catholic teaching about heterosexual gender complementarity will become increasingly contentious as its foundation in sexual dimorphism is challenged by emerging scientific data. Let me explain. During the second half of the twentieth century, the church gradually came to argue for the equality of women and men both at home and in society.[13] At the same time, the church began to emphasize gender differences more and more, concluding that women have a "special nature," essentially different from, yet complementary to, that of men. The church grounded this theory of heterosexual gender complementarity in what it took to be the axiomatic "fact" of sexual dimorphism.

In this binary paradigm for human sexuality, all ("normal") people are presumed to be unequivocally and exclusively male or unequivocally and exclusively female. Of course, humans have long recognized that there were persons who did not fit well into dichotomous categories of male or female. For most of church history, such "exceptions" to this binary paradigm were seen as persons who perverted God's design for human sexuality and threatened to pollute the wider community. Hermaphrodites and other intersexed persons were often seen as embodiments of personal or parental sin. Transgendered persons who did not successfully closet their condition were often persecuted. In the twentieth century, more pastoral approaches emerged: "exceptions" to the rule of sexual dimorphism were seen as suffering from congenital defects or diseased developmental dysfunctions. While they may have little or no subjective moral culpability for their "condition," the sexual identity of such persons remains "disordered." Such experiences of sexuality are "problematic" and "tragic" as such.

Are Humans Sexually Polymorphic?

However, it is precisely this framework that at the close of the twentieth century began to be challenged in many medical circles. Many studies of human sexual variation challenge the adequacy of this organizing metaphor. We now know that several biological factors contribute to the transgendered person's identity appearing (at least from within a bipolar system) to be "indeterminate" or "shifting." In addition to a person's external genitalia and internal reproductive organs, our gonadal sex and the sex of our brains, along with multiple chromosomal and hormonal factors, all combine and contribute variously to a range of sexual identities far more diverse than suggested by the dimorphic model. We now know there are many types of intersexuality and we have a much clearer picture of the extent of the phenomenon.[14]

For example, consider just what we now know about the genetic basis for human sexuality. While it is true that the vast majority of people are genetically either male (XY) or female (XX), nevertheless, it is estimated that across the globe five and a half million people have chromosomal patterns that vary from this binary pattern.[15] This is just the tip of the iceberg of biological evidence "against" (that is, not comprehended adequately by) the standard dimorphic paradigm.

Diseased, Defective, or Different?

Of course, logically it is not necessary to abandon the notion of sexual dimorphism on the basis of this data. The existence of anomalies does not necessarily undermine the presumption of a paradigm. Relatively speaking, intersexuality is still rare. Until very recently the scientific community treated such "exceptions" to the dimorphic paradigm as unquestionably diseased or defective.[16] Now, however, there is considerable debate within the medical community about whether there is any "need" for "treatments" at all. With a few exceptions, intersexuality per se is usually not associated with higher than average rates of morbidity or mortality.[17] Since these are the standard criteria for identifying a variation as a defective, many in the medical community question whether there is anything "wrong" with being intersexed.

Still, every difference is not natural in a normative sense. Whether what is statistically anomalous is interpreted as a monstrous abomination, a tragic defect, or a delightful variation depends upon the concepts through which it is interpreted. Human responses to difference are a function of the paradigmatic lens through which they are interpreted. What this new scientific information surfaces are questions about the adequacy of sexual dimorphism as an interpretative lens.

Much is at stake in this conversation. The church's basic teachings about procreativity and heterosexual gender complementarity are rooted in the paradigm of sexual dimorphism. It is on this foundation that the use of artificial forms of contraception, sterilization, and (intentionally) childfree marriages are condemned. It is on this foundation that the church condemns homosexual behavior, describes gay, lesbian, and bisexual orientations as disordered, outlaws same-sex marriage, and excludes from eligibility for ordination anyone who is not predominantly heterosexual as well as a vowed celibate. Though there is not much official teaching about gender-bending and gender-blending behaviors, most confessors conclude on the basis of this framework that such activity is morally proscribed as well.

The Sanctification of Sexual Dimorphism

In the West, sexual dimorphism has been religiously reinforced. It is thought to reflect a divinely established order for human sexuality, revealed in sacred Scriptures and evident in God's natural law. In Catholic teaching gender is thought to be determined at least to a significant degree by stable and essentially dimorphic biological differences. The church teaches that perspectives suggestive of human sexual polymorphism obscure this difference or duality of the sexes and are condemned. Biblical stories of creation are interpreted as revealing sexual dimorphism.

In its 2004 "Letter to the Bishops of the Catholic Church on the Collaboration of Men and Women in the Church and in the World," the Vatican interprets the opening chapter of Genesis as describing humanity "as articulated in the male-female relationship. This is the humanity, sexually differentiated, which is explicitly declared 'the image of God.' "[18] To be created in the image of God is to be created not only for relationship but for relationship precisely as only either male or female. The second creation story is said to confirm this as the significance of sexual difference. At first man was created in a state of original solitude and experienced loneliness there. This is resolved only when woman is created as a suitable life companion. "God's creation of woman characterizes humanity as a relational reality." Sexual "difference is oriented toward communion."[19]

The Vatican contends that the inscription of this vital difference onto humanity carries more than biological or psychological import. It is ontological in significance. This claim is asserted despite the fact that biologically, men and women are far more alike than different, and that individual differences tend to outweigh group differences. Quoting Pope John Paul II's letter "On the Dignity and Vocation of Women," the Vatican argues that " 'man and woman are called from the beginning not only to exist 'side by side' or 'together,' but they are also called to exist mutually 'one for the other.' "[20] All of human history unfolds within the context of the spousal significance of the body. All of humankind is set within this spousal call to be mutually for the other in interpersonal communion. And this must be heterosexual. The Vatican concludes: there is developing within "humanity itself, in accordance with God's will, the integration of what is 'masculine' and what is 'feminine.' "[21] In their review of the principal elements of the biblical vision of the meaning of sexual difference, the Vatican concludes that sexual dimorphism characterizes men and women on the physical, psychological, and spiritual level. It cannot be reduced to mere biological "fact," because sexual complementarity is a fundamental component of the human capacity to love. "This capacity to love — reflection and image of God who is love — is disclosed in the spousal character of the body, in which the masculinity or femininity of the person is expressed."[22]

For Christians it is always true that, as the Vatican notes, "the human dimension of sexuality is inseparable from the theological dimension."[23] For Christians anthropology is always really theological anthropology. People can truly understand who they are only in light of who God is. Hence, it is not surprising that this anthropological argument is rooted in and sanctified by a nuptial metaphor for God's relationship to humanity. The Vatican suggests that God is most aptly portrayed as a divine Bridegroom eagerly pursuing and making love to His bride (that is, all of humanity).[24] "God makes himself known as the Bridegroom who loves Israel his Bride."[25]

In a truly extraordinary move — that is, against the grain of long-standing patterns of biblical interpretation and many ancient traditions — the Vatican began to argue in this letter that the distinction between male and female will not be erased at the end time in Christ.[26] Only "the rivalry, enmity and violence which disfigured the relationship between men and women" will be overcome at the end time. Sexual dimorphism is so inscribed into creation's design that the Vatican argues that "male and female are thus revealed as *belonging ontologically to creation* and destined therefore *to outlast the present time,* evidently in a transfigured form."[27]

Christian Convictions about the Discernment of Truth

As evident above, the church's claims about sexual dimorphism no longer rest upon an uncontested account of human sexuality as "naturally" dimorphic. Rather, they rest largely upon a direct and straightforward appeal to and interpretation of biblical revelation. In this sense the Catholic framework for sexual ethics rests upon "revealed" natural law.

As evidenced above, when considered apart from the emerging scientific challenges to dimorphism, the biblical texts frequently cited in support of sexual dimorphism can be reasonably interpreted to do so. However, the question of what constitutes the criteria for *reasonable* biblical interpretation is significant. It has always been the Roman Catholic position that the discernment of the living Tradition is rooted in the consilience of insights, not only from traditional sources (such as the Bible and official church teachings) but also from secular (scientific, legal, philosophical, and other academic disciplines) and human (personal and communal) experiences.[28] Catholic Christians believe that truth is such that it is faithful to expect *reasonable* biblical interpretations to cohere not only with cogent church teachings but also with the wisdom emerging from sound scientific studies, well-constructed normative analyses, and properly interpreted human experiences.[29]

From a Catholic perspective it is reasonable to expect magisterial interpretations of biblical texts to be readily corroborated not only by the best of biblical scholarship but also to cohere with cogent interpretations of relevant human experiences and with the best scientific data and philosophical arguments available. When this expectation is not fulfilled, in theory at least, the genuine appreciation of official church interpretations of the Bible is not antithetical to their critical analysis. In fact, the absence of this consilience should spark further inquiry into and deliberation about how best to understand God's normative design for human sexuality and complementarity. Again, what follows is a taste of what such arguments may look like.

Gender in Heaven?

Since there are clear scientific and experiential grounds for reexamining these official interpretations, I hope by way of conclusion to demonstrate that the notion of sexual polymorphism is not necessarily incompatible with the creation accounts found in the opening chapters of Genesis.[30] In fact, those texts can be shown to be congruent with sexual polymorphism, just as the Scriptures are now readily seen to be compatible with a number of scientific concepts, such as the notions of a heliocentric solar system, polygenism, and the ongoing, evolutionary development of the universe, etc.

While both creation accounts specify that God created people "male **and** female" (Gen. 1:27; 2:23), nowhere does the Bible specify that God created people as *only either* male *or* female. The Bible is in fact silent about the existence of transgendered and intersexed persons, but the Bible is also largely silent about most of the astonishing biodiversity that flavors creation as a whole and the human community therein. Furthermore, what is theologically central to both biblical accounts of sexual differentiation — the linking of difference to the human longing not to exist in isolation but to live in intimate, passionate, tenderhearted, and delightful companionship with others — could remain applicable to all persons, whether they are intersexed, male or female. Such an interpretation affirms the human call to interpersonal communion that images God's own Triune dance and is more compatible with emerging scientific data about sexuality.

As conversations about both priestly celibacy and gender complementarity take new turns in the decades to come, there are new voices and perspectives that must be invited to the conversation. The ways we understand priestly celibacy and gender complementarity will have implications for our perspectives on issues such as the use of contraceptives and the prohibition of faithful homosexual unions. A new understanding of gender, free from the bounds of sexual dimorphism, would create space to celebrate our common life in Christ, where there is "neither male nor female." A new understanding of spousal love developed apart from rigid theories of gender complementarity would permit the blessing of both faithful heterosexual and homosexual unions. While it is true that church teachings may not develop in these directions, such dialogue is necessary if we want to witness faithfully to God's passionate and "promiscuous" love, in both this life and in the life to come.

Chapter 22

Practical Theology
in Global Christian Contexts

Susan Abraham

T HE *New Yorker* OF THE WEEK of February 12, 2007 carried a full-page
advertisement of a conference to take place in May 2007, called "Conference 2012: Stories from the Near Future," sponsored by Microsoft. It said: "See
what happens when the right brain meets the left brain at the first New Yorker
Conference, a dynamic day and two nights of new ideas, forward thinking, and
eye-opening innovation" and had among the complete list of presenters the
following: Theorists, Designers, Economists, Philosophers, Ethicists, Anima-
tors, Inventors, Musicians, Entrepreneurs, Philanthropists, Scientists, Artists,
Politicians, Engineers, and Financiers. Glaringly absent are theologians, pastors, priests, and ministers in the attempt to collectively think about shaping
a shared future. The life of communities of faith, their thoughts and insights
as they struggle for the same future, their creativity and commitment to such
work obviously seem to offer little by way of anything new, groundbreaking,
or surprising to this think tank.

The Microsoft logo at the end of the page says "People ready" and presumably they are ready for such a future, especially a new, innovative, and creative
technological future. Is there no place at all for theologians and pastors and
ministers and community leaders at such a table? Do communities of faith have
a stake at all in the future that will be midwived here by the Microsoft Corpora-
tion? Do the practical theological perspectives emerging out of communities of
faith have any thing to do with "real life" as a technological and instrumental
rationality imagines it?

"Christian beliefs have nothing to do with real life," declares my Wiccan
friend at the women's book club that I belong to in Allegany, New York, after
the group had read Elaine Pagels's book *Beyond Belief*. This group of women is
diverse in religious convictions, education levels, marital status, national identities, and race, but is homogenous in terms of class. Our conversation around
the book began with the pagan and the atheist launching into a spirited support
of the book's primary thesis: that it was distasteful and impossible to possess an
uncritical acceptance of a single set of authorized beliefs. The women were in
complete agreement with Pagels's denial that it is assent to Christian belief alone
that will lead us to God.[1] Two theologians in the group agreed that the book's
argument attempted to polarize belief and practice. Others in the group were

dismayed that the complex history of arguments that Pagels traces between the Gospels of John and Thomas, and the consequent establishment of the canon by its chief architect Irenaeus, is largely unknown to many. The mood during the discussion led me to wonder at the depth of insouciance at those elements of belief and assent that official Christianity holds dear.

The problem it seemed to me was the narrow "cognitivist" understanding of belief that seemed to be the basis for rejection by the Wiccan and the atheist. Do Christian beliefs indeed have the status of inerrant or infallible knowledge that consequently implicate Christian practice? The Wiccan and atheist rejected such infallible knowledge since both highly educated women had learned to be critical of "supernatural" bases for knowledge and any claims of infallibility. When the narrow cognitivist basis of their rejection was pointed out, they volleyed a much more pertinent charge. The church treats women terribly, they said, and argued that beliefs about women and women's "place" in religion and society have led to the subordination of women in multiple ways. Others in the group concurred. Most are "lukewarm" Christians or Catholics who were of the mind that assenting to a list of beliefs "authorized" by a celibate male hierarchy that could not see the worth and value of women could not possibly make the claim of infallibility. Here, I thought that what we had begun to talk about was a matter of ethics. Ethical relating to the "differences" we experience in everyday life seemed to trump the requirement for uncritical belief for all the women in the group.

It was obvious that our embodied experience as women in the Catholic and other Christian churches had led to the interrogation of beliefs as the ground for Christian practice. We chewed on the question of what our "ideal" church looked like, and there was unanimity in the vision that Catholics and Christians ought to move from a "preservation" model of church to a "dynamic, organic, and relational" model of church. Such a church would reflect how beliefs and practices existed in a dialectical relationship and would also reflect the community's capacity to hear and listen church into being as it continued to struggle with immediate and pressing questions that arise in real life.

Miroslav Volf and Dorothy Bass, in their book *Practicing Theology,* examine the plaintive question often asked in centers of theological instruction or education: But what does that [theology] have to do with real life?[2] As the authors argue, it is true that theologians often seem to be presenting "knowledge" of a particular sort, but in reality, theology has indeed much to do with real life — the often tragic and comic human realm of work, love, celebration, and suffering.[3] The volume, which is a collection of reflections on the relationship between beliefs and practices by professors of systematic theology, is a defense of the relevance of Christian theology, and the reflective and coherent system of doctrines, narratives, and propositions that form Christian belief.

Bass, in her introductory statements, asserts that all of the contributors to the volume are "convinced that Christian beliefs are already deeply implicated in the actual lives of Christian individuals, families and communities."[4] In other words, these authors are writing for and to a particular constituency and do not attempt in their work to make connections to groups such as a future think

tank sponsored by Microsoft or to irate and intelligent women who simply have
chosen to walk away from Christianity.

It seems to me, therefore, that the task at hand requires theologians of practice to demonstrate, firstly, that the cognitivist basis for belief is too narrow
and constrictive in scope. The automatic rejection of beliefs as the ground of
practice seems to be a precipitous move. Sharon Daloz Parks in this regard
suggests that when belief becomes mere intellectual assent to abstract propositions, a corresponding erosion of the meaning of "faith" obtains as well.[5]
Thus, the "narrowly cognitive connotations [of "belief"] separate faith from
the personal, visceral and passional dimensions of being and knowing."[6] The
cognitivist reduction of belief reduces faith to an assent to a set of beliefs touted
as the "truth" whereas faith really is the *search* for truth, which may require
a revision of beliefs if necessary. In other words, attention paid to faith and its
expressions in language, ritual, and practice will provide us with the vision to
re-vision beliefs. The notion of "belief" expands then to underscore the action
component of the verb "believe" and includes practices of trust, hope, and love.

Similarly, the notion of "practice" expands to include practices other than
"sacramental" or "ecclesiastical" or "parish" practices. In *Practicing Theology,* for example, Craig Dykstra argues that immersing ourselves fully in the
practices of hope and trust can lead us to comprehend how Christian belief is
right and true about the abundant giftedness of God's grace,[7] which then leads
to comprehending what right belief is for Christians. "Belief" in his view is not
rigidly construed as a laundry list of items to be assented to, but is the clearest
possible articulation of what practices of hope and trust bring as insight about
the nature of a giving God, Christ, creation, and one's place in the universe.
Kathryn Tanner's essay in the same volume considers how practices can arise in
the negotiations and improvisations by the ordinary, non-elite, and untidy processes of everyday life between people. These negotiated, ambiguous, and often
contradictory modes of relating practice and belief lead Christian practices to
remain "fluid, processual and ... bifocal."[8] Tanner writes:

> Called to the difficult work of being a disciple and witness of Christ in a way
> appropriate to one's own time and circumstance, one comes, by way of theological
> investigation into Christian practices, to understand more fully what one is doing
> and why, and to have a sense for how all that one believes and does as a Christian
> holds together.[9]

A theological reflection on practices then allows us the critical distance to
evaluate whether the beliefs we hold need reconstruction or reconsideration.
Both beliefs and practices are intended to demonstrate the potential for transformation in the present moment. Beliefs and practices that lead to hope, trust,
and love have the potential to transform each person as well as the community
of faith that sustains and supports them. Theology done from this perspective
begins with real life, and the relationship between beliefs and practices is coherent and relevant to the questions that consume Christian believers in a world
of multiple and contradictory claims.

Consequently, I suggest in this essay that theological reflection on practices,
which is to ask how a particular practice is relevant to being a disciple in the

world today, is indispensable to any rumination about the shared future of our world. If the boundaries of practices are fluid and processual, they point not to the arbitrariness of Christian practice, but rather to the vitality and dynamism of the tradition that can imagine the relationship between beliefs and practices more capaciously. Practices that are marked by living boundaries rather than rigid ones make it possible to imagine the organic, relational, and dynamic communities that Christians must negotiate today.

Belief and Practices: The Transformative Requirement

The vignettes above alert us to the imperative to present Christian — or indeed religious — truth claims in a plural society and thus contribute both faithfully and boldly to contemporary cultural debates on our shared future. Dykstra's assertion that it is our immersion in practice that will open up our comprehension of core beliefs invites us to reflect more on practice. The women's reading group's assertion that their practices of trust, hope, and joy in God are more important to them than dogmatic beliefs inflicted on them by church hierarchy alerts us to the shifting terrain in theological reflection, from intellectual niceties to practical narratives of struggle and perseverance. The technological giant Microsoft's marginalization of input from living communities of faith points to the extent to which theology has become the language of an inward-looking tribe, its idiom understandable only to the insiders. Practical theology that is attentive to this positioning in the current cultural context has much work to do to advance vigorous visions for a vital and shared future.

Consequently, theology as practical — which, as Robert Schreiter says is not merely about applying systematic theology to pastoral situations, but is about theologizing about practice — examines those practices that arise from faith communities.[10] Some of these faith communities may have a tenuous relationship with regulatory processes and official powers. Nevertheless, their critical stance is able to re-create the boundaries drawn by belief, particularly in relation to identity boundaries. In an earlier moment, such practical critical theologies were called "contextual theologies." The term "contextual theology" of course underwent further disciplining moves in the manner that academic theologies at the center commodified them, limited their prophetic potential, and ghettoized them.[11] Yet the deep yearning for a world of justice and peace has continued to challenge academic theology to consider what was at the heart of these contextual theologies — not the exoticizing of context or identity, but an ethical and immensely practical vision of human community and life as created and gifted by God.

That theology be practical — that is, related to "real life" — is the foundational urging in the volume *Practicing Theology*. Miroslav Volf, in his essay titled "Theology for a Way of Life," advances the idea that at the heart of every good theology is both "a plausible intellectual vision" as well as a "compelling account of a way of life."[12] Following the Scotian insight that theology is a practical science, Volf argues that those practices that arise from "authentic doctrines" should properly be called sacraments. Sacraments are of a different order than "practices [which are]...cooperative and meaningful human endeavors that seek to satisfy fundamental human needs and conditions...that people do together and over time."[13] Beliefs relate differently to sacraments than to practices since "core Christian beliefs are by definition normatively inscribed in sacraments but not in 'practices.' "[14] Some Christian practices, such as that of hospitality or welcome, do not even need any deep knowledge of Christian beliefs.[15] On a first reading, this assertion seems to be saying that Christian practices could rest on some anonymous Christian source. However, Volf goes on to clarify his position as referring solely to Christian practices by Christian people.

Analyzing the relationship between beliefs and practices from the angle of practices, Volf argues that the relationship between beliefs and practices is best understood through a correspondence relationship: "*as* God has received us in Christ, *so* we too are to receive our fellow human beings."[16] The as-so structure informs the practice of hospitality and welcome. Thus, by definition, what Christian practice is depends on what Christian belief is; in this case, the practice of hospitality depends on our belief in the nature of Christ. But are only Christians capable of having or doing Christian practices? To put it another way, can an incarnational practice of treating people like Christ would treat us necessitate assent in the set of core beliefs about Christ, the second person of the Trinity and the fullness of the revelation of God? The boundary marked by assent to beliefs in this scheme does not seem to be flexible at all.

In my view, Volf introduces a rather rigid stance on the relationship between beliefs and practices by making the correspondence model a narrow one. By making a distinction between Christian and non-Christian practices, Volf argues that someone who is not a Christian cannot practice Christian practices. Non-Christian practices are not Christian practices because Christian practice requires belief in Christ and a commitment to follow him. Non-Christian practices can be Christomorphic, but not Christian. His argument rests on the defense of Christian practices as normed by Christian beliefs. The Christian practice of hospitality as he articulates it cannot be such a uniquely different practice of hospitality that no Hindu or Muslim or atheist could ever replicate it. However, what Volf does not want to work out is how Christomorphic practices may relate to beliefs that are not necessarily Christian. The as-so principle, that is, the incarnational principle, can transgress the confines of Christian identity. Its universal transformative capacity has tremendous appeal to those who may not subscribe to the requirement for assent to Christian beliefs, but who believe that its transformative potential is invaluable in liberation or emancipatory efforts. Take Gandhi, for example. His Christomorphic actions of refusing to dehumanize the colonizer gave flesh to the incarnational principle in the colonial context. Yet he absolutely refused to convert to Christianity even as he assiduously read and quoted from the Christian Bible. As he was fond of saying, he could well appreciate Christianity, but could not appreciate Christians who could not practice in the manner of Christ. In his view, Christian belief did not lead necessarily to Christian practice. Rather, Christian belief was hijacked by the more mundane and ordinary aspirations to superiority, triumphalism, and imperialism.

Christianity as a way of life cannot ignore its embeddedness in the present context of unequal power and the forceful arguments made by contextual and liberation theologians against this reality. The ability to critically think of the relationship between beliefs and practices arises from an ethical demand for the transformation of human practices, particularly our practices toward the "other" such as hospitality and welcome. For Christian practical theology, reconceiving the as-so principle as representing the deepest insights into the human/divine relationship and the human/human relationship in practice, allows us to imagine the connection between belief and practice more capaciously. We are Christians, and our welcome of other human beings into our community makes of our boundaries a living line that is constantly redrawn to be inclusive in imitation of the as-so principle. The redrawing of boundaries in this manner requires reflection on the manner in which the practice hews to belief. And, when we do *not* do this well, we can learn from those Christomorphic examples of hospitality that may put our meager attempts to shame.

Beliefs and Practices: Transformative Strategies

Hospitality, that is, our disposition toward the strange other to be inclusive, welcoming, and generous, is a vital ingredient of global Christian relations. The as-so principle that enjoins us to stand in the Christic space of beholding another in their full humanity permits the acute awareness of relationality undergirding traditional beliefs such as the doctrines of the Incarnation, the Trinity, God, theological anthropology, creation, and church. Constructive and practical theologians have attempted to explain these doctrines as primarily relational.[17] The moments of ambiguity, paradox, and discontinuity that arise in such explorations provide a keenness to their analyses. Every Christian denomination is involved in these explorations.

For example, Christianity in its present world and global configuration continues to be of tremendous interest to theologians and scholars of religion, especially as its numerical strength seems to be increasing exponentially. Relative growth figures for various Christian denominations are presented in volumes such as *World Christian Encyclopedia: A Comparative Study of Churches and Religions in the Modern World,*[18] and studies such as Phil Jenkins's *The Next Christendom: The Coming of Global Christianity.*[19] However, the manner in which this growth is charted highlights the context in which beliefs and practices are articulated in global flows of power. The *World Christian Encyclopedia,* for example, is carefully studied by Rome to make sense of the rapidly declining numbers of Roman Catholics in South America, Asia, and Africa. Jenkins's book, on the other hand, manages to be both alarmist and racist in speaking of the coming hordes of culturally and racially different Christians. Further, the precise nomenclature with which to address this new development is under scholarly consideration.

Lamin Sanneh argues that this new phenomenon of growth leads us to the awareness of world Christianity,[20] which is different from "global" Christianity. Sanneh is more concerned to show that the pluriform Christian practices that arise in world Christianity are simply evidence of the manner in which Christianity is being inculturated in various parts of the world. Robert Schreiter, who prefers the term "global Christianity," is more of the mind that economic, cultural, and political globalization have led to alliances and negotiations with Christianity that reveal practices that definitely seem to be in tension with the preferred beliefs of ecclesiastical institutions.[21] He argues that theologians of practice who take the category of "culture" seriously cannot yet make the move Sanneh is suggesting. Instead, when one takes into account the global relations modifying cultural, racial, gendered, sexual, and religious identities, the dynamics of power that create and sustain these identities mandate us to think about redrawing the lines of belief. Theologians of practice therefore need to have interdisciplinary skills to forge strategies to counter the rigid logics of institutions that guard the boundaries of authorized belief and acceptable practice.

One such strategy requires theologians of practice to be skilled in critical theories that interrogate the manner in which institutions structure arguments against change. Thus, the primacy of the as-so principle and the principle of hospitality in ecclesiastical or academic institutions is seriously compromised when one thinks of gender, race, class, and sexual dynamics. The practices that compromise the as-so principle, which are shored up by particular beliefs about human relations, reveal the extent to which the boundary of Christian identity is drawn with an eye to maintaining traditional forms of superiority and dominance.

Feminist theologians examining the as-so principle, or the incarnational principle, have consistently pointed out that traditional beliefs about women's bodies, sexuality and sexual rights, and their relationship to God have been articulated by patriarchal theologies fully invested in maintaining gender dominance. Precisely because women have realized the extent to which systemic exclusion operates through a logic of gender dominance, constructive and practical proposals redrawing the lines of belief and practice challenge and test the rigidity of ecclesiastical structures. Nowhere is this more clearly evident than in the feminist critiques of Roman Catholic authoritarianism.

Here, Tina Beattie's book *New Catholic Feminism: Theology and Theory* is a good conversation partner as it challenges the manner in which beliefs about women engender and sustain the exclusionary tactics of the Roman Catholic Church.[22] The explicit heterosexist paradigm for embodied relations as articulated by the official church reveals that women are coerced into a complementary relationship to men. Such a thoroughly repressive sexual ideology saturating the view of gendered relations in church performs a distortion of the vocation to be church. Feminist critiques of such hetero-normative moves have invited the ire of the CDF, which blamed the hostility of these critiques as responsible for creating antagonism between the sexes.[23] Full of confidence in the wisdom and the authority of the church's view of embodied relations between human beings, as an "expert in humanity," the official response of the CDF to the challenge of feminism is to be manifestly antifeminist.

The CDF's antifeminist stance is clear in the manner that it provides prescriptive norms for women's conduct by failing to explicate how gendered and embodied relations between women and men unfold in the lived reality of church. Its reactive mode is clear in the manner that it lays the blame squarely on feminism for the deterioration of relationships between men and women. As Beattie demonstrates, the letter seeks to frame feminist questions as deliberately provoking the abuse of power. The analytic strengths of feminism as a sustained investigation of the abuse of power in the manner in which gendered and embodied relationships have been institutionalized in the church, the synthesizing strengths of forms of feminism that continue to argue for a positive retrieval of the principles of Catholicism that would be significant for the collaboration of men and women in the church, are ignored in favor of presenting feminism in an antagonistic relationship to Catholic theology.

It is important, however, not to think that feminist critiques exist only in supreme opposition to ecclesiastical or social institutions. As Beattie demonstrates, feminist critiques based in Western secular ideals of equality and justice have given rise to a reaction by women professing allegiance to the church to develop what is being called in Roman Catholic circles the "new feminism." These conservative theologians are indeed paying attention to questions of sexuality, gender, and embodiment, but they repudiate analyses of power in favor of retrieving aspects of the Catholic tradition with full confidence in its wisdom and authority.[24] Such a development need not be a cause for angst among feminist theologians. The development to redraw the lines of beliefs and practices is coming out of an engaged membership in a community of faith in the attempt to repristinate the deepest insights of the tradition and is as good a definition of practical theology as any.

As Beattie argues, there are positive elements to "new feminism." The constructive vision of "new feminism" draws on official Catholic tradition to set out a vision of women's dignity and sexual mutuality as persons made in the image of God. The new feminism also seriously engages with the nihilistic and materialistic tendencies of Western culture and is deeply concerned with the declining numbers in mainstream churches. Finally, "new feminism" points to a serious lack in liberal and secular feminism, which has continued to be arid in regard to the actual practices of faith and belief, such as the language of prayer, underscoring the love and desire that one may have for God.

Obviously, "new feminism" does not investigate the power dynamics infusing the Catholic tradition when it comes to the gendered and sexual roles imposed on women. Neither does it investigate the rhetorical topos in which such assertions are created and sustained. Nevertheless, their emphasis on the practices of prayer and other forms of engaged discipline that allow the depth of the incarnational reality to be revealed cannot be dismissed out of hand as merely conservative or consolidating. Surely prayer and one's desire for God can subvert and undercut the defensive authoritarianism of even the Roman

Catholic hierarchy by challenging the lack of hospitality and the compromise of the as-so principle in its ecclesiastical structures.

What Beattie is arguing for is not an uncritical acceptance of the "new feminism." However, she is arguing that overtly political feminist strategies are currently stagnating. Instead, she is imagining new strategies to include those investigations of language and knowledge to uncover how culture, language, politics, economics, and subjectivity are implicated in the global flows of power inscribing patriarchal values on the bodies of women. Her solution is to remake the symbolic world of Catholicism, giving it theologically denser possibilities for subversion and transformation. She retrieves Julia Kristeva and Luce Irigaray to argue that sacramentality exists in the postmodern sexual body's in-carnality. Such redeemed sacramentality then can allow woman and her body to incarnate the divine to imagine the Catholic Mass as the site of reconciliation of all things in Christ. Consequently what she wants is a maternal theology of the priesthood alongside the masculine theology of the priesthood.[25] Such a maternal theology of the priesthood will provide much needed balance as well as reveal the refulgence of the incarnational relation to humanity.

Beattie's argument is persuasive; however, the emphasis on the maternal relationship to repristinate the incarnational relation to humanity does not address the problem of multiple axes of determination on women's relationality in our global context. The symbolic transformations she hopes will effect change will not happen if the masculinist bases of sacramental principles rest solely on reproductive processes within a heterosexist framework alone. Third world postcolonial feminists will point out that heterosexism in global relations is thoroughly embedded in larger economic, cultural, social, and political milieus that work to vitiate the liberatory potential of women's life-giving capacities. In other words, for postcolonial feminist theologians, the case that Beattie makes for a maternal theology of the priesthood may be making the case for hospitality within ecclesiastical structures but does not make as good a case for hospitality toward women as women from the third world in other social structures where the as-so principle ought to work as well.

As Gayatri Chakravorty Spivak explains, the "uterine social organization" that is at the heart of capitalist negotiations in the globalized economies of our world demands that such a uterine social organization support the "phallic norm of capitalism."[26] Postcolonial practical and feminist theologians cannot but help notice how economic and cultural relations then continue to order religious and theological perspectives leaving third world women in an even greater bind. The issue here is that third world women have to additionally prove that their reproductive capacities are in service to not simply the family or the church but also as a requirement to participate in the global economy. As Spivak comments, capitalism is shored up by the uterine norm of womanhood by creating a network of global economic relations in which everything we consume — homes, cars, cosmetics, sports gear, and everything else — is aimed at reproductive logics. Strategically then, starting with the uterine norm of social organization to address systemic exclusion does not examine how such social organization shores up global economic, political, and cultural relations. It may be of use where a primary experience of being woman can be cherished and subversively utilized for particular forms of agency. However, without adequate theorization, uterine norms of social organization simply are in cahoots with global systems of superexploitation. Spivak's solution is that there is no one strategy; feminist strategies have to be uncompromisingly heterogeneous. However, in her work these heterogeneous strategies are informed by one practice — the practice of love.[27]

Heterogeneity as a norm for constructive feminist practical theology will fly in the face of academic requirements to provide unified and coherent analyses and solutions to the systemic exclusions faced by women everywhere. Heterogeneity as a norm will certainly fly in the face of ecclesiastical requirements for unambiguous truth as defining the boundaries of the believing community. It will raise the specter of relativism; this will be true only if "belief" is taken in its narrow cognitivist sense. It will raise the problem of pluralism and that of adjudicating mutually exclusive claims for agency and representation in the cultural and political context and redemption and salvation in the theological and religious one. But these conversations of practical theology will continue to shape our world, and holding on to the as-so principle as we navigate these contradictory, ambiguous, and paradoxical conversations must yield paradigms of relations that can transform our present impoverished forms.

Most importantly, heterogeneity makes room for Christomorphic practices that theologians such as Volf dismiss. In fact, it could be heterogeneous and Christomorphic practices of loving and responsible relation that repristinate Christian beliefs in the global multireligious context. The real life conundrums faced by people and communities of faith in their attempt to avoid the dread of dehumanizing violence permit their religious imaginations to draw on wide sources. When Christianity becomes such a source, it will result in a plethora of Christomorphic practices. Retrieving these heterogeneous Christomorphic practices to redraw the boundaries of belief and identity is the shape that practical theology in the third millennium will take. It is Christomorphic practices, by hewing close to the boundary of ethical relation, that must challenge the followers of Christ to practice what they believe. *As* we love then, *so* we believe in the love of Christ vivifying and enlivening our world. We will be known by our love.

Conclusion

UPHOLDING HOPE

Chapter 23

On Not Losing Heart

Catherine of Siena and the
Strategies of Prayer and Friendship

MARY CATHERINE HILKERT

THIS VOLUME FOCUSES on women's strategies for change for the pilgrim church, which is always in need of transformation if it is to be faithful to its mission to be sacrament of salvation in and for the world. Dreams and prophecies from daughters as well as sons, young and old alike, are part of the promise of the Spirit at Pentecost to "pour out a portion of my spirit on all humankind" (Acts 2:17–18). Concrete plans and strategies are essential to the work of the Spirit in our day. But for many women — and men — today, the strategies we are most in need of are resources for hope and courage for the long haul. Contemporary Catholic women, especially those who have been engaged in efforts for reform and renewal in a variety of social and ecclesial settings for years and even decades, may well identify with the persistent widow in Jesus' parable in Luke 18. As the text describes her situation and perseverance:

> Once there was a judge in a certain city who respected neither God nor man. A widow in that city kept coming to him saying, "Give me my rights against my opponent." For a time he refused, but finally he thought, "I care little for God or man, but this widow is wearing me out. I am going to settle in her favor or she will end by doing me violence." (Luke 18:2–5)

While the woman's victory in the cause of justice may be encouraging, the parable can't be turned into a simple allegory. Neither does it offer a concrete way forward for women operating in difficult situations or in systems where they hold little influence or power to bring about change. Luke's introduction to the parable, however, makes clear that Jesus relates the story in an effort to remind his followers on their journey to Jerusalem of the one non-negotiable strategy for all Christian disciples. "[Jesus] told them a parable on the necessity of praying always and not losing heart" (Luke 18:1). The danger of "losing heart" is perhaps the most serious threat facing those who have worked long hours — and years — for a vision of a renewed church as "sacrament of salvation in and for the world" and for liturgical celebrations that engage the "full, active, and conscious participation" of all of the members of the baptized assembly. Both of those hopes from the Second Vatican Council seem — at least to many who lived through the conciliar transition — more difficult to sustain today than in the first decades after the Council.

Ecclesial and liturgical reform are not the only concerns, or even the primary concerns, for many in search of resources for hope today. Work on behalf of justice and peace (including the integrity of creation), which the 1971 Synod of Bishops recognized as "essential to the preaching of the gospel," is difficult to sustain over the course of a lifetime. Many once-devoted disciples have experienced forms of psychological and spiritual burnout. As Thomas Merton noted during the era of the Vietnam War, it is possible for ministers, activists, and reformers to succumb to a kind of inner violence that drains their own spirits. In Merton's words,

> The rush and pressure of modern life are a form of its innate violence. To allow myself to be carried away by a multitude of conflicting concerns, to surrender to too many projects, to want to help everyone in everything...is to succumb to violence. The frenzy of the activist...destroys the fruitfulness of one's own work because it kills the root of inner wisdom which makes work fruitful.[1]

Unable to find the roots of wisdom in their original ecclesial homes or troubled by injustice in the church's own structures and modes of operation, some now disassociate their efforts for justice and peace — and their own identities — from the public ministry of the church. Others search for ways of "praying always," but find themselves without moorings in liturgical celebrations from which they feel excluded in terms of language, imagery, and liturgical roles. Some remain in their parish or ecclesial communities, but can be described best as "defecting in place."[2] Still others remain actively engaged, but hunger for more spiritual nourishment to sustain them on their journeys.

In our search for the kind of inner wisdom that can sustain us in our limited, but important, efforts to transform ecclesial and social structures, we would do well to turn to the spiritual classics of our tradition, especially the wisdom of women who were engaged in strategies for change in the church and world of their own day. One Christian mystic who initially thought that her call to contemplative union with God meant withdrawal from the difficult challenges of ecclesial and political reform, as well as from engagement in direct ministry to the poor and suffering of her day, was the fourteenth-century lay Dominican tertiary Catherine of Siena. But the "tremendous desire for the love of God" that fueled her mystical search led her to a deeper grasp of the inseparability of the two great commandments of love of God and love of neighbor. As her friend, spiritual director, and biographer Raymond of Capua reports it, just after Catherine's experience of mystical espousal with Christ, she received the revelation and commission: "on two feet you must walk my way; on two wings you must fly to heaven."[3]

From that time on Catherine turned her attention to the needs of her family, to nursing the sick in their homes and hospitals, and to caring for the poor of Siena. She embraced a preaching ministry throughout the Sienese countryside that was so effective that priests were appointed to accompany her as confessors since large numbers of those who heard her message responded to her calls for conversion. Her contemplative wisdom was recognized by many, and she soon became a political advisor and spiritual counselor not only to kings and queens and the heads of warring Italian city-states, but also to popes, cardinals, bishops, monks, and contemplative nuns.

This is not to say that Catherine's strategies for political or spiritual reform were always heeded. Some of the very leaders who initially had sought her advice and support later dismissed her as a naive and meddling woman who was partially responsible for the failure of her efforts.

Nevertheless, in both her active ministries and the spiritual darkness she herself endured, Catherine was sustained by a contemplative union with God born of a life of prayer. The wisdom for which Catherine was recognized in 1970 as the first lay woman to be named a Doctor of the Church can provide a resource for contemporary women and men who struggle to remain faithful to their own vocation as active participants in the church's mission in the world, even when that vocation is not recognized or celebrated.

The wisdom that guided Catherine of Siena in her efforts on behalf of political and ecclesial reform is evident in her prayers and letters as well as in the major work of mystical wisdom for which she is known, her *Dialogue with Divine Providence*. The *Dialogue* is structured as a conversation in which God replies to four prayers that Catherine, like the widow in the Gospel of Luke, prayed persistently. A closer look at the focus of the fourfold petition that she prayed "without ceasing" can provide insight into the kind of prayer that is needed today if contemporary disciples are not to lose heart on our own journeys.

Dwelling in the Cell of Self-Knowledge

It may be something of a surprise to note that Catherine's first prayer was for herself, but it is a clear reminder that the call to personal conversion is integral to the vocation of the prophet or reformer. Catherine describes the heart of her own spiritual journey in the opening paragraph of the Prologue to the *Dialogue*:

> A soul rises up, restless with tremendous desire for God's honor and the salvation of souls. She has for some time exercised herself in virtue and has become accustomed to dwelling in the cell of self-knowledge in order to know better God's goodness toward her, since upon knowledge follows love. And loving, she seeks to pursue truth and clothe herself in it.[4]

Catherine's passionate calls for reform in church and government, as well as her preaching and her ministry on behalf of the poor and the sick, were rooted ultimately in a deeper passion—her desire for God. Even as a young child in a large Sienese family, Catherine wanted to dwell in the solitude of her room (her "cell") so that she could focus on and delight in God's goodness and love. That passion for God never left her. In her contemplative search for God, however, she came to two clear realizations: the love of God is impossible without love of neighbor, and experience of God brings a deeper self-knowledge that is at once delightful and painful.

The desire to "clothe herself in truth" led Catherine to an experiential knowledge that she and all of God's beloved creatures are created in the image of God and destined for communion with God. That realization led to an extravagant prayer of praise to God as "mad lover":

> O fire of love!
> Was it not enough to gift us
> with creation in your image and likeness,
> and to create us anew to grace in your Son's blood,
> without giving us yourself as food,
> the whole of divine being,
> the whole of God?
> What drove you?
> Nothing but your charity,
> mad with love as you are![5]

This keen awareness of God's love for every human person and for creation itself was at the heart of all of Catherine's efforts to reform the church and the social and political factions of her day. Her political strategies — sometimes fruitful, sometimes misguided — were motivated by love and a vision of what is possible for human life and for the church that was given to her in prayer. She tried to envision the church and world of her day through the eyes of God's own love for them and God's desire for their reform.

One image of the personal transformation that is necessary if our human efforts are to participate in the work of Spirit can be found in Catherine's description of a diver entering the sea: "A person who dives down into the sea, and is swimming under its water, does not see or touch anything except the water of the sea and the things that are in the water. If things outside fall in or on the water, then the diver sees them, but only in the water and as they look in the water."[6] According to Catherine, the person who "plunges totally into God" is herself "transformed into God" so that her thoughts, understanding, love, and memory are taken up exclusively with God. As a result, "She sees herself and others only in God, and she thinks of them and of herself exclusively in God."[7]

Catherine called for conversion and courage on the part of popes, politicians, political leaders, and even her own mother. But she knew well that she herself was in need of that same transformation. The self-knowledge and conversion to which Catherine was called led her to embrace an identity and mission that did not fit the stereotypical roles of women in her day. According to Raymond's account, Catherine's mystical espousal to Christ was followed by the kind of challenge she herself later exhorted other women and men to embrace: "From now on you must never falter about accepting any task my providence may lay upon your shoulders."[8]

At the same time her unflinching search for truth also led Catherine to a painful awareness of her own limits and her sinfulness. She spoke with the kind of boldness (*parrhesia*) that is a gift of the Spirit, but she also struggled to align her own strong and sometimes stubborn will with the will of God. She prayed to Jesus, who experienced his own temptations in the desert and agony in the garden, to remove her own will and give her his will. Catherine's descriptions of her own sinfulness are vivid, but they are always surrounded by an ever deeper awareness of God's mercy and unconditional forgiveness. Thus although she acknowledged her solidarity with all of sinful humanity and writes of her own "filth" and wretchedness as well as that of corrupt ecclesial and civil leaders, she concludes her *Dialogue* by thanking God for God's infinite mercy toward her and all of humankind:

> You, Light, have disregarded by darksomeness; you Life, have not considered that I am death; nor you, Doctor, considered these grave weaknesses of mine. You, eternal Purity, have disregarded my wretched filthiness; you are infinite and have overlooked the fact that I am finite, and you, Wisdom, the fact that I am foolishness. For all these and so many other endless evils and sins of mine, your wisdom, your kindness, your mercy, your infinite goodness have not despised me. No in your light, you have given me light. In your wisdom, I have come to know the truth; in your mercy I have found your charity and affection for my neighbors. What has compelled you? Not my virtues, but only your charity.[9]

Catherine's prayer that she might know better God's infinite love for her was at the same time a desire to remain faithful to prayer and to the truth that she learned in the "cell of self-knowledge" so that she might truly become "another Christ."[10]

Reform of "Holy Church"

Catherine's prayer that she herself might follow in the footsteps of Christ crucified so that "through desire and affection and the union of love he [might make] of her another himself," was the same petition that she prayed for the church that she loved deeply. Her bold criticisms of church leaders and structures when they failed to incarnate the Body of Christ or to carry out the church's mission in the world were grounded in the vocation she had been given to "speak the truth in love." Catherine never doubted that the Holy Spirit would be faithful to the church and to church leaders in spite of their limitations and sinful failures. She prayed faithfully for the reform of "holy church," which she believed to be not merely a human institution, but the Body of Christ at work in the world. That same conviction about the church's identity and vocation fueled her calls for reform when ecclesial leaders who, in her words, were meant to be "flowers in the garden of the Church," were instead "stinking weeds."

In the church of the twenty-first century, in which one finds patterns of sexual abuse and financial corruption, manifestations of dishonesty and raw ambition among high-ranking church officials, and a lack of transparency and accountability in aspects of ecclesial structures, Catherine's love and prayer for a sinful church and its leaders is not easy to embrace. But it was that love that empowered her to speak so frankly and that enabled those she addressed to hear a call to conversion, rather than simply a harsh judgment. Repeatedly in her prayer, Catherine heard God telling her not to judge sinners, but to pray for them and work for their conversion. Catherine was convinced that only the love of God could bring about a change of heart and life in the sinner, whether within or outside the church. Her awareness of her own sinfulness gave her the ability to speak with conviction of both the transforming power of love and the clear demands of the Holy Spirit for reform and change. She placed even her strongest critiques of the church and its leaders in the context of affection, concern, and the possibility of conversion.

Catherine had great respect for hierarchical authority within the church, but she also believed all members of the church were called to be obedient to the higher authority that comes from the Holy Spirit, source of all truth. She held herself accountable to church authorities, but she also criticized explicitly the selection of poor pastors and cardinals for the church. Although she insisted that she would not defy the pope even if he were the "devil incarnate," she wrote to him with freedom and frankness, even advising him to resign if he could not exercise his authority properly:

> My dearest *babbo,* forgive my presumption in saying what I've said — what I am compelled by gentle First Truth to say. This is his will, father; this is what he is asking of you. . . . Since he has given you authority and you have accepted it, you ought to be using the power and strength that is yours. If you don't intend to use it, it would be better and more to God's honor and the good of your soul to resign.[11]

On one occasion when the pope expressed his disapproval of her, Catherine maintained that even if the pope were to abandon her, she was confident that the crucified Christ would receive her, emphasizing that she and Gregory XI were both servants of the same Christ. She saw her authority, like that of the pope and all ministers of Christ, as rooted ultimately in the truth and love that constitute the very mystery of God.

Catherine's prayer for and love of the church brought clarity and boldness to her calls for reform. She was not concerned about offending others, nor did she limit her speech to what others wanted to hear. She criticized popes and even her dear friends when they did not have the courage of their own convictions. She spoke of being a lover of the truth and a spouse of the truth and had little patience with those she saw as compromising truth in a misguided attempt to "keep peace." Thus she wrote to Pope Gregory, censuring the failure of the church's pastors and leaders to speak difficult truths:

> They are forever afraid of offending and making enemies — and all of this because of self-love. Sometimes it's just that they would like to keep peace, and this, I tell you, is the worst cruelty one can inflict. If a sore is not cauterized or excised when necessary, but only ointment is applied, not only will it not heal, but it will infect the whole [body], often fatally.[12]

Catherine respected the fact that the pope and all the church's ministers were entrusted with a unique office and responsibility. Yet precisely for that reason she argued that they were in need of consultation and discernment in discovering the truth of God's will for the church. On that basis, Catherine proposed to Pope Urban VI that he should have a "council of the servants of God" to advise him in addition to his cardinals and political advisors.[13] She reminded the pope of the importance of exercising his authority with patience and of listening to the wisdom of those who offered criticism of the abuses in the church. Otherwise, she warned, he might make mistakes of judgment that they could have spared him. As she remarked to Urban after he had rebuffed one of his critics, "so far as authority is concerned you can do everything, but in terms of vision, you can see no more than any one person can."[14]

Part of the reason that Catherine was so insistent on the responsibility of all members of the body of Christ to speak the truth in love was that she was convinced that no one member, not even the pope, had full access to the truth that rests in God alone. Reflecting on that reality in her *Dialogue,* Catherine came to the insight that God has given unique gifts to each member of the body of Christ, but that no one member has all of the gifts necessary for the life of that body, precisely so that we would realize our interdependence. Her prayer for the church was not only a prayer for the conversion of its leaders, but a prayer that the baptized would realize that we are indeed one body with many diverse gifts and responsibilities. Here too she was convinced that in spite of human sinfulness and resistance, God's Holy Spirit would guide the church in its mission and would empower — and require — collaboration in that mission:

> In this mortal life, so long as you are pilgrims, I have bound you with the chain of charity. Whether you want it or not, you are so bound. If you should break loose by not wanting to live in charity for your neighbors, you will still be bound by it by force.... That you may practice charity in action and in will, I in my providence did not give to any one person or to each individually the knowledge for doing everything necessary for human life. No, I gave something to one, something else to another, so that each one's need would be reason to have recourse to the other.... Though you may lose your will for charity because of your wickedness, you will at least be forced by your own need to practice it in action.[15]

Catherine's desire that the church of her day might experience and reflect the trinitarian life of love more fully was a desire that extended to her prayer for the world and that empowered her many missions on behalf of peace.

Prayer for the World, Especially for Peace

Catherine's third prayer — for "the entire world" and especially for peace — was related to her love of the church and her desire for its unity. She understood her call to preach the Gospel as at the same time a mission of peacemaking. In a letter to Raymond in April 1376 she described a vision she experienced in which Christ gave her a cross and an olive branch and called her to the mission of the angels at the time of the birth of Christ — to announce great joy to all. But as Catherine frequently reminded both civil and ecclesial leaders, joy and peace follow from right relationships, the exercise of justice, and concern for the common good. Thus her constant prayer for peace was accompanied by her ministry of exhortation through preaching, letters, and political advocacy.

Catherine's best-known ecclesiastical intervention — her travel to Avignon to urge Pope Gregory XI to resist the pressures of his papal court and return to Rome for the sake of the unity of the church — was clearly a political act as well. Catherine was convinced that the pope's return to Rome and reform of church administration were important not only for church unity, but also to put an end to the rebellion against the papacy by the Tuscan city-states, the so-called "War of Eight Saints," which continued to be waged throughout her life in spite of her interventions.

As independent city-states warred with one another for supremacy in Italy and throughout Western Europe, Catherine consistently advocated for what she perceived to be the will of God for the unity of the church, peace and co-operation among rival city-states, and the well-being of the poor. In her role as political negotiator, Catherine attempted to remain open to both sides in difficult conflicts and to call both to reform and dialogue. In spite of her own loyalties, she was convinced that human beings and societies are necessarily interdependent and called to cooperation for the good of all. A devoted daughter of Siena, she nevertheless accepted an invitation to visit the rival city of Pisa because she thought she could be an advocate there for collaboration and peace although her visit was seen by others as "a source of scandal."[16] Likewise she stood in solidarity with the Perugian Niccolo di Tuldo at the time of his execution although he had been condemned to death for incendiary remarks against the government of Siena. In the conflict between the pro-papal Guelph merchants and the pro-empire aristocratic Ghibellines of her day, Catherine called for unity with the pope, but also criticized both the Guelph bishop of Florence and a prominent Guelph leader for not working more actively for peace.

Catherine's well-known support of the crusades is troubling in light of her vocation as peacemaker. This aspect of her fourteenth-century worldview is clearly problematic from the perspective of present-day interreligious and intercultural dialogue and a growing awareness of how religious absolutism fuels and perpetuates violence in the name of God. There is no denying that Catherine's perspective on the relationship of Christianity to Judaism and Islam was shaped by the biases of the time — a reminder that even the most committed reformers in one area are often blinded to their own forms of bias in other arenas. What is worth noting, however, is that although Catherine advocated the conversion of Jews and Muslims to Christianity, her prayer suggested a wider and more complex vision of the wideness of God's mercy. In the *Dialogue* Catherine hears God telling her that the good of the church and of humankind will come about "not by the sword or by war or by violence," but through "peace and constant and humble prayers."[17] On the occasion that she saw herself as entrusted with both the cross and the olive branch as symbols of her dual vocation as preacher and peacemaker, she also had an image of Muslims and Christians together entering the wounded side of Christ. As she described her vision in a letter to Raymond, "The fire of holy desire was growing within me as I gazed. And I saw the people, Christians and unbelievers, entering the side of Christ crucified."[18]

In Catherine's prayer, as well as in her prophetic missions, this preacher of peace was led where she would not have gone on her own. Once again we are reminded that the strategy of "praying always" is crucial not only so that reformers may not lose heart, but also so that they might have their hearts expanded and their vision clarified. The habit of constant prayer leads political and ecclesial reformers to insights they could not fathom in the context of their own limited imaginations. Likewise, prayer beckons prophets to an encounter with "the other" that can shift preestablished boundaries in light of a greater good or wider vision.

At the same time, contemporary reformers find another kind of challenge in the realization that this fervent advocate for peace and church unity and woman of unfailing prayer was not always successful in her efforts. At the time of Catherine's death, the Italian city-states remained at war, the church was in schism, and she admitted to her own "dark night of hope," confessing to Raymond that she was no longer sure what God was doing with her. The energy to stay committed to the neighbor in need and to remain engaged in what appear to be fruitless efforts for peace and justice in church or society requires the conviction that more than human effort is at work. Catherine's exhortation to solidarity with all those who suffer — to "join one's wounds with the wounds of Jesus" — was grounded in her unflinching conviction that the power of love had overcome the powers of evil in the death and resurrection of Jesus. But that conviction did not spare this reformer from her own experiences of darkness, doubt, and failure or her own need to experience compassion.

Prayer for Friends and Those We Love with a "Particular Love"

Although Catherine wrestled with darkness at the end of her life, she died surrounded by her close followers and in the arms of one of her dearest friends and companions in ministry, Alessa Saracini. Catherine's many friendships were the source of deep joy in her life. Thus it comes as no surprise that her final petition was for those she had been given to love "with a particular love." Her friendships also provided a kind of "school of right relationship" in which Catherine experienced her own need for the unconditional trust in God's providence that she preached so powerfully to others. The wisdom that Catherine promoted in the political and ecclesial arenas came not only from her life of "unceasing prayer" but also from her concrete experience of the joys and struggles involved in all deep human relationships.

Friendship was, for Catherine, one of God's greatest gifts to us. She spoke of her friends and wrote to them with deep affection, loving them as God loves us: "unspeakably much." She was convinced that human friendships are a sacrament of the divine friendship that God offers to us in grace. According to Catherine, the God who "fell in love with the beauty of creation" draws us into the divine mystery of love through the experience of "falling in love" with God's creatures, especially those we have been given to love "with a particular love." Every friend is to be cherished since each is a gift from God and a unique image of God.

In the Prologue to the *Dialogue* Catherine asked divine providence to supply "in general and in particular" for "a certain case which had arisen." The specific reference is unclear, but what is clear is that throughout her life Catherine treasured and prayed for all those whom she had been given to love in a special way — her family, her many dear friends, the numerous members of her "famiglia" who accompanied her on her journeys, and those who sought her counsel and support. Catherine had a unique relationship with each of them and she interceded for each of them in a particular way. That was in itself a ministry as well as a form of love.

Catherine had a special bond with the friends who were also her partners in the service of the Gospel, such as her companion in service to the sick and the poor, the young widow Alessa Saracini, and her closest friend to whom she confided even her intimate mystical experiences, Raymond of Capua.[19] Even while she was actively engaged in political negotiations or peacekeeping missions, Catherine found time to send letters to her friends, and she expressed her sadness when they were separated for long periods of time. A particularly poignant example of this is Catherine's final letter to Raymond when he was on a papal mission in the north of Italy and Catherine was experiencing great suffering during her final days in Rome. Nevertheless, she encouraged Raymond and all of her friends to be faithful to their vocations and calls to ministry and was bold in her words of challenge when she thought they were shirking their responsibilities.[20]

Catherine notes that we are given friends that we love "with a singular love" so that we might grow in grace and virtue. Through her friendships, Catherine herself learned painful lessons about "right relationship" that bore fruit in her efforts at political reconciliation and her calls for unity and reform among all the members of the one Body of Christ. Her own struggle to keep her love for others rooted in her love for God is perceptible in her advice to Alessa in one of her letters:

> Take, for example, a jug that you'd fill in the fountain and drink from in the fountain. For although you might have drawn love from God, who is the fountain of living water, unless you drank from it always in God it would end up empty. And this will be the sign that you are not drinking entirely in God: that the person or thing you love becomes a source of pain to you, either because of a conversation you have, or because you have been deprived of some comfort you are used to receiving, or because of something else that happens. When these things — or anything other than offense against God — cause you pain, it is a clear sign that this love is still imperfect, drawn outside the fountain.[21]

In a similar section of her *Dialogue,* where she is reflecting on divine providence, Catherine refers to the attraction of friendship as "God's holy trick" meant to draw us more deeply into love, but also to convert us from all forms of "disordered love." Catherine remarks that the struggles that are inevitable in human relationships as we grow in freedom, self-knowledge, and love are God's most intimate way of teaching us about the mystery of divine providence, because in the pain of learning to love, we *experience* divine providence, whereas before this we only believed in it. Speaking of God's ways with her, Catherine writes,

> I even make use of a holy trick, just to raise her up from imperfection: I make her conceive a special love for certain people, beyond a general spiritual love. In this way she practices virtue, lets go of her imperfection, strips her heart of every other sensual love for creatures — even any selfish passion for her father and mother, sisters and brothers — and she loves them for my sake. And with this well-ordered love I have given her she chases out the disordered love with which she had loved creatures in the beginning.[22]

Later in the same passage, Catherine is more specific about the sources of pain that often arise in close friendships as well as the way that the lessons learned in relationships of "special love" carry over to the call to love of neighbor, solidarity with those who suffer, and work for the common good — all of which she includes in her understanding of "a greater and more perfect love for others in general":

> Whenever the soul loves someone with a special love, she feels pain when the pleasure or comfort or companionship she has become accustomed to, and which gives her great consolation, is lessened. Or she suffers if she sees that person keeping more company with someone else than with her. This pain makes her enter into knowledge of herself. And if she is willing to walk wisely in the light as she ought, she will come to love that special person more perfectly, for with self-knowledge and the contempt she has conceived for her selfish feelings, she will cast off imperfection and come to perfection. Once she is more perfect, a greater and more perfect love for others in general will follow, as well as for the special person my goodness has given her.[23]

Catherine knew from experience that the mutual love of dear friends is a source of energy and support that enables us to grow in compassion for those to whom we are not naturally attracted and even those who have betrayed us or are our enemies. What we learn in our most intimate relationships bears fruit in our work for peace and the reform of the body of Christ since these too are ultimately matters of rightly ordered relationships. The experience of mutual human love and the deeper love it reveals of God's offer to us of mutual friendship in grace enables us to come to see others as God sees them and to widen the tent of our love and concern. Thus Catherine notes in her *Dialogue* that our sufferings, including the sufferings experienced in friendships, are intended to make us "compassionate instead of cruel toward [our] neighbors."[24]

In that sense, those we have been given to love "with a particular love" include not only family members, close friends, and companions in ministry, but also all those in our lives who make a special claim on our compassion. Some speculate that Catherine's specific prayer at the beginning of the *Dialogue* for a "special case" referred not to one of her intimate friends or family members, but to the political prisoner Niccolo di Tuldo, whom she accompanied to the gallows for his execution in Siena. Raymond's *Life of Catherine of Siena* reports multiple other examples of those that Catherine befriended in her life of ministry. In each case she came to see others with God's own "eye of compassion" in spite of their unreasonable demands, their misinterpretation of her motives, and the slanderous rumors they circulated about her lack of integrity.[25] Catherine's ministry to others was rooted in love and concern for the person and an attempt to respond to their needs even when they rejected or mocked that love. Her experience of mutual friendship with others and of God's unlimited friendship for her that she "tasted" in her mystical prayer developed her capacity to love others even when that love was not reciprocated. In her *Dialogue* Catherine returned repeatedly to the theme of the inseparability of love of God and love of neighbor that had been revealed to her in her mystical prayer:

You cannot give me the kind of love I ask of you. This is why I have put you among your neighbors: so that you can do for them what you cannot do for me — that is, love them without any concern for thanks and without looking for any profit for yourself. And whatever you do for them I will consider done for me.[26]

In all of her relationships, both those of deep and mutual love and those in which she was rejected or scorned, Catherine experienced the transformation symbolized in her mystical espousal with Christ. Although the image is pictured as an exchange of hearts, Catherine describes it in one of her prayers not as a giving up or replacement of her human heart, but rather as its gradual transformation. She gives thanks for the way that the God "mad with love" expands our hearts in charity so that our compassion might extend beyond those we have been given to love in a special and mutual way to all those whom God loves:

> You, light, make the heart simple,
> not two-faced.
> You make it big, not stingy —
> so big that it has room in its loving charity for everyone:
> with well-ordered charity
> it seeks everyone's salvation.[27]

Conclusion

The church of the twenty-first century is not the church of the fourteenth. The politics of the Italian city-states are not those of a multicultural, globalized international world where even negotiations among nation-states cannot guarantee world peace. The strategies of the lay reformer Catherine of Siena cannot serve as a template for achieving unity in the church and the integrity of its leaders, much less for advancing political reform in today's complex world. Even her admirers readily admit that in her own time Catherine's strategies were sometimes naive or misguided and that often they were ignored or failed.

Nevertheless, Catherine's twenty-first-century sisters — and brothers — have much to learn from this woman whose persistence in speaking the truth and calling for right relationships in church and world was rooted in her relationship with God in contemplative prayer. As Carmelite Constance FitzGerald reminds contemporary women and men who are experiencing impenetrable forms of impasse in their personal relationships, ministries, ecclesial lives, or political efforts, the only way forward in some situations is "holding this impasse in our bodies and hearts before the inner God we reach for in the dark of shattered symbols."[28]

Catherine of Siena does not offer concrete strategies for ecclesial, social, or political change. But her *Dialogue,* prayers, and letters do provide strategies for the kind of prayer that is necessary to sustain efforts for reform and renewal of church and world. Catherine's fourfold prayer reminds us that the Holy Spirit is the source of all genuine reform of the church and the source of the energy to work for right relationship in the broader world as well. Prophetic wisdom in both arenas is rooted not only in keen analysis of what is blocking the common good in each situation, but also in keen awareness of the forms of bias that are ours as well.

Catherine's ability to call others to conversion was grounded in her desire to grow in self-knowledge and virtue and her love and concern for those whose behavior she criticized. The prayer that sustained Catherine of Siena's strategies for change widened her vision and tempered her judgments of others, even as it strengthened her voice and empowered bold action. Catherine was a peace-maker, but she never sacrificed truth for a false peace. She desired the unity of the church and supported even weak leaders of the church of her day, but that love and desire prompted her frank calls for their reform as well.

At the heart of Catherine's work as an ecclesial and political reformer was her experience of friendship, her friendship with God and her friendship with those she had been given to love "with a special love." Her experience of love, both human and divine, sustained her in ministry and led her to a wider love and concern for the salvation of all. Here, too, she reminds us that friendships with other women and men and networks of relationship, support, and collab-oration are essential to the work of justice, peace, and ecclesial reform. In our experiences of companionship, joy, and shared mission we taste the joy of the life we anticipate and gain strength for the journey ahead.

We are in need of multiple strategies for change if the church of the twenty-first century is to be a more vital witness to the Gospel in today's world. But only strategies of prayer and friendship will sustain us along the way.

Notes

Introduction / Colleen M. Griffith

1. For a discussion of the rights and responsibilities of laypeople in the 1983 Code of Canon Law, see Lynn Jarrell's essay in this volume.

2. Emilie Townes, "Womanist Theology: Dancing with Twisted Hip," in *Introduction to Christian Theology,* ed. Roger A. Badham (Louisville: Westminster John Knox Press, 1998), 219.

3. Aristotle, *Nicomachean Ethics,* book 6, chapter 5:4, Loeb Classical Library, 1982.

4. See Margaret R. Miles, *Fullness of Life: Historical Foundations for a New Asceticism* (Philadelphia: Westminster Press, 1981).

Chapter 1: Articulating the Vision Anew / Elizabeth A. Johnson

1. See Augustine, "Sermon 306c," in John E. Rotelle, ed., *The Works of St. Augustine: A Translation for the 21st Century,* part 3, vol. 9 (*Sermons on the Saints: 306–340A*), trans. Edmund Hill (Brooklyn, N.Y.: New City Press, 1990), 36.

2. Karl Rahner, *Theological Investigations,* vol. 7: *Further Theology of the Spiritual Life I* (New York: Herder and Herder, 1971), 15.

3. Rabbi Abraham Joshua Heschel, "Vocation of the Cantor," in *The Insecurity of Freedom: Essays on Human Existence* (New York: Farrar, Straus & Giroux, 1966), 245.

4. See Gerard Manley Hopkins, "God's Grandeur," in D. H. S. Nicholson and A. H. E. Lee, eds., *The Oxford Book of English Mystical Verse* (Oxford: Clarendon Press, 1917), 194.

5. See Pope John Paul II, "1990 World Day of Peace Message," *Origins* 19, no. 28 (December 14, 1989): 465–68, par. 16.

6. See Frederic and Mary Ann Brussat, *Spiritual Literacy: Reading the Sacred in Everyday Life* (New York: Scribner Book Company, 1996), 93.

7. See Homer, *The Odyssey, 800 B.C.E.,* trans. Edward McCrorie (Baltimore: Johns Hopkins University Press, 2004).

8. See Geiko Muller-Fahrenholz, "Turn to the God of Mercy: New Perspectives on Reconciliation and Forgiveness," *Ecumenical Review* (April 1998).

9. Gustavo Gutiérrez, "Christ's History, and Ours," in *The God of Life* (Maryknoll, N.Y.: Orbis Books, 1991).

10. See Augustine, "Sermon 227," in *Sermons on the Liturgical Seasons,* trans. Mary Sarah Muldowney (New York: Fathers of the Church, Inc., 1959), 196. For more in Augustine's sermons on the working of the Spirit, see also Sermon 225 in the same volume (pages 189–94).

11. Edward Schillebeeckx, *Christ: The Experience of Jesus as Lord* (New York: Seabury Press, 1980), 641.

12. See Rabbi Professor Jonathan Sacks, "The Dignity of Difference: How to Avoid the Clash of Civilizations," Seventh Annual Templeton Lecture on Religion and World Affairs (Philadelphia: Foreign Policy Research Institute, May 21, 2002).

Chapter 2: Knit Together by the Spirit as Church / M. Shawn Copeland

1. Bernard Lonergan, *Method in Theology* (New York: Herder & Herder, 1972), 361.

2. Bernard Cooke, *Power and the Spirit of God: Toward an Experience-Based Pneumatology* (Oxford: Oxford University Press, 2004), 25.

3. Robert Hood, *Begrimed and Black: Christian Tradition on Blacks and Blackness* (Minneapolis: Fortress Press, 1994). My use of the term "bias" in this essay coincides with that of Bernard Lonergan; see his *Insight: A Study of Human Understanding*, vol. 3, *Collected Works of Bernard Lonergan,* ed. Frederick E. Crowe and Robert M. Doran (Toronto: University of Toronto Press, 1992), chaps. 6 and 7.

4. David M. Goldenberg, *The Curse of Ham: Race and Slavery in Early Judaism, Christianity, and Islam* (Princeton, N.J.: Princeton University Press, 2003), 196.

5. Gay L. Byron, *Symbolic Blackness and Ethnic Difference in Early Christian Literature* (New York: Routledge, 2002), 123.

6. Kim F. Hall, *Things of Darkness: Economies of Race and Gender in Early Modern England* (Ithaca, N.Y.: Cornell University Press, 1995), 4.

7. Orlando O. Espín, "A Multicultural Church? Theological Reflection from Below," in *The Multicultural Church: A New Landscape in U.S. Theologies,* ed. William Cenkner (New York: Paulist Press, 1996), 58; see also his *Grace and Humanness: Theological Reflections Because of Culture* (Maryknoll, N.Y.: Orbis Books, 2007).

8. Espín, "A Multicultural Church?" 62.

9. Ibid., 63.

10. Iris Marion Young, *Justice and the Politics of Difference* (Princeton, N.J.: Princeton University Press, 1990), 157.

11. David Theo Goldberg, *Racist Culture: Philosophy and the Politics of Meaning* (Oxford: Blackwell Publishers, 1993), 8.

12. Jonathan Sacks, *The Dignity of Difference: How to Avoid the Clash of Civilizations* (New York: Continuum, 2003), 62.

13. Ibid., 60.

14. Ibid., 65.

15. *Brothers and Sisters to Us: U.S. Bishops' Pastoral Letter on Racism in Our Day* (Washington, D.C.: United States Catholic Conference, November 14, 1979), 3.

16. C. F. D. Moule, *The Holy Spirit* (Grand Rapids: Wm. B. Eerdmans, 1978), 33.

17. Yves Congar, *Tradition and Traditions: An Historical and Theological Essay* (London: Burns & Oates, 1966).

18. Michael Schmauss, "The Gifts of the Spirit," in *Encyclopedia of Theology: The Concise Sacramentum Mundi,* ed. Karl Rahner (New York: Crossroad, 1984), 649.

19. Jürgen Moltmann, *The Spirit of Life: A Universal Affirmation* (Minneapolis: Fortress Press, 1993), 193.

20. William Johnston, *The Inner Eye of Love: Mysticism and Religion* (San Francisco: Harper & Row, 1978), 176.

21. Bernard Lonergan, *Insight, A Study of Human Understanding,* 422; idem, "Finality, Love, Marriage," in *Collection: Papers by Bernard Lonergan, S.J.,* ed. Frederick E. Crowe (Montreal: Palm Publishers, 1967), 16–53.

Chapter 3: The Possibilities of Creating Church / Rosemary Radford Ruether

1. For more on Rosemary Radford Ruether's thoughts regarding women and church, see *Sexism and God-Talk: Toward a Feminist Theology* (Boston: Beacon Press, 1983); *Integrating Ecofeminism, Globalization, and World Religions* (Lanham, Md.: Rowman & Littlefield Publishing, 2005); *Woman-Church: Theology and Practice*

of Feminist Liturgical Communities (Eugene, Ore.: Wipf & Stock Publishers, 2001); *Introducing Redemption in Christian Feminism* (Cleveland: Pilgrim Press, 2000).

Chapter 4: Biblical Interpretation and Women's Experience / Karen A. Barta

1. Monika Hellwig, *Whose Experience Counts in Theological Reflection?* (Milwaukee: Marquette University Press, 1982). The lecture series showcases "distinguished theologians of international reputations." Since then only three other women have been so honored.

2. Ibid., 29.

3. This concern has been raised by a number of feminist, womanist, mujerista, and Asian feminine theologians since. See, for example, the section titled "The Scriptures" found in part 5, in *Lift Every Voice: Constructing Christian Theologies from the Underside,* ed. Susan Brooks Thistlethwaite and Mary Potter Engel (Maryknoll N.Y.: Orbis, 1998), 265–97.

4. Hellwig, *Whose Experience,* 39.

5. Sharon Ringe, "Reading from Context to Context: Contributions of a Feminist Hermeneutic to Theologies of Liberation," in Thistlethwaite and Engel, eds., *Lift Every Voice,* 292.

6. Elisabeth Schüssler Fiorenza, *Wisdom Ways: Introducing Feminist Biblical Interpretation* (Maryknoll, N.Y.: Orbis, 2001), 4.

7. See Musimbi R. A. Kanyoro, "Cultural Hermeneutics: An African Contribution," in *Other Ways of Reading: African Women and the Bible,* ed. Musa W. Dube (Atlanta: Society of Biblical Literature; Geneva, World Council of Churches Publications, 2001), 107–8.

8. How one woman described her Christian experience. See Patricia O'Connell Killen, *Finding Our Voices: Women, Wisdom, and Faith* (New York: Crossroad, 1997), 1.

9. See the classic works of Sallie McFague, *Metaphorical Theology: Models of God in Religious Language* (Philadelphia: Fortress Press, 1982); Rosemary Ruether, *Sexism and God-Talk* (Boston: Beacon Press, 1983); and Elizabeth A. Johnson, *She Who Is: The Mystery of God in Feminist Theological Discourse* (New York: Crossroad, 1992).

10. See Sandra M. Schneiders, *Women and the Word: The Gender of God in the New Testament and the Spirituality of Women* (New York: Paulist Press, 1986), 50–66; also Rosemary Radford Ruether, "Christology: Can a Male Savior Save Women?" in *Sexism and God-Talk: Toward a Feminist Theology* (Boston: Beacon Press, 1983), 116–38.

11. Vatican II, Dogmatic Constitution on Divine Revelation (*Dei verbum*), VI, 21.

12. Elizabeth Cady Stanton, *The Woman's Bible,* 2 vols. (New York: European Publishing Co., 1895–98; reprint, Boston: Northeastern University Press, 1993).

13. Michael Fishbane, *Text and Texture: Close Readings of Selected Biblical Texts* (New York: Schocken Books, 1979), xiii.

14. Sandra M. Schneiders, *The Revelatory Text: Interpreting the New Testament as Sacred Scripture,* 2nd ed. (Collegeville, Minn.: Liturgical Press, 1999), 29.

15. Historian Gerda Lerner argues against using the term "patriarchy" in a narrow sense as a system derived from Greek and Roman law that gave absolute legal and economic rights to a male head of the household over his dependent female and male family members. Lerner opposes the suggestion that patriarchy existed only from classical times to the nineteenth century when women obtained civil rights. She claims that this usage distorts historical reality: "The patriarchal dominance of male family heads over their kin is much older than classical antiquity; it begins in the third millennium B.C. and is well established at the time of the writing of the Hebrew Bible." See Gerda Lerner, *The Creation of Patriarchy* (New York: Oxford University Press, 1986), 239.

16. A vivid example of how "social location" affects biblical interpretation is Bob Ekblad's *Reading the Bible with the Damned* (Louisville: Westminster John Knox Press, 2005), which grew out of his work in prison ministry. See also Miguel De La Torre, *Reading the Bible from the Margins* (Maryknoll, N.Y.: Orbis Books, 2002).

17. See, e.g., Daniel Patte, ed., *Global Bible Commentary* (Nashville: Abingdon Press, 2004); Fernando F. Segovia and Mary Ann Tolbert, eds., *Reading from this Place*, 2 vols. (Minneapolis: Fortress Press, 1995); Musa W. Dube, ed., *Other Ways of Reading: African Women and the Bible* (Atlanta: SBL Publications, 2001).

18. Sandra M. Schneiders, "The Bible and Feminism," in *Freeing Theology: The Essentials of Theology in Feminist Perspective* (New York: HarperSanFrancisco, 1993), 40.

19. Schneiders, *The Revelatory Text*, 35.

20. Ibid.

21. Ibid.

22. Victor Roland Gold et al., *The New Testament and Psalms: An Inclusive Version* (New York: Oxford University Press, 1995).

23. Available through Alta Mira Press, a division of Rowman & Littlefield Publishers.

24. Implementing suggestions in Brian Wren's 1993 classic *What Language Shall I Borrow? God-Talk in Worship: A Male Response to Feminist Theology* (New York: Crossroad, 1993) would make a huge difference in our communities of faith. An example of a translation empowering for women is Marchiene Vroon Rienstra's book of psalm-prayers, *Swallow's Nest*, in which all references to God and Her people are feminine. See Marchiene Vroon Rienstra, *Swallow's Nest: A Feminine Reading of the Psalms* (Grand Rapids: Wm. B. Eerdmans, 1992, 2003).

25. See Phyllis Trible, *God and the Rhetoric of Sexuality* (Philadelphia: Fortress Press, 1978).

26. Ibid., 94–105.

27. See Elisabeth Schüssler Fiorenza, *In Memory of Her: A Feminist Reconstruction of Christian Origins* (New York: Crossroad, 1983, 1994).

28. For an excellent "workbook" approach to the essential steps and stages within the practice of feminist biblical hermeneutics as envisioned by Elisabeth Schüssler Fiorenza, see *Wisdom Ways: Introducing Feminist Biblical Interpretation* (Maryknoll, N.Y.: Orbis Books, 2001). Chapter 7 briefly describes the various practices of hermeneutics as retrieval, suspicion, experience, social location, remembrance and reconstruction, etc. But the value of the book lies in its careful grounding of these hermeneutical moves in theory and analysis, and amply illustrated by examples.

29. Phyllis A. Bird, "What Makes a Feminist Reading Feminist? A Qualified Answer," in *Escaping Eden: New Feminist Perspectives on the Bible,* ed. Harold C. Washington, Susan Lochrie Graham, and Pamela Thimmes (Sheffield: Sheffield Academic Press, 1998), 129–30.

30. See Jane Schaberg with Melanie Johnson-DeBaufre, *Mary Magdalene Understood* (New York: Continuum, 2006).

31. See Warren Carter, "Getting Martha out of the Kitchen: Luke 10:38–42 Again," *Catholic Biblical Quarterly* 58 (April 1996): 264–80; see also *Women in Scripture: A Dictionary of Named and Unnamed Women in the Hebrew Bible, the Apocryphal/Deuterocanonical Books, and the New Testament,* ed. Carol Meyers, Toni Craven, and Ross S. Kraemer (Boston: Houghton Mifflin, 2000), 114–16.

32. Warren Carter, *Matthew and the Margins: A Sociopolitical and Religious Reading* (Maryknoll, N.Y.: Orbis Books, 2001), 59–61.

Chapter 5: Sisters of Thecla /
Francine Cardman

1. Thecla's story is incorporated into the extracanonical *Acts of Paul;* the standard translation is in *New Testament Apocrypha,* vol. 2: *Writings Relating to the Apostles;*

Apocalypses and Related Subjects, ed. Wilhelm Schneemelcher, ed. and trans. Robert McL. Wilson (Louisville: Westminster John Knox Press, 2003), 235–46.

2. Teresa of Avila, *The Book of Her Life* 1.4 (missionaries); 32.6 (Lutherans), *The Collected Works of St. Teresa of Avila,* vol. 1, trans. Kieran Kavanaugh, O.C.D., and Otilio Rodriguez, O.C.D. (Washington, D.C.: ICS Publications, 1976).

3. Thérèse of Lisieux, *Story of a Soul: The Autobiography of Thérèse of Lisieux* 9, trans. John Clarke, O.C.D., 3rd ed. (Washington, D.C.: ICS Publications, 1996): "I feel the *vocation* of the WARRIOR, THE PRIEST, THE APOSTLE, THE DOCTOR, THE MARTYR" (emphasis hers), 192.

4. Miriam Therese Winter, *Out of the Depths: The Story of Ludmila Javorova, Ordained Roman Catholic Priest* (New York: Crossroad, 2001); Petr Fiala and Jiří Hanuš, "Dossier: The Practice of Ordaining Women in the Present Church. Theological Preparation and Establishment of the Ordination of Women in the Clandestine Church in Czechoslovakia," in *The Non-Ordination of Women and the Politics of Power,* ed. Elisabeth Schüssler Fiorenza and Hermann Häring (*Concilium* 3 [1993]: 126–38).

5. On these ordained women see online *www.romancatholicwomenpriests.org; www.womenpriests.org/index.asp; www.virtuelle-dioezese.de/newsletter.* See also the Women's Ordination Conference, founded in the United States in 1975: *www.womensordination.org/index.html* (January 15, 2007).

6. Gerda Lerner, *Women and History* (New York and Oxford: Oxford University Press), vol. 1, *The Creation of Patriarchy* (1986); vol. 2, *The Creation of Feminist Consciousness* (1993), vii, viii.

7. Michel Foucault, "Truth and Power," in *Power/Knowledge: Selected Interviews and Other Writings 1972–1977,* ed. Colin Gordon (New York: Pantheon Books, 1980), 109–33; also in *The Foucault Reader,* ed. Paul Rabinow (New York: Pantheon Books, 1984), 51–75.

8. See introduction to *Acts of Paul* in Schneemelcher, *New Testament Apocrypha,* 2:213–35. See also *The Apocryphal Acts of Paul and Thecla,* ed. Jan N. Bremmer (Kampen: Pharos, 1996). For Thecla's memory and cult, see Stephen J. Davis, *The Cult of St. Thecla: A Tradition of Women's Piety in Late Antiquity,* Oxford Early Christian Studies (Oxford and New York: Oxford University Press, 2001).

9. See, e.g., Bernadette Brooten, " 'Junia … Outstanding among the Apostles' (Romans 16:7)," in *Women Priests: A Catholic Commentary on the Vatican Declaration,* ed. Leonard Swidler and Arlene Swidler (New York: Paulist Press, 1977), 141–44; see also Mary Rose D'Angelo, "Women Partners in the New Testament," *Journal of Feminist Studies in Religion* 6 (Spring 1990): 65–86.

10. Wilson, *New Testament Apocrypha,* vol. 2, thinks there was a woman named Thecla converted by Paul, but that the *Acts of Thecla* cannot be historically verified (222); he rejects the view of scholars who hold that the story reflects a movement among second-century women (236, n. 19). I discuss Thecla in the context of women's ministries in this period: "Women, Ministry, and Church Order in Early Christianity," in *Women and Christian Origins,* ed. Ross Shepherd Kraemer and Mary Rose D'Angelo (New York and Oxford: Oxford University Press, 1999), 300–329.

11. The longer ending is available online in an antiquated translation from an uncritical text at *www.monachos.net/library/Thecla_the_Great-Martyr,_Acts_and_ Life* (July 6, 2006) and in a more recent but unattributed translation at *www .atheavensgate.com/ocwa/25-Protomartyr%20Thecla.html* (January 6, 2007).

12. *http://orthodoxwiki.org/Thekla_the_Protomartyr* (January 6, 2007). Although the title is readily noted, it is also often downplayed.

13. Tertullian, *On Baptism* 17: "And if certain Acts of Paul, which are falsely so named, claim the example of Thecla for allowing women to teach and baptize, let men know that in Asia the presbyter who compiled that document, thinking to add his own to Paul's reputation, was found out, and though he professed he had done it for love of Paul, was deposed from his position. How could we believe that Paul should give a female power to teach and to baptize, when he did not allow a woman even to learn by

her own right? *Let them keep silence,* he says, *and ask their husbands at home*" (1 Cor. 14:35). *Tertullian's Homily on Baptism,* text, translation, commentary by Ernest Evans (London: SPCK, 1964), 37.

14. The phrase was made widely known by Johann Baptist Metz in *Faith in History and Society,* trans. David Smith (New York: Seabury Press, 1980).

15. See Flora Keshgegian, *Redeeming Memories: A Theology of Healing and Transformation* (Nashville: Abingdon Press, 2000), 151: "Memory is not only dangerous but endangered," as is often the case in regard to "remembrance of resistance to oppression and of acts of historical agency."

16. For an overview of the movement, see Maureen Fiedler and Dolly Pomerleau, "The Women's Ordination Movement in the Roman Catholic Church," in *Encyclopedia of Women and Religion in North America,* ed. Rosemary Skinner Keller and Rosemary Radford Ruether (Bloomington: Indiana University Press, 2006), 2:951–60.

17. The declaration is *not* among the CDF texts on the Vatican website, but can be found online, e.g., *www.papalencyclicals.net/Paul06/p6interi.htm* (January 20, 2007) and in the collections in n. 18 and n. 19.

18. The commentary, by an unnamed "expert theologian," can be found, along with Latin texts and translations of other documents, in *From "Inter Insigniores" to "Ordinatio Sacerdotalis": Documents and Commentaries* (Washington, D.C.: United States Catholic Conference, 1998), 55–76.

19. For essays on nearly every significant argument of the declaration, see Swidler and Swidler, eds., *Women Priests.* For a review of all the relevant ecclesial documents through 2002, and translations of many of them, see Deborah Halter, *The Papal "No": A Comprehensive Guide to the Vatican's Rejection of Women's Ordination* (New York: Crossroad, 2004), which also includes the commentary on the declaration.

20. In *From "Inter Insigniores" to "Ordinatio Sacerdotalis,"* 184–91, and Halter, *The Papal "No,"* 211–13.

21. *Reply to the Dubium,* in *From "Inter Insigniores" to "Ordinatio Sacredotalis,"* 196–7, and Halter, *The Papal "No,"* 225.

22. Francis A. Sullivan, "Guideposts from Catholic Tradition," *America* (December 9, 1995): 5–6, argues that it is not an infallible teaching; see also Ladislas Orsy, "The Congregation's 'Response': Its Authority and Meaning," *America* (December 9, 1995): 4–5.

23. For an overview see Suzanne Radley Hiatt, "Women's Ordination in the Anglican Communion: Can This Church Be Saved?" in *Religious Institutions and Women's Leadership: New Roles inside the Mainstream,* ed. Catherine Weissinger (Columbia: University of South Carolina Press, 1996), 211–27.

24. Code of Canon Law available at *www.vatican.va/archive/eng1104/_index.htm* (December 13, 2006).

25. See Mark 10:27; Matt. 19:26.

26. Javorova was ordered by her bishop in 1996 not to preside at the Eucharist (Winter, *Out of the Depths,* 211); I can find no explicit statements from the Vatican about the invalidity of her ordination or the other women's, which presumably were understood to be covered by *Inter Insigniores* and *Ordinatio Sacerdotalis.* The men's ordinations were declared invalid in the "Declaration of the Congregation for the Doctrine of the Faith on Bishops and Priests Ordained Secretly in the Czech Republic," February 11, 2000; available at *www.zenit.org/english/archive/documents/CDF_ordenations.html* [*sic*] (March 15, 2007).

27. See *www.spirituschristi.org/history.html* for the history of Spiritus Christi parish and the ordinations (March 29, 2007).

28. The "Danube Seven" were warned by the CDF that they would be excommunicated if by July 22 they did not admit that their ordinations ("the simulation of a sacrament") were void and repent for the scandal their actions caused the faithful; *www.ewtn.com/vnews/getstory.asp?number=28041* (March 15, 2007). On August 6, 2002, they were formally declared excommunicated; see

www.hartford-hwp.com/archives/62/279.html (March 15, 2007). Communications with and from the Vatican are available in German at *www.virtuelle-dioezese.de/* (March 15, 2007).

29. For information about or links to all these ordinations, see n. 5 above.

30. Michael Paulson, "Making a Stand for Women Priests," *Boston Globe,* July 28, 2006, B1.

31. "Prophetic Obedience: The Experience and Vision of R.C. Womenpriests," address at the Southeast Pennsylvania Women's Ordination Conference, March 12, 2005; online at *www.womensordination.org/pages/art_pages/art_Fresen2005.htm* (April 11, 2007).

Chapter 6: Women within Church Law / Lynn Jarrell

1. Sue Bender, *Everyday Sacred: A Woman's Journey Home* (New York: HarperCollins, 1995), 15–16.

2. The discussion will be guided by the content of the 1983 Code of Canon Law in the following translation: *Code of Canon Law — Latin-English Edition* (Washington, D.C.: Canon Law Society of America, 1999). Translation prepared under the auspices of the Canon Law Society of America. Particular canons will be referenced by the abbreviations of "c" or "cc" followed by the appropriate canon number.

3. C. 208.

4. While there had been centuries of legal texts addressing all aspects of the life of the church, it was only in the twentieth century that the legal texts were organized into what is called a code of canon law. The first code was published in 1917 and then revised in 1983 in light of the directions and teachings developed at the Second Vatican Council.

5. *Codex Iuris Canonici* (Rome: Typis Polyglottis Vaticanis, 1917), approved by Pope Benedict XV. It was authorized only to be published in Latin, but there were English commentaries that offered unofficial translations of the canons.

6. One other duty is also stated: not to wear clerical garb since this was a privilege that belonged only to the clergy. The right and duties listed for women were the same for lay men. The key differences were that women were not eligible to petition to enter the clerical state and were viewed as inferior to men in the exercise of authority.

7. This is the same role that lay men had in the 1917 Code.

8. This perspective in this canon was the mind-set, throughout much of first two centuries of the church. Women were viewed as seductive, intellectually inferior in administrative matters, timid, scrupulous, and in need of protection. See the following study of this earlier perspective: Nancy Reynolds, S.P., "A Comparison of the Specific Juridic Status of Women in the 1917 and 1983 Codes of Canon Law" (Washington, D.C.: Licentiate Dissertation on depose in the John K. Mullen of Denver Memorial Library, Catholic University of America, 1985).

9. The one exception to this was when women held the role of major superiors in their religious institutes, which enabled them, for the most part, to exercise autonomy in governing the internal life of their institutes.

10. See n. 1. Parallel canons are available but not referenced in this essay for those of the Eastern Rites from the following text: *Code of Canons of the Eastern Churches, Latin–English Edition* (Washington, D.C.: Canon Law Society of America, 1996). Translation prepared under the auspices of the Canon Law Society of America.

11. See cc. 209–23 for the listing of the duties and rights of the Christian faithful and cc. 224–31 for a listing of duties and rights particular to the laity. There is also a listing for rights, duties, eligibilities, and formation of the clergy in cc. 232–93. The footnotes for canons 209–31 are primarily the documents of Vatican Council II, in particular *Lumen gentium*, November 21, 1964 (AAS 57 [1965] 32, and *Gaudium et spes,* December 7, 1966; AAS 60 [1966] 49 and 61). Examples of other documents

and statements of the church that have expressed this same shift over the years are: Apostolic Constitution on the Christian Faithful Laity (*Christifideles laici*) in 1988, the U.S. bishops' document on women in 1994, and Pope Benedict XVI's statement on women on March 13, 2006.

12. C. 129 §2.

13. A comparison of the content of canon 145 in both the 1917 and 1983 Codes demonstrates this shift. Canon 150 in the 1983 Code states that only those offices that involve the full care of souls are reserved solely to the clergy.

14. An example of this distinction between lay women and men is in c. 230 §1 which says only lay men can be *stably installed* as acolytes since only men can move on to the clerical state.

15. C. 96.

16. C. 204 §1.

17. Cc. 146 and 208.

18. C. 205.

19. C. 212 §1.

20. C. 204 §1.

21. Cc. 781 and 211.

22. Cc. 781 and 225 §2.

23. For clear, concise discussion of this topic see Sharon Euart, R.S.M., and Lynn Jarrell, O.S.U., "The Church's Legal Position concerning Women for Ministry," in *Creating a Home: Benchmarks for Church Leadership Roles for Women — A Special LCWR Report*, ed. Jeanean D. Merkel (Silver Spring, Md.: Leadership Conference of Women Religious, 1996).

24. Cc. 211, 214, 225, 226. See also Merkel, *Creating a Home,* 53.

25. C. 149. See also Merkel, *Creating a Home,* 53.

26. C. 129. See also Merkel, *Creating a Home,* 54–55.

27. C. 145 §2.

28. For example, of the ministries in the listing in this section women could hold the positions of finance officer, judge with some restriction, and superintendent of schools if qualified and appointed.

29. For a thorough description of custom see John Huels, "Back to the Future: The Role of Custom in a World Church," *Canon Law Society of America Proceedings* 59 (1997): 1–25.

30. C. 27.

31. C. 26.

32. Enculturation presumes a certain dynamism that defies prescribing more than general boundaries in most cases or particular boundaries that can be altered as the circumstances warrant.

33. Cc. 213 and 217.

34. Cc. 209–10.

35. Cc. 748 and 219.

36. C. 223.

37. C. 212. At the same time all members are required to accept the teaching role of the church authorities. This teaching role belongs to the church always and everywhere to announce moral principles, even in the social order, and to render judgment concerning human affairs insofar as the fundamental rights of the human person or the salvation of souls requires it. It includes preaching the Gospel to all people and making use of the effective means of social communication available for evangelization.

38. C. 229.

39. C. 1282. See canons 1273–89 for the responsibilities of an administrator in the church. While church administration is governed by the civil law of the given geographical area, the individuals overseeing ecclesiastical goods are bound to fulfill their functions in the name of the church according to the norms of canon law (C. 22).

40. C. 1254 §2.

41. The necessary formation will vary. Current legal texts present structured seminary programs for individuals who seek ordination. Eventually, as the ordained, these individuals will hold official church offices and/or exercise official church functions. In addition, preparation for perpetual incorporation into a religious institute is directed by norms in both universal law and the proper law of the particular institute. Commonly, these formation programs involve a life commitment on the part of the individual.

42. Cc. 149 §1 and 229 §2.

43. In most cases it is not the law itself that is the barrier but the mind-sets and the interpretations of texts that create unnecessary limitations on the fuller participation of women within the church's ministerial life.

Chapter 7: *Wise as Serpents, Innocent as Doves /* Margaret R. Pfeil

1. Helen Prejean, *Dead Man Walking* (New York: Vintage Books, 1994), 5.

2. Ibid.

3. Ibid., 5–6.

4. See Sandra Harding, "Rethinking Standpoint Epistemology: What Is 'Strong Objectivity'?" in *Feminist Epistemologies,* ed. Linda Alcoff and Elizabeth Potter (New York: Routledge, 1993), 54.

5. Rosita deAnn Mathews, "Using Power from the Periphery: An Alternative Theological Model for Survival in Systems," in *A Troubling in My Soul: Womanist Perspectives on Evil and Suffering,* ed. Emilie M. Townes (Maryknoll, N.Y.: Orbis Books, 1993), 99.

6. John Paul II, *Sollicitudo rei socialis,* in *Catholic Social Thought: The Documentary Heritage,* ed. David J. O'Brien and Thomas A. Shannon (Maryknoll, N.Y.: Orbis Books, 1992), 421–22 (par. 38). Unless otherwise noted, all subsequent references to Catholic social teaching texts will be taken from this source and parenthetically cited by paragraph number.

7. John Paul II, *Sollicitudo rei socialis,* 421–22 (par. 38).

8. On the power of coercive influence, see John R. P. French Jr. and Bertram Raven, "The Bases of Social Power," in *Studies in Social Power,* ed. Dorwin Cartwright (Ann Arbor: University of Michigan, 1959), 157.

9. See Peter J. Henriot, Edward P. DeBerri, and Michael J. Schultheis, *Catholic Social Teaching: Our Best Kept Secret,* 3rd rev. ed. (Maryknoll, N.Y.: Orbis Books, 1992).

10. John Paul II, *Evangelium vitae* (Washington, D.C.: U.S. Catholic Conference, 1995), 99–100 (par. 56). See also Pontifical Council for Justice and Peace, *Compendium of the Social Doctrine of the Church* (Vatican City: Libreria Editrice Vaticana, 2004), par. 405.

11. Helen Prejean, *The Death of Innocents: An Eyewitness Account of Wrongful Executions* (New York: Vintage Books, 1996), 126.

12. Ibid., 117.

13. Ibid., 124.

14. Ibid., 125.

15. Ibid., 127.

16. Ibid., 126.

17. Ibid., 129–30.

18. Cardinal Renato Martino, president of the Pontifical Council for Justice and Peace, has likened the evolution of Catholic teaching on just war theory to that on capital punishment, noting that the church is moving toward a "quasi-abolitionist stance" on war. See John L. Allen Jr., "Pope's 'Answer to Rumsfeld' Pulls No Punches in Opposing War," *National Catholic Reporter,* February 14, 2003.

19. Prejean, *Death of Innocents,* 134.

20. Walter Brueggemann, *The Prophetic Imagination*, 2nd ed. (Minneapolis: Fortress Press, 2001), 40.

21. Ibid., 116.

22. John Dear, "One Woman Talking: An Interview with Sister Helen Prejean," available at *www.ottawainnercityministries.ca/biographies/srPREJEAN.htm* (January 9, 2007).

23. Dogmatic Constitution on the Church (*Lumen gentium*), in *Vatican Council II: The Conciliar and Post-Conciliar Documents*, vol. 1, rev. ed., ed. Austin Flannery (Collegeville, Minn.: Liturgical Press, 1992), 363 (par. 12). See also the Decree on the Apostolate of Lay People (*Apostolicam actuositatem*), 768–69 (par. 3).

24. See Hans Küng, "The Charismatic Structure of the Church," in *The Church and Ecumenism*, Concilium vol. 4 (New York: Paulist Press, 1965), 51. See also the following contributions in *Retrieving Charisms for the Twenty-First Century*, ed. Doris Donnelly (Collegeville, Minn.: Liturgical Press, 1999): Margaret M. Mitchell, " 'Be Zealous for the Greater Charismata': Pauline Advice for the Church of the Twenty-First Century," 22; John C. Haughey, "Charisms: An Ecclesiological Exploration," 2; and Avery Dulles, "The Charism of the New Evangelizer," 36. Finally, see René Laurentin, "Charisms: Terminological Precision," trans. Theo Weston, in *Charisms in the Church*, Concilium, ed. Christian Duquoc and Casiano Floristan (New York: Seabury Press, 1978), 7–8.

25. Michel Foucault, "Powers and Strategies," in *Power/Knowledge: Selected Interviews and Other Writings 1972–1977*, ed. Colin Gordon, trans. Colin Gordon, Leo Marshall, John Mepham, and Kate Soper (New York: Pantheon Books, 1980), 142.

26. Donal Dorr, *Option for the Poor: A Hundred Years of Vatican Social Teaching*, rev. ed. (Maryknoll, N.Y.: Orbis Books, 1992), 332.

27. Prejean, *Dead Man Walking*, 7.

28. Prejean, *The Death of Innocents*, 121.

29. Charles Curran, "The Changing Anthropological Bases of Catholic Social Ethics," *The Thomist* 45, no. 2 (1981): 284–318.

30. See Barbara Ward, "Looking Back on *Populorum Progressio*," *Doctrine and Life* 29, no. 4 (1978): 196–212, and Allan Figueroa Deck, "Commentary on *Populorum progressio (On the Development of Peoples)*," in *Modern Catholic Social Teaching: Commentaries and Interpretations*, ed. Kenneth Himes (Washington, D.C.: Georgetown University Press, 2005), 292–314.

31. "Benedetto XVI al Clero della Diocesi di Roma (March 2, 2006)," *L'Osservatore Romano*, March 3, 2006 (supplement). The English translation used here is that of Matthew Sherry and may be found at *http://chiesa.espresso.repubblica .it/dettaglio.jsp?id=46491&eng=y* (February 12, 2007).

Chapter 8: Unknowing in the Place of Understanding / Jeannine Hill Fletcher

1. Examples of Catholic initiatives in interfaith dialogue range from the grassroots (for example, the women's Islamic-Catholic dialogues in Milwaukee) to the high-profile (including those initiated by the Vatican). Catholics can be encouraged by the statements of Vatican II and Pope Benedict XVI, who has publicly recognized as among the "positive elements characteristic of the modern age," "the growing awareness of the importance of dialogue between cultures and between religions." "Address of his Holiness Pope Benedict XVI to the Diplomatic Corps Accredited to the Holy See for the Traditional Exchange of New Year Greetings," January 8, 2007, *www.vatican.va* (January 11, 2007), §8.

2. Miroslav Volf, "Your Scripture Meets Mine," *Christian Century* 121, no. 21 (October 19, 2004): 43.

3. Sallie King, "A Pluralistic View of Religious Pluralism," in *The Myth of Religious Superiority: A Multifaith Exploration,* ed. Paul F. Knitter (Maryknoll, N.Y.: Orbis Books, 2005), 99–100.

4. For example, in *The Dialogical Imperative: A Christian Reflection on Interfaith Encounter,* David Lochhead writes, "The purpose of dialogue is understanding" (Maryknoll, N.Y.: Orbis Books, 1988), 65.

5. George Lindbeck, *The Nature of Doctrine: Religion and Theology in a Postliberal Age* (Philadelphia: Westminster Press, 1984); see especially chap. 6, 112–35.

6. George Lindbeck, "The Story-Shaped Church: Critical Exegesis and Theological Interpretation," in *Scriptural Authority and Narrative Interpretation,* ed. Garrett Green (Philadelphia: Fortress Press, 1987), 161–78.

7. George Lindbeck, "The Gospel's Uniqueness: Election and Untranslatability," *Modern Theology* 13, no. 4 (October 1997): 432.

8. King, "A Pluralistic View," 99–100.

9. Volf, "Your Scripture Meets Mine," 43.

10. Judith Plaskow, *Standing Again at Sinai: Judaism from a Feminist Perspective* (San Francisco: HarperSanFrancisco, 1991), 57.

11. The work of Francis Clooney at the intersection of Hinduism and Christianity is one example of scholarly achievement of this rare bilingualism; individuals like Roshi Robert Kennedy, S.J., and Sallie King demonstrate the lifelong commitment of understanding through practice of dual religious systems. Chung Hyun Kyung and Raimon Panikkar give witness to the way Christians in many parts of the globe are shaped by the multiple religious traditions of their native place.

12. Lindbeck, "Gospel's Uniqueness," 426–27.

13. Aquinas, *Summa Theologica,* I.I, Question 12, Article 7, in *Basic Writings of St. Thomas Aquinas,* trans. Anton C. Pegis (New York: Random House, 1945), 101.

14. Teresa of Avila, "Spiritual Testimonies," in *The Collected Works of St. Teresa of Avila,* trans. Kieran Kavanaugh and Otilio Rodriguez (Washington D.C.: ICS Publications, 1976), 322–28.

15. Karl Rahner, "An Investigation of the Incomprehensibility of God in St. Thomas Aquinas," in *Theological Investigations* 16, trans. David Morland (New York: Seabury Press, 1979), 246.

16. Aquinas, *Summa Contra Gentiles,* chapter 62, Pegis, vol. 2, 110.

17. Morwenna Griffiths, *Feminisms and the Self: The Web of Identity* (London: Routledge, 1995), 2.

18. Martha Minnow, *Not Only for Myself: Identity, Politics and the Law* (New York: New Press, 1997), 40.

19. Helene Egnell, *Other Voices: A Study of Christian Feminist Approaches to Religious Plurality East and West* (Uppsala, Sweden: Studia Missionalia Svecana C, 2006), 168.

20. The concept of "integral salvation" is taken from Gustavo Gutiérrez, *A Theology of Liberation: History, Politics, and Salvation,* rev. ed., trans. and ed. Caridad Inda and John Eagleson (Maryknoll, N.Y.: Orbis Books, 1988).

21. Kwok Pui-lan, "Beyond Pluralism: Toward a Postcolonial Theology of Religious Difference," in *Postcolonial Imagination and Feminist Theology* (Louisville: Westminster John Knox Press, 2005), 205.

22. In her essay "On Relationship as a Key to Interreligious Dialogue" in *Many and Diverse Ways: In Honor of Jacques Dupuis,* ed. Daniel Kendall and Gerald O'Collins (Maryknoll, N.Y.: Orbis Books, 2003), 133–45, Doris Donnelly affirms Leonard Swidler, who cites Vatican II to articulate that "dialogue can take place only between equals." See Swidler, "Interreligious and Interideological Dialogue: The Matrix for All Systematic Reflection Today," in *Toward a Universal Theology of Religion,* ed. Leonard Swidler (Maryknoll, N.Y.: Orbis Books, 1987).

23. Homi Bhabha, keynote address of conference on "Sex and Religion in Migration," Yale University, September 15, 2005.

24. In envisioning what it means to pattern our future on a witness to Christ and the tradition of the Christian past, the work of Elisabeth Schüssler Fiorenza has been formative to my understanding of the foundations of the church. See *In Memory of Her: A Feminist Theological Reconstruction of Christian Origins* (New York: Crossroad, 1992).

Chapter 9: The Dialogical Imperative / Teresia M. Hinga

1. Methodologically, Circle women have prioritized story telling, even the telling of personal stories, as a tool to interrupt prevailing androcentric methodologies that prioritize detachment, and analyses of religious texts and phenomena that are without adequate reference to the contexts in which those religions are daily negotiated and experienced. Prioritizing what they have referred to as narrative theology, the Circle published an anthology suitably entitled *Her Stories: Hidden Histories of Women of Faith in Africa* (Pietermaritzburg, South Africa: Cluster, 2002). As a way of narrating and analyzing their own untold stories of struggle, hope, and vision, the Circle also elevates and retells stories of women integral to the scriptural and oral traditions of Africa's triple heritage of Islam, Christianity, and Indigenous religions. For example, the story of Jairus's daughter, in which Jesus calls the apparently dead girl to arise, is adopted metaphorically as the story of African women, as daughters of Africa, responding to God's call to action. Similarly, the story of Anowa, a prophetic female leader featured in Akan mythology, is also adopted by African women seeking female role models to emulate in their struggles for freedom and empowerment today. It is also noteworthy that in their analyses of contemporary crises like violence and HIV/AIDS, women often preface their analyses with stories of actual women facing such crises, such as Njeri below. Their work, therefore, has an embodied feel, rather than an anonymous and abstract tone, as has been the tendency of the more prevalent methodologies. For more detailed examples of this narrative methodology at work, see Fulata Moyo's essay, "Navigating Experiences of Healing: A Narrative Theology of Eschatological Hope and Healing," in *African Women, Religion and Health,* ed. Isabel Apawo Phiri et al. (Maryknoll, N.Y.: Orbis Books, 2006), 243–57. For an analysis of the role of narrative methodology in Circle thought, see Dube Musa, ed., *Other Ways of Reading* (Geneva: WCC Publications, 2001), 3.

2. Survivors of the Rwandan genocide, among other situations of hot violence in Africa, are beginning to tell the stories of their experiences of terror under such circumstances. Women in these situations were subjected to rape and sexual assault by enemy combatants. For an example of one such harrowing story of women's double jeopardy in situations of armed conflict, see Ilibagiza Immacule, *Left to Tell: Discovering God Amidst the Rwanda Holocaust* (Carlsbad, Calif.: Hay House, 2006). In the book she narrates in heartrending detail how in many instances, when faced with the prospect of rape and sexual assault, she would pray to die by the gun or machete rather than face the intimate terror of rape and sexual torture, often a prelude to being killed anyway.

3. For details of this story of resilience, courage, and hope, see chaps. 6 to 11 in Wangari Maathai's autobiography, simply and appropriately titled *Unbowed: A Memoir* (New York: Alfred A. Knopf, 2006).

4. In several of his literary works, Ngugi WA Thiongo, one of the most articulate social critics in Kenya, has addressed this problem of distributive malpractice and land grabbing and the very subtle ways in which these are executed in Kenya. For details of this analysis, see his novel *Devil on the Cross* (London: Heinemann, 1982). The novel chronicles and dramatizes the heartrending conditions of peasants and workers in Kenya under the colonial and neocolonial systems of domination prevailing there. It also narrates how sexism compounds the pain of women under such exploitative circumstances. His prophetic critique of society is formed in this regard by the author's

own experience of being tortured, detained without trial, and forced into exile, where he has been for the last thirty years.

5. Maathai, *Unbowed*, 294–95.

6. It is noteworthy that in founding the Circle, Mercy was responding to preliminary overtures from the World Council of Churches to engage women more as they launched "A Decade of Churches in Solidarity with Women." In turn, the outreach from the WCC seems to have been prompted by the recommendations made by women themselves, clamoring for their voices to be heard in church and society during the 1985 UN Conference on Women in Nairobi. For more details and analysis of the events that preceded and fostered the emergence of the Circle, see M. Kanyoro's essay "Beads and Strands: Threading More Beads in the Story of the Circle," in *African Women, Religion and Health*, ed. Phiri et al., 19–23.

7. The term "Ubuntu," signifying specifically African notions of the human person, has been adopted in the context of the discourse on African liberation and reconstruction, otherwise referred to as "African Renaissance." African anthropology defines true or ideal humanity in terms of interconnectedness and interrelationships, what Laurenti Magesa calls the relationship imperative (see Magesa, *African Religions: The Moral Traditions of Abundant Life* [Maryknoll, N.Y.: Orbis Books, 1997], 64). This is contrasted with Western notions of personhood, which emphasize rationality, individualism, and mental prowess as its defining features. This notion is well captured in the often-cited Cartesian quote, "I think therefore I am." In the African context, however, it is in the embrace of interconnectedness and interrelationship with others (in the divine, human, and even the nonhuman world) that one finds Ubuntu, true humanity. This is the thought that John Mbiti (*African Religions and Philosophy* [London: Heinemann, 2000], 106) tries to capture in his often cited quote: in the African context, the individual can only say, "I am because we are and since we are, therefore I am." Ubuntu anthropology is increasingly championed as part of the solution to issues arising out of the radical and deadly individualism that has percolated through African societies since European colonialism. For a detailed account of how Ubuntu has informed and shaped the thought and practice of one of the most prominent moral exemplars of our time, see Michael Battle, *Reconciliation: The Ubuntu Theology of Desmond Tutu* (Cleveland: Pilgrim Press, 1997), 35f; for a proposal for the urgent reclamation and application of Ubuntu anthropology in the reconstruction of a post-apartheid South Africa, see Mbigi Lovemore, *Ubuntu: The African Dream in Management* (Pretoria, South Africa: Knowledge Resources, 1997).

8. For details, see M. Oduyoye, ed., *Transforming Power: Women in the Household of God* (Accra-North, Ghana: Samwoode, 1997), 5.

9. As I write this paragraph, the Circle's fourth Pan-African conference is taking place in Yaoundé, Cameroon (September 2–9, 2007). Thematically, this conference continues the Circle's analysis of the crisis of HIV/AIDS started in the 2002 Pan-African conference, focusing this time on the plight of young girls. Structurally, the conference is designed to celebrate and highlight various ways the dialogical roundtable has expanded to include the fruitful partnerships with concerned others for purposes of building solidarity beyond the Circle's initial boundaries. For details of this conference and its goals, see the *Circle Newsletter,* no. 7 (December 2007): 2.

10. M. Oduyoye and M. Kanyoro, *The Will to Arise: Women, Tradition, and the Church in Africa* (Maryknoll, N.Y.: Orbis Books, 1992), 10.

11. Ibid., 1.

12. Women consider the cumulative and multiplier effect of other social issues, metaphorically called "viruses," such as poverty, sexism, and ignorance as they analyze the complexities of HIV/AIDS in Africa.

13. The 2001 Pan-African conference, "Overcoming Violence: Women of Faith Speak," was held at the Talitha Qumi Center in Ghana. Subsequently, at the national level, the Kenyan chapter published a book entitled *Violence against Women* (Nairobi: Acton, 1996), while the Nigerian chapter researched and published on cultural factors

that militate against women's human rights and that are therefore both causative and symptomatic factors in violence against women.

14. M. Oduyoye, *Daughters of Anowa* (Maryknoll, N.Y.: Orbis Books, 1995), 170.

15. Ibid., 171.

16. One such opportunity for mutual education about faith availed itself during the 1996 Pan-African conference. Determined to be inclusive, the organizers of the conference had scheduled a prayer session each morning at 8:00 to be led by women from the various faith traditions represented at the conference, including Islam and Indigenous African religions. When their turn to lead prayers came, the Muslim women took the podium, but instead of leading the group in prayer, they took the opportunity to explain Muslim prayer patterns and the notion that Muslims pray five times a day, often reminded to do so by a muezzin. They also explained that their prayer schedule follows a different timetable and rhythm than the one the organizers of the Circle conference had assumed in assigning 8:00 a.m. as the universal prayer time. Similarly, the practitioners of Indigenous African religions spent their time slot explaining and demonstrating some of the most misunderstood aspects of their faith such as divination, ritual/sacred dance, and the use of material objects in prayer. While these insiders' views and explanations did not necessarily dispel all the mysteries and misunderstandings regarding each other's faith, they represented a significant step toward mutual understanding.

17. Circle conferences have always included participants from outside of Africa. In 1989, Katie Geneva Cannon and Jacquelyn Grant, both prominent black feminist theologians, were in attendance. In addition, Carrie Pemberton, a 1996 participant from the United States, wrote the first comprehensive study of Circle thought and practice based on her interaction with Circle women. See Carrie Pemberton, *Circle Thinking: African Women Theologians in Dialogue with the West* (Boston: Brill, 2003). Recently, the inclusion of male participants as dialogue partners has also been deliberately nurtured. See also n. 26 below.

18. See Elisabeth Schüssler-Fiorenza, *The Power of Naming: A Concilium Reader in Feminist Liberation Theology* (Maryknoll, N.Y.: Orbis Books, 1996), xxi.

19. Such reconsideration of the question of power within the church is urged by Letty Russell in *Church in the Round: Feminist Interpretations of the Church* (Louisville: John Knox, 1993). Russell invokes the metaphor of a round kitchen table and the possibility of face-to-face conversations around such tables to signify the kind of ecclesiology that concerned women, even in Western feminist circles, long for. For details see Russell, *Church in the Round*, 12.

20. It is always refreshing and reassuring to receive communication from Circle members and coordinators in which the addressees are saluted as "Dear Sisters," while the writers sign off as "Yours in the Circle." This contrasts with the rather harsh language more prevalent in the contemporary world where a corporate mind-set dominates and where people are hierarchically categorized as board of directors, presidents, chairmen, and CEOs. In such corporations, power is not shared but wielded from the top down.

21. D. Akintunde, ed., *African Culture and the Quest for Women's Rights* (Ibadan, Nigeria: Sefer Books, 2001), 103.

22. Ibid., 108.

23. Significantly, one of the two keynote speakers invited to the fourth Pan-African Circle conference (Yaoundé, Cameroon, September 1–8, 2007) was Tinyiko Maluleke, a male theologian from South Africa who specifically addressed African notions of manhood and the prevailing notions of masculinity and their implications in the Age of AIDS. Other dialogue partners in the Cameroon meeting include representatives of WCC and its HIV/AIDS programs, as well as colleagues from Yale University, such as Margaret Farley, who have partnered with the Circle in the last five years to help them access the resources at Yale Divinity School, the Yale University Public Health Program,

and USAID to strengthen their research and responses to the crisis of HIV/AIDS. For details of this partnership, see *Circle Newsletter* (December 2006): 3.

24. The acronyms stand for Ecumenical Association of Third World Theologians (EATWOT), All Africa Conference of Churches (AACC), and Organization of African Independent Churches (OAIC).

Chapter 10: *Asian Women and Dialogue* / Gemma T. Cruz

1. James Kroeger, *Asia-Church in Mission* (Quezon City, Philippines: Claretian Publications, 2002), 3.

2. See Jonathan Tan, "Local Churches and the Task of Christian Mission in Asia," in *Dialogue: Resource Manual for Catholics in Asia*, ed. Edmund Chia (Bangkok: Federation of Asian Bishops' Conferences-OEIA, 2001), 106.

3. Gaudencio Rosales and C. G. Arevalo, eds., *For All the Peoples of Asia: Federation of Asian Bishops' Conferences, Documents from 1970–1991,* vol. 1 (Quezon City, Philippines: Claretian Publications, 1992), 94, section III, §9.

4. See Sebastian Painadath, S.J., "Federation of Asian Bishops' Conferences Theology of Dialogue," in Chia, *Dialogue,* 102.

5. *For All the Peoples of Asia*, 16, section V, §22.

6. Ibid., 23, §18.

7. *Christian Discipleship in Asia Today: Service to Life,* final statement of the Sixth Federation of Asian Bishops' Conferences Plenary Assembly, no. 14.2, as quoted in *For All the Peoples of Asia: Federation of Asian Bishops' Conferences, Documents from 1992–1996,* ed. Franz-Josef Eilers, vol. 2 (Quezon City, Philippines: Claretian Publications, 1997), 8.

8. See especially Peter Phan, *Christianity with an Asian Face: Asian American Theology in the Making* (Maryknoll, N.Y.: Orbis Books, 2003), 186. His other two books are *In Our Own Tongues: Perspectives from Asia on Mission and Inculturation* (Maryknoll, N.Y.: Orbis Books, 2003), and *Being Religious Interreligiously: Asian Perspectives on Interfaith Dialogue* (Maryknoll, N.Y.: Orbis Books, 2004).

9. Painadath himself speaks of the poor as meeting point in the Federation of Asian Bishops' Conferences three forms of dialogue. See Painadath, "Federation of Asian Bishops' Conferences Theology of Dialogue," 104.

10. Phan, *Christianity with an Asian Face,* 199.

11. Michael Tan, "Global Mamas," *www.inq7.net* (May 12, 2006).

12. *For All the Peoples of Asia,* vol. 1, 58, §9.7–9.8.

13. Amelia Vasquez, R.S.C.J., "Towards Fullness of Life: Women's Resources for the Transformation of the Church," *East Asian Pastoral Review* 41, no. 3 (2004): 285.

14. See Theresa Lim Chin Chin et al., "A Feminist Vision of a Participatory Church," in *Ecclesia of Women in Asia: Gathering the Voices of the Silenced,* ed. Evelyn Monteiro, S.C., and Antoinette Gutzler (New Delhi: ISPCK, 2005), 199–209.

15. See also Gemma Cruz and Christine Burke, "Asian Women Theologians Make Voices Heard," *National Catholic Reporter,* December 27, 2002, 10.

16. The women observers in the last Federation of Asian Bishops' Conferences plenary assembly were actually EWA coordinators (we don't call them presidents or chairpersons because we are interested in a governance that is less hierarchical). And the Federation of Asian Bishops' Conferences Commission on Women and the Laity, in partnership with the Office for Theological Concerns, has begun a dialogue between Asian Catholic women theologians and the bishops on feminism.

17. Emmanuel Guzman, "A Lay Educator's Ecclesiological Reading, Philippines," in *Charting the Future of Theology and Theological Education in Asian Contexts*, ed. David Kwang-sun Suh (Delhi: ISPCK, 2004), 192.

18. This is not to say that the Asian hierarchy has not exerted any effort toward a more egalitarian and participatory church. Christine Tse, "New Ways of Being Church:

A Catholic Perspective," in *With Passion and Compassion: Third World Women Doing Theology,* ed. Virginia Fabella and Mercy Amba Oduyoye (Eugene, Ore.: Wipf and Stock Publishers, 2006), 96, shares, for example, how the attempts by the Asian Catholic Church to team up both priests and women for spiritual direction (traditionally the domain of male clergy) have produced new and very positive experiences.

19. Mananzan shares: "My own impression of the dialogue we had with our male colleagues in the Philippines was that although they seemed to understand the women's perspective as we explained to them, they have not actually taken it into consideration in their own theologizing. They consider it as primarily the business of the Women's Commission." See Mary John Mananzan, "Gender Dialogue in EATWOT: An Asian Perspective," *Voices from the Third World* 19, no. 1 (June 1996): 76.

20. Sun Ai Lee-Park, "A Short History of Asian Feminist Theology," in *Women's Visions: Theological Reflection, Celebration, Action,* ed. Ofelia Ortega (Geneva: WCC Publications, 1995), 38. See also Virginia Fabella, M.M., *Beyond Bonding: A Third World Women's Theological Journey* (Manila: EATWOT and Institute of Women's Studies, 1993).

21. FIRE was founded by Angeline Bones-Fernandez, who also founded DAWN (Divorced and Widowed Network) and is also the founder and coordinator of EMPOWERMENT — a group that focuses on providing theological training for the laity. Though parish-based, FIRE holds activities on a national and even international level. See Angeline Bones-Fernandez, "Experiment in Inter-religious Dialogue: Voice from Grassroots Women," in Monteiro and Gutzler, *Ecclesia of Women in Asia,* 367–83, for more details on this group.

22. D'Souza used to be involved with the Henry Martyn Institute, an international ecumenical center for research, interfaith relations, and reconciliation in Hyderabad, India; see n. 23 below. See Diane D'Souza, "Inter-faith Dialogue: New Insights from Women's Perspectives," in Monteiro and Gutzler, *Ecclesia of Women in Asia,* 441–45, for more details on the project.

23. Ibid., 442.

24. Mary John Mananzan and Sun Ai Lee-Park, "Emerging Spirituality of Asian Women," in *With Passion and Compassion,* ed. Fabella and Oduyoye, 85.

25. Mananzan and Lee-Park, "Emerging Spirituality of Asian Women," 85.

26. Pope John Paul II directly pointed to this laudable character of the Asian peoples in the synodal document *Ecclesia in Asia.* "Asian peoples," John Paul II says, "are known for their spirit of religious tolerance and peaceful co-existence." See *Ecclesia in Asia,* no. 6 as quoted in Phan, *Being Religious Interreligiously,* 118.

27. I have written on this elsewhere. See Gemma T. Cruz, "Toward a Mosaic Society: The Praxis of Interculturality from an Asian Perspective," in *Utopie hat einen Ort: Beiträge für eine interkulturelle Welt aus vier Kontinenten.* Festschrift für Raúl Fornet-Betancourt, ed. Elisabeth Steffens and Annette Meuthrath (Frankfurt a.M., London: IKO, 2006): 135–43.

28. See Mananzan and Lee-Park, "Emerging Spirituality of Asian Women," 86.

29. See Vasquez, "Towards Fullness of Life," 286.

Chapter 11: Feeling through the Limits of Conversation / Michele Saracino

1. Luke 5:30 (NRSV).
2. Luke 14:13 (NRSV).
3. Thomas L. Friedman uses "flat" to refer to the interconnectedness of people due to globalization. See *The World Is Flat: A Brief History of the Twenty-First Century* (New York: Farrar, Straus, & Giroux, 2005).
4. Stephanie Paulsell describes bodily practices, such as eating and bathing, as potential openings for God's presence. See *Honoring the Body: Meditations on a*

Christian Practice (San Francisco: John Wiley & Sons, 2002). Here, I am thinking of dialogue as a similar sacramental bodily practice.

5. Deborah Tannen, *That's Not What I Meant: How Conversation Style Makes or Breaks Relationships* (New York: Ballantine Books, 1986).

6. See Luce Irigaray, *To Speak Is Never Neutral,* trans. Gail Schwab (New York: Routledge, 2002).

7. For Irigaray's analysis of how gender influences language, see *An Ethics of Sexual Difference,* trans. Carolyn Burke and Gillian C. Gill (Ithaca, N.Y.: Cornell University Press, 1993), and *This Sex Which Is Not One,* trans. Catherine Porter with Carolyn Burke (Ithaca, N.Y.: Cornell University Press, 1985).

8. Emmanuel Levinas, *Alterity and Transcendence,* trans. Michael B. Smith (New York: Columbia University Press, 1999), 26.

9. For more on how language squelches another's desire, see Jean-François Lyotard, *The Differend: Phrases in Dispute,* trans. Georges Van Den Abbeele (Minneapolis: University of Minnesota Press, 1988); *Just Gaming,* with Jean-Loup Thebaud, trans. Wlad Godzich (Minneapolis: University of Minnesota Press, 1985); *Discours, Figure* (Paris: Klincksieck, 1971); and *Libidinal Economy,* trans. Iain Hamilton Grant (London: Athlone, 1993).

10. Lyotard, *Libidinal Economy,* 262.

11. *Lost in Translation,* DVD, directed by Sofia Coppola (2003; Universal City, Calif.: Universal Studios Home Video, 2003).

12. *The Godfather, Part III* (Widescreen Edition), DVD, directed by Francis Ford Coppola (1990; Los Angeles: Paramount, 2005).

13. In relation to our everyday encounters with others, Jeannine Hill Fletcher writes about how our "hybrid" identities allow us to make connections with people with whom we might expect to have nothing in common. See *Monopoly on Salvation: A Feminist Approach to Religious Pluralism* (New York: Continuum, 2005), 89–101, 134.

14. For an in-depth account of her life, see Waltraud Herbstrith, *Edith Stein: A Biography,* 2nd English ed., trans. Bernard Bonowitz (San Francisco: Ignatius Press, 1992). Her experience of being female, Jewish, and then later Catholic in a predominately male field influenced her life's work and writings to the extent that she is regarded by some as one of the most important feminist voices of the twentieth century. See Edith Stein, *Essays on Woman: The Collected Works of Edith Stein,* vol. 2, ed. L. Gelber and Romaeus Leuven, trans. Freda Mary Oben, 2nd rev. ed. (Washington, D.C.: ICS Publications, 1996).

15. For an interesting look at Stein's life and reactions to her beatification from both Christian and Jewish communities, see Waltraud Herbstrith, ed., *Never Forget: Christian and Jewish Perspectives on Edith Stein,* trans. Susanne Batzdorff (Washington, D.C.: ICS Publications/Institute of Carmelite Studies, 1998).

16. Craig Driscoll, *Of the Cross: The Life of Blessed Edith Stein* (Manila, Philippines: Sinag-tala Publishers, 1987), 34.

17. Invoking the term "lessons" at this juncture brings to mind Bradford E. Hinze's comprehensive work on dialogue as an ecclesial practice, in which he both problematizes the notion of dialogue from a variety of theoretical perspectives and evaluates actual situations of dialogue that have occurred in the church since Vatican II. See *Practices of Dialogue in the Roman Catholic Church: Aims and Obstacles, Lessons and Laments* (New York: Continuum International Publishing Group, 2006), 245. In my essay, I consider his point that "lament" in dialogue marks the "unconscious dimensions" in our struggle to engage others in conversation, and I simply try to imagine practices that might help us negotiate conscious and unconscious affective dimensions of dialogue.

18. Lyotard defines a *differend* as "a case of conflict, between (at least) two parties, that cannot be equitably resolved for a lack of rule of judgment applicable to both parties," in *The Differend,* xi.

19. Levinas, *Alterity and Transcendence,* 79.

20. See Andrew Greeley, *The Catholic Imagination* (Berkeley: University of California Press, 2000).

21. See Bessel A. van der Kolk, "Beyond the Talking Cure: Somatic Experience and Subcortical Imprints in the Treatment of Trauma," in *EMDR as an Integrative Psychotherapy Approach: Experts of Diverse Orientations Explore the Paradigm Prism,* ed. Francine Shapiro (Washington, D.C.: American Psychological Association Press, 2002), 57–83.

22. Studies engaging trauma, particularly around the Shoah, 9/11, and even the recent tsunami, have transcended the fields of psychiatry and psychology and are now part of the humanities. For work on trauma in literary theory, see Cathy Caruth, *Unclaimed Experience: Trauma, Narrative, and History* (Baltimore: Johns Hopkins University Press, 1996); for a historical approach, see Dominick LaCapra, *Writing History, Writing Trauma* (Baltimore: Johns Hopkins University Press, 2001). More recently, the field of trauma studies has impacted scholars of pedagogy and writing composition. See Shane Borrowman, ed., *Teaching and the Trauma of Writing* (Albany: State University of New York Press, 2005).

23. Bessel A. van der Kolk, "Posttraumatic Therapy in the Age of Neuroscience," *Psychoanalytic Dialogues* 12, no. 3 (2002): 382.

24. Van der Kolk, "Posttraumatic Stress Disorder and the Nature of Trauma," in *Healing Trauma: Attachment, Mind, Body, and Brain,* ed. Marion F. Solomon and Daniel J. Siegel (New York: W. W. Norton, 2003), 187.

25. Ibid., 381.

26. Relying on the work of van der Kolk, Marion F. Solomon posits goals for treating trauma, including its effects on interpersonal relations, in "Connection, Disruption, Repair: Treating the Effects of Attachment Trauma on Intimate Relationships," in *Healing Trauma,* 324. Also, my husband, Kenneth Einhorn, who works with traumatized children and families at New York Foundling, was of great assistance in helping me conceptualize these clinical goals in terms of an everyday spirituality.

27. For more on the importance of being attentive to body processes in treatment sessions, see van der Kolk, "Posttraumatic Therapy," 389.

Chapter 12: For the Sins of the Parents / Cristina Traina

1. This essay could not have come into being without helpful advice from Karen Barbour, Carol Clay, Marion Flynn, Carol Gaetjens, Jan Kay, Kim Reed, Andrew Sagartz, and Elena Segura, and diligent, patient research by Meghan Courtney. It would also be much the poorer without the suggestions of David Clairmont, Jennifer Herdt, Gerald McKenny, Jean Porter, Maura Ryan, Todd Whitmore, and the student members of the Notre Dame graduate colloquium in moral theology. I have not responded to all questions or incorporated all suggestions adequately. Finally, writing on families takes time from family; Bill, David, Maggie, Kate, Louise, Polly, and Dick have all graciously granted it.

2. Pontifical Council for Justice and Peace, *Compendium of the Social Doctrine of the Church* (Washington, D.C.: United States Conference of Catholic Bishops for the Libreria Editrice Vaticana, 2005).

3. On the assumed link between normal adult development and parenthood, see Lucy M. Candib, M.D., *Medicine and the Family: A Feminist Perspective* (New York: Basic Books, 1995), 18–55.

4. See Barbara Katz Rothman, *Recreating Motherhood: Ideology and Technology in a Patriarchal Society* (New York: W. W. Norton, 1989), 65–81.

5. Sharon Parrott and Arloc Sherman, "TANF at 10: Program Results Are More Mixed Than Often Understood" (Washington, D.C.: Center on Budget and Policy Priorities, August 17, 2006), *www.cbpp.org/8-17-06tanf.htm* (February 14, 2007).

6. Annalyn Lacombe, "Welfare Reform and Access to Jobs in Boston," US Department of Transportation, Bureau of Transportation Statistics (January 1998), BTS98 A-02, 1, *www.bts.dot.gov/publications/welfare_reform_and_access_to_jobs_in_boston/pdf/entire.pdf* (February 14, 2007), 1.

7. Parrott and Sherman, "TANF at 10."

8. Ibid. Most of these cuts remain in effect.

9. On current participation rules and thresholds, see Elizabeth Lower-Basch, Evelyn Ganzglass, Elisa Minoff, Sharon Parrott, and Liz Schott, "Analysis of New Interim Final TANF Rules" (Washington, D.C.: Center on Budget and Policy Priorities/Center for Law and Social Policy [Summer 2006]), *www.clasp.org/publications/final_tanf_rules_analysis.pdf* (February 14, 2007).

10. Parrott and Sherman, "TANF at 10."

11. Ibid.

12. Department of Transitional Assistance 2005 Annual Report, Commonwealth of Massachusetts Executive Office of Health and Human Services (April 2006), *www.masslegalservices.org/docs/g_new_annualreport.pdf* (February 14, 2007); Lacombe, "Welfare Reform"; and Parrott and Sherman, "TANF at 10."

13. James Jennings, "Welfare Reform and Neighborhoods: Race and Civic Participation," *Annals of the American Academy of Political and Social Science* 577 (September 2001): 94–106. See also James Jennings, *Welfare Reform and the Revitalization of Inner City Neighborhoods,* Black American and Diasporic Studies (East Lansing: Michigan State University Press, 2003).

14. Lacombe, "Welfare Reform."

15. Steven G. Anderson, Anthony P. Halter, and Brian M. Gryzlak, "Difficulties after Leaving TANF: Inner-City Women Talk about Reasons for Returning to Welfare," *Social Work* 49, no. 2 (April 2004): 185–94.

16. See *Welfare Reform: Rural TANF Programs Have Developed Many Strategies to Address Rural Challenges,* GAO-04-921 (Washington, D.C.: United States Government Accountability Office, September 2004). The report's conclusion admits that declining caseloads indicate nothing about the self-sufficiency of families no longer on TANF; *www.gao.gov/new.items/d04921.pdf* (February 14, 2007), 37.

17. USCCB, *A Place at the Table: A Catholic Recommitment to Overcome Poverty and to Respect the Dignity of All God's Children,* November 13, 2002, section V, *www.usccb.org/bishops/table.shtml* (January 28, 2007). On solidarity, see also John Paul II, *Sollicitudo Rei Socialis,* December 30, 1987, pars. 38–40.

18. *A Place at the Table,* section VI.

19. Ibid. See also Pontifical Council for Justice and Peace, *Compendium,* 105, par. 214: "Public authorities may not take away from the family tasks which it can accomplish well by itself or in free association with other families; on the other hand, these same authorities have the duty to sustain the family, ensuring that it has all the assistance that it needs to fulfill properly its responsibilities."

20. *A Place at the Table,* section VI.

21. Poor women tend to value marriage highly but often make prudential decisions not to marry their children's fathers: a husband with an unsteady job or none at all endangers his children's material welfare by draining family resources. See Stephanie Coontz, *Marriage, A History: From Obedience to Intimacy or How Love Conquered Marriage* (New York: Viking, 2005), 288–89. See also Paula Roberts, "Out of Order? Factors Influencing the Sequence of Marriage and Childbirth among Disadvantaged Americans," Center for Law and Social Policy, Policy Brief, Couples and Marriage Series Brief No. 9 (January 2007), *www.clasp.org/publications/out_of_order.pdf* (February 14, 2007).

22. "Children of Immigrants: Facts and Figures" (Washington, D.C.: Urban Institute, May 2006), *www.urban.org/publications/900955.html* (February 14, 2007).

23. Randy Capps, "Five Questions for Randy Capps," *www.urban.org/toolkit/fivequestions/RCapps.cfm* (February 14, 2007). See also "Efforts to Promote

Children's Economic Security Must Address Needs of Hard-Working Immigrant Families" (Washington, D.C.: National Center for Children in Poverty, October 2005), *www.nccp.org/media/epc05_text.pdf;* "Children of Low-Income, Recent Immigrants" (Washington, D.C.: National Center for Children in Poverty, December 2004), *www.nccp.org/pub_cli04.html;* "Children of Immigrants: Facts and Figures" (Washington, D.C.: Urban Institute, May 2006), *www.urban.org/publications/900955.html;* Randolph Capps et al., "The Health and Well-Being of Young Children of Immigrants" (Washington, D.C.: Urban Institute, February 8, 2005), *www.urban.org/UploadedPDF/311139_ChildrenImmigrants.pdf;* Jeffrey S. Passel, "The Size and Characteristics of the Unauthorized Migrant Population in the United States: Estimates Based on the March 2005 Current Population Survey" (Washington, D.C.: Pew Hispanic Center, March 7, 2006), *http://pewhispanic.org/files/reports/61.pdf.*

24. For children between six and seventeen nearly three times as many children of immigrants suffered fair or poor health as children of natives, and nearly four times as many were without a usual source of health care. Capps et al., "The Health and Well-Being of Young Children of Immigrants."

25. Ibid.

26. Based on projections by Amanda Levinson in "Alone in America" (Women's Commission for Refugee Women and Children, August 23, 2005), see online *www.womenscommission.org/archive/05/news_stories/Alternet.shtml,* (February 14, 2007).

27. "Strangers No Longer: A Pastoral Letter concerning Migration from the Catholic Bishops of Mexico and the United States," January 22, 2003, pars. 6, 18, *www.usccb.org/mrs/strangershtml* (February 14, 2007).

28. "Strangers No Longer," pars. 2, 4, 65–67; see also *Compendium,* 130–31, par. 298.

29. Ibid., pars. 34, 56–62.

30. Ibid., par. 35. See also *Compendium,* 128–29, pars. 294; 130–31, pars. 297–98.

31. *www.gaydemographics.org/USA/PUMS/nationalintro.htm* (February 15, 2007). This does not count the 2 percent of households that care for grandchildren; *www.gaydemographics.org/USA/ACS/2002/index.htm* (February 15, 2007).

32. For an excellent summary of the privileges marriage accords spouses and children, see Michael S. Wald, "Same-Sex Couples: Marriage, Families, and Children," Stanford Public Law and Legal Theory Working Paper Series, no. 6 (December 1999), *http://papers.ssrn.com/paper.taf?abstract_id=203649* (January 2, 2005).

33. The complexities involved are explored in detail in Andrew Koppelman, *Same Sex, Different States: When Same-Sex Marriages Cross State Lines* (New Haven, Conn.: Yale University Press, 2006).

34. *www.lambdalegal.org/cgi-bin/iowa/documents/record2.html?record=1923* (February 14, 2007). Elsewhere, second-parent adoption is either expressly forbidden or granted on a case-by-case basis.

35. *www.gaydemographics.org/USA/PUMS/nationalintro.htm* (accessed February 15, 2007).

36. Justice Barry Albin, quoted by David W. Chen, "New Jersey Court Backs Full Rights for Gay Couples," *New York Times,* October 26, 2006 (electronic archive).

37. *Compendium,* 114, par. 253.

38. Ibid., 106, par. 235.

39. Congregation for the Doctrine of the Faith, "Considerations Regarding Proposals to Give Legal Recognition to Unions between Homosexual Persons" (March 28, 2003), *www.vatican.va/roman_curia/congregations/cfaith/documents/rc_con_cfaith_doc_20030731_homosexual-unions_en.html,* pars. 6–9.

40. The Vatican's additional putative claims about the large-scale effects of gay and lesbian marriage on social mores are distinct from its children's rights claims.

41. "U.S. Married Couples Drop to Minority Status in Survey," *Chicago Tribune*, October 25, 2006, Section 1, 7.

42. *Compendium*, 114, par. 253, italics in original.

43. Ibid., 103, par. 228.

44. Thanks to Julie Hanlon Rubio of St. Louis University for this insight.

45. *Compendium*, 108, par. 239, some italics removed.

46. Ibid., 106, par. 235, italics removed. See also 111, par. 244.

Chapter 13: Children and the Common Good / Mary M. Doyle Roche

1. Elements of this chapter were part of a paper given at the 2006 Annual Meeting of the American Academy of Religion, Children and Childhood in Religion Consultation, "Children's Rights and the Common Good in Catholic Social Teaching." I am thankful to the other members of the panel for their comments, Marcia Bunge, Don Browning, John Wall, Zayn Kassam, and the late Robert Drinan, S.J., who graciously served as our principal respondent.

2. Information about Catholics in Alliance for the Common Good can be found at *www.thecatholicalliance.org*. The most recent edition of *Faithful Citizenship*, which is revised every four years by the United States Conference of Catholic Bishops, can be found at *www.usccb.org/faithfulcitizenship/* (February 1, 2007).

3. David Hollenbach, *The Global Face of Public Faith: Politics, Human Rights, and Christian Ethics* (Washington, D.C.: Georgetown University Press, 2003), and *The Common Good and Christian Ethics* (New York: Cambridge University Press, 2002). Lisa Sowle Cahill, *Theological Bioethics: Participation, Justice, and Change* (Washington, D.C.: Georgetown University Press, 2005).

4. Lisa Sowle Cahill has initiated an application of the common good to family life in *Family: A Christian Social Perspective* (Minneapolis: Fortress Press, 2000). Other contributions include Florence Caffrey Bourg, *Where Two or Three Are Gathered: Christian Families as Domestic Churches* (Notre Dame, Ind.: University of Notre Dame Press, 2004); David Matzko McCarthy, *The Good Life: Genuine Christianity for the Middle Class (The Christian Practice of Everyday Life)* (Grand Rapids: Brazos Press, 2004); and Julie Hanlon Rubio, *A Christian Theology of Marriage and Family* (New York and Mahwah, N.J.: Paulist Press, 2003).

5. For a clear and accessible discussion of the history, documents, themes, sources, and methods of Catholic social teaching, see Thomas Massaro, S.J., *Living Justice: Catholic Social Teaching in Action* (Franklin, Wisc.: Sheed and Ward, 2000).

6. See Children's Defense Fund, "Each Day in America," *www.childrensdefense.org/site/PageServer?pagename=research_national_data_each_day* (accessed February 1, 2007).

7. Jonathan Kozol's provocative writings include *Ordinary Resurrections: Children in the Years of Hope* (New York: Crown Publishers, 2000), and *Savage Inequalities: Children in America's Schools* (New York: HarperPerennial, 1992).

8. See Cristina L. H. Traina in this volume.

9. Facts about children can be found at *www.unicef.org/media/media_fastfacts.html* (February 1, 2007).

10. UNICEF, *The State of the World's Children 2007: The Double Dividend of Gender Inequality,* available at *www.unicef.org/publications/index_3658.html* (February 6, 2007).

11. Pontifical Council for Justice and Peace, *Compendium of the Social Doctrine of the Church* (Washington, D.C.: United States Conference of Catholic Bishops for the Libreria Editrice Vaticana, 2005), par. 152.

12. James F. Keenan and Jon D. Fuller, "The International AIDS Conference in Bangkok: Two Views," *America* 191, no. 5 (August 30–September 6, 2004): 13–16.

13. *Economic Justice For All,* 1986; emphasis added.

14. Keenan and Fuller, "The International AIDS Conference in Bangkok."

15. For an example of this line of argument see Bruce C. Hafen and Jonathan O. Hafen, "Abandoning Children to Their Rights," *First Things* (August/September 1995): 18–24.

16. *Children: Springtime of the Family and Society, Conclusion of the Theological-Pastoral Congress,* Third World Meeting of the Holy Father with Families, Jubilee of Families (Vatican, October 14–15, 2000).

17. Christine E. Gudorf, "Children, Rights of," in *The New Dictionary of Catholic Social Thought,* ed. Judith A. Dwyer and Elizabeth L. Montgomery (Collegeville, Minn.: Liturgical Press, 1994), 143–48.

18. *Vatican Charter on the Rights of the Family,* Article 4, *www.vatican.va/roman_curia/pontifical_councils/family/documents/rc_pc_family_doc_19831022_family-rights_en.html* (November 9, 2006).

19. *Vatican Charter,* Preamble, 198.

20. Ibid.

21. John Paul II, "Address to the Committee of European Journalists for the Rights of the Child" (January 13, 1979): *L'Osservatore Romano,* English Edition, January 22, 1979.

22. Christine E. Gudorf and Regina Wentzel Wolfe, eds., *Ethics and World Religions: Cross-Cultural Case Studies* (Maryknoll, N.Y.: Orbis Books, 1999).

23. Cristo Rey Center for the Working Child, *http://barrioperu.terra.com.pe/ccrnt/Ingles/default.htm* (November 9, 2006).

24. Bonnie J. Miller-McLemore, *Let the Children Come: Reimagining Childhood from a Christian Perspective* (San Francisco: Jossey-Bass, 2003).

25. See Susan Linn, *Consuming Kids: The Hostile Takeover of Childhood* (New York: New Press, 2004), and Juliet B. Schor, *Born to Buy: The Commercialized Child and the New Consumer Culture* (New York: Scribner, 2004).

26. For a reflection on this tension between the experiences of poor and wealthy children with respect to their participation in communities, see Craig Kielburger with Kevin Major, *Free the Children: A Young Man Fights against Child Labor and Proves That Children Can Change the World* (New York: HarperPerennial, 2000).

27. United States Conference of Catholic Bishops, *Renewing Our Commitment to Catholic Elementary and Secondary Schools in the Third Millennium* (Washington, D.C.: USCCB Publishing, 2005).

28. Information about the network can be found at *www.cristoreynetwork.org/* (February 6, 2007). Cristo Rey was also featured in *Newsweek* (December 25, 2006). The article is available online at *www.msnbc.msn.com/id/16242487/site/newsweek/* (February 6, 2007).

29. Thanks to Meg Florentine, superintendent of schools for the New England province of the Society of Jesus, for providing information and insight into these initiatives.

Chapter 14: When Pregnancy Hits Home / Angela Senander

1. This term comes from Mary Ann Glendon, *Rights Talk: The Impoverishment of Political Discourse* (New York: Free Press, 1991), 47–66.

2. While a politics of the hearth also invites reflection on the solidarity experienced within marriage, regardless of age, we will limit our focus to those who are young and single, which is the experience of the majority of women whose crisis pregnancies end with abortion. According to the Center for Disease Control's statistics, women under twenty-five have the majority of abortions in the United States and the vast majority of these women are single. According to their report, more than 80 percent of all women who have abortions are not married. Center for Disease Control, "Abortion Surveillance–United States, 2003," *MMWR Surveillance Summaries* 55 (SS11,

November 24, 2006): 1–32, *www.cdc.gov/mmwr/preview/mmwrhtml/ss5511a1.htm* (January 27, 2007).

3. Catholics engage in the listening ministry of crisis pregnancy counseling through diocesan organizations like Pregnancy Help in the Archdiocese of Boston (*www.rcab.org/ProLife/PregnancyHelp/HomePage.html*) as well as through ecumenical organizations like Birthright (*http://birthright.com/htmpages/index.htm*). The primary way in which the Catholic Church has entered into solidarity with women who are grieving after an abortion is through a ministry of listening called Project Rachel (*http://hopeafterabortion.com/*), which offers spiritual healing (often including the sacrament of reconciliation) and emotional healing. Priests and professional counselors who participate in this network accompany those who seek healing. See National Conference of Catholic Bishops, Secretariat for Priestly Life and Ministry and Secretariat for Pro-Life Activities, *Post-Abortion Ministry: A Resource Manual for Priests* (Washington, D.C.: United States Catholic Conference, 1999), 8–17.

4. All scriptural references are to the New American Bible.

5. National Conference of Catholic Bishops, "Pastoral Plan for Pro-Life Activities," *Origins* 5 (December 4, 1975): 372–73.

6. With regard to the question of raising the child, Todd Whitmore notes: "The Catholic Church calls on women who are faced with pregnancy in difficult circumstances to exhibit heroism. The responsibility approach reveals that there is no intrinsic reason why this cannot be asked — indeed, required — of the rest of us." See Todd David Whitmore, "Moral Methodology and Pastoral Responsiveness: The Case of Abortion and the Care of Children," *Theological Studies* 54, no. 2 (June 1993): 338.

7. Given the reference to Rachel in the title of this listening ministry, one might assume that it is only for women. This, however, is not the case. As Joanne Angelo notes, the name Project Rachel was inspired by a passage from Jeremiah: 'Rachel mourns her children; she refuses to be consoled because her children are no more. Thus says the Lord: Cease your cries of mourning. Wipe the tears from your eyes. The sorrow you have shown shall have its reward. There is hope for your future" (Jer. 31:15–17). See J. Angelo, "Project Rachel: Post-Abortion Ministry in the Jubilee Year in the United States," in *La Cultura della Vita: Fondamenti e Dimensioni, Supplemento al Volume degli atti della VII Assemblea Generale* (Vatican City: Libreria Editrice Vaticana, 2002), 33. The poetic language of mourning the loss of the northern kingdom of Israel to Assyrian occupation sets the stage for the prophetic message of God's desire that mourning be transformed into hope. While the circumstances for the mourning of mothers, fathers, grandparents, siblings, and other family members of the aborted child are different from those described here in Jeremiah, those engaged in the post-abortion ministry of Project Rachel want to communicate God's desire that mourning change to hope for all grieving after an abortion. This ministry serves men as well as women, grandparents as well as parents, and those who learned about the abortion only after the fact as well as those who played a role in the choice.

8. Theresa Burke with David C. Reardon, *Forbidden Grief: The Unspoken Pain of Abortion* (Springfield, Ill.: Acorn Books, 2002), 24.

9. See Project Rachel's "Hope after Abortion" website, focusing in particular on the section "In Their Own Words" at *www.hopeafterabortion.com/hope.cfm?sel= A31Q* (February 13, 2007).

10. As the Catholic Church develops a pastoral care outreach to those troubled to learn they are grandparents (described below), an initial phase in the preparation of volunteers could be participation in this interdisciplinary training program.

11. Since the first pastoral plan, the bishops have recognized the need for opportunities for unwed mothers to continue their education. This did not necessarily call for much change and adaptation on the part of the institution, for the school could help unwed mothers continue their education at home. By the third pastoral plan, the language about continuation of education has developed to include the fathers, to refer to college and graduate school as well as high school, and to name the need for changes in school

policies, though what this might look like concretely is not mentioned. See United States Conference of Catholic Bishops, "A Pastoral Plan for Pro-life Activities: A Campaign in Support of Life" (Washington, D.C.: United States Conference of Catholic Bishops, 2001), 21.

12. Angela Senander, "Standing with Pregnant Students: A Response to Standing for the Unborn," *America* 190, no. 18 (May 24, 2004): 17.

13. Michelle McCusker, "Statement," Fall 2005, at *www.nyclu.org/mccusker_ personal_stmnt_112105.html* (February 20, 2007); Theresa Andersen, "Letter from Saint Rose of Lima to Michelle McCusker," October 11, 2005. *www.nyclu.org/pdfs/ mccusker_termination_letter_112105.pdf* (February 20, 2007); Michelle McCusker, "Equal Employment Opportunity Commission Charge of Discrimination," November 21, 2005, *www.nyclu.org/pdfs/mccusker_eeoc_complaint_112105.pdf* (February 20, 2007); Spencer Lewis, "EEOC Determination," October 5, 2006, *www.nyclu.org/pdfs/mccusker_eeoc_determination_101106.pdf* (accessed February 20, 2007).

14. Robert J. Karris, O.F.M., "The Gospel According to Luke," in *The New Jerome Biblical Commentary,* ed. Raymond Brown, Joseph Fitzmyer, and Roland E. Murphy (Englewood Cliffs, N.J.: Prentice Hall, 1990), 721.

Chapter 15: Fostering the Next Generation of Faithful Women / Jane E. Regan

1. While much of what is included in this essay is applicable to sons and fathers, boys and men, the specific focus for this essay is daughters and mothers. Therefore, I use the feminine gender when third-person singular pronouns are needed.

2. Tillich writes, "Faith is the state of being ultimately concerned. Faith as being ultimately concerned is a centered act of the whole personality." See *Dynamics of Faith* (San Francisco: Harper and Row, 1957), 45–46.

3. For a fuller examination of developmental theory and the dynamics of adult faith, see Jane E. Regan, *Toward an Adult Church: A Vision of Faith Formation* (Chicago: Loyola Press, 2002), particularly chap. 2: "The Adult as Person of Faith."

4. James W. Fowler, *Stages of Faith: The Psychology of Human Development and the Quest for Meaning* (San Francisco: Harper and Row, 1981), 4.

5. James W. Fowler, "Faith and the Structuring of Meaning," in *Faith Development and Fowler,* ed. Craig Dykstra and Sharon Parks (Birmingham: Religious Education Press, 1986), 15.

6. The clearest and most developed articulations of Fowler's stages of faith are found in his *Life Maps* and *Stages of Faith,* 117–213. The stages are briefly revisited with slight nuance in later works in which he examines the reality of adult faith. See, for example, James W. Fowler, *Becoming Adult, Becoming Christian: Adult Development and Christian Faith,* 1st ed. (San Francisco: Harper & Row, 1984). For a consideration of implications for a public church, see James W. Fowler, *Weaving the New Creation: Stages of Faith and the Public Church,* 1st ed. (San Francisco: Harper, 1991).

7. Fowler, *Stages of Faith,* 182.

8. Ibid., 179.

9. Ibid., 183.

10. Helpful in understanding this shift in engagement with the symbolic is the work of Paul Ricoeur. His description of the movement from a "hermeneutic of suspicion" to a "willed naiveté" or "second naiveté" makes clear the critical perspective of Stage Five interpretation. But for a person interpreting from the position of a second naiveté, there is an embrace of the realization that the critical analysis, which marks a hermeneutic of suspicion, does not disclose all that is present in the symbol. From the perspective of a second naiveté, there is the recognition that the full referent of the symbol can never be revealed; the symbol as symbol must be allowed to speak in its own voice and to be embraced on its own terms.

11. Fowler, *Stages of Faith,* 185.

12. Ibid., 186.

13. The data from Fowler's research reported in *Stages of Faith* indicates that only one person out of 359 moved beyond Stage Five to either Five-Six transition or Stage Six (see page 322). The fact of the rarity of persons embodying a Stage Six faith in Fowler's study and the tendency for him to point to very public people whose recognition is as much for their political impact and their rhetoric as their faith perspective raises some serious questions about the validity of this stage and its continuity with the prior stages. The problematic nature of this final stage, described by Fowler as the "normative endpoint, culminating image of mature faith in this theory" (*Stages of Faith,* 199) does raise questions concerning the total enterprise. See John M. Broughton, "The Political Psychology of Faith Development Theory," in *Faith Development and Fowler,* particularly 95–97.

14. For a fuller discussion of the place of conversation in adult faith formation, see my book *Toward an Adult Church,* particularly chap. 3: "Transformative Learning: Insights from Adult Education."

Chapter 16: *Making Room for Beauty /* Susan A. Ross

1. See, e.g., Sheila Jeffreys, *Beauty and Misogyny: Harmful Cultural Practices in the West* (London and New York: Routledge, 2005).

2. Richard John Neuhaus, "In the Beauty of Holiness," *First Things* 75 (August–September 1997): 74–75.

3. See John Paul II's writings on womanhood, especially *Mulieris dignitatem,* and the July 31, 2004, letter of the Congregation for the Doctrine of the Faith; see also Benedict XVI's *Deus Caritas Est,* especially the last section, which discusses Mary as a model for humans.

4. See "Some Questions Regarding Collaboration of Nonordained Faithful in Priests' Sacred Ministry," *Origins* 27, no. 24 (November 27, 1997).

5. See Michelle A. Gonzalez, *Sor Juana: Beauty and Justice in the Americas* (Maryknoll, N.Y.: Orbis Books, 2003), and Roberto S. Goizueta, *Caminemos con Jésus: Toward a Hispanic/Latino Theology of Accompaniment* (Maryknoll, N.Y.: Orbis Books, 1995).

6. See Maria Antonaccio, "Asceticism and the Ethics of Consumption," *Journal of the Society of Christian Ethics* 26, no. 1 (Spring–Summer 2006): 79–96; L. Shannon Jung, *Food for Life: The Spirituality and Ethics of Eating* (Minneapolis: Fortress Press, 2004).

7. See my *For the Beauty of the Earth: Women, Sacramentality, and Justice* (Mahwah, N.J.: Paulist Press, 2006).

8. Elizabeth A. Johnson, *Truly Our Sister: A Theology of Mary in the Communion of Saints* (New York: Continuum, 2003), 57–60.

9. See Wendy Steiner, *Venus in Exile: The Rejection of Beauty in 20th-Century Art* (New York: Free Press, 2001).

10. Ross, *For the Beauty of the Earth,* x.

11. Margaret Miles, *Image as Insight: Visual Understanding in Western Christianity and Secular Culture* (Boston: Beacon Press, 1985).

12. See Susan S. Jorgensen, *Knitting into the Mystery: A Guide to the Shawl-Knitting Ministry* (Harrisburg, Pa.: Morehouse Publishing, 2003).

13. Elaine Scarry, *On Beauty and Being Just* (Princeton: Princeton University Press, 1999), 23–28.

14. John de Gruchy, *Christianity, Art, and Transformation: Theological Aesthetics in the Struggle for Justice* (New York: Cambridge University Press, 2001), 78.

15. Ivone Gebara, *Longing for Running Water: Ecofeminism and Liberation* (Minneapolis: Fortress Press, 1999).

16. Ross, *For the Beauty of the Earth*, 32–60.

17. See Ross, *Extravagant Affections: A Feminist Sacramental Theology* (New York: Continuum, 1998), especially chap. 5.

18. See Mary Catherine Hilkert, *Naming Grace: Preaching and the Sacramental Imagination* (New York: Continuum, 1997).

19. Vatican II, Constitution on the Sacred Liturgy (*Sacrosanctum concilium*), in *Vatican Council II,* new revised edition, vol. 1, ed. Austin Flannery, O.P. (Northport, N.Y.: Costello Publishing, 1996), 6.

20. See the Wangari website: *http://nobelprize.org/nobel_prizes/peace/laureates/2004/maathai-bio.html* (accessed July 26, 2007).

21. Margaret Pfeil, "Liturgy and Ethics: The Liturgical Asceticism of Energy Conservation," *Journal of the Society of Christian Ethics* 27, no. 2 (Fall–Winter 2007).

22. With respect to fashion shows, it is interesting to note that Spain has forbidden too-thin models to work.

Chapter 17: Insistent Inclusion / Diana Hayes

1. Margaret L. Hunter, *Race, Gender, and the Politics of Skin Tone* (New York: Routledge, 2005), 31.

2. "Womanist" is a reference to the distinctive theology of black women.

3. Delores Williams, *Sisters in the Wilderness: The Challenge of Womanist God-Talk* (Maryknoll, N.Y.: Orbis Books, 1995), 118.

4. Williams, *Sisters in the Wilderness,* 119.

5. Patricia Hill Collins, *Black Feminist Thought: Knowledge, Consciousness, and the Politics of Empowerment,* 2nd ed. (New York: Routledge, 2000), 12; also see the fuller discussion in 11–13.

6. With regard to racism, Pope John Paul II apologized for the devastation of slavery and the church's role in its implementation in Africa and the Americas in 2000, but the impact of this apology has been minimal in the worldwide church.

7. Collins, *Black Feminist Thought,* 9.

8. Loretta Ross, "A Feminist Perspective on Katrina," *www.zmag.org* (October 10, 2005).

9. Ibid.

Chapter 18: Practicing Justice with Spirit / Mary Jo Leddy

1. St. Augustine, "Letter 111," in *Letters* (*Volume* 2), ed. John E. Rotelle, trans. Roland Teske (Hyde Park, N.Y.: New City Press, 2001–2005).

2. Michael Lerner's concept of "surplus powerlessness" is developed throughout his book *Surplus Powerlessness: The Psychodynamics of Everyday Life — and the Psychology of Individual and Social Transformation* (Oakland, Calif.: Institute for Labor & Mental Health, 1986).

3. More extended reflections on power can be found in Mary Jo Leddy, *Radical Gratitude* (Maryknoll, N.Y.: Orbis Books, 2002), chap. 4.

4. This is a maxim that Atwood has repeated often in radio interviews and talks. It is "fleshed out" in her novel *The Robber Bride* (New York: Nan A. Talese/Doubleday, 1993).

5. My indebtedness to Hannah Arendt will be evident throughout. Her analysis of systematic evil was first presented in her now-classic work *Origins of Totalitarianism* (New York: Harcourt, Brace, 1951). Her notions of action, interaction, and power were first developed in her seminal book on political thought, *The Human Condition* (Chicago: University of Chicago Press, 1958).

6. I also take this bias to be true, although in a slightly different way, for Canadians who live in a somewhat friendly, somewhat powerful colony of this empire.

Chapter 19: *Claiming and Imagining /*
Rosemary P. Carbine

1. Martin E. Marty, *The Public Church: Mainline, Evangelical, Catholic* (New York: Crossroad, 1981), 3.

2. On civil society as a shared space of public debate in democratic societies, see Hannah Arendt, *The Human Condition,* 2nd ed. (Chicago: University of Chicago Press, 1998); Richard J. Bernstein, "The Meaning of Public Life," in *Religion and American Public Life: Interpretations and Explorations,* ed. Robin Lovin (New York: Paulist Press, 1986), 29–52; and Gary Simpson, *Critical Social Theory: Prophetic Reason, Civil Society, and Christian Imagination* (Minneapolis: Fortress Press, 2002).

3. This paragraph identifies emerging criticisms of patriarchal norms in the public church, which are addressed at length in Rosemary P. Carbine, "Ekklesial Work: Toward a Feminist Public Theology," *Harvard Theological Review* 99, no. 4 (October 2006): 433–55, especially 442–45, 455.

4. Feminist theologies already critically engage with church structures of governance and participation in light of democratic principles and processes. See, for example, Eugene C. Bianchi and Rosemary Radford Ruether, eds., *A Democratic Catholic Church: The Reconstruction of Roman Catholicism* (New York: Crossroad, 1992), and Mary E. Hines, "Community for Liberation — Church," in *Freeing Theology: The Essentials of Theology in Feminist Perspective,* ed. Catherine Mowry LaCugna (San Francisco: HarperSanFrancisco, 1993), 161–84. Much more feminist theological reflection is needed regarding how theological discourses and practices of public engagement aim to transform the U.S. political order.

5. Carbine, "Ekklesial Work," 434, 436–37.

6. These initial paragraphs summarize Carbine, ibid., 437–41.

7. Rather than simply situate a person within multiple communities, including political communities, that shape human identity, *Gaudium et spes* offers a theological anthropology that holds that becoming fully human entails political agency and public engagement. Pastoral Constitution on the Church in the Modern World (*Gaudium et spes*), in *Vatican Council II: The Basic Sixteen Documents: Constitutions, Decrees, Declarations,* ed. Austin Flannery, O.P. (Northport, N.Y.: Costello Publishing, 1996), pars. 24–25, 46, 73–75.

8. Such measures of political effectiveness are often applied in analyzing Catholic political advocacy groups. See Kristin E. Heyer, *Prophetic and Public: The Social Witness of U.S. Catholicism* (Washington, D.C.: Georgetown University Press, 2006), 128, 136, 147–48.

9. Iris Marion Young, *Inclusion and Democracy* (Oxford: Oxford University Press, 2000), 65, 70–77.

10. Roger S. Gottlieb, *Joining Hands: Politics and Religion Together for Social Change* (Boulder, Colo.: Westview Press, 2002), 3–23.

11. Craig Dykstra and Dorothy Bass, "A Theological Understanding of Christian Practices," in *Practicing Theology: Beliefs and Practices in Christian Life,* ed. Miroslav Volf and Dorothy C. Bass (Grand Rapids: Wm. B. Eerdmans, 2002), 18; cf. 6.

12. Rebecca S. Chopp, "Reimagining Public Discourse," in *Black Faith and Public Talk: Critical Essays on James Cone's Black Theology and Black Power,* ed. Dwight N. Hopkins (Maryknoll, N.Y.: Orbis, 1999), 152.

13. Testimonies "have criticized and reshaped who 'we' are, as a social public and as Christianity, by making public the memories of suffering and giving public hearing to new voices, experiences, and expressions of life, while calling into question essentialist and hegemonic definitions of these publics." See Chopp, "Reimagining Public Discourse," 154. For a similar argument regarding narrative theology in Catholic womanist, *mujerista,* and feminist theologies, see Diana Hayes, *And Still We Rise: An Introduction to Black Liberation Theology* (New York: Paulist Press, 1996), 116–34, Ada María Isasi-Díaz, *La Lucha Continues: Mujerista Theology* (Maryknoll, N.Y.:

Orbis Books, 2004), 47–68, and Mary Ann Hinsdale, *Women Shaping Theology* (New York: Paulist Press, 2006), especially 2, 59–64, 94–111.

14. Chopp, "Reimagining Public Discourse," 157.

15. Ibid.

16. Ibid., 160–63.

17. Martin Luther King Jr., *I Have a Dream: Writings and Speeches That Changed the World,* ed. James M. Washington (San Francisco: HarperSanFrancisco, 1992), 83–100. On the far-reaching impact of King's alternative vision of U.S. society on subsequent social justice movements, see Charles Marsh, *The Beloved Community: How Faith Shapes Social Justice, from the Civil Rights Movement to Today* (New York: Basic Books, 2005).

18. David Hollenbach, S.J., "Editor's Conclusion," in "Theology and Philosophy in Public: A Symposium on John Courtney Murray's Unfinished Agenda," *Theological Studies* 40 (1979): 714, as quoted in Michael J. Himes and Kenneth R. Himes, O.F.M., *Fullness of Faith: The Public Significance of Theology* (New York: Paulist, 1993), 4.

19. As sociologist of religion Sharon Erickson Nepstad observes, religious activists who seek to end rather than engender violence "integrate religiously inspired principles of justice and respect for all people into the fabric of society." See Nepstad, "Religion, Violence, and Peacemaking," *Journal for the Scientific Study of Religion* 43, no. 3 (2004): 301. See also Robin Lovin, "Religion and American Public Life: Three Relationships," in *Religion and American Public Life,* ed. Robin Lovin (New York: Paulist Press, 1986), 7–28.

20. Linell Cady, *Religion, Theology and American Public Life* (Albany: State University of New York Press, 1993), 51–56, 62–64, and "H. Richard Niebuhr and the Task of Public Theology," in *The Legacy of H. Richard Niebuhr,* ed. Ronald Thiemann (Minneapolis: Fortress Press, 1991), 107–29.

21. *Economic Justice for All: Pastoral Letter on Catholic Social Teaching and the U.S. Economy: A Catholic Framework for Economic Life* (Washington, D.C.: U.S. Catholic Conference, 1997 [1986]), pars. 15–19.

22. Cady, *Religion, Theology and American Public Life,* 99–109; Himes and Himes, *Fullness of Faith,* 55–61.

23. *Economic Justice for All,* pars. 13–15, cf. chap. 2, pars. 28, 31–34.

24. Himes and Himes, *Fullness of Faith,* 61–62. See also J. Milburn Thompson, *Justice and Peace: A Christian Primer,* 2nd ed. (Maryknoll, N.Y.: Orbis Books, 2003), 92–102.

25. Walter Brueggemann, *The Prophetic Imagination* (Philadelphia: Fortress Press, 1978), 11–14, 27, 44–45.

26. Ibid., 67–69.

27. Mark Lewis Taylor, *The Executed God: The Way of the Cross in Lockdown America* (Minneapolis: Fortress Press, 2001), especially 70–78, 90–118, 127–33.

28. Sponsored by the Boston May Day Coalition, *www.bostonmayday.org/* (March 3, 2007).

29. Public theology constitutes "a perennial struggle to reform this life in light of the eschatological goal toward which creation, it may be hoped, asymptotically moves." See Cady, *Religion, Theology, and American Public Life,* 111.

30. This eschatological orientation characterizes many feminist theologies. Rebecca Chopp, "Feminism's Theological Pragmatics: A Social Naturalism of Women's Experience," *Journal of Religion* 67, no. 2 (1987): 239–56; Chopp, "Christian Moral Imagination: A Feminist Practical Theology and the Future of Theological Education," *International Journal of Practical Theology* 1, no. 1 (1997): 97–109; and Serene Jones, *Feminist Theory and Christian Theology: Cartographies of Grace* (Minneapolis: Fortress Press, 2000), 9–10, 75–76.

31. Scholarly studies of Berrigan include Jason C. Bivins, *The Fracture of Good Order: Christian Anti-Liberalism and the Challenge to American Politics* (Chapel Hill: University of North Carolina Press, 2003); Murray Polner and Jim O'Grady,

Disarmed and Dangerous: The Radical Lives and Times of Daniel and Philip Berrigan (Boulder, Colo.: Westview Press, 1998); Patricia McNeal, *Harder Than War: Catholic Peacemaking in Twentieth-Century America* (New Brunswick, N.J.: Rutgers University Press, 1992); Fred A. Wilcox, *Uncommon Martyrs: The Berrigans, the Catholic Left, and the Plowshares Movement* (Reading, Mass.: Addison-Wesley, 1991); Charles A. Meconis, *With Clumsy Grace: The American Catholic Left, 1961–1975* (New York: Seabury Press, 1979). For a summary of Philip Berrigan's lifelong commitment to antiwar activism, see *www.democracynow.org/berrigan.shtml* (March 3, 2007).

32. Philip Berrigan with Fred A. Wilcox, *Fighting The Lamb's War: Skirmishes with the American Empire: The Autobiography of Philip Berrigan* (Monroe, Maine: Common Courage Press, 1996), 183–85, 191.

33. Arthur Laffin and Anne Montgomery, *Swords into Plowshares: Nonviolent Direct Action for Disarmament* (San Francisco: Harper & Row, 1987); Arthur J. Laffin, *Swords into Plowshares: A Chronology of Plowshares Actions, 1980–2003* (Marion, S.Dak.: Rose Hill Books, 2003); and *www.plowsharesactions.org/* (March 3, 2007).

34. Brenda Truelson Fox, *Conviction* (Boulder, Colo.: Zero to Sixty Productions, 2006).

35. On the "politics of moral witness," see Sharon Erickson Nepstad, "Disciples and Dissenters: Tactical Choice and Consequences in the Plowshares Movement," in *Authority in Contention,* ed. Daniel J. Meyers and Daniel M. Cress (Amsterdam: Elsevier, 2004), 144, 157. The Plowshares movement seeks to upend a militarist sociopolitical order and at the same time to create an alternative community to it. Jonah House, a nonviolent resistance community located in Baltimore, and founded by Berrigan, McAlister, and others in 1973, signifies such an alternative community. See Berrigan, *Lamb's War,* 166–68, 170–72, 175. Community building in the Plowshares movement takes place at Jonah House, because it provides material, affective, and spiritual support for Plowshares activists both in and out of jail; see Berrigan, *Lamb's War,* 166–67, 219; Sharon Erickson Nepstad, "Persistent Resistance: Commitment and Community in the Plowshares Movement," *Social Problems* 51, no. 1 (2004): 43–60, especially 50–59; and Bivins, *Fracture of Good Order,* 145–51. My essay argues that Plowshares actions based on their theological underpinnings constitute a form of community building; for a similar argument, see Bivins, *Fracture of Good Order,* 128–39.

36. Phil rejected the role of a priest in perpetuating such irrational public discourse: "As a priest, I stood square in the middle of the power pyramid.... My job was to interpret the capitalist, expansionist, war-driven paradigm of America's military-industrial complex, making it appear rational, when in fact it is destructively irrational." See Berrigan, *Lamb's War,* 36.

37. Bivins, *Fracture of Good Order,* 139–45.

38. "Yes, I came / to the conclusion / that I was in direct line / with American democratic tradition / in choosing civil disobedience.... / There have been times in our history / when in order to get redress / in order to get a voice *vox populi* / arising from the roots / people have so acted. / From the Boston Tea Party / ... through the civil rights movement / we have a rich tradition / of civil disobedience." See Berrigan, *Lamb's War,* 106, cf. 85.

39. Ibid., 187.

40. Berrigan, *Lamb's War,* 193–95; Philip Berrigan and Elizabeth McAlister, *The Time's Discipline: The Beatitudes and Nuclear Resistance* (Baltimore: Fortkamp, 1989), 133.

41. Berrigan, *Lamb's War,* 201–2.

42. On the sociopolitical and historical context and interpretations of Isaiah, see Daniel Berrigan, S.J., *Testimony: The Word Made Fresh* (Maryknoll, N.Y.: Orbis Books, 2004), 3–22.

43. Berrigan, *Lamb's War,* 175, 188; quote at 180.

44. Ibid., 211.

45. Jail could be considered among the repertoire of Plowshares prophetic practices to subvert a war-making society. While prison is designed to undermine community through alienation and isolation, Plowshares activists tried to create community through jail; Berrigan, *Lamb's War,* 164–67, and Nepstad, "Persistent Resistance," 49. Moreover, Philip interpreted jail as prophetic witness to a different world, based on biblical and Christian themes of the desert and wilderness as sites of marginality and social change; Berrigan, *Lamb's War,* 96–97, 225–26.

46. Ibid., 98, 109, 169.

47. Ibid., 204–5.

48. Ibid., 96, 209–11.

49. Even though later in life Phil connected militarism with sexism and global ecological crises, women were largely responsible for expanding the Plowshares agenda and actions beyond antiwar protests. In July 1969, women anti-war activists, called the New York 5, staged and led a draft board raid in midtown Manhattan to explicitly link militarism and patriarchy. The New York 5 challenged women's roles in patriarchal militarist societies and in antimilitarist movements; according to their statement, Berrigan and other Plowshares leaders reinforced a masculinist pacifism and an antifeminist patriarchal Catholicism, to the detriment of the movement and its goals. These women were ostracized by Berrigan and other male Catholic Left leaders, proving that "masculine identity indelibly shaped the culture of American radical dissent." See Marian Mollin, "Communities of Resistance: Women and the Catholic Left of the Late 1960s," *Oral History Review* 31, no. 2 (2004): 29–51, especially 40–51, quote at 51; and Marian Mollin, *Radical Pacifism in Modern America: Egalitarianism and Protest* (Philadelphia: University of Pennsylvania Press, 2006).

50. My understanding of the church as critical witness and healing presence is drawn from models of the church as herald and sacrament, described by Avery Dulles, *Models of the Church,* expanded ed. (New York: Doubleday, 2002).

Chapter 20: *Through the Leaven of Popular Catholic Practices / Nancy Pineda-Madrid*

1. Miriam Therese Winter, "Feminist Women's Spirituality: Breaking New Ground in the Church," in *The Church Women Want: Catholic Women in Dialogue,* ed. Elizabeth A. Johnson (New York: Crossroad, 2002), 23.

2. Elisabeth Schüssler Fiorenza, ed., *The Power of Naming: A Concilium Reader in Feminist Liberation Theology* (Maryknoll, N.Y.: Orbis Books, 1996), 10.

3. Elisabeth Schüssler Fiorenza clarifies the meaning of kyriarchy as distinct from patriarchy. Kyriarchy refers to "the Greek word for the domination of elite propertied men over women and other men, whereas patriarchy is generally understood in feminist discourses in terms of the western sex/gender system which posits a man/woman opposition. In contrast, I understand patriarchy as a structure of kyriarchy, as a social and discursive system that interstructures gender, race, class, and colonialist oppressions and has as its focal point women at the bottom of the sociopolitical and religious pyramid." See Elisabeth Schüssler Fiorenza, *Bread Not Stone: The Challenge of Feminist Biblical Interpretation* (Boston: Beacon Press, 1984), 211, n. 6.

4. Craig Dykstra and Dorothy C. Bass, "A Theological Understanding of Christian Practices," in *Practicing Theology: Beliefs and Practices in Christian Life,* ed. Miroslav Volf and Dorothy C. Bass (Grand Rapids: Wm. B. Eerdmans, 2002), 18.

5. Dykstra and Bass, "A Theological Understanding of Christian Practices," 16.

6. Dorothy C. Bass, "Introduction," in *Practicing Theology: Beliefs and Practices in Christian Life,* 6.

7. Roberto S. Goizueta, *Caminemos con Jesus: Toward a Hispanic/Latino Theology of Accompaniment* (Maryknoll, N.Y.: Orbis Books, 1995), 21.

8. Orlando O. Espín, *The Faith of the People: Theological Reflections on Popular Catholicism* (Maryknoll, N.Y.: Orbis Books, 1997), 162.

9. Timothy Matovina and Gerald E. Poyo, eds., *¡Presente! U.S. Latino Catholics from Colonial Origins to the Present* (Maryknoll, N.Y.: Orbis Books, 2000); Moises Sandoval, *On the Move: A History of the Hispanic Church in the United States* (Maryknoll, N.Y.: Orbis Books, 1990).

10. Goizueta, *Caminemos Con Jesus,* 23.

11. Rosemary Houghton, *The Re-Creation of Eve* (Springfield, Ill.: Templegate, 1985), 119.

12. Berta Esperanza Hernández-Truyol, "Culture and Economic Violence," in *The Latino Condition: A Critical Reader,* ed. Richard Delgado and Jean Stefancic (New York: New York University Press, 1998), 536.

13. Alvina E. Quintana, *Home Girls: Chicana Literary Voices* (Philadelphia: Temple University Press, 1996), 101.

14. Nora O. Lozano-Díaz, "Ignored Virgin or Unaware Women: A Mexican-American Protestant Reflection on the Virgin of Guadalupe," in *A Reader in Latina Feminist Theology: Religion and Justice,* ed. María Pilar Aquino, Daisy L. Machado, and Jeanette Rodríguez (Austin: University of Texas Press, 2002), 211. See also Rosa Maria Gil and Carmen Inoa Vazquez, *The Maria Paradox: How Latinas Can Merge Old World Traditions into New World Self-Esteem* (New York: G. P. Putnam's Sons, 1996), 7–8; Anna Nieto Gomez, "La Chicana — Legacy of Suffering and Self-Denial," in *Chicana Feminist Thought: The Basic Historical Writings,* ed. Alma M. García (New York: Routledge, 1997), 48–50; Consuelo Nieto, "The Chicana and the Women's Rights Movement," in García, *Chicana Feminist Thought,* 208–9; Tey Diana Rebolledo, *Women Singing in the Snow: A Cultural Analysis of Chicana Literature* (Tucson: University of Arizona Press, 1995), 49–81.

15. There are a few recent exceptions. See Michelle A. Gonzalez, *Afro-Cuban Theology: Religion, Race, Culture and Identity* (Gainesville: University Press of Florida, 2006); Anita De Luna, "Popular Religion and Spirituality," in *Handbook of Latina/o Theologies,* ed. Edwin David Aponte and Miguel A. De la Torre (St. Louis: Chalice Press, 2006), 105–13; and Jeanette Rodriguez, "Latina Popular Catholicism," in *Encyclopedia of Women and Religion in North America,* vol. 1, ed. Rosemary Skinner Keller and Rosemary Radford Ruether (Bloomington: Indiana University Press, 2006), 168–78.

16. María Pilar Aquino, *Our Cry for Life: Feminist Theology from Latin America* (Maryknoll, N.Y.: Orbis Books, 1993), 179.

17. Carolyn G. Heilbrun, *Writing a Woman's Life* (New York: Norton, 1988), 18.

18. See Schüssler Fiorenza, *The Power of Naming.*

19. Ada María Isasi-Díaz, *Mujerista Theology: A Theology for the Twenty-First Century* (Maryknoll, N.Y.: Orbis Books, 1996), 74–75.

20. Ibid.

21. Susan A. Ross, *Extravagant Affections: A Feminist Sacramental Theology* (New York: Continuum, 1998), 34.

22. Elizabeth A. Johnson, *Women, Earth, and Creator Spirit* (New York: Paulist Press, 1993), 68. See also Sallie McFague, *Life Abundant: Rethinking Theology and Economy for a Planet in Peril* (Minneapolis: Fortress Press, 2001); McFague, *Super, Natural Christians: How We Should Love Nature* (Minneapolis: Fortress Press, 1997); Rosemary Radford Ruether, "Dualism and the Nature of Evil in Feminist Theology," *Studies in Christian Ethics* (Edinburgh, Scotland) 5, no. 1 (1992): 26–39.

23. Ross, *Extravagant Affections,* 75–83, 217.

24. Elisabeth Schüssler Fiorenza, *Discipleship of Equals: A Critical Feminist Ekklesia-Logy of Liberation* (New York: Crossroad, 1993).

25. Schüssler Fiorenza, *Bread Not Stone,* 21.

26. Ibid.

27. Feminist theologians long ago identified this insight. See for example Mary Collins, "Principles of Feminist Liturgy," in *Women at Worship: Interpretations of North American Diversity,* ed. Marjorie Procter-Smith and Janet R. Walton (Louisville:

Westminster John Knox Press, 1993), 9–26; Diane Neu, *Women-Church Sourcebook* (Silver Spring, Md.: WaterWorks Press, 1993); Ada María Isasi-Díaz, *En La Lucha = In the Struggle: A Hispanic Women's Liberation Theology* (Minneapolis: Fortress Press, 1993).

28. Ross, *Extravagant Affections,* 224.

29. Schüssler Fiorenza, *The Power of Naming,* 10.

30. Ibid., 11.

Chapter 21: Catholic Sexual Ethics in the Twenty-First Century / Patricia Beattie Jung

1. On the contrary, he too viewed celibacy as a path of discipleship superior to marriage, but he believed that only a rare few were truly called to and gifted for such a life by the Spirit. Consequently, most monks and nuns in fact failed to keep their sexual vows; when viewed realistically, Luther concluded, most convents and monasteries simply occasioned sin. Luther viewed marriage as a "hospital" for all those sickened by sexual lust and commended it to most of the faithful.

2. In fact in his theology of the body, Pope John Paul II claims that in its ideal form, such spousal love is celibate, if not virginal. For example, John Paul II did not find in sexual desire and delight any clues about resurrected life. While he found "rumors of angels" in dimorphic sexual differentiation, in the complementarity of maleness and femaleness, he found no eschatological destiny for sexual desire or pleasure. For him, the nuptial meaning of the body is virginal. In heaven we will love, but as Pope John Paul II foresaw it, this will not involve sexual desire or delight. It is precisely such a vision that valorizes celibacy as superior to marriage and that is used to bolster the requirement for priestly celibacy. See Pope John Paul II, *On the Dignity and Vocation of Women* (*Mulieris dignitatem*), 1988, pars. 20 and 22.

3. Pope Benedict XVI, *Sacramentum Caritas,* apostolic exhortation (Libreria Editrice Vaticana, 2007), par. 81.

4. Jovinian in the late fourth century and Julian of Eclanum in the early fifth went against this tide and argued powerfully for the equality of marriage with celibacy. Both were eventually condemned as heretics.

5. In his text *The Body and Society* Peter Brown indicates that at the end of his life Augustine may have conceded as a hypothetical possibility the presence of sinless experiences of sexual desire in Paradise, that is, prior to "the Fall." See Peter Brown, *The Body and Society: Men, Women, and Sexual Renunciation in Early Christianity* (New York: Columbia University Press, 1988), 423–25.

6. It has never been part of Christian belief that personal continuity is established through reproduction or ensured by ancestor worship. Hence, marriage and/or procreation were never required. They were not essential to the call to witness to life of the world to come.

7. Though in the end I think them incompatible with the best of Christian convictions about human embodiment, such dualistic modes of thought "make sense" of some of our experience of sexuality. The fact is that all sexual contact is boundary blurring, but when such contact is disordered, it is boundary violating. So while Stoicism distorted early Christian views of sexuality, it is not completely mistaken to hold some sexual desires in suspicion. The distinction between the desire for sexual pleasure and lust does as a matter of fact blur easily. There is, as Susan A. Ross has underscored in her book, *Extravagant Affections,* a profound ambiguity about human embodiment. See Ross, *Extravagant Affections: A Feminist Sacramental Theology* (New York: Continuum, 1998), 64ff.

8. My own thinking in this regard was sparked by a remarkable presentation delivered by David Cloutier. Some of his thought on this topic can be found in "Heaven Is a Place on Earth? Analyzing the Popularity of Pope John Paul II's Theology of the

Body," in *Sexuality and the U.S. Catholic Church: Crisis and Renewal*, ed. Lisa Sowle Cahill, John Garvey, and T. Frank Kennedy, S.J. (New York: Crossroad, 2006), 18–31.

9. Vatican II, Pastoral Constitution on the Church in the Modern World (*Gaudium et spes*), no. 48.

10. It is interesting to note that the Church has always taught that it is the ability to engage in sexual intercourse, and not the ability to reproduce, that is the essential requirement for marriage.

11. Elizabeth Stuart, "Sex in Heaven: The Queering of Theological Discourse on Sexuality," in *Sex These Days: Essays on Theology, Sexuality, and Society*, ed. Jon Davies and Gerald Loughlin (Sheffield: Sheffield Academic Press, 1997).

12. Ronald E. Long, "Heavenly Sex: The Moral Authority of an Impossible Dream," *Theology and Sexuality* 11, no. 3 (2005): 31–46.

13. Pope Pius XII noted in the 1950s that both sexes were equal in the eyes of God, because they were essentially different; women belonged at home, where they would flourish under the benevolent male headship of their fathers and/or husbands. In the 1960s Pope John XXIII would teach that women should, for the most part, be treated as equal to men in the public sphere, but because of their "different nature," women should remain subject to men at home. Similarly, Pope Paul VI affirmed the equality of the sexes in society, but defended their differential treatment in the church. (He did not address the issue of women's comparative status authority and power at home.) In a truly remarkable reversal of nearly nineteen hundred years of constant church teaching, Pope John Paul II taught in his apostolic letter *On the Dignity and Vocation of Women* (*Mulieris dignitatem*) that women should be considered equal to men both in the wider society and at home. (Like his predecessor, Pope Paul VI, Pope John Paul II would argue that women's iconic inability to represent Christ required that they be treated differentially in the church.)

14. How often does intersexuality occur? Of course, that depends upon how broadly intersexuality is defined. Only now are we becoming aware of the sheer number of cases in which the multiple factors that contribute to sexuality neither agree with each other nor correspond to the dimorphic model. In her review of the literature Heather Looy noted that "estimates range widely from 0.07 percent to 4 percent of the population, depending upon whether they include conditions with clearly identifiable causes, or any case of 'ambiguous genitalia' ('enlarged' clitoris or micropenis) whether or not the cause is identified" (see Heather Looy, "Male and Female God Created Them: The Challenge of Intersexuality," *Journal of Psychology and Christianity* 21, no. 1 [2002]: 10–20, 12). Anthropologist William O. Beeman has suggested that this means that in the United States alone "between 3 million and 10 million Americans are neither male nor female at birth" (see William O. Beeman, "What Are You? Male, Merm, Herm, Ferm or Female?" *Baltimore Sun*, March 17, 1996).

15. In addition to Looy and Beeman, see Stephen F. Kemp, M.D., Ph.D., "The Role of Genes and Hormones in Sexual Differentiation," in *Ethics and Intersex*, ed. Sharon E. Systema (Dordrecht, The Netherlands: Springer, 2006), 1–16.

16. Since the 1950s medical treatments have been offered as soon as a person was identified as "ambiguously" sexed. Until the last decade, the virtually unquestioned standard care for intersexed persons was to surgically limit (insofar as possible) their anatomy to either a male or female (usually the latter) model, even if such "treatments" reduced or destroyed their capacity for sexual pleasure and left them feeling "out of sync" with the sex to which they had been clinically assigned.

17. There is a higher rate incidence of cancer associated with undescended or malformed testicles. One exception may be the high rate of infertility, both congenital and iatrogenic in origin, frequently associated with intersexuality. But of course, how infertility is experienced depends upon the framework through which it is interpreted. Within a polymorphous paradigm, it may not be seen as problematic that some individuals are not biologically reproductive; they may be given different roles within the community.

18. Congregation for the Doctrine of the Faith, "Letter to the Bishops of the Catholic Church on the Collaboration of Men and Women in the Church and in the World" (2004), 5.

19. Ibid., 6.

20. Ibid.

21. Ibid.

22. Ibid., 8.

23. Ibid.

24. Among the many biblical books cited are Hosea, Song of Songs, John, 2 Corinthians, Ephesians, and Revelation. Of course, other images of God abound in the Christian Bible.

25. CDF, "Men and Women in the Church," 9.

26. At least in part on the basis of the baptismal formula found in Galatians 3:28 the church has traditionally taught that sexual, like ethnic and master/slave, distinctions would be erased in the new creation at the end time.

27. CDF, "Men and Women in the Church," 12.

28. Though such a claim in our present postmodern climate is somewhat unfashionable, arguably one of the twentieth century's most prominent scientists operates with and argues for a similar epistemological vision. See Edward O. Wilson, *Consilience: The Unity of Knowledge* (New York: Alfred A. Knopf, 1998).

29. For more information about this approach to biblical interpretation, see Carolyn Osiek, R.S.C.J., "The New Handmaid: The Bible and Social Sciences," *Theological Studies* 50 (1989): 260–78.

30. Before proceeding, note well that nothing in a polymorphic model of human sexuality denies that God created most people either mostly male or mostly female. What sexual polymorphism does deny is that sexual dimorphism is the exclusive, or more precisely, the only normative form of human sexual differentiation.

Chapter 22: Practical Theology in Global Christian Contexts / Susan Abraham

1. Elaine Pagels, *Beyond Belief: The Secret Gospel of Thomas* (New York: Random House, 2003), 29.

2. Miroslav Volf and Dorothy Bass, eds., *Practicing Theology: Beliefs and Practices in Christian Life* (Grand Rapids: Wm. B. Eerdmans, 2002).

3. Ibid., 1.

4. Ibid., 2.

5. Sharon Daloz Parks, *Big Questions, Worthy Dreams: Mentoring Young Adults in Their Search for Meaning, Purpose and Faith* (San Francisco: Jossey-Bass, 2000).

6. Ibid., 17.

7. Volf and Bass, *Practicing Theology*, 13–32.

8. Ibid., 230–31.

9. Ibid., 234.

10. Robert Schreiter, *The New Catholicity: Theology between the Global and the Local* (Maryknoll, N.Y.: Orbis Books, 1997), 85.

11. R. S. Sugirtharajah, *Postcolonial Reconfigurations: An Alternative Way of Reading the Bible and Doing Theology* (St. Louis: Chalice Press, 2003), 166–72.

12. Volf, "Theology for a Way of Life," in Volf and Bass, *Practicing Theology*, 247.

13. Ibid., 248.

14. Ibid.

15. Volf narrates a story of his parents welcoming someone to their home, a person who would not ordinarily have been present at this family's table. Volf says that in his parents' agapic meal, the original unity of the eucharistic celebration and the agape meal were retained, even though he is not sure they possessed any strong understanding

of this unity. In other words, they were simply practicing their Christian convictions without really "knowing" the belief.

16. Volf, "Theology for a Way of Life," 250.

17. See, for example, Mary Grey: *Prophecy and Mysticism: The Heart of the Postmodern Church* (Edinburgh: T & T Clark, 1997); Lisa Isherwood and Elizabeth Stuart, *Introducing Body Theology* (Sheffield: Sheffield Academic Press, 1998); Serene Jones, *Feminist Theory and Christian Theology: Cartographies of Grace* (Minneapolis: Fortress Press, 2000); Ann Loades, *Feminist Theology: Voices from the Past* (Cambridge: Polity Press, 2000); Natalie Watson, *Introducing Feminist Ecclesiology* (Cleveland: Sheffield Press, 2002).

18. David B. Barrett, George T. Kurian, and Todd M. Johnson, eds., *World Christian Encyclopedia: A Comparative Survey of Churches and Religions in the Modern World,* 2nd ed. (New York: Oxford University Press, 2001).

19. Philip Jenkins, *The Next Christendom: The Coming of Global Christianity* (New York: Oxford University Press, 2002).

20. Lamin Sanneh, *Whose Religion Is Christianity? The Gospel beyond the West* (Grand Rapids: Wm. B. Eerdmans, 2003), 22.

21. See Schreiter, *The New Catholicity,* 62–83. Of particular interest here is the story of how the Asmat in Irin Jaya came to Christianity.

22. Tina Beattie, *New Catholic Feminism: Theology and Theory* (New York: Routledge, 2006).

23. Cardinal J. Ratzinger, "Letter to the Bishops of the Catholic Church on the Collaboration of Men and Women in the Church and in the World," Congregation for the Doctrine for Faith, July 31, 2004.

24. Beattie, *New Catholic Feminism,* 19.

25. Ibid., 290–311.

26. Gayatri Chakravorty Spivak, *In Other Worlds: Essays in Cultural Politics* (New York: Methuen, 1987), 152–53.

27. Gayatri Chakravorty Spivak, *A Critique of Postcolonial Reason: Toward a History of the Vanishing Present* (Cambridge, Mass.: Harvard University Press, 1999).

Chapter 23: On Not Losing Heart / Mary Catherine Hilkert

1. Quoted by Paul Connolly in "The Violence of Everyday Living," *Commonweal* 110 (October 21, 1983): 555.

2. See Miriam Therese Winter, Adair Lummis, and Allison Stokes, *Defecting in Place: Women Claiming Responsibility for Their Own Spiritual Lives* (New York: Crossroad, 1995).

3. Raymond of Capua, *The Life of Catherine of Siena,* part 2, chapter 1, no. 121, trans. Conleth Kearns (Wilmington, Del.: Michael Glazier, 1980), 116.

4. Catherine of Siena, *The Dialogue,* trans. Suzanne Noffke (New York: Paulist Press, 1980), Prologue (no. 1), 25.

5. Prayer 10, lines 36–45, in *The Prayers of Catherine of Siena,* ed. Suzanne Noffke (New York: Paulist Press, 1983), 79.

6. Raymond of Capua, *The Life of Catherine of Siena,* part 1, chapter 10, no. 100, in *Catherine of Siena,* trans. Mary O'Driscoll (Santa Sabina: Éditions du Signe, 1994), 17.

7. Ibid.

8. Ibid., part 1, chapter 12, no. 115.

9. *Dialogue,* no. 167, 364.

10. Ibid., Prologue (no. 1), 25.

11. Letter to Pope Gregory XI, (T255) June 18–22, 1376, *The Letters of Catherine of Siena,* vol. 2, trans. Suzanne Noffke (Tempe: Arizona Center for Medieval and Renaissance Studies, 2001), 193.

12. Letter to Gregory XI (T185), January 1376, *The Letters of St. Catherine of Siena,* 1:245–46.

13. See Prayer 12, lines 174–78, p. 103, and Noffke's note in *The Prayers of Catherine of Siena,* 106, n. 11.

14. Letter to Pope Urban VI (T302), trans. Suzanne Noffke in unpublished anthology.

15. *Dialogue* (no. 148), 311.

16. Letter to Piero Gambacorta (T149), 1374, *Letters,* vol. 1, 62.

17. *Dialogue* (no. 15), 54.

18. Letter to Raymond of Capua and Others (T219), *Letters* 2:92. On this point, see Karen Scott, "St. Catherine of Siena, 'Apostola,' " *Church History* 61, no. 1 (March 1992): 37; and Marygrace Peters, "Catherine of Siena: Broker of Relationships," *Listening: Journal of Religion and Culture* 38 (Fall 2003): 225–35.

19. See Mary O'Driscoll, *Catherine of Siena* (London: Catholic Truth Society, 2007), 23–27 and 39–46.

20. See Letter to Raymond of Capua (T267), 1377, *Letters* 2:472–76. See also Catherine's letter to William Flete and Antonio da Nizza (T326), forthcoming in vol. 4 of *The Letters of Catherine of Siena,* trans. Suzanne Noffke.

21. Letter to Alessa dei Saracini (T49), November 1377, *Letters* 2:601.

22. *Dialogue* (no. 144), 302.

23. Ibid. (no. 144), 302–3.

24. Ibid. (no. 145), 305.

25. See Raymond of Capua, *Life of Catherine,* part 2, chapter 4, 138–57.

26. *Dialogue* (no. 64), 121.

27. Prayer 15, lines 182–89, 131.

28. Constance FitzGerald, "Impasse and Dark Night," in *Living with Apocalypse: Spiritual Resources for Social Compassion,* ed. Tilden Edwards (New York: HarperCollins, 1984), 112.

Index

Of Related Interest

Elizabeth A. Johnson

SHE WHO IS

*The Mystery of God
in Feminist Theological Discourse*

Tenth Anniversary Edition

Winner of the Louisville Gravemeyer Award in Religion!

This classic explains what feminist theology is and how we can rediscover the feminine God within the Christian tradition. A profound vision of Christian theology, women's experience, and emancipation.

"As perhaps the best book of feminist theology to date, *She Who Is* is at once thoroughly orthodox, grounded in classical Christian thought, liberatingly contemporary, and rooted in women's experience."   — *Library Journal*

978-0-8245-1925-4, paperback

crossroad

Also in the Series

Lisa Sowle Cahill, John Garvey,
and T. Frank Kennedy, Editors

SEXUALITY AND
THE U.S. CATHOLIC CHURCH

Crisis and Renewal

No issue in the contemporary church evokes more controversy than sexuality. In the wake of the clerical abuse scandals, the Catholic Church has come under intense scrutiny, criticized for being either too repressive or too lenient in its approach to human sexuality. In *Sexuality and the U.S. Catholic Church,* Lisa Sowle Cahill, John Garvey, and T. Frank Kennedy, S.J., introduce the work of leading Catholic theologians, writers, and scholars to help ground the conversation in the tradition, identify modern-day challenges, and point to resources for the future.

978-0-8245-2408-1, paperback

crossroad

Also in the Series

Robert P. Imbelli, ed.

HANDING ON THE FAITH

The Church's Mission and Challenge

Catholic Press Award Winner!

- ◆ What is the substance of Catholic faith and hope?
- ◆ What are the best means for conveying the faith, particularly in North America?

The Crossroad Publishing Company presents the first volume of The Church in the 21st Century series sponsored by Boston College. In *Handing on the Faith* Robert P. Imbelli, a renowned theologian and teacher, introduces the work of leading Catholic theologians, writers, and scholars to discuss the challenges of handing on the faith and the opportunity it creates for Catholics to rethink the essential core of their identity.

This volume includes original contributions by figures such as Robert P. Imbelli, Mary Johnson, William D. Dinges, Paul J. Griffiths, Luke Timothy Johnson, Robert Barron, Robert Louis Wilken, Michael J. Himes, Christopher and Deborah Ruddy, Terrence W. Tilley, Thomas Groome, Bishop Blase Cupich, and John C. Cavadini.

0-8245-2409-8, paperback

crossroad

Of Related Interest

Sidney Callahan

CREATED FOR JOY

A Christian View of Suffering

Catholic Press Award Winner!

In the face of suffering, is it possible to believe in God? In this heartfelt and thoughtful new book, revered Catholic columnist Sidney Callahan answers yes, offering a reflection on suffering from a Christian perspective. Taking on C. S. Lewis and other traditional writers, she introduces the reader to new insights from fields such as the psychology of human emotion and evolutionary biology. Drawing from her own harrowing experience of a mother's loss, she shows that Christians view suffering in a different way, with the expectation — in the face of all evidence to the contrary — that we are created to experience joy. Topics include September 11, traditional justifications, a new story of God and creation, Jesus man of sorrows, suffering and joy in Christian practice, the emotions, prayer, and transformation.

978-0-8245-2566-8, paperback

Check your local bookstore for availability.
To order directly from the publisher,
please call 1-800-707-0670 for Customer Service
or visit our Web site at *www.cpcbooks.com.*
For catalog orders, please send your request to the address below.

THE CROSSROAD PUBLISHING COMPANY
16 Penn Plaza, Suite 1550
New York, NY 10001

All prices subject to change.

crossroad